BEYOND A MOUNTAIN VALLEY

Paula Brown overlooking the Simbu valley, 1958. Photo by Harold Brookfield.

Beyond a Mountain Valley

THE SIMBU OF PAPUA NEW GUINEA

Paula Brown

UNIVERSITY OF HAWAI'I PRESS

HONOLULU

© 1995 University of Hawai'i Press
All rights reserved
Printed in the United States of America

00 99 98 97 96 95   5 4 3 2 1

Library of Congress Cataloging-in-Publication Data
Brown, Paula, 1925–
    Beyond a mountain valley : the Simbu of Papua
New Guinea / Paula Brown.
        p.   cm.
    Includes bibliographical references and index.
    ISBN 0–8248–1701–X (alk. paper)
    1. Chimbu (New Guinea people)—History.
2. Chimbu (New Guinea people)—Folklore.
3. Chimbu (New Guinea people)—Politics and
government.   4. Big man (Melanesia)   5. Folk-
lore—Papua New Guinea—Chimbu Province—
Performance.   6. Acculturation—Papua New
Guinea—Chimbu Province.   7. Chimbu Province
(Papua New Guinea)—Social life and customs.
I. Title.
DU740.42.B76   1995
995.3—dc20   95–19834
                                            CIP

University of Hawai'i Press books are printed on
acid-free paper and meet the guidelines for
permanence and durability of the Council
on Library Resources

Cartography by Dale Williams

Designed by Paula Newcomb

To the Simbu People

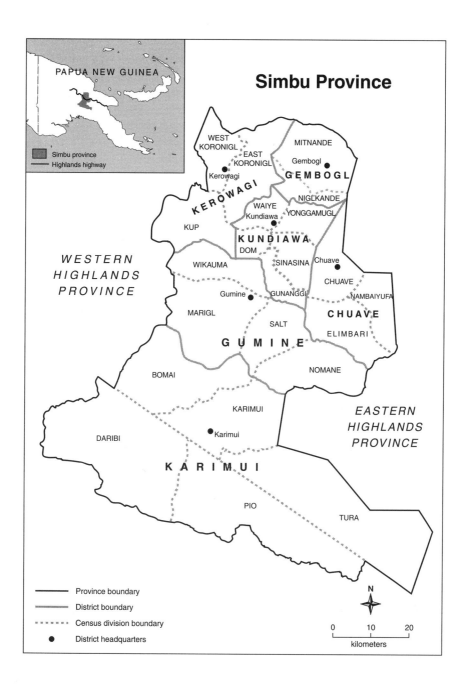

PAPUA NEW GUINEA

Simbu province

Highlands highway

Simbu Province

WEST KORONIGL

MITNANDE

EAST KORONIGL

Gembogl

GEMBOGL

Kerowagi

KEROWAGI

NIGLKANDE

WAIYE

YONGGAMUGL

Kundiawa

KUP

KUNDIAWA

DOM

WESTERN

WIKAUMA

SINASINA

Chuave

HIGHLANDS

CHUAVE

PROVINCE

Gumine

GUNANGGL

NAMBAIYUFA

MARIGL

CHUAVE

SALT

ELIMBARI

GUMINE

BOMAI

NOMANE

EASTERN

KARIMUI

HIGHLANDS

Karimui

PROVINCE

DARIBI

KARIMUI

PIO

TURA

N

Province boundary

District boundary

Census division boundary

District headquarters

0   10   20

kilometers

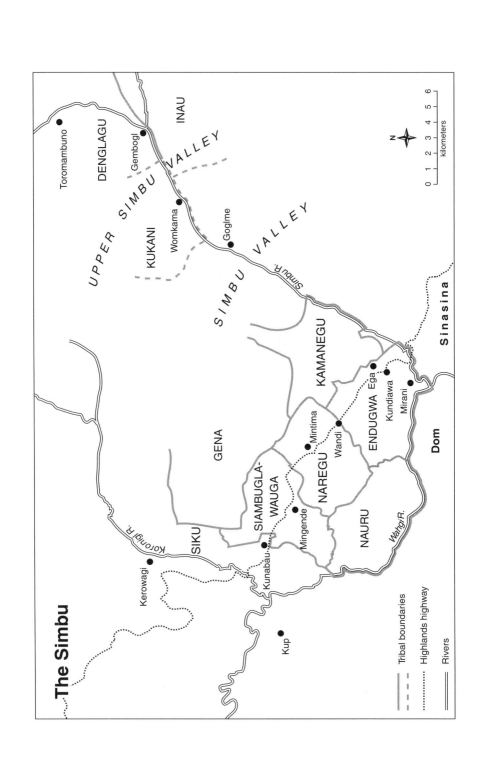

The Simbu

Toromambuno

DENGLAGU

Gembogl

INAU

UPPER SIMBU VALLEY

KUKANI

Womkama

Goglme

SIMBU VALLEY

Simbu R.

Kerowagi

Koronigl R.

SIKU

GENA

KAMANEGU

Sinasina

Mintima

Wandi

ENDUGWA

Ega

Kundiawa

Mirani

SIAMBUGLA-
WAUGA

NAREGU

Kunabau

Mingende

NAURU

Dom

Wahgi R.

Kup

N

0 1 2 3 4 5 6
kilometers

——— Tribal boundaries

- - - Highlands highway

········ Rivers

CONTENTS

PREFACE

For some years it seemed that my life was with the Simbu.[1] When I was a fellow in anthropology at the Australian National University, my visits to Simbu were frequent. Among the Naregu I was known as Mintimamam (woman/mother of Mintima) or *ambara* (S. sister). I had no sooner returned to Canberra than my friends and colleagues asked, "When are you going back to New Guinea?" To them Simbu was my true home.

The New Guinea highlands was an exciting new field for anthropologists in the 1950s. Several field studies preceded my own,[2] and a 1956 Association of Social Anthropologists conference at the Australian National University, just after my arrival, was my introduction to the area. The group discussed the terms and categories of social structure; in the light of contemporary social anthropological concepts, patrilineality seemed the major characteristic. The general outlines of social organization were defined, and field research could be more specific and problem-oriented. My choice of Simbu for highlands fieldwork in 1958 was a matter of access, both to location and to some early anthropological reports that I saw as providing information from their first observers, the missionaries Schäfer, Nilles, and Aufenanger.[3] Something of the Simbu and their twenty-five-year contact history was known through patrol reports and descriptive and anthropological papers and books.

The highland and mountain peoples of New Guinea are of extraordinary interest to historians and anthropologists. They were among the world's last large populations to be discovered; thus we can tap memories of the 1930s, written and spoken. This is exceptional, for although travelers often report their observations and we may have accounts of their first impressions of contact, we can rarely match such observations with those of the other party, the nonliterate tribal peoples whose perceptions of the first intruders are lost in generations of subaltern colonial status and interethnic relations.

I had a rare opportunity to consult many historical sources: documents, writings of mission and government officials, field notes, memory of my experience and conversations in the field. Besides my own notes and the writings of Europeans and Simbu available to most highlands researchers, I guided the collection of statements of elders and accounts made by some literate young people, who interviewed, recorded, and wrote comments about Simbu and about themselves at my request.

Another difference between my work and that of others in the highlands at that time was my collaboration with Harold Brookfield, a geographer colleague at the Australian National University. We were drawn to Simbu because of its very high population density on steep mountain valley gardens. The agricultural system had been called "shifting agriculture," consisting of long- or short-fallow, sweet-potato subsistence along with pig husbandry and large feasts. Looking at stereoscopic air photographs in Canberra, we agreed to select an area with a range of soil types and altitude, accessible by road. The Simbu and Upper Koronigl valleys were very difficult of access. Government rest houses at Mintima were repaired, and some were added, as arranged by the *kiap* [P. government officer]. From our field site at Mintima we discovered marks of agricultural ditches throughout the Wahgi valley, Simbu techniques of intensive agriculture on steep mountainsides, territorial land rights, individual land holdings, and land use. Together, we studied the mountain environment, population distribution and movements, settlement pattern, agriculture, land tenure, and the introduction of coffee and cash crops. The opportunity to study a community's land use and succession over a generation made the results a contribution to agriculture, geography, ecology, ethnography, culture change, the introduction of cash crops, and their interrelations (Brown and Brookfield 1959; Brookfield and Brown, 1963; Brown, Brookfield, and Grau, 1990).

I was to move beyond descriptive ethnography into the dynamic field of social and cultural change, as it was then conceived, and to follow these changes through time. My data base of settlement, residence, family census, group activities, and leadership of a group of several subclans was updated in frequent visits (Brown 1979b, 1984:241–247). Our studies of land tenure and settlement were built from a solid base of maps and census in Mintima.

In my field trips, supported by the Australian National University (1958–1965), I followed what is usually known as participant observation,[4] a "modernist" social anthropology. I observed community life, attended weddings, funerals, political gatherings, and celebrations of all kinds at Mintima. In 1959–1960, pig feasts were held by many Simbu tribes, and I attended all I could. I wrote about unilineal groups, tribes, intergroup relations and exchange transactions, nonagnates, the changing economy, and the early phases of local government. In the 1960s, highlands ethnography began to attend to new concerns: gift exchange,[5] gender, and change (cf. Read 1965; Lederman 1986; A. Strathern 1971; M. Strathern 1972, 1988).

A special interest in politics and leadership also influenced my choice of location. Naregu is the home tribe of Kondom, an important Simbu leader whose career I followed at Mintima and Wandi for some years (Brown 1963, 1966b, 1990b). My presence with notebook, as official recorder, was often demanded. Whenever a meeting was called at Mintima or Wandi by Wamugl (the Mintima headman) or Kondom to inform the people of council, government, or other matters, I was summoned and given a chair (usually one I had discarded some time earlier) and a pidgin[6] translator. Then the speeches could be suitably recorded in my notebooks. I made some record of informal court proceedings too. I think the very act of my photographing and recording (later confirmed in publications, for example, Brown 1972) meant that the occasion was official and authoritative, and the speaker's esteem recognized.

My repeated visits, as I planned the study in consultation with John Barnes, the professor of anthropology at the Australian National University in 1957–1958, were at first intended as a continuing study of social/cultural change, a running chronicle of Simbu life. Of course, the Naregu of Mintima are no more or less "typical" Simbu than any others. Our optimistic plan did not recognize the difficulty of contextualizing the complexities and many currents of change: intermittent observations in one locality cannot be generalized in such studies. Brookfield and I found that some things we had diagnosed as trends were discovered at the next visit to be false trails. I did not then anticipate certain developments of the 1970s and 1980s: a new phase of tribal warfare, incipient stratification, accusations of witchcraft, Papua New Guinea independence, and the electoral practices of candidates for office.

Nor did I envision the changes of interests in the next thirty years. Still less did I set out to resolve the problems of realist or experimental ethnography.[7] I have moved from a study of Simbu, or perhaps more correctly the Simbu of Mintima, with notes from other parts of the highlands, in two ways: (1) Over time: While my early study was of the contemporary and changing Simbu, I have, through years of field notebooks, interviews, personal recall, and document study, assembled reports from the beginning of contact history (1930s) to the present. (2) By examining the relationships, interactions, and intergroup perceptions of Simbu and strangers—how the Simbu have become involved with and participate in the world beyond the valley. Some of my methods of data collection in the 1980s were designed to attain greater breadth through gathering statements from Simbu and highland people of other tribes and areas.

The assemblage of this wealth of material has brought new insights and observations. Some tales that I recorded in my first notebooks (1958–1960) were repeated many years later. I have also observed differences and shifts in opinions and statements, from the same person, from contemporaries, and from others. The accumulation of historical information, my observations, and the memories or impressions of others come together here.

In writing this book I selected the multivocal accounts, as does any creator of ethnographic montage or collage. My objective is to gain a historical perspective on Simbu, neighbors, and newcomers in the highlands of Papua New Guinea. This history, studded with events, announcements, and performances, is memory and record, rather than my judgment of "what actually happened." Of many versions, recollections, and reports, all add new perspectives. There is surely no single truth.

Fieldwork was supported by the Australian National University for the first years. We stayed at government rest houses by invitation of the local people and by arrangement with government officers until 1964, when the Australian National University acquired a land lease at the invitation of the people at Bamugl near Mintima, and we stayed in the house built there, as did other university research people. After I left the Australian National University in 1965, frequent field trips were no longer possible. I made a brief visit in 1971 and had another opportunity of leave from Stony Brook, with support from the State University of New York, for fieldwork in 1976, when I attempted to catch up with local affairs, politics, and celebrations. This was a year after the independence of Papua New Guinea; provincial government and magistrates' courts were beginning. A new generation and new interests were evident, and I could see how the people of Mintima and Simbu were no longer confined to their mountain valley. Reactions against economic problems, political change, and tribal conflicts appeared. It was clear that my early goal of writing a history from field observations was unattainable: not only were gaps in fieldwork insurmountable (proof, perhaps, was that I was no longer able to follow conversations and speeches in Kuman Simbu), but new leaders and situations in Simbu and the new nation created a different world for my friends and their children. Our friends of the 1960s became elders, and their children's experiences extend beyond local affairs.

I have always enjoyed the friendship and hospitality of Simbu. Among the elders at Mintima and Bamugl my greatest friends have been Wamugl, Yere, Dogoba, Mua, Waim, Kaglwaim, Tagumba, Kia, Kama, and Kagl. Over many years my closest companions and confidants of all ages include Waine, Bomai, Wagai, Goiye, Kawagl, Burugl, Witni Michael, Gendua, Kum, Bomaiambu Clara, and Ninmongo. Some of these will appear in the brief life stories of a later chapter.

Then, in 1984, a grant from the Wenner-Gren Foundation offered another opportunity to return to the field. The Australian National University allowed me to use the field house at Bamugl in 1984 and a vehicle in 1984, and in later trips in 1985 and 1987. Work was concentrated on leadership, stratification, and the provincial election, as well as local Mintima affairs. I constructed a detailed life-history questionnaire that elicited information on family, education, career, travel, religion, and political and economic activities, and in the course of an interview asked (and had interviewers ask or report) about particular interests, experiences, and concerns. The results were wide-ranging, analyzed statistically through another grant from Wenner-Gren, and were related to candidacy and election to the Provincial Assembly.

On assignment by Andrew Strathern, then director of the Institute of Papua New Guinea Studies, Rex Okona joined in the study. We selected a number of research assistants and supervised their work. In Simbu Province, Peter Golla, Philip Kai Moore, Anton Goie, Paul Dage, Robert Kuno, James Bile, Mogia Taiya, John Waine, Peter Nuglai Frazer, Boniface Nua Benson, and Sister Agnes collected information from candidates and leaders, following the questionnaire form, throughout the province (see Brown 1987a). With the assistance of Elizabeth Jimmy, I also conducted a brief questionnaire inquiry at the Kundiawa market. When Harold Brookfield joined us, Mintima land use, settlement, and residence were resurveyed for our long-term study of land tenure and land use (Brown, Brookfield, and Grau 1990).

In 1985 a brief field trip (undertaken with the assistance of an American Council of Learned Societies fellowship) again concentrated on political and social change; Moro, a young woman of eastern Simbu, and I interviewed leading women and elders (Brown 1988) with the help of other young people.

The thirteenth field trip in 1987 was specifically to gather historical and life-history information on a Fulbright research fellowship. I stayed in Kundiawa; Rick Giddings, the magistrate on leave, kindly allowed me to use his house. This time a number of young Simbu men and women, some on leave from Goroka Teachers' College and the Lae University of Technology, others resident in different parts of the province, took part in the inquiry. The interviewers were carefully selected with the assistance of some good friends in Simbu, whose knowledge of the educated and available young people in their home areas was invaluable. I also visited,

interviewed, and had some assistance in the Eastern and Western Highlands. Additional information has come from high school students at
Chuave, Kondiu, Muaina, and Kerowagi.

I prepared several lists of questions for the interviewers, including a
guide to life history from childhood through courtship, marriage, family,
participation in feasts, political activities, movements, work experiences,
travel. Other questions were geared to tap the memories elders had of
their early views about and experiences with newcomers—missionaries,
kiaps, police, Papua New Guineans from other areas, government
appointments, elections. Questions were designed to collect traditional
myths, tribal origins, wars and movements, group and tribe compositions.
I went over the question lists with each interviewer, and the purpose of
the inquiry was fully explained to them. In many cases I jointly interviewed one or more informants with them and checked their reports
against my own notes. At first, interviewers wrote up their material in
Simbu and translated it into English; I checked the information and
translations,[8] as well as the consistency, exact locations, and identities of
people. Most interviewers began with family elders or distinguished elders
in their home community, people well known to them, and spent many
hours over the recording and translation. Some interviewers enjoyed the
work and covered a range of subjects with several informants; others, few
of whom are quoted here, seemed casual and less reliable. Many of the
stories of tribal traditions and historical accounts tell much the same tale,
duplicated in my notes from people I have known for many years. Others
speak from a specific tribe and locality in tracing a personal and tribal
story. At this time I was also interested in the memories and legends of
Kondom (Brown 1990b), which I studied with the help of some of these
interviewers and also schoolchildren. I myself conducted many interviews on all of these questions, and others, interviewing and observing
the campaign for the 1987 parliamentary election (Brown 1989), as well
as revisiting the Mintima area to update local community affairs and see
my friends there.

Lawrence Gigmai often accompanied me, and together we inter-
viewed many people for life histories and traditions.[9] I am grateful for
information, interviews, tribal traditions, legends, friendship, and help
from: Arnold Nai, Moses Geno, Michael Gandi, John Karl, Paul Kawage
Livingstone, Francis Kombugun, Paul Nombi, John Kaile, Joe Gelua,
Dilu Siune, Moro, Ruth Kega, Paul San, Nogai Luke, Paul Ambani,
Joseph Mando, Peter Kamis, Kerry Mua, Elisabeth Bomai, Ruth Gigmai,
Godfrid Harry, Thomas Ombi, Mugua Michael, Matthias Kiu, Naur Wai
Philip, Aglua Jenny, Gabriel Apa, Edward Gumba, Moses Parkay, Tobias

Apa, Bruce Mondo Kair, Dilu Deck, Samson Appiua, Waikama Essy, Jim McPhersen, Fred Eremuga, Peter Seifa, Raia Tesine, Carol Jenkins, Maggie Wilson, and Michael Mel. The quotations in the text indicate the speaker and the interviewer. These accounts from interviews show the responses of older people to my young literate assistants, who recorded life-history information in an open interview form so that the interests and personal experiences of the informant, often a relative, could be pursued.

The collected information gave me a breadth of material from different areas and ages, and in them I hoped to overcome some bias or restriction that might occur because of my age, color, and sex, especially when I did not know the person well.[10] More specifically, I felt that the Simbu interviewers might bring out a different viewpoint than I could, for in my experience Simbu often told me what they expected me to want to hear. Although I might be confident that my relations with my old friends at Mintima would, after these years, enable me to evaluate their responses, I could not be sure of new acquaintances. I found, from my close and long relations with the people of Mintima and Bamugl and field notes from 1958 to 1987, that stories, experiences, and legends are often retold with surprising consistency.

The interview plans were varied. Some followed a life-history outline: "What do you remember about your childhood, your youth? Did you fight or see fighting? What do you remember about your first view of the white man? Did you ever go out of the district to work?" and so on. Some collected tribal origin traditions, legends, stories of personal experiences, and questions of special interest to the interviewee (or sometimes interviewer). A few were taped and later translated by the interviewer or an assistant. There are some differences in the approach and collaboration of interviewer and interviewee: the personal interests and sometimes the interpretations of the interviewers come through.

The results provide a variety of styles and forms, as compared to the more formally structured interviews of 1984. I found that a few men (John Akunai of Goroka, for example) took the stance of a group storyteller, gathering a small audience and telling what they regarded as important experiences, such as the killing at Kunabau or going to work as a policeman. A few assistants wrote longer essays, integrating information from several people and their own knowledge. The collected records have provided many versions of some common stories of origin, tribal traditions, mythical and legendary characters, as well as varied statements and opinions about Simbu life. Several interviewers pursued subjects they chose.[11]

The individual quotations in the text cite the interviewer; I had especially detailed material and reports from Paul Dage, Philip Kai Moore, Lawrence Gigmai, Dilu Deck, and Moro. The quotations usually follow the style and spelling used by the writer, so that at times place-names have different spellings. These are usually obvious. Where I think the meaning might be in doubt, I have occasionally modified the English spelling and syntax. The results of interviews, of course, fill many note-books and files. With my own observations as background, I show how Simbu describe themselves, their experiences, and interpretations of their experiences.

Documentary sources are an essential dimension of this work. These include historical studies, reports, diaries, fiction, and personal accounts —official and unofficial, published and unpublished. In 1989, with a Travel to Collections grant from the National Endowment for the Humanities, I was able to consult materials in the Australian Archives (ACT) and National Library, including manuscripts, and to use the Aus-tralian National University library. On a return visit in 1993 some further material was obtained and references checked. Another important source of documentary and unpublished writings has been the Pacific Manu-scripts Bureau, and through the help of Kathryn Creely at Melanesian Studies Resource Center, University of California, San Diego, I have had access to these and other documents. Papua New Guinea patrol reports of Kundiawa and Simbu from the Papua New Guinea Archives were made available to me by archivist-librarian Nancy Lutton. A visit to the Fryer Library, University of Queensland, with the help of Margaret O'Hagen, made a significant addition. Correspondence, conversation, and access to or copies of private letters, diaries and other sources have been gener-ously given me by the John Black family, Harold Brookfield, Bill Gam-mage, Rick Giddings, Jim Griffin, Terry Hays, Robin Hide, Diana How-lett, Bob Hueter, Kerry Pataki-Schweizer, Michael Leahy family, John Murphy, Fr. John Nilles, Michael O'Hanlon, Anton Ploeg, Bill Standish, Meg Taylor, and the archives collection of the University of Papua New Guinea. I can never fully express my debt to the Simbu, members of the Papua New Guinea administration, my friends and colleagues, and my gratitude for the dedicated and devoted support and encouragement of Ira Glick.

I begin the book with some observations about the ancestral world, myths, legends, and cultural life of the Simbu, not as a static precontact ethnography but to describe certain practices and meanings that persist or adapt in new circumstances. I think of them as a mirror in which expe-riences are reflected and from which reinterpretations are made.

Several following sections are built around chronology, taking up both time periods and topics from the 1930s through the 1980s. The work ends with life stories, legendary characters and their place in Simbu thought, and an overview of phases of change and Simbu evaluation of these changes. I present early contact experiences of the patrol and intrusion: the first views of Simbu and white man, impressions of the airplane, the dramatic and violent events in 1933–1935, killings and arrests, and the different memories of and evaluations by government, mission, and Simbu. I have referred to the interaction and views of Simbu and stranger as "no dialogue" (Brown 1990a). Subsequent chapters continue a chronological account of relations and experiences, pacification, establishing colonial control, and missions. I examine government officers' reports and attitudes, and the effect of these and mission activities on Simbu life. After World War II, new goals and government programs, labor migration, schools, political and economic programs are considered. The preparations for and experience of independence, later field observations, and Simbu views of their lives and times comprise the final sections.

1

Introduction

In the past sixty years the Simbu have ventured beyond their mountain valley, and strangers live among them. Beginning in 1958, I have made numerous field trips, assembled documents and private papers, observed Simbu and
others in action, and collected life stories, personal accounts, and memories
of this period. This book describes and analyzes experiences, encounters, and
relations of Simbu people and outsiders, and the changes that have occurred
in the time-span of study. The story is told in terms of action and event:
memories, reports, deeds, and performances of men and women, leaders,
administrators, and missionaries. I present a living history or ethnohistory of
the Simbu—their actions and interactions, their statements about their
experiences and memories, the performances they recall. This work, then,
pertains to a specific or local people and the happenings and events that
shape change: the interrelation of structure, action, and event (cf. Ortner
1984).

In a series of papers, books, and comments, Marshall Sahlins (1981,
1985, 1991, and 1992) discusses relations between incidents or happenings
and structures. His work has enlivened a decade of discussion in historical
anthropology (M. Strathern 1984, 1990a; Toren 1989; Biersack, ed. 1991;
Obeyesekere 1992). Sahlins says of the relations between event and structure or symbolic system: "[a]n event is not just a happening in the world; it is
a *relation* between a certain happening and a given symbolic system. . . . An
event is a happening interpreted—and interpretations vary" (1985:153). I
find this last qualification crucial: it opens the structure/event relationship
to many interpreters. Sahlins' view has been taken to hold the culture/struc-
ture/symbolic system as stable. In his analysis, he seems to consider structure
as both durable and affected by events. The examples and case studies in Fiji
(1991, 1993) show both changes and continuities in structures. The several
observers and interpreters may be identified in records or by an observing
ethnographer.

The idea reappears: "an endogenous event is a relation between an incident and a structure" (Sahlins 1991:45). Marilyn Strathern argues that

Sahlins' "focus on the events as interpreted action" takes the event as an artefact; "an event is seen as a culturally interpreted happening" (1990a:28).[1] In her view of event and social action as performance or artefact, the observer's voice interpreting social/cultural context is silenced; for her, an artefact is recognized as the effect of an event on witnesses and their subsequent actions: "An event taken as a performance is to be known by its effect: it is understood in terms of what it contains . . . registered in the actions of those who witness it" (1990a:28–29).[2] The analysis might go on to record the reactions of witnesses, in order to assess their interpretation of event and artefact.

My observations in Simbu will show how the performance of a leader or big man who makes an announcement at a meeting and directs the display and distribution of goods and food at a ceremony, for ceremonial distributions and speeches become events: he proclaims a payment, rewards allies, manages compensation. The recipient is a messenger who takes food or goods to distribute and spreads the news at home. By recalling the occasion, Simbu informants make it into an event. A Melanesian penchant for pronouncement and display as authority has been examined by Lindstrom (1990b); Mosko (1991) would call these "messages." In this history of Simbu, I see action or performance and its impact on the future as a major force for change; this results, too, in underplaying structure.

Strathern's view of performance as artefact invites interpretation of innovations; I see that this applies to my view of Simbu. My long and multivoiced account of the Simbu and the others who have entered their world covers over fifty years, with voices of several generations. Many events and performances could be identified as separate occurrences within a changing cultural context. In Simbu, I will show that there can be a cumulative effect of leaders' performances and pronouncements in which memory of individual events may merge into a general image of a leader. The models of Sahlins and Strathern seem best suited to singular instances and few actors.

A second distinction of this study is its focus upon the situation of contact, the conceptions and interactions of Simbu and the outside agents of contact—administrators, missionaries, police, and others. In historical situations of culture contact, participants interact in a domain of multiple structures and cultural understandings. Early colonial encounters might best be seen as interactions between people of different preconceptions and expectations. If practice is fashioned by culture, then action springs from distinct cultural systems: each participant's act is a performance that signifies his/her system.

Max Gluckman defined "social situation" as whites and Zulu together in the same social field. I was reminded of Gluckman (1958:7) when in 1959–1960 I attended cricket matches at Kundiawa, Chimbu Subdistrict, Papua New Guinea, which were described to me by the Assistant District Officer (A.D.O.) as matches between the Australians and the natives. One end of the airstrip was the playing field. The cricket match proceeded like any village affair; in this case the native players were all educated government employees from other areas, as sports were taught in schools that no Simbu had yet attended. Australian officers, wives, and children watched the match from chairs placed in a shaded shelter, and the wives served a buffet at halftime to the players and white guests. The Papua New Guinean players took their plates to the sidelines. Papua New Guinean spectators, including families of players, sat on the sidelines to watch. Conversation among groups was minimal. The few Simbu observers were even farther from the action. This interracial match and separation of the several groups on this occasion impressed me greatly; it is a keynote for this book.

Jayawardena finds in the social situation an opportunity to "study both events in human affairs as well as the regularities in human interaction. The concept of social situation interlocks the interest of the historian and the anthropologist/sociologist" (1987:41).

Cohn's discussion of "situation," apparently independent of Gluckman, specifies that the "colonial situation . . . is . . . to be viewed as a situation in which the European colonialist and the indigene are united in one analytical field" (1980:218).

In an impressive number of anthropological studies, dramatic events and confrontations within or among groups indicate conflicting values and are enduring reminders of significant turning points in relationships. In Simbu the incident at Kunabau and the killings of Father Morschheuser and Brother Eugene (Chaps. 3 and 4) are such events.

In Sahlins' (1981) discussion of the meeting of Captain James Cook and Hawaiians, the participants had different understandings and expectations. Sahlins prefaces his account with: a "confrontation of cultures affords a privileged occasion for seeing very common types of historical change *en clair*" (1981:vii). He goes on to observe, "[p]eople act upon circumstances according to their own cultural presuppositions, the socially given categories of persons and things" (1981:67) and continues: "I argue too that such effects as transformation and reproduction are maximally distinguishable in situations of culture contact, although the processes involved are by no means unique to these situations. For here, in the clash of cultural understandings and interests, both change and resistance to change are themselves historic issues" (1981:68).

Dening comments: "It seemed to me that the British discovery in their histories that Cook was a hero was not very different from the Hawaiian discovery in their histories that he was a god" (1991:375).

Historical events are particularly subject to conflicting interpretation and later revision. Sahlins, in his analysis of the death of Captain Cook (1981, 1985), states that Cook was viewed as the dying god Lono by Hawaiians and as the slain commander by the British. This interpretation has been widely accepted by scholars for many years. His analysis portrays persistent symbolic significance of this event and the disparate understandings of the Hawaiians and Cook's shipmates. Obeyesekere's (1992) critical historical review of Sahlins' evidence and interpretation calls for a new assessment of Sahlins' conclusions. Obeyesekere's reanalysis of the Captain Cook myth, and his conclusion that Cook at the time of his death was an angry, vengeful commander, is based on a different reading of diaries, logs, and other texts. It is nevertheless without support from contemporary eighteenth-century Hawaiian texts, which do not exist. In commenting, Sahlins responds that "nothing can be taken for granted . . . the violence that attends early contacts has no self-evident meaning . . . without the indigenous understandings of what happened . . . nothing can be deduced . . . from our own moral sentiments" (1992: 6). This confrontation forcefully demonstrates contradictions that may arise in cultural interpretation when data consist of European documents, often first views, and ethnographic observations or reports of a later period.[3]

The label "event" may also be an analytic tool to set out something that the anthropologist-author has identified as significant. But community members may not remember it. There are puzzling instances where inquiry in a community is unable to identify what is recognized by outsiders as an event —the nonrecognition contradicts other evidence (Schieffelin and Kurita 1988; Ballard and Allen 1991).[4] Natural disasters, floods, volcanic eruptions, or epidemics that have been identified by scientists and observers may not be considered memorable events in a local community. Although the 1943–1945 dysentery epidemic in the New Guinea highlands was of great concern to the military government, and was responsible for thousands of deaths (Burton 1983), decades later not all of the people had any recollection of it. In a discussion of events and non-events, Fogelson says:

> . . . the lack of an authenticated history for many of these groups [American Indians] begs fundamental questions about the authority of history. Who determines it? Who sets the criteria? or, in a literal sense, Who *possesses* history? (1989:142).

Personal experience is the basis of an event, interpreted by a participant. In telling and retelling, it may further enter a group's store of legend and oral tradition: it becomes social memory (Fentress and Wickham 1992). The meaning of the event is shared in memory and retelling. As Ardener put it, oral history is the memory of events restructured and structuring is the registration of events (1989).

Historians who study early contact in order to reevaluate or reinterpret conquest and colonial domination may introduce new historical documentary evidence or interpret the situation in a new way: new data sources invite reinterpretation. Yet these can rarely reveal history as it is known to the non-literate native; rather, they present the Western-trained writer's view of a history and its revision. Anthropologists, from field observation and local legend, may see how violent events have continuing historic significance.[5]

Anthropological studies in Papua New Guinea that attempt to recapture reactions to early contact and intercultural encounters have uncovered many different memories (Schieffelin and Crittenden 1991). In the highlands of Papua New Guinea, because of their myth that the white giant Souw would return to punish them, the Daribi were shocked into giving food and pigs to the first white men to enter their home area, Leahy and Dwyer (Willis 1969; Wagner 1972, 1989). In Simbu, as I describe below, the sacred flute and bird (S. *kua*) myth attained new significance when the first airplanes, seen as giant birds, flew over the area at the time of the first exploratory patrols. Such events in early contact initiated new relationships and meanings.

Violent interactions and conflicting interpretations were surely more common than most western historians and writers of the colonial era have known. The fear and inarticulateness of native people in early contact, their inability or reluctance to voice their objections to their conquerers, and the late development of anticolonial sentiments all have muted the natives. Reactions in the form of small-scale rebellions and "cargo cults" are better known. A "dark side" of colonialism is only now emerging to the general knowledge of the west.[6]

Ethnohistory has been called the intersection of anthropology and history.[7] Ethnohistorical scholarship dedicated to showing "what actually happened"—in itself a possibility denied by many—often includes traditional and recorded data from the "native point of view." Taking as a guide Malinowski's famous definition of the anthropologist's task, Cohn (1981:233–234) states that ethnohistorians try to write the history of their traditional subjects from the natives' own standpoint, using as sources everything from documents of European observers to oral traditions and archaeology. He comments: "Traditional historians who have studied the history of the American Indians have been limited in their perspective because they used documents which were generated by white conquerors; hence, they accepted many of the assumptions of those who produced these sources" (1981:234).

A rare joint effort (Keesing and Corris 1980) brings together historical reports and native commentary on the events and circumstances surrounding what is known as the "Bell massacre." In commenting on this, Keesing calls colonial history "contested ground":

> Who represents the history, what history is represented or left buried, how it is narrated, and from whose perspective are not simply matters of fact, matters of power, matters of authority, or matters of truth. There is and can be no "true" and authoritative account of the Bell massacre and its consequences. The events of 1927 will not speak for themselves. (1990:299)

Vansina's claim (1985) that the historian can use oral tradition as a hypothetical or approximate historical truth[8] is questioned by Neumann. That is, the scholar's care and caution does not assure historical truth: the question of whose voice and purpose remains. Neumann suggests that when oral testimony becomes written history, it is accepted as historical truth, rather than praxis (1992:106–124).

Oral history is a most important component of recent historical studies in Pacific island communities. Concerning oral material, Parmentier concludes: "in speaking of any cultural phenomena, one can never consider 'what happens' apart from uncovering the meaningful categorizations that specify the significance of events for social actors" (1987: 306). As Wagner says: "The . . . creation of history is . . . an intended and contrived act . . . , something produced by human beings" (1991:345).

Anthropologists need to consider the significance and effect of their inquiries upon a community and upon their informants. Howe (1984), Borofsky (1987), and Parmentier (1987), working in small island communities in these reflexive times, are especially sensitive to their relations with informants. Parmentier (1987) found a recognized traditional narrator of Belau sacred history, whereas many potential informants were reluctant to claim the authority to tell the stories to him.

Scrutinizing his methods in historical study of the Tolai, Neumann believes that he may codify oral history by writing it (1989). Kiste remarks in his introduction that Neumann: "is concerned to write a history of the Tolai's colonial experience through a series of incidents and a variety of reports or memories of them. The result is not a single history, but rather multiple histories that are themselves montages of varying complexity. . . . For Neumann, there is no such thing as an objective history, of 'the way it really was' " (1992:vii). As Neumann puts it, "Tolai histories differ depending on who tells them, when, and where" (1992: 260). Documents and oral statements about an event are seen from different viewpoints and cultures (Schutte 1991; Neumann 1992). I found in the reports and oral testimonies of Simbu participants and observers that each may have his/her own view of what happened and why.

Dening considered ethnohistory a subdivision of anthropology that concentrates its interest upon the native peoples and their culture. He said: "I take my historical task to be to describe what *actually* happened in the past. I call that ethnography. . . . I do ethnographic history. . . . It begins with the most difficult thing of all to see: the experience of past actors as they experienced it, and not that experience as we in hindsight experience it for them" (1988a:99). He comments that "ethnohistorians are not quite ready to admit that soldiers and missionaries are also the objects of their inquiry and methods" (1980:37).

Similarly, Axtell observes that history, anthropology, and ethnohistory "tend to focus on one society or culture at a time" (1979:2). Depth in time and meaning are often achieved by combining later writings of Europeans and natives with observations of travelers and anthropologists while basing the main interpretations upon native memory and tradition. Axtell differs from both anthropologists and historians by identifying the task of ethnohistory, in treating the contact of two cultures, as the recognition of conflicting values and the understanding of ethnocentric bias and motives in interaction (1979:9–10). In Axtell's view, history is imagining—the encounters of Europeans and Native Americans, Indian–white relations, involve each group imagining the other (1992).

Most studies in historical anthropology are situated in a colonial time, when visitors recorded their observations and before the native people began to write for historical record. The data are mainly of two types: written observations of westerners and oral narratives of natives. Few of them can quote indigenous witnesses to the events reported. Critical evaluation of historical anthropology has accused writers of essentialism, forms of Orientalism, authenticity,[9] and other academicians' faults (cf. Carrier 1992b).

The anthropologist/historian critically collects and reviews the narrators' tales, assesses the evidence available, and evaluates conflicting statements and interpretations about incidents and happenings. It is the reporter of it who makes a happening into an event. In identifying processes, policies, and forces of change, we harness the incidents and acts to control the data and organize observations, statements, and records into what appears to be a coherent aggregate, synchronic or diachronic. We see how people may revise and reinterpret practices to fit a new situation (Borofsky 1984; A. Strathern 1991; Sahlins 1995). If the investigator is cautious in drawing conclusions, it is no solution to let the people "speak for themselves" (Keesing and Jolly 1992): every observation, statement, and informant quoted is both happenstance and selected.

Pacific islanders met outsiders on the beaches: explorers and whalers refueling their ships, traders in sandalwood and bêche-de-mer, recruiters to sugar plantations, and government visitors. These brief encounters, in which tantalizing western manufactures were traded for food, water, wood, and ships' supplies, were later followed by colonial and government settlement, plantations, mission settlements, and laboring work. The distance between the white men's riches and power and the natives' life was experienced in many ways, over long periods of occasional, sometimes frequent, encounters. The arrival of a ship in the cove could bring metal goods, guns, clothing, preachers, opportunity, disease, or death. At best, our knowledge of these encounters resides in the tales, diaries, and reports of the European visitors and what can now be recovered from native oral tradition (Salmond 1991). A rich Pacific historical literature attests to the significance of the encounters and events to one or all parties, with multiple and divergent interpretations.[10]

Records and reports of inland encounters between natives and visitors traveling on foot or in small river boats sometimes lack drama and are not memorable. Perhaps a small traveling party is less of a surprise, but it also seems that inquiry in remote places has just begun to elicit from informants the impact of these visits (Wagner 1972; Ballard 1992). However, as we shall see, the Taylor-Leahy patrol, with its long procession of carriers, police, and volunteers, the airplanes associated with them, and their trading of shells for pigs, is memorable to the people of Simbu.

Some Melanesian historical work, where contact began only one or two generations ago, can include personal accounts as recollected events are recorded. Connolly and Anderson (1987) interviewed, and recorded, Papua New Guineans of the Western Highlands about their memories of the first contact Bena-Hagen patrol and M. J. Leahy. Taking the 1935 Strickland-Purari patrol of Hides and O'Malley as their basic text, Schieffelin, Crittenden, and their collaborators (1992) collected field interviews and memories of their movements and encounters with people in Papua. In the New Guinea highlands, several studies utilize interviews with local participants (Munster 1975, 1979, 1983; Mennis 1982; Radford 1987). Ballard and Allen (1991) tell the story of the Huli's first encounter with white men, the Fox brothers.[11]

This work similarly centers upon a highlands area. Simbu's short history of contact has been documented in many ways. These narratives that form a foundation for Simbu oral history show that certain violent events of early contact had decisive effects on attitudes and perceptions; I am interested in the diverse perceptions of the participants; the effect of events, actions, and behavior upon responses in intercultural contact; and how perceptions of self and other changed. The statements of Australian officers, missionaries, and other writers are presented to illustrate their views and observations, not to indicate a systematic European world of thought, as in Salmond (1991).

My goal here is not limited to a historical understanding of the native people, but rather, following Axtell and Dening, intends to examine the intercultural interactions and conceptions of one another that emerged following first contact in what was then a remote Papua New Guinea highlands area. The written records, recollections, and second- and third-hand reports of Simbu and outsiders speak of the same times and events; but they are not all there is to the history of the last sixty years in Simbu. Rather, the reports and memory statements provide multiple aspects of the past, from many viewpoints.

History and ethnohistory in Melanesia were much advanced by Gewertz and Schieffelin, who state: "we cannot really understand the nature of events from an objective point of view, but can only grasp their significance when we understand how the people themselves experienced and understood them at the time, and in retrospect" (1985:2). Observations and historical accounts must be evaluated and combined to compose group or regional oral history (Biersack 1991) or a "collective biography" (Gewertz and Errington 1991). A. Strathern, taking as his example the Hagen Moka, finds history imbued with local values. Melpa people "make their history . . . in terms of the exchanges they hold and the meanings they attach to them" (1991:227). Here the main reference must be a single person's experience and memory. In Simbu it has been possible to record oral tradition in personal recollection of experiences in early contact.

Simbu stories, memories, and thinking about their place in their world, take many forms, both as social memory[12] and as individual recollection of experience:

1. Myth, creation story, origin of the Simbu, beginnings of humanity and society, pigs, agriculture, technology.
2. Traditional history of the tribe or group—places and conquests, movements. The incidents, wars, places of settlement and movements of the group. Their traditions are embedded in stories of pre-contact wars and migrations. Place-names carry the identity of people and their settlements.

3. Folk tales and legends about persons and actions in the time before contact.[13]
4. Remembered and significant events: tales that circulate about witnesses and significant events.[14]
5. Heroes and significant historical figures. These characters, their actions, their descendants, their communities, the intergroup relations and consequences of those actions, are Simbu historical tales. In these tales a named historic person gives a performance that the observers and reporters make the event, and may transform Simbu society.
6. Simbu in school, and later as authors, have become their own recorders and editors of traditional and semifictional history.

My materials are what is preserved in recall and retrospect: writing the past in the present. It is not simply that contact initiates a new episode or era in the lives of such isolated people as the Simbu were before 1933. Our understanding of peoples' worldviews—the premises of their community, culture, and social life—is derived from what has been heard and seen in the field, years after contact.[15]

The changing conditions of precontact and early colonial contact life are accessible in the New Guinea highlands as in few other places. In this study I examine both Simbu and newcomers' views of the situation of contact, how they see the introductions, legislations, discards, and changes. Simbu experiences of intrusion, missions, and colonial rule are within living memory and accessible through reports and interviews. I have observed their views of this changing situation, the independent indigenous adaptation to it, and innovations over thirty years.

I look for the Simbu view of their own history, the imprint of events and their perceived consequences. Their history is punctuated by events of change, introductions, and adaptations. Events may be turning points, the beginning of episodes of transformation:[16] myths and stories of the first man and woman; migration and conquest; a group's settlement in its present area; the arrival of the white man; colonial lives; Papua New Guinea independence; and travel to other places.

Memory embedded in the names of people and locations commemorates significant events. These are the materials of Simbu history. In the history of Simbu people, certain incidents are unforgettable: they live now in legend and social memory. In legendary accounts, time and duration are rarely noted; an episode may be the marking between events. The experience is the basis of the tale, and an important, named person creates the event. A Simbu orator, a big man, announces the conditions, relations, and decision to his audience, thus initiating a war or a gift. A leader's arrangement of a ceremonial prestation may establish new groups and relationships. The images of heroes and their acts are the substance of Simbu memory and their folk history. The heroic accomplishments are to be understood in a double context of their importance in their own time and the ways in which they are now retold as memorable events to the narrators and audience.

In Simbu, oratory and performance are male attributes. The stories of women are delivered in a shy monotone; those of men, often in a strong manner, as pronouncements, whether addressing a single ethnographer or a group. Women's stories are about themselves and their families; men's are about travels, wars, exchanges, activities. To each individual, initiation, marriage, places of settlement, fights with enemy groups, and participation in group exchanges are the materials of a life story.

I pay particular attention to the differing perceptions of the participants and the effect of events and actions upon responses in intercultural contact. I shall examine what has been an Australian myth of benign colonialism in the highlands of Papua New Guinea. Three generations—the cohorts of elders, of people born after the white man came, some of whom have been to school or worked outside the area, and of those born in the early days of independence—have different sets of experiences, and often different views of themselves and the world outside the province.

The ethnographer may generalize a cultural and community interpretation of the events of contact and speak of community adaptation to new things—the guns, the missionaries, the police and government officers. In fact, experience is personal. A dramatic, intense experience is, for the individual, often a catalyst for life change, a new interpretation of the world and him/herself. Each individual has his/her memories, experiences, and reactions. Each person's stories may be told to relatives or inquiring anthropologists or historians; a few are recorded in notes and an occasional published account. These narratives are not only valued personal memories; some are the materials of group legends and folk histories. Memory is the raw material of oral history; repeated performances of narratives become a group's story (Connerton 1989).

2

The Simbu and Their Traditions

I was a great warrior.
I led many victorious battles over rival tribes near and far.
—GULL KUMUGL OF ENDUGWA
    (interviewer Godfrid Harry, 1987)[1]

Placing Simbu in New Guinea

Although there has been little archaeological work in the area, Simbu clearly share in highlands prehistory. None of the present New Guinea highlands peoples has been fully isolated or static; tribal histories tell of wars, movements, and innovations everywhere. The large island of New Guinea has been populated for about forty thousand years, and the Trans New Guinea language phylum that includes Chimbu language is widespread in the interior and the high valleys of Papua New Guinea and Irian Jaya. Settlement in the Western Highlands site of Kuk began nearly ten thousand years ago; pigs appear by 6,000 B.P. Analysis of materials from the Kuk and other highlands sites has established a long history of agriculture and dense settlement in the Wahgi valley region (Golson and Gardner 1990). Many highlands groups trace their origin to present or nearby highlands sites. Sweet potato was introduced through trade from the coast only three centuries ago. Highlanders trade regionally distributed items—salt, stone, shell, feathers, and plumes (Hughes 1977; Burton 1984). The redistribution of population to the higher slopes and its growth, the expansion of pig production, and a florescence of ceremonial exchange probably followed the growth of sweet potato as the staple crop. Highlands people stand out among Melanesians for their technologically advanced agriculture with fencing, full clearing, tillage, short fallow, drains, terraces, and mounds, all constructed with polished stone tools, wooden hoes, and digging sticks. Throughout the highlands there is more or less intensive agriculture, pig husbandry, and dense settlement (Brookfield and Brown 1963; Brown and Podolefsky 1976; Brown 1978; Feil 1987). Simbu cultivators plant their sweet potato and vegetable gardens in steep valleys and mountainous terrain over 1,500 m in altitude.

Simbu,[2] one of the largest linguistic and cultural groups in New Guinea, have diversified linguistically and culturally from a common foundation, maintaining some cultural similarities and common features over thousands of years in their mountainous home. Most of the languages spoken in Simbu and Western Highlands Provinces are of the Hagen-Wahgi-Jimi-Chimbu language family[3] (Wurm 1975). Simbu are particularly close to the Wahgi valley Kuma (Reay 1959) and Nangamp (O'Hanlon 1989) in language and ceremonial practice; they share some ritual forms (for example, male initiation and *gerua* symbolism) with peoples to the east.

Simbu provincial population in 1990 was 186,109 (Deck 1991:7) in Gembogl, Kerowagi, Kundiawa, Chuave, Gumine, and Karimui Districts. Simbu recognize several subareas: Kombugl—East, Kuman—West, Geregl—North, and Bomai—South. These are regions and language or dialect groups. My interviews and observations are mainly in Kuman Simbu, with a little information about Sinasina and Chuave to the east, and less on the Bomai and Gumine. Most of the Kombugl and Kuman share in the myth of origin at Womkama.[4] Geregl is used as a directional term that refers to the Gende people as well as to the upper Simbu valley. South Simbu (Bomai and Karimui) was not in continuous contact with government and mission until the 1950s, and the people are still little known in cultural detail.[5]

Many specific beliefs and cultural differences distinguish these groups, and within the groups there are some dialectic and cultural differences. Kuman Simbu see the sun (S. *ande*) as the protector of people and gardens (Aufenanger 1962b); for the Sinasina people, sky and earth are the supreme spirits. Local and specific spirits, legends, and magical practices set tribes and clans apart. Kuman settlement is dispersed with large centrally placed men's houses and women's houses located in garden areas and along fences. Chuave and Sinasina now follow the eastern highlands settlement patterns of nucleated villages, some of considerable size; however, they had dispersed settlements in the past. Kuman Simbu build feast villages at ceremonial sites for their pig feasts; eastern Simbu and Chuave hold pig festivals at their village sites. The upper Bomai area, at a lower altitude, has extensive fruit pandanus trees and groves that are valued for feasts and exchanges. Other areas have some different resource specialties, such as nut pandanus at high altitude, cassowary, game, stone for axe blades, salt, and birds valued for plumes.

Kuman Simbu

In the 1930s, about fifty thousand Kuman Simbu, divided into some fifty-five tribes, lived in the Simbu and Koronigl valleys and a section of the Waghi valley. Some tribal populations have reached over four thousand. The largest named groups, Yonggamugl and Dom, are congeries of clans and units like subtribes that have a cultural and linguistic identity but, as far as I know, not joint activities. The tribe is named (S. *kangie pondo*) and coordinates pig feast celebrations and other ceremonial distributions; the people think of their tribe or a major subdivision (subtribe) as a unit in warfare and defense of territory. A tribe may be a kind of phratry when descent is traced from a founder and his clan-founding sons (Podolefsky 1992) or an alliance of clans (Brown 1960). Clans are usually exogamous subdivisions of tribes, not always at peace with one another.

Segments within the clan have some dispersed land holding, which when not in use are claimed for the group and allocated as required by the ground father (S. *magan nim*). Individual plots are held by men in a family (Brookfield and Brown 1963; Brown, Brookfield, and Grau 1990).

The mythic tale of origin and cultural creation is centered in Womkama in the Simbu valley. Each tribe and settlement group has a particular story of expansion through successive generations of sons, differentiation into clans and subgroups, migration, warfare, and dispersal in defeat. Mythic themes of growth, magical plentitude, the origin and multiplication of pigs, fights between brothers, and ancestral spirit powers sustain the great pig festivals and intergroup relations.

Tales of Origin

From my earliest efforts to record Simbu traditional stories (S. *kumbu kaman*), I saw how a group is identified with a locality. Names are the crucial memory-hooks of Simbu narrative and commemorate events. The storyteller names the persons, groups, and sites of each scene or element of the tale, and these represent actions and movements. Simbu thus document their history and territorial claims with place-names; ceremonial ground sites and cemeteries are of special importance.[6]

Simbu traditional stories include spirits, heroes, and remembered persons whose deeds, actions, and exploits originated practices and relationships. Some themes are often repeated: on the theme of primitive/cultured are stories of the beginnings of Simbu culture, the origin of pigs, fire, agriculture, and cultural teaching of a tribe founder by a stranger; and the creation of human characteristics and relations between peoples. Giving food is a common feature: the food or pig multiplies to provide for everyone. In a number of stories, a spirit man or woman mates with a human to found a tribe.

Over the years of interviewing Simbu elders, I have collected many *kumbu kaman* of the origin of the Simbu, of tribes and clans, and the history of particular groups and people. These stories were augmented by the stories taken down by young assistants in 1987. In many cases the same tale, with minor variations, was told by several people at different times, in different parts of Kuman Simbu area, and in different circumstances. I recorded some narratives many times from 1958 to 1987. The Simbu and tribe origin story and the origin-of-pigs tale are particularly widespread and basic to Simbu ideas of their cultural identity and tribal history.[7] The origin myth always contains an image of primitiveness in the first couple—incomplete bodies and ignorance of agriculture. Ignorance and primitiveness is also attributed to other peoples, especially the Bomai.

The characters are eponymous, human more than spirit. Kuman Simbu origins are in most stories traced to Womkama; some few groups of other Simbu start at Goroka, Bundi, Madang; and others go through Womkama to reach their present location. The common form of myth of Kuman Simbu origin includes a statement about real Simbu and pre-Simbu human conditions. The husband of the primal couple is named, and the narrator is usually a member of the tribe that bears his name. The story goes as follows:

A primitive, cultureless, and incomplete first man and first woman live at Womkama without fire by hunting, collecting, and sitting on food to warm it. The primal couple is in a way wild, lacking the cultural refinements of civilized Simbu life: settlement, pigs, good agricultural techniques, cooking, as well as the full complement of body parts and functions.

When the husband goes out to hunt marsupials, Siambugla, a cultured stranger, arrives. He instructs and humanizes the woman in the husband's absence. He cuts her to make a vagina, has intercourse with her, and cuts ears and other orifices. He demonstrates how to make fire and they eat cooked food. When the husband returns and discovers this, he is incensed that the stranger has had intercourse with his wife and fights with the stranger. The outcome is that the winner remains; the defeated has to find a new home. When a Siambugla tells the story, it is a Siambugla hero who evicts the couple from Womkama and later travels to found the many branches and descendants of Siambugla who have migrated all over the Simbu and Wahgi area of the highlands. In most of the stories and tales of other tribes, the wife accompanies her husband on his migration, and the several sons born to the primal couple found the clans of the tribe.

Nilles (1977) reports a story from the upper Simbu that is a preamble to the origin story. Mother Earth drank water and became pregnant, giving birth to a son, Siambugla. This son went hunting and discovered the couple at Womkama. Ancestors (S. *kovane avane*) are spirits who continue to dwell in Simbu cemeteries. Pigs are sacrificed at ancestral places and in cemeteries to please the spirits and for community or personal welfare.

The idea of a culturally deficient primitive occurs widely in Simbu origin stories; agriculture and pig husbandry are Simbu cultural achievements. Simbu warfare aims to destroy houses and gardens and capture pigs in order to reduce the losers to a return to primitive reliance upon wild foods. As the elders tell it, the humiliating and despicable result of defeat is loss of territory, crops, and garden land. The making of fire is a popular pantomime dance at the pig feast. There is a general view that the people to the south, "Bomai," are backward and primitive. The stories of origin of Endugwa and Dom carry this theme. All reinforce the idea of Kuman cultural development emanating from Womkama. Womkama plays a central role in all Simbu tribal traditions.

The Origin of Pigs

A widespread origin of pigs story begins with two brothers who have tree names, Mondo and Gandi. They live together in a bush area and go together to work in gardens. However, Mondo, the elder (spirit) brother disappears into the forest during the day and returns home after dark. Becoming curious, the younger brother, Gandi, follows Mondo and sees him remove his decorative clothing and begin to root in the ground like a pig; he turns into a pig, but toward nightfall reverts to human form, dons his clothing, and returns home to join his brother. Mondo knows that he has been seen and tells Gandi to fence and clear the land to prepare the place, and something wonderful will happen. On the next day, Mondo is killed by his brother, and in his place many pigs spring up to be the basis of Simbu pig herds. The brother Gandi brings all the people to this place to get pigs, and it becomes a famous ceremonial ground where many pigs are killed for the ancestors at time of the great pig feast.[8] The theme of plenitude (S. *merekinde*) is always linked to the multiplication of pigs at the ceremonial feast site. The significance of the name *mondo* is that it is a strong wood, a well-known tree, and is also a common name for men. A club of *mondo* is used to kill pigs by striking them on the snout; *mondo* wood is also often used in the construction of the *bolum* house at the ceremonial ground.[9]

Yopumil Konowemin Womai, a Sinasina of eastern Simbu (interviewed by Walkaima Essy) said his tribe traces its origin from Madang through Bundi and Womkama to this eastern Simbu area: "When man came they brought the pigs with them. Despite tribal fights and bad times people never let the pigs go. They say, pig is a big brother because it brings wealth and pride to the owners. There is no happiness without pigs and women. If things go bad with these two things tribal fights would erupt in no time."

Dama Caspar Daka of Bogo, Kerowagi (interviewer Naur Awi Philip), told a version in which the older brother turned into a pig so that at the time of the pig feast the younger brother would kill him and have a pig for the feast. He said: "So now the people in my area believed that pig was a human being, so they loved the pig very much as their first brother, and they valued pig much more than money."

Tribal Historical Tales

The several tribes maintain somewhat different versions of the basic tales, particularly in the names and locations of the main events, in the routes of migration following the fight between Siambugla and the primal husband, and in the names and locations of the pig transformation. The specific tribal and local histories have both mythic elements and details about locations and subgroups.[10] Some account for the incorporation of groups and alliances.[11]

Stories, dense in group- and place-names defining members of tribes and settlement at places, are a common form that declare old and renewed conflicts and claims to territory, intergroup hostilities, and the establishment of groups at locations.[12] Such tradition is the backbone of tribal alliance, exchange relations, and continuous retaliation. The general form of highland social groupings is patrilineal and patrilocal, so that sons and brothers continue as members of identified social units, tribes, and clans, and their marriage and exchange relations are with others. Support and assistance in war are derived from extraclan kinship and affinity, and the injuries or losses of extratribal supporters must be compensated.

In the traditional stories of different Simbu tribes—among the Naregu, Kamanegu, Endugwa, and others—the next phase of tribal origin story is the family *nimangigl* (S. father, brothers, and sons) story. This carries into clan and subclan, with names of founders stated as sons and brothers, and sometimes including seniority among brothers. Localities, especially ceremonial grounds and cemeteries, are named and linked with territorial claims of tribes, clans, and subclans. Thus the origin tales and recent ritual locations provide a charter for land claims of groups.

Some stories tie together groups that have separated, migrated, and later allied with other groups. In 1958 I was told that the Siku, Kombuku, Gamgani, and Naregu were once a single clan; after disputes and migrations, some Kombuku went into the western Wahgi valley, where they are now known as Komblo (Kondwai and Trompf 1976; O'Hanlon 1989, 1993), and Gamgani have gone to other Wahgi locations.

Naregu origin and migration begin when the Naregu are settled at Pari, in the Singga valley. Their defeat by Kamanegu, still within the memory of our oldest informants in 1958–1959, ties into detailed statements of settlement, land occupation, and recent land gifts, transfers, and movements. These merge into our data on land in the area of study where repeated land surveys confirm transfers (Brookfield and Brown 1963; Brown, Brookfield, and Grau 1990).

The elder Wamugl of Sungwakani, Kombaku clan, Naregu tribe (interviewer Paula Brown), in 1958 told a characteristic tale of origin and movements, identifying many places of settlement, gardens, fights, cemeteries, and ceremonial grounds familiar to his listeners.

> This land at Damar had no inhabitants. It was water. The Simbu were at Wulim, Keglsugl, Wom. We came from Womatne, Gembogl, Kaire, in the mountains. Then the water drained from this valley. The Naregu went to Kurumugl and Pare, long ago. When I married I was at Singgare, where there was a big men's house. We were at Agl, Yugu, Kungare, Daruwa, Bandagl, and Yomba Yaundo. There was a burial ground at Tambagl for Naregu. That's where my father and ancestors were, and they all died there. After a fight with Kamanegu and Naregu, the Endugwa and Endugwa-Nauru left the area. Then there was a fight between Kamanegu and Naregu. The fight was over my pig. The Kamanegu stole it, killed it, and some men ate it. Everyone was angry, and in the fight, the Kamanegu chased the Naregu out. They stopped at Guye; the Sungwakani went to Gondamakane; the Domkani went to Agumbaya; and the Komniambugo to Wayankemambuno. My father and I were at Yombakangwa and Dibinmugl where we had a house. We came here later. The Gamgane had left this place Damar; the ground was unoccupied. Wagai's father and Dogoba's father went to Mintima to find land, and many of the Sungwakani were still at Guye; they were asked by Wagai's father to come to Mintima and Dibinmugl. The Pentagu went to Wandi, Bindekombugl, Guye, Manga, Mi, Druamugl, Bongolungu. Duwagi, Kanindemambuno, Okenagoli, Darali. They all found land in all these places. The Pentagu, Bindegu, Toglkane, Kendagagu, Kigungaumo, Sumbaingaumo found land. They kept it and stayed. Then the Numambugu came, and Gamgani and Kombaku gave them land. They are not patrilineal fathers and sons, but brothers [S. *angra*] here, all the Naregu. The others—Siambugla, Wauga, Gena, Kamanegu, Endugwa are not brothers of Naregu.

Endugwa is now composed of numerous clans in three distinct tribes, with different locations (Kugame Tange interviewed by Lawrence Gigmai; nearly identical story from Wagl Ombo, and from Kiugl Waguo). An

Endugwa origin story follows a line similar to that of Siambugla, the first cultured man. In this version, Naregu people from the Simbu valley taught the Endugwa cultivation when they came to the Endugwa tribal area. Another variant of this tale names some other specific locations. The Endugwa were wild men living in trees at Kogo on bush fruits, leaves, and plant roots. One night they were discovered by some men from the Naregu (Kombaku clan, Domkane subclan), hunting for *cuscus* (marsupial). The hunter shot an Endugwa man with an arrow and then took the wounded man to Pari, where he stayed for two days, entertained and feasted by the Naregu on pigs and decent food (cultivated food).[13]

The next episode is the Endugwa dispersal story. Two friends at Kogo, Bengande and Wawe, looked alike. At the time of a ceremony, Tokai, the wife of Wawe, spent a night out with Bengande and committed adultery with him. They lay on some edible leaves. When he returned, the husband Wawe saw the leaves and was told by his wife that they must not be used for food. Thus he discovered the deceit, was angry, so fought and drove the adulterer off; thus originated the Bandi branch of Endugwa at Neragaima, Bomai, and Mongoma. The Nauru Endugwa later divided and some crossed the Wahgi.[14]

The Reverend Bergmann was told that Kamanegu occupied land won from the Endugwa. The Endugwa went to Mirani and continued to fight over land. Both groups welcomed the Lutheran mission and gave them Ega, a tribal battleground, for their station. Both Kamanegu and Endugwa wanted the mission nearby to continue to provide gifts and offered this disputed territory so as to become a protected frontier. Many years later there were claims and requests for further payment from both Kamanegu and Endugwa.

Another type of tribal origin story is that of a magical spirit, the *kangi ambu* of Wauga. The spirit woman and her daughter are found by a man; the daughter mates with this first man and has many children, who found the clans of Wauga. In some variants there are clan groups that join the Wauga but had a different place of origin and parentage; thus five clans of Wauga were founded by these sons, while two Wauga clans are said to be adopted.

The Dom origin story begins with smoke seen on the mountain by a young woman. In following the smoke she discovered a man, food, and became his wife. The couple then gave birth to the founders of the clans of Dom.[15]

These tribal traditions are realistic and localized; they include movements, fights, alliances, marriage, trade, and hostilities. Local conflicts and movements were active at the time of discovery. According to Vial (1942), war destroys houses, crops, trees, fences, cassowaries, and pigs. Some Simbu had migrated to the middle Wahgi valley well before 1930, and others have continued to do so, as land there is available for the Simbu who live at high altitudes where pig raising and coffee growing are difficult. Local groups' tradition merges with remembered events, movements, and fights. Every story links a person and group to a place of settlement. In my early days of fieldwork I interviewed elders for their war stories and now can quote from these notebooks.

Agai, in 1958 (interviewer Paula Brown), told how he had been a famous Naregu fighter:

> Many men like to fight. . . . At night I went to all the enemies. When I looked in a house and saw a man inside, I went inside, hit him on the head with a stick, so he died. This was at Kamanegu. Then the Kamanegu brought a fight at night to Mi above Agumbaya. They surrounded the house. The men in the house did not know that I was there. When they saw me they ran away. I killed one and was going to burn him, as that was the practice with enemies. But they said not to burn him but take him back to Ogondie. Then there were other fights. Agai proceeded to count all the men he killed of Kamanegu, Siambugla, Bundi, Gena, Wauga; some of these were staying with their hosts at Kagai and were killed there. Agai would go out at night, steal up to a house, and kill the men inside. All the others were afraid but Agai went and killed people: men, women, children. He broke a stick to count all those he killed—total count 67. Some were to avenge Naregu war deaths.

Kama, Tultul in Naregu (1959 notebook 5), commented on this:

> I have seen these fights. We fought together, the Bau-Aundugu and Komun-Kani. Diunde killed with bow and arrow, spear. Endugwa did not fight against Naregu. We drove them to Dom. Also drove out the Nauru and the Gena. We took Gena gardens, then some kinsmen gave it back to their sisters. We burned their land and kept our enemies out.

In 1959 I recorded in the Upper Simbu that they had married sisters and sisters' sons at Bundi and had planted *marita* (P. oil pandanus) there.

In the remote parts of Simbu Province, the areas called Salt, Nomani, and Bomai are inhabited by people who claim diverse origin and migration from several directions. It seems that the Kuman Simbu expanded from the Simbu River valley and pressed south, west, and southeast, forcing the occupants of these areas into more remote and less productive areas, some with less healthy (for example, malarial) conditions. Kuman are more numerous than other dialect and cultural groups within Simbu.

The Ancestral World of Simbu

The New Guinea highland cultural area is the setting for the Kuman Simbu elaboration of a competitive economy, in which rare wild resources, cultivated food, livestock, pandanus nuts and oil fruits, salt, stone axes, feathers, plumes, shells, dog-tooth necklaces, and other goods are exchanged as valuables (Hughes 1977). Ritual feasts are celebrated by each tribe for its welfare, growth, and fertility. Clan and tribe are linked in patrilineal ancestor cult ritual; bamboo flutes are the symbolic center of the male cult, revealed to youths at initiation to teach men to support the group and fight enemies. Sexual segregation, with men sharing large central houses and women living in dispersed houses with their children and pigs, exogamy, and the exchange of goods and pigs upon marriage are supported by intergroup male competition. Warfare and feasts perpetuate the rivalry of groups. Marriage is the first step of a new intergroup and interpersonal exchange relationship, followed by gifts and return gifts at the birth of children, deaths, and group ceremonial distributions.

In 1958, an elder *luluai* (P. appointed native official, head of a tribe or large clan), Kiagenem of Pari, a Kamanegu (interviewer Paula Brown), said:

> Our ancestors were fighters. They did not fight for nothing, but fought because of stolen pigs, stealing food, and women. If a woman ran away to another man, her husband's group would fight with the new husband's group. We Kamanegu were strong, we held onto our land, and when we fought the Naregu over a runaway wife, we kept the land. (From my notebook)

Ulka Baglau, upper Simbu (interviewer Michael Gandi in 1987):

> [During initiation] we were in the small bush learning when the fight broke out so we did not learn [to play] the bamboo [flute] properly, we left the bamboo and then we took for the fight. We got our bows and arrows and we followed our bigger brothers and we fought. The boys of my age we all enjoyed fighting because it was like a game of shooting and courting. Some of my mates were killed but I was still alive and used to go fighting.

Kaglwaim of Naregu, a former fighter and *tultul* (P. native official, head of a clan or subclan) in the 1950s (interviewer Bruce Mondo Kair):

> He first went to a fight at a place called Kumbo with a big tribe called Waugla and killed a man called Per who was a headman of the Waugla. The relatives of Per are still complaining about the killing of Per which was done by Kaglwaim Kumugl. He then killed a man from another tribe during a very big tribal fight.

He speared a man called Kawagle Kondo and the spear went through the knee. That man was a great warrior and used to lead tribal fights with his tribesmen. The fighting took place at Damar. The dead man's family still kept his bones and are still keeping them in their area. He then went to Guo and grabbed a man and brought him to his place and his men killed him. The men grabbed were from Endugwa tribe. It was about a mile away from Gadaimino village still in the Guo area. He killed so many people but couldn't remember them all. He was a good warrior ... [story continues with names and places of other men killed]. People complained a lot about "kumos"[16] so that's why he killed those two men.

Francis Gaglu of Wauga (interviewer Francis Kombugun):

My father used to tell me that in order to become a responsible and respected member of my clan, the food I ate was to make me grow and gives me strength. I must work hard in work like fetching drinking water, breaking firewood, keep guarding over our pigs during the day.

The role and activities of big men were summarized by Anton Wuka (interviewer John Karl):

The role of the leaders in the past was that they talk on behalf of the people during feasts, pig killing, food exchange, giving advice to young boys who are going to be initiated. They are the brave ones who lead the rest of the people to fight. They lead feasts, are the guest speakers when invited to other ceremonies. They are the key people of the whole village. They are respected by their own clan and also others. . . . They show their respect . . . and they are also scared of them because if they say something bad than the big ones will hang them or burn them in their house. . . . What they do is lead discussions about feasts, bride price, giving advice, solving problems.

A local big man of eastern Simbu was described by his son Talaba Sinne to Fred Eremuge:

Once upon a time there lived a great man called Sine Kumil. He was a great warrior and a very wealthy man. He had many wives and several valuable traditional wealths such as *kina* (P. goldlip mother-of-pearl) shells, pigs, feathers, and stone axes. As it used to be in the olden days, people who have all these valuable things are always highly respected. That is why Sine Kumil was appointed chief of our clan . . . Sine Kumil is a famous and very active man in our clan. He goes out to fight by himself. He can even kill more than ten men a day from the enemy clan. People used to be afraid of him because they know he is a very dangerous man. He had two wives and about ten to twenty concubines. His two wives had six kids each. I am from the first wife. Finally my father Sine Kumil died in Kundiawa hospital in 1971 due to liver problem.

Yere William of Naregu (interviewer Peter Aglua):

Initiation. . . . Put in men's house at Bamugl. In the house the men made big fire and the boys stayed close around the fire and were not to move away from the fire. If they do they will be belted by the men and push them towards the fire. They were there and big men (*yagl kande*) give them talks on how they should live when they are married, how to go about when there is tribal fighting, to help others in their works and needs, to be polite and kind. After the talk the boys were taken to the river Mindimanigl, taught how to play the bamboo flute. At the end they have a feast to celebrate their initiation.

Kamanau of Sinasina (interviewer Paula Brown 1987):

Sun is our god. It looks after us when we work garden. We stop thieves by appealing to Ande; call the name of Ande so pigs and garden come up well. Our spirits are called *dewe* and *kangi*. . . .

Tell young people how to behave, don't make trouble with young girls or pull their breasts or your eyes will be hurt, bones weak, skin no good.

Guwand Kombugun, a Gena elder, moved to Endugwa (interviewer Harry Godfrid):

I was a great warrior during my young days. I fought in so many battles against various rival tribes near or distant. One such fight took place at a place called Mingelle. We fought with Mitnande due to a dispute over a lady. I later speared three other enemies. I was a hero.

In the first discussions of the New Guinea highlands (Read 1951; Salisbury 1956; Meggitt 1958), patrilineality seemed a basic feature. Detailed ethnography began to show how these societies differed from the African lineage systems as defined by Fortes (1953), and the variations were explored (Reay 1959; Barnes 1962; Brown 1962; Langness 1964; Glasse 1968). The highlanders' version of patrilineality accepted family mobility, invited nonagnates to share land and settlements, and sometimes incorporated them into the local and clan group of the hosts.

Northern Simbu Province is characterized by individually held, patrilineally inherited land on steep slopes and very high population density—that is, over 300 per square mile. Land was fought over, conquered, and claimed by the victor tribe; then a *bugla ingu* (S. pig-feast site) was made on a choice flat site. The honoring of ancestors at the pig feast confirmed the holding.

The general origin story centering on Womkama is held by Kuman Simbu of the Gembogl-Kundiawa and Kerowagi districts and, sometimes in different outline, by Sinasina and Marigl valley Simbu too. The shared traditions are perpetuated in exchange relations with affines and kin. Although these practices have changed much (Schäfer 1981) and some rites are now rarely celebrated, I describe the traditional forms in present tense. Many of the ceremonial and symbolic forms and paraphernalia, such as the bamboo flutes and *gerua* boards representing family and patrilineal continuity, are found throughout a larger cultural area. The symbols of *gerua* ancestors and *kua* flutes were major elements of the differentiation of men from boys and women. Simbu kill pigs at cemetery sites to honor ancestors, claim territory, assert group continuity, and promote the health, fertility, and welfare of people and pigs. These claims to sites and territory are the foundation of land disputes and wars. Whatever great changes in everyday life the Simbu have undergone, land, locality, and local monuments still serve to define territorial and homeland claims and the sentiments of local ties. On great ceremonial occasions leaders define groups and assert rights over places.

Kua, the generic word for bird, has a wide significance. It is the sacred bird of the Simbu, and is represented in the *gerua* ritual symbols at male initiation and pig feast. *Kua kambu*, the spirit flutes, are blown in pairs that represent male and female on ritual occasions. Whereas boys are shown and taught how to blow them at initiation, women and uninitiated boys are told that these are sacred bird calls (Nilles 1939, 1940, 1943, 1944).

Kua is also important in marking puberty for girls, when it is said "she has seen the *kua*." *Kua*, the flute, has the additional meaning of men's genitals, as well as symbolizing wealth, the exchange process, group prestige, and plenty. This powerful concept was actualized when the airplane appeared (see Chap. 3).

Bird feathers and plumes of birds of paradise, parrots, and cassowaries, both traded and imported, are important valuables in marriage transactions and also used in spectacular headdresses in ritual dances. Birds symbolize beauty, freedom, and wealth; the most important and valuable birds are often the names of men (Nilles 1977). Some—like the Princess Stephanie long, black plume *miuge*, the sicklebill *siune*, and the lesser bird of paradise *yombagl*[17]—are still valued, traded, and worn for ceremony (Dilu Deck 1992).

The greatest Melanesian ceremonials are occasions for massive assemblies, displays, and distributions of food and goods. These exchange ceremonies and other transactions have appeared to some writers[18] as being of a singular character. The several types include traveling fleets trading in valuables as well as rare and useful goods not available in other communities, ceremonial exchanges that mark intergroup competitions, and interpersonal exchanges to win prestige and confirm relationships. Many transactions in Melanesia originate a relationship or signify a continuing relationship between the involved parties. Marriage, birth, death, intergroup relations, and tribal affairs are announced by a transaction that confirms and publicizes. The gift marks the event; Simbu keep the jaws and bones of pigs received until a return ceremony and gift removes the debt. A larger gift extends the reciprocal obligation; bones are a measure and a reminder. Exchanges most often consist of giving an object, food, or pig that has been made or raised by the donor and in some sense represents the person (Strathern 1988). The value lies in the persons and the relationship.

Gregory (1982) and Strathern (1988) would distinguish gifts from commodity transactions, in which the value is in the object transacted. The idea of commodity is said not to be indigenous to Melanesia. This seems to me too sharp and universal a distinction (see Bloch and Parry 1989). Tueting's survey (1935), as well as Malinowski's study of the Trobriand *kula* (1922:176–194), describe several types of transactions, including trade and barter, throughout Melanesia. Open markets and trade were certainly not rare there (see Harding 1967; Epstein 1968).

Exchange and competition preoccupy every Simbu. Agriculture was not for subsistence alone; they raised food and especially pigs for ceremonial feasts, in which large quantities of both were presented to individuals of other clans and tribes. Exchange of shells, feathers, stone axes, and other valuables is based upon trade and production of agricultural goods. Competition for agricultural land and interpersonal conflict create frequent fights and permanent hostilities between tribes. Friendly relations involve marriage and reciprocal exchange of valuables and feasts of foodstuffs and pigs. Quarrels and hostility among clans and tribes lead to fighting and retaliation for injuries. Some battles involve thousands of warriors armed with bows, arrows, spears, and axes.

In all of their affairs and relationships, Simbu are cognizant of the group—which is a clan or tribe (sometimes identified as the followers of a big man, sometimes as a group from a certain place)—and the person. Although individuals are not submerged in their clan, neither do they stand only as individuals. The youths of a clan, clan segment, and subclan are age mates who were initiated together. They call one another *yaglkuna* (S. man, age-mate) and form a lifelong support group, work parties, and courting parties, and sing and dance together at ceremonies, help one another to assemble food and goods for ceremonies, and fight for the clan and tribe. The big men (S. *yagl kangi*, the man with a big name) are outstanding individuals who become icons of the clan and tribe. Ordinary men, or men of slight distinction, form the support for group enterprises such as war and peace, instigated and led by the big men. When a man is brash and recklessly attacks enemies or travelers, his action may lead the group into an undesirable war that endangers them all. In the relations among tribes neutrality is unknown.

Relations between individuals and groups in Simbu are marked by the giving and receiving of food, pigs, cassowaries, and valuable goods, many of which are not available in the local environment and reached the highlands through long-distance trade (Hughes 1977). Exchange, gift, trade, and other sorts of transactions are interwoven with social, group, and interpersonal relations. Not every transaction must be between people in a long-term relationship, however. Plume trade to distant areas is undertaken by small groups of men, often with affines, friends, or relatives in distant tribes (Bulmer 1962). Highly valued are feathers and plumes of parrots, cassowaries, and, above all, birds of paradise, shells, the small *tambu* and *girigiri* (P. cowries), and whole or fragments of goldlip mother-of-pearl, bailer, green snail, and other large shells. Large, thin, ground stone axe blades affixed to decorative handles are valuables, whereas the shorter and thicker work axes are essential tools and weapons. Both are obtained from local Wahgi valley and distant (for example, Jimi) quarries, and are traded (Burton 1984). Simbu both give and trade tools, shields, bows, arrows, flutes, bags, and items of clothing and decoration—woven belts, skirts, aprons, and armbands.

Occasions and Transactions of Foods and Goods

Marriage is the key to the arena of exchange. A gift marks the event and the relationship. Bride-price is translated by Simbu into pidgin as *baiim meri*. The content of marriage payments has changed over the years from dog's-teeth necklaces and stone axes to shells and steel. Now money, several thousand kina, is the chief item. Pigs have been a constant. At weddings, shells, feathers, plumes, axes, pigs, and often other rare valuables are given to the bride's group and exchanged between the groups of bride and groom; funerals also are occasions for the giving and sharing of valuables and foods. Small celebrations of births and the maturing of young people are occasions for gifts of food and payment of debts. Kinsmen and affines of the donors are the principal exchange partners, who repay the gifts at the next occasion of intergroup celebration.

The Kuman Simbu hold two distinct kinds of intergroup exchange ceremony. *Mogenabiri* alternate between tribes or clans: the gifts are given by one individual to another in the recipient group, the whole ceremony organized by and given to one tribe or clan. The pig feast, *bugla gende*, is held by a tribe for all of the members' friends and exchange partners. Kuman Simbu have several times proclaimed that pig feasts will no longer be held, and there have been none since the 1970s. The *mogenabiri*, however, is adaptable to new goods and valuables, and to new circumstances involving group gifts and payments.

The *mogenabiri* is a huge display of food, often including rare types not available in the territory of the recipients: pandanus, especially valued bananas, sugarcane, yams, taro, and hunted animals, cuscus, and other marsupials. The composition of the vegetable heap varies in different regions. The very important exchange goods, nuts and fruits of two species of pandanus, grow at different altitudes in the Simbu area. The distribution of one variety to friendly tribes at a different altitude is an important tie between groups, and intermarriage was thus stimulated. *Mogenabiri* are not held at fixed intervals; rather, each tribe plans a distribution when it has the food and resources to make a suitable return for a previous *mogenabiri*. The exchange has in recent years included peanuts, cartons of beer, horses, cows, coconuts, display boards of money, stacks of canned fish and meats, frozen meat, and other purchased foods (see also Bergmann 1971, 4:130–135; Gande 1974).

The tribal leaders announce the plan, designating the tribe to receive the return payment. The gift must be at least equal to that received at a former occasion, but largesse is mandatory, and honor requires increment. Leading men direct the planting of a large communal garden of special festive foods and set the date for the display and distribution. Then each man plants bananas, sugarcane, and other special foods to make a show of plenty. When the display pile is constructed, each member contributes gift foods for his friends and relatives in the recipient group. In the case of the largest intertribal gifts, a series of contributing gift presentations are solicited and ceremonially given by friends of the donors in nearby clans and tribes not involved in the main gift. This may occur over a period of weeks, as I observed in 1976. In this way, members of all the tribes in a region are included. The spectacle of dance, song, oratory, and the massing of food gifts is a major event for participants and audience. The huge pile of food gifts, assembled on one day, is dismantled item by item over many hours, the name of the recipient being shouted out by the big man in charge. It is a distribution from each donor to each of his personal friends, affines, and relatives in the recipient group. Women attend to enjoy visiting with their kin and receive the gifts donated to their husbands and themselves with cheers of appreciation. A woman whose brothers are members of the donor group receives many gifts in her husband's name.

For the *bugla gende* or *bugla ingu* (S. pig-house), pigs for ceremonial distribution, which are raised and fattened on a long ceremonial cycle of seven to ten years, are the central item. Simbu measure success in the display, slaughter, and distribution of many very large fat pigs.[19] Pigs are taken for fattening by extratribal relatives, who may also help in the butchering and cooking and will receive pork. It is a tribal rite (Aufenanger 1965), with gifts made to individuals in all clans and tribes, including, nowadays, relatives and friends of distant, non-Simbu groups. When the feast plan is announced, ritual flutes are blown, and over a period of months houses then are built at the donor tribe's ceremonial grounds, both for the men of the donor group and for the many guest families who will come to enjoy the festival and receive pigs at the distribution. The final ritual is preceded by many weeks of visits to the ceremonial sites by richly adorned, weapon-carrying clan and tribe dance troupes from all surrounding tribes.

An important element in the *bugla gende* is the ancestral ritual, for the ancestors are responsible for the welfare, fertility, and reproduction of people, food, and pigs (Gande 1974). Ceremonial paraphernalia of *gerua* (S. headboards painted with ancestral insignia), specially constructed *arigl* (S. wigs) and pairs of *kua* (S. bamboo flutes) symbolize men and patrilineal ancestry. During the ritual, young men and boys are initiated through ordeals of heat and thirst and are taught to play the ancestral flute tunes. The men wear *gerua* representing their particular patrilineal ancestors, and patrilineal groups hold traditional rights to certain dance performances and flute tunes. Signs of wealth are the plume and feather headdresses, shell ornaments, and axes. Pigs are killed in the ceremonial ground and nearby cemeteries as a sacrificial demonstration of their dedication to the ancestors. The pigs are arranged like the spokes of a wheel from the central *bolum* house, proclaiming the size and value of each subclan's production and distribution of pigs. Some special distributions are announced to honor and compensate allies, repay group debts, and seal marriages. Invited guests assist in butchering and cooking the meat, and then carry their portions home, where they are divided and distributed with announcements.[20]

Banduo Monguai, Endugwa (interviewed by his grandson, Paul Ambani), said: "Pigs are used as prestige. The more you have, the more status you have in the village. Dead ancestors are believed to be alive in the cemetery. They are assumed to live as spirits. They are believed to be help in certain case. The pigs are killed in cemetery to seek help."

In a story, Toby Waim Kagl explained warfare. When one tribe challenged another because of a rape, theft of a pig, or a very humiliating insult, they put the strength and resources of the whole tribe, their collective effort, to the test. If one tribe lost, it would call on its allies to come to its rescue. The winning tribe, further to contain any reprisal, would do likewise.

So what had been an argument or a war between two rival tribes very soon became warfare for a whole region (Kagl 1976:70).

Intertribal alliance, amity, and hostility are related to the competitive relations among them. Debts, insults, and responsibility for deaths in warfare are transformed by ceremonial payments. Goods, food, and pigs are presented ceremonially to be distributed and consumed; there is no prestige in accumulation. A poor or excessively delayed return of *mogenabiri* or *bugla gende* is tribal shame. The prestige of individuals and of tribes is linked to the state of debt and credit in intertribal exchange, and to the killing of enemies in warfare. The tribal exchange system is regulated by the specific types of payment required at weddings, funerals, and the delayed exchanges of the large food and pig festivals.

Simbu individual and group relations are ever-shifting, constantly being renegotiated in the give-and-take of competitive exchange that is the basis of power. In the prestige exchange system, individual men seek exchange-friends who can provide valuables and access to rare resources. Exchange cycles interconnect clans and tribes as donor and recipient throughout a region. Each tribe has affinal and kinship ties to all of its neighbors and some distant groups. Marriages, trade, visits, and migration cross language and cultural barriers between the upper Simbu valley and the Asaro and Gende areas.

There does not appear to be a separate sphere of commodities or trade relations. At the conclusion of a pig ceremony, when the donor tribe has killed all of its grown pigs and many families have no pigs, the donors trade plumes, and other valuables used in the ceremony for small pigs, with visitors who are not necessarily kin or friends.[21] Visitors come to obtain valuable shells and plumes for their transactions. Nilles (1944) describes a market between Simbu and Gende peoples at the head of the Simbu valley.[22] Long-distant trading expeditions are organized and conducted by men who have some personal, kinship, or affinal link with distant people. Simbu traveled to distant places for trade in plumes, feathers, and products of other areas (Bulmer 1962; Hughes 1977). Travel is hazardous because strangers and enemies might attack to steal and kill small traveling parties.

Men and Spirits

In their everyday interactions, Simbu seem remarkably outspoken and direct in their dealings with people and in their expressions of anger, animosity, and conflict with others. Warry (1987:185) sees Simbu as argumentative, aggressive, and litigious; Podolefsky, as contentious (1992: 52). Simbu talk and interests concentrate on competition and confrontation: warfare, fights, competitive feasts and exchanges. Yet there is always suspicion of clandestine acts, magic, and hidden meanings. Mystical forces are seen by Simbu as powerful, as are potentially dangerous spirits (S. *gigl, kangi, dewe, yogondo, dinggan;* cf. Nilles 1950, 1977; Aufenanger 1960, 1971; Bergmann 1971; Hughes 1985) in the mountains and bush, and people may control some powerful forces.

Simbu beliefs about *kumo* (S. witchcraft) are significant in understanding their relations with one another and their reactions to contact. The concept *boromai suara* (S. one blood) distinguishes the local section of a subclan, represented ideationally as the men's house (S. *yagl ingu*) group—that is, a group of five to fifteen closely related men and their wives and children. *Kumo* does not act upon more distant clansmen, unrelated persons, or distant relatives. This close group should be a model of solidarity, a source of constant help in daily activities, obligations of payments and gifts, and defense of land and family. Betrayal and *kumo* destroy unity and harmony (see O'Hanlon 1989 for a Wahgi version of this).

Relations with other groups, beyond the clan and tribe, are intrinsically distrustful, competitive, and potentially hostile. But within these outside groups are affines, matrikin, and friendly relatives who support and assist in payments, generously offer sanctuary, and help when illness or defeat creates special needs, and so must be always treated with respect and friendship. To insult or neglect a close kinsman is to court danger; his angry resentful thoughts can harm the family. There are thus several different kinds of reprisal for misconduct or mistreatment of other people: the *kumo* of a member of the men's-house group; the harmful thoughts of kin; and the assault of enemies. The Simbu feel that malefactors are all around them; they need protection and exercise caution in their relations with others. Although local group solidarity should be constant, jealousy, betrayal, and *kumo* do happen: there is always suspicion and mistrust.

Statements by and interviews with those who claim to be *kumo* (S. witches) or know it well (Bergmann 1971; Hughes 1985; Sterly 1987) are not consistent but demonstrate a range and variety of beliefs. These and my own inquiries (Brown 1977) agree that *kumo* is witchcraft: a familiar spirit-animal (rat, bat, marsupial) inside the chest or body of the witch takes a vital organ or injures the victim. *Kumo* is the person who is a witch, the spirit-creature that makes the witchcraft, and the act of causing harm. The Simbu say that the *kumo* person may not be in full control of his/her *kumo*; however, he or she joins with the secret band of *kumo* that plan and execute killings and share the flesh of victims.[23]

Simbu terminology for sorcery, magic, and medicine carries a complex meaning. *Kirai* is a power within a plant, potion, or object that is medicine and magic. Perhaps combined with a spell (S. *nimbine*), or as a charm (Bergmann 1971, 4:35–50), it may cure an illness, restore good health, make a person fall in love, bring good fortune to a marriage, make a woman pregnant, cause infertility, or win a war (Philip Kai Moore 1985, 1987; Dage 1988).

Many of these magical medicines are eaten. A kind of earth (S. *mondono*) is fed to pigs for growth and health. Many foods and special varieties of common foods are eaten at particular times; for example, certain greens are fed to mothers after childbirth to make the mother and her milk strong. Ginger (S. *gene*) is often used in magic and medicine, and as a condiment at feasts, as it is powerful and gives strength. Such materials may be beneficial or harmful; some are called poison. The most powerful magic medicines are used in warfare.

The first travelers in the highlands saw bodies they thought were war victims that had been thrown into fast-flowing rivers. They are more likely to have been persons who died of certain dreaded diseases associated with *kumo* and sorcery, or persons accused of *kumo*, as this was the usual way in which Simbu disposed of them. In the 1960s Simbu spoke of these beliefs and regretted that executions were forbidden by the government. Still more recently, several accused witches have been attacked (Giddings 1990). My field notes record cases when Simbu suspicions and accusations of witchcraft were made after the death of a young person. Then the accused and his/her family might be exiled from the local group, to live with relatives. They often visited their home area, continued to garden on their land, and to participate in exchanges, activities, and payments of the local men's house and subclan group. *Kumo* operates only within a subclan group and locality, so this move is seen as protecting the survivors in a local group without endangering the new hosts. The Simbu believe that *kumo* is rancor in the men's-house group, a kind of interpersonal malice, not a haphazard attack on a neighbor.

The first white men to visit the area, Jim Taylor and his party, were watched closely for indications of otherworldly connections.[24] Their discarded tins, paper, excretions, and so on were prized for possible magical powers, and as late as 1958, when I was first in the area, there were attempts to obtain my goods for their magical value. During my first fieldwork my household discards were treasured and I was thought to bring friends luck in card games. Once I discovered an attempt to collect my excretions. While Simbu, at least at Mintima, no longer collect these objects as far as I know, the knowledge gained in school and in contact with western things does still have a magical quality that brings success to the owner and enhances his worth. Today Simbu feel that an educated person, whose family has invested resources in her or him, should command a large bride-price or compensation for injury (Dage 1985).

The wide variation and piecemeal information I obtained over the years suggest that magic and sorcery in Simbu consist in hints, impressions, suspicions, and fears that they are ever imperiled by fiends. Although sometimes translated to *pidgin sangguma*, I believe that among the Simbu these ideas, more than any other kind of cultural knowledge, are often individually invented and modified. Meanings are often concealed (Aufenanger 1962a). Simbu spells, *ka nimbine*, are often simple sentences like "Do this," "Make this." Magical/medicinal materials, herbs, and so on can be selected or created by the practitioner. Like folktales, sorcery incantations and practices may be individual, passed on within families, taught, invented, or modified in use. Although contagious and imitative magic ideas are evident, Simbu do not display the obsessive concern with protection of personal leavings or constant suspicion of unfaithful wives and hidden enemies that have been reported in some Melanesian communities, nor do they hold endless moots or divinations after every death (Brison 1992).

Big Men in War and Exchange

Simbu big men (S. *yagl kande* or *yomba pondo*) are prominent in all group activities: they are physically large and forceful in manner. In the past, they often had several wives and many followers who could produce large amounts of special foods and pigs for ceremonial exchange. When they speak at gatherings, they declare their preeminence and define relations and group alignments.

Big men have a magical power that gives them their strength and capacity to injure others. For Simbu, the big man's power is a kind of *mana*, in a Melanesian context. In himself he represents tribal strength and invincibility: he cannot be killed or injured by enemies. Agai, in 1958, said: "I walked about, men did not see me. I shot them at night." A big man's powerful control of magic protects him so that he is impervious to arrows or spears; they cannot penetrate his skin. His own arrows and spears are under his power, magical and physical. This makes his aim accurate and kills his enemies. Thus a war is also a contest between the physical and magical powers of big men.

The big man is the enemy's prime target in war. He is always more exposed than his followers; in ceremonies and in war he stands prominently before his followers. By injuring or killing a big man in battle the conqueror demonstrates his superior magic. The big man is proven unable to defend and protect himself and his followers. When a big man is killed in warfare, the enemies celebrate their greatest success. When a big man dies suddenly, especially after a ceremonial feast, it is believed that he was killed by some form of poison magic. The corpse and burial place of a big man is guarded against attempts to steal his powerful substance, and it may be collected by relatives for magical uses.

Kaglwaim of Naregu (interviewer Bruce Mondo Kair):

Arime died so he [Kaglwaim] went to Kundiawa because many people were talking about "kumo" so kiap asked him not to bury the dead body because talks were going on that Sanguma or Kumo were going to take his body away. They laid his dead body on a big shelf made of four bush vines and because he was such a very big person, people collect his body liquid from what their customs say so had to get the liquid to look after pigs. They had to keep the liquid in the house and had to produce big fat pigs, big fat crops, etc.

Warfare was never a simple opposition between two parties. Simbu tribes, and their blocks of land, are among the largest in Melanesia. Marriage and kinship ally the close relatives of bride and groom, and they become friends and supporters. Every tribe is divided by individual loyalties to members of each side in a war of large scale or long duration. Although the big man should be strong, powerful, and magically protected, members of his group and allies remain vulnerable; the big man may fail to protect them all. If a man dies in support of allies, compensation is demanded. The payment should consist of pigs; and a girl, to be a bride in the victim's group, was included if possible.[25] This is an inescapable obligation, for which any delay or neglect of responsibility may lead to retaliation or war. Mistrust and censure characterize the relations between men of different clans and tribes.

There are multiple obligations and support patterns within a clan, among friendly clans (normally within a tribe, sometimes in another tribe), and in clans or tribes at war. Tensions and apprehension, fraught with magical suspicions, characterize apparently friendly or neutral clans. In contrast, one's own clan, and often tribe (except at times of conflict), should be trustworthy; enemies may use any means to inflict revenge and injure a clan or tribe in opposition. The operation of sorcery is in a middle zone where outright physical attack is not permitted but allegiances are unreliable. Here motives are uncertain; friendship and competition, affinity and kinship prevail, but not unquestioned solidarity.

Unexplained deaths and anxieties about trust in fellow tribesmen, allies, and affines underlie the urgency of death payments and compensation for losses of allies. Big men attending ceremonies of their kinsmen and affines were in special danger, in need of magical protection as much as that of weapons in intertribal meetings. There is a pervasive awareness of the dangers of sorcery and the vulnerability of men. In a people with a wide reputation as outspoken, direct, and active in physical retaliation for any insult or wrong, this underlying apprehension and fear are not readily observed. It seems to prove a general Melanesian characteristic concealed beneath a forceful cultural facade.

This mixture of spiritual power and forceful leadership sums up the Simbu idea of the character of the big man. It descends through the generations as success in war and in display and exchange, the pride of the tribe.

Although some Simbu big-man attributes may fit Godelier's (1982) definition of "great men," a wide range of leadership characteristics in Melanesian societies is evident, as further discussion demonstrates (Brown 1990b; Godelier and Strathern, eds. 1991). The great man/big man discussion involves a contrast of sister exchange and bridewealth, male initiation ritual and organized large-scale exchange by leaders in the name of groups, and payments that imply an equivalence or substitution of valuables and pigs for men and women. Commentaries and examples of big-man societies and great-man societies are comparative and evolutionary; they concentrate on precontact practices and concepts. However, few case studies (cf. Godelier and Strathern, ed. 1991) discuss changes during and after the colonial period in Papua New Guinea. I shall show how the colonial officers imposed peacemaking ceremonies with compensation and gift exchanges upon the Simbu, transforming their concepts and values.

3

White Spirits and Cargo

The kiaps came with police;
the missionaries came with dogs.
—KIUGL WAGUO, ENDUGWA, 1987
(interviewer Lawrence Gigmai)

The Highlands Area and Contact History

In the 1920s the Australians had only recently taken charge of German New Guinea and began to extend administration from the coast and islands, with Rabaul and Salamaua as centers. The Australian Mandated Territory of New Guinea administration was responsible to the League of Nations for a territory only partly explored; the large populations of the inland were little known. Tribal fighting, pacification, and prevention of attacks on miners, missionaries, and administration officers were their concerns, as the New Guinea administration developed policies for the extension of authority and control. Each tribe and group was to come under administrative control and be subject to native regulations; a first step was "influence."

Official policy adapted to new situations. Papua was for the most part a longer established territory. Administrative policy developed for small communities of less warlike, coastal peoples, and in 1935 the hostility that Hides and O'Malley encountered in the southern highlands was unexpected. J. Walstab, D.O.[1] reported in 1924 on his Sepik expedition to deal with tribal conflicts. He commanded native police in night strikes to arrest killers, used rifles against spears, and took captives. His report suggested how to bring the people under influence and then under control. It was his view that the administration should not punish fighting among tribes that were not "under influence." A year later, Ambunti station had a celebratory *singsing* (P. festival), which was well attended and peaceable, to the satisfaction of A.D.O. Townsend.[2]

The ideas and practices of officers were shaped by official policy and experience in the service. Field and headquarters officers differed in their definition of and approval of punitive sanctions against those involved in tribal

fighting, raids, and murders. Everyone knew about, and many had some experience of, violent exchanges with and among Kukukuku, highlands, and Sepik
groups in the 1920s and 1930s; mining and administrative history of the New
Guinea mandate is full of such clashes. The people were seen by many administrators as belligerent and resistant to pacification, so that officers were ap-
prehensive in their conducting of patrols and investigations. Police had many
opportunities to observe fights and come into conflict with newly contacted
natives whose attacks were under investigation (see Chapters 4 and 5).

The publicity and questions raised about tribal fighting, punitive measures, and killings of white men in the Australian press and parliament during the League of Nations mandate made the Australians sensitive to public
and international criticism. The New Guinea administration was held responsible for protecting the missionaries, miners, and other white men. Australian policy of control of violence, both between tribal communities and
against white men and visitors, was cautious. Throughout the history of the
Australian New Guinea extension of administration contact and control
there were violent clashes and incidents to investigate.

Newly contacted natives were not subject to the native regulations set
by the Australian administration, which were enforced only after administrative control had been established. Incidents of tribal fighting were investigated, and the officers worked to bring the communities under peaceful government influence without punitive expeditions. Those known to have been
fighting and killing enemies might be arrested but not harmed, and weapons,
but not other property, might be seized and destroyed. After a group was considered to be under control, tribal fighting, killing, and attacks could lead to
arrest, trial, and imprisonment.

First Contact in the Eastern Highlands

Morobe District stretched inland from the Huon peninsula and gulf to the
Papuan border; Madang District crossed the Finisterre range and included
the western highlands to the Papuan border; there were no highlands districts. The first European to enter the highlands area was probably H. Detz-
ner, a German officer in World War I who attempted to escape arrest.
H. Baum, a former German officer, turned prospector after that war. In the
acts of expansion and penetration, Lutheran missionaries established Kaiapit
in 1917 and entered the highlands through Binumarien and Pundibassa, proceeding to Gadsup and other eastern highlands areas after 1919 and throughout the 1920s. The "Gadsup fringe" of the eastern highlands was reached by
gold prospectors and Lutheran missionaries in the 1920s (Radford 1987).
Australian extension of administration and control came afterward.

The fame of the Leahy-Dwyer discoveries in 1930–1931 and the great exploratory patrols—the Leahy-Taylor Bena-Hagen patrol of 1933 and the Hagen-Sepik patrol of 1938–1939—have overshadowed the history of penetration of the Upper Ramu by Lutheran missionaries and private gold prospectors (Radford 1987). Eastern highlanders met Lutheran missionaries from Kaiapit on the Markham in 1920 and later. Several early attempts to set up mission stations were unsuccessful, for there were intertribal hostilities, and Gadsup and other eastern highlands peoples resisted the intrusion. Australian policy under the League of Nations mandate concerning the control of fighting among inland people was still being developed.

The first Europeans to settle in the highlands had quite different interests and goals: miners were seeking new gold sources beyond Bulolo and Wau after the discovery of Edie Creek in 1926, and the Lutherans sought to develop missions (Radford 1987:56). In 1928 Rev. L. Flierl crossed the Arona valley. The Lutherans placed native evangelists from the Finschhafen area in several Gadsup and Tairora villages, probably in the 1920s (Watson 1992). Binumarian station was established in 1923 (Bergmann 1971, 1:3). Many visits to eastern highlands communities were made by Lutherans L. Flierl, W. Flierl, Pilhofer, and Bergmann between 1926 and 1933. There is some evidence that cattle and pack animals were introduced by miners, and coffee by German missionaries (Watson 1992).

One of the first prospectors, Ned Rowlands, camped at Arona in 1928 and was seen by the Lutheran missionaries Pilhofer and Bergmann in 1929 (Radford 1987:64). Rowlands' prospecting in the Arona and Kainantu valleys attracted the interest of Levien, an experienced prospector. When his most promising finds were valuated, Rowlands settled at Ornapinka. The Peadon brothers, Lance and Lex, Ted Ubank, and others began mining in the Ornapinka, Barola, and Yonki areas. The independent prospectors set up their camps with a few native workers. As O'Neill (1979) points out, in New Guinea gold is usually found in areas that are cold, damp, and not promising for habitation. There was little contact with natives in the Bulolo and Watut areas. However, the mining activities at Kainantu and Mount Hagen were close to highlands settlements, and the prospectors depended upon local communities for some supplies and labor. Conflicts with local communities arose over the intrusion and use of local resources by miners. Thefts of their goods by natives, retaliation for theft, and treatment of native employees could also bring about violent reactions. A few incidents between miners and natives ended in the withdrawal of the miners' permit to camp in an uncontrolled area. According to M. Leahy's diary notes for 27 October 1932, "Met Lea Ashton who got his permit cancelled for shooting a nig after they opened fire on him." On 29 November "Taylor arrested 4 nigs who shot the missionaries dogs. Sent 3 to Wau very sorry looking for themselves."[3] George Chester killed one of his employees by striking him, and P.O. C. D. Bates brought him in for trial; he was sentenced in 1934.

Michael Leahy was determined to extend prospecting into the highlands. In 1930 he and Michael Dwyer made their "epic journey" (Willis 1969) into unknown territory, discovering large unknown populations west and south of Kainantu. In another prospecting trip in 1931, after H. Baum had been killed and robbed by Kukukukus, Leahy, with his brother Pat, killed a Kukukuku native in the Tauri area; an attack was driven off after three were killed.[4] Leahy made several more prospecting trips into the highlands between 1930 and 1933 (Leahy 1935b; Leahy and Crain 1937; Leahy 1991).

> In Barabuna (Northern Tairora), many villagers recall their first experiences with "contact." The first whites into the area were two missionaries (in 1928). . . . One woman recalled the visit as follows: When they came, people ran into the forest in fear—they thought the missionaries were ghosts. They also smeared pig blood and grease over their hands, face, hair, etc. to protect themselves. They feared they would die because they were seeing the dead. (Grossman 1992)

Watson (1992) suggests that the missionaries may have been Pilhofer and Bergmann.

In February 1933, Mick and Dan Leahy and Charles Marshall climbed to the top of Mount "Irambadi" (Elimbari) to see the vista of Mount Wilhelm and the Simbu and Wahgi valleys. On 16 February 1933 they were enthusiastically greeted by men and women, some women claiming that they were returned from the dead. They saw fighting spears, black palm bows, and green stone axes. On the eighteenth, as they were returning toward the Garfuka River headwaters, hundreds of armed and decorated men and women threatened the group (Marshall 1983). Ewunga, a native employee of Leahy who accompanied them, told Munster: "His lasting memory of this journey is the view of dozens of Chuave warriors taking up slabs of wood from their garden fences, tying pieces of bush rope to them and slinging them across their backs, in imitation of the rifles" (Munster 1975:7).

Warry's study of the Duma people near Chuave describes their first contact as meeting with Leahy's patrol and observing the Europeans trading pearl shells for pigs (Warry 1987:1) They took shavings from the firewood chopped with steel axes by members of the patrol and hung them from the rafters in the men's house where they could be used to rub on the stone axes to make them strong. This magical aura surrounding the first patrol takes many forms in the stories of first contact. My talks in the Goroka area include stories of stealing mirrors, flour, rice, and whatever could be taken from the patrol. The purpose or use of the object was often not known. Anything associated with the strangers was appropriated and kept for its possible magical value. As late as 1958–1959, on my first visits, I frequently saw tin lids and paper goods attached to highlanders' skin or clothing.

This excursion was shortly followed by the joint New Guinea Goldfields Company/New Guinea administration patrol from Bena post to Mount Hagen, which established the existence of fertile valleys and a large population not previously known.

White Men's Attitudes and Observations in Early Contact

White men in Papua New Guinea, whether they were administrative officers, missionaries, or private settlers and prospectors, had as their most urgent concerns health, safety, and food supply for themselves and those government employees and contract laborers from coastal areas who worked for them. They depended upon native goodwill for their necessities. By paying for local supplies with shells and bringing some tools for mining and building, their immediate needs could be met. The shells, cloth, knives, and axes used in gifts and trade were greatly desired by the local people.

> Our dependence on a supply of native food was one cogent reason why we valued friendly relations with the local inhabitants. We just could not have existed in a hostile environment, apart from the danger of being bumped off. (O'Neill 1979:70)

> We white men treated our boys as inferiors, . . . but it was impossible to harbour such attitudes towards these wild, free people. They were just men; most very likeable. Looking back, I fear we gave these people much less than they gave us. (O'Neill 1979:77)

The men engaged in mining and prospecting maintained contact with coastal stations, mining interests, and friends through radio and frequent air visits. Unlike the missionaries and government officers, they needed no continuing contact with village communities. To mine, they camped near local communities, took some supplies, traded for food, cut trees, and gave the natives much desired shells, cloth, and metal goods. The miners found that local villagers were often at war with neighbors and were tempted to steal from the mining camp.

There grew up a white man's legend that on first sight the natives were awestruck and thought that white men and unknown New Guineans were spirits; on further acquaintance they would attack and steal shells and other goods.[5]

> First contact with people who had not seen whites before always made both sides equally cautious and nervous of the other's capabilities. On second contact, the young bucks and/or locals, seeing the treasure in our hands often became ambitious to possess it. On the third meeting one had to be on guard against an unexpected attack, unless a psychological and physical superiority had been established.[6]

The belief was shared by Ewunga, Waria "boss-boy" who accompanied Mick Leahy on many trips: "They were new fellows, they never fought us the first time they saw us. If we came back a second time we had to watch out, because then they realized we were just ordinary people, not spirits or ancestors."[7] This generalization is not confirmed in all cases. Taylor and Leahy recorded that the first Simbu they encountered seemed awed and lethargic, and later were eager to trade. People of the Bomai area of Simbu, many years later, greeted the first patrols with gifts and enthusiasm.

Retaliation by shooting, thus showing the power of guns, was thought by many to be an appropriate response to such attempts at theft. Leahy expresses his attitude in reviewing a 1932 incident near the Bena River:

> Familiarity began to breed the contempt that primitive people have for seemingly unarmed and defenseless members of any community outside their own village relatives and allies of the moment. The idea that we wielded magic began to take a second place to avarice and acquisitiveness intensified by the uniqueness and evident utilitarian and decorative value of our camp gear. The theft of a knife along a straight stretch of the river gave us a good opportunity to demonstrate the power of the rifle to the gathered hundreds who had scattered from around the camp and were watching to see the outcome of this daring effort to plunder our property. (Leahy 1991:59)

The Australian government opened the Upper Ramu patrol post at what is now Kainantu in 1932. Local hostility to intrusion in the area where miners had established camps, and hindsight of misunderstanding, brought killings and intensified concern on the part of the Australian government. The New Guinea administration, responsible for the lives and welfare of the natives and few Europeans of this vast inland region, had focused on administering longer contacted groups. Most officers and headquarters were in coastal stations, engaged in managing communications and services in areas better known and longer under administrative control. The highlands experience was shared by a small handful of miners and officers. There was a post at Bena airstrip called Purari base camp in 1933. By 1934, Kainantu had become the highlands administrative center and power base. From diaries and reports it is clear that, although they may all have been newcomers and strangers to the native peoples, they were distinct individuals with varied attitudes. Most especially, the personalities and ways of dealing with natives exhibited by several miners and government officers were quite varied.

A key incident was the killing of Ian Mack; in March 1933 he was P.O. at Upper Ramu police post (Kainantu), having followed P.O. J. L. Taylor. When he tried to stop the tribal fighting of Aiamontina Agarabi with a line of police boys, leading a village raid to effect arrests, he was shot with an arrow when entering a house. Taken back to the post, and later to a hospital, he died (Radford 1987:119). P.O. A. F. Kyle arranged a peace ceremony and was determined not to punish the people. However, "The people of Aiamontinas bore the brunt of government reprisal for insubordination" (Radford 1987:120–121). They abandoned their villages for a time, but this did not end intertribal hostilities and attempts to regain lost territory.

Lutheran missionaries set up stations and airstrips, and traveled extensively (Flierl 1927, Bergmann n.d.). Their native evangelists from coastal and island communities of New Guinea, spread among many villages, each making a distinct impression in a local community. In 1934 the Seventh-Day Adventists established a mission in the eastern highlands.

One phase of developing administrative control was the appointment of native leaders as luluais, who had the responsibility of conveying government orders and maintaining peace and order in their communities. The first paramount luluai (P. higher native official), Anarai'i of Agarabi, was appointed in 1936. His group had been ousted by the Aiamontinas and Unantu. With support, he raided the Unantu area. P.O. Nurton gathered people and displayed gunfire by drilling a kerosene can with bullets. Then, to discourage fighting, he and C.P.O. Aitchison brought force to Unantu, killing four men and taking weapons. He warned that there would be immediate retribution for any attack against people under government control such as Anarai'i (Radford 1987:124).

Several of the Europeans in the area attempted to maintain white prestige by "teaching the natives a lesson" from time to time (Radford 1987:113) and impressed the natives with displays of gun power. When the property of a European was stolen and he was attacked, guns were fired against arrows. It is suggested (Radford 1987:114) that at times prospectors threatened villagers with kiap intervention. Government officers, including Bates in 1933, were sometimes caught in intervillage hostilities, and also between native villagers and miners. Conflicts between upper Ramu villagers and newcomers, miners, and government resulted in many deaths; the European community reacted with punitive actions, intervention in intercommunity conflicts, and attempts to pacify and disarm the natives. The miners of the area formed a friendly band that gathered at Kainantu, and the Australian government officers often met with them. Australian officers Nurton, Bates, Black, Taylor, and Kyle were posted at Kainantu in the 1930s. Connolly and Anderson suggest that Taylor was regarded with distrust by the Leahy brothers, and that M. Leahy wished to be the sole leader and director of prospecting and exploration in the Wahgi valley expedition (1987:205ff.).

The killing of his fellow prospector, Bernard McGrath, may have marked a turning point in Leahy's attitude. The death was discovered by Dan and Mick Leahy when they arrived at Ekanofe (Henganofi) and found the native people alarmed. They later determined that there had been thefts of knives and axes, which the people refused to return, then attacking McGrath, who fired above their heads and was killed (Leahy 1991:151–153). Leahy said that McGrath had

> forfeited his life through his reluctance to inflict harm on the natives. If he had killed or wounded a few with his first shots, instead of firing over their heads, he could probably have beaten off the attack. . . . But Captain McGrath was a humane man, as well as a brave one, and so his name was added to the long list of pioneers killed by the natives—who are incapable of understanding a white man's very curious reluctance to take human life. (Leahy and Crain 1937: 206–207)

In this incident, soon after McGrath was found by Mick and Dan Leahy, Ted Ubank, Bob Dugan, Lance Peadon, and later, Cadet Tom Aitchison arrived. D.O. E. Taylor and Officer J. Black then came and took administrative charge of the situation.

After the killing of McGrath, Leahy said, in his diary of 21 February 1934: "Murder is an everyday occurrence with these people and they forget it quick. Wives will kill children if the father is not there. I wish we had a free hand here to do some murdering of the murdering bastards."

When his prospecting efforts failed to turn up important sources of gold, Leahy began to write about his other discoveries and seek recognition as an explorer. He presented an account of his observations to the Royal Geographical Society in 1935. In his diaries, and as quoted in *First Contact* (Connolly and Anderson 1987:186ff.), his attitude in 1934 seems to have changed from optimism and excitement over discovery to anger at thefts and difficulties. In his diary of 1934 Leahy frequently refers to the highlanders as "nigs" and "coons," and he reacted to insolence by thrashing and to theft with reprisal. The latest published version of his diary-based story of the exploration (Leahy 1991) does not detail the sexual encounters described in the diaries, but clearly expresses his contempt for natives as primitive (Brown 1994).

Beyond the Upper Ramu other airfields, base camps, and police posts were temporarily and intermittently staffed but were not permanently established for some years. Thus control was uneven and inconsistently extended into the highlands, although it was an essential link to the densely populated areas of Simbu, Wahgi valley, and Mount Hagen as they were explored and pacified. There were no private settlers to the west except for Dan and Mick Leahy at Kuta. In 1937 the road from Gadsup to Simbu was 480 kilometers long; another 103 kilometers were added the following year. It was essentially a path of contact and influence.

The Fox brothers, Jack and Tom, traveled independently with a small party of carriers and covered a large area west of Mount Hagen between August and December 1934. J. Fox's diary notes that they moved rapidly and often camped away from native villages, stopping at settlements only long enough to purchase some foodstuffs. Pigs were shot with rifles to impress the natives. They noted cannibalism, tribal warfare, weapons, houses, and clothing. J. Fox attributes their safe passage to rapid movement, so that they did not give the native community an opportunity to observe their store of trade goods or ponder on their weaknesses. When they mistrusted the local people they placed a rope barrier around their campsite to keep them out.[8] When Ballard (1992) traced their passage through Huli, he found the visit remembered there as one during which many Huli had been shot by the intruders.[9]

Jack and Tom Fox, so long missing, were sought by the Leahy brothers and appeared in late December 1934 to report that they had found no signs of gold in their prospecting trip all the way to the Dutch border and beyond (reports are unclear about the actual route). They all heard of the killings in the Simbu valley from the pilot in January 1935 (see Chap. 4). M. Leahy took a strong white supremacist stand that would punish the natives and "show them who is boss" (letter to Leo Tracey, 1935a).

At Korgua (Western Highlands) in 1987, Dan Leahy described joining up with J. Taylor to have one big line of carriers and ten police on the Bena-Hagen patrol (interviewer Paula Brown).

> The people didn't know what to make of us. They took the hairs off the back of my legs. We were always very strict with the carriers, and tried to keep things secure. They couldn't just rush up and steal a knife. We'd stop that. We said we pay you for food and work. Some places looked as though they would fight. We'd go to the headman and bargain. They liked goldlip shells best. Had some worn down knives; we'd buy a pig for an axe. We'd see different people every

three or four days. They had no cloth, but bark belts, rope, bilum. On the first trip we found gold at Kuta. Then we got people to work, made boxes for sluicing. The workers were coastals, and some of the Hagen people were good, and worked, learned *pidgin* quickly.[10]

When Tom and Jack Fox returned from their western highlands prospecting trip with no successful gold finds in December 1934, Michael Leahy gave up further prospecting in the highlands. He and his brother Dan continued to work gold and farm at the Mount Hagen site, and he later farmed at Zenag in Morobe District until his death in 1979.

In the western highlands, Catholic and Lutheran missions and Leahy mining—later farming—were the only European establishments. Administration first was an extension from Simbu. The western highlands post opened in 1938 when Greathead was stationed as the officer and became the headquarters for the Hagen-Sepik patrol. The great impact of European coffee production, which took over much Wahgi and Hagen area land, occurred after 1950.

For prospectors the motive was profit, to find and extract gold, and for later settlers, agriculture and trade stores. The Leahy brothers employed Hagen men as carriers and laborers, paying them in shell. Their activities at Mount Hagen introduced great quantities of shells, and the kina mother-of-pearl shell became an especially important mark of wealth and exchange valuable, supplanting pigs in some respects (A. Strathern 1979). Soon after their acceptance of the strangers as humans who exchanged (M. Strathern 1992), the Hagen people had so much shell[11] from labor, food, and sexual payments that they were a wealth center for the Hagen region and bought pigs from surrounding peoples to trade for shell. In the 1930s large quantities of all kinds of shells were brought in.

Although Leahy cannot be taken as representing the attitudes held by all prospectors in the 1930s, his view that the natives had to learn who was boss is clearly quite different from that expressed by government officers and missionaries. Lutheran missionaries and evangelists promoted peace. In fact, a "peace movement" was sponsored by missionaries and P.O. Aitchison in the eastern highlands: weapons and sorcery bundles were collected and destroyed, and people promised to stop tribal warfare in 1936–1937 (Radford 1977).

Employment opportunities were limited; mining mostly employed non-local laborers on contract.[12] Only a few could work on the Aiyura agricultural station after 1937; one opportunity was in police recruitment. Although there may have been some labor recruitment of highlanders in the 1930s, concern for health and malaria control prevented relocating many highlanders to lower altitudes.

Highlands administration and contact was concentrated along the road from Arona to Hagen, and neither exploration nor control reached far beyond this strip. Okapa, Marigl, Karimui, Kubor, Bismarck, Jimi, Baiyer, and other major areas were hardly seen until after World War II; southern highland and Enga areas were visited by some exploratory patrols, but only short-term posts and base camps were occupied. Lutheran missionaries in the region around Kainantu have left little record of the extent of their explorations and did not establish posts in Simbu west of Onerunka and Kambaidam until September 1934, after the Taylor-Leahy expedition had explored the highlands to Mount Hagen.

The policies and methods of dealing with native communities that developed in the New Guinea administration in the 1920s and 1930s were to determine the program of influence and control of highlanders. Jim Taylor played an important role in the development of a peaceful approach, which required the cessation of tribal warfare and the gradual introduction of Australian control through the influence of Australian kiaps and New Guinea police, as can be seen in his 1938–1939 report of the Hagen-Sepik patrol. Simbu had little contact with private settlers or miners; their relations were mostly with missionaries and administrators.

First Encounters

Exploratory air flights and patrols of 1933 were the first that Simbu could know of white people and coastal New Guinea natives. Simbu tell many stories of their first views of the newcomers. The eyewitness accounts, memories, legends, and writings show many reactions to the first sightings of the airplane, white men, and patrols. The experience was interpreted, in local cultural terms, as the miraculous return of ancestral spirits, enemy magic and retaliation, or a new opportunity for trade. By the time of my first field trip in 1958, some of the stories had assumed the form of legends. There was a first air reconnaissance flight of Leahy and the New Guinea Goldfields Company, and a second of Leahy with Taylor on 27 March 1933: the first white men's view of the Wahgi valley. The sacred bird of Simbu suddenly took the form of a noisy giant, from which women and children were made to hide.

Throughout Simbu Province the legendary first priest, Fr. Schäfer, and the first kiap, Jim Taylor, have become iconic names for early priest and kiap (see Chap. 9). The experiences of first contact, the first sight of white men, police, and carriers, and the dogs of missionaries and Australians have become stories that may be performed for an audience. In 1958–1960 I was told by Simbu that the visitors gave them many marvelous things of shell, steel, and cloth. They thought the white men were dead people or spirits.

The first air reconnaissance trips were followed by the patrol of J. L. Taylor, Michael and Dan Leahy, and Ken Spinks, with carriers and police from Bena to Mount Hagen. They crossed the Simbu River near Mirani on 3 April 1933 and continued up the Wahgi valley.

Rumors of the white strangers spread from Bundi, where the Catholics had a station in 1932, and from the Chimbu-Wahgi expedition group as they traversed the area. People of the Simbu valley had their first experience with Catholic missionaries in November 1933, when three Siambugla men—Kawagl, Mondia and Witne—with a party of several hundred Simbu, led Fr. Schäfer, Fr. Cransen, and Br. Anton from Bundi over Mondia pass to Kangrie, and down the Simbu valley via Womkama (also called Womatne) and Goglme, to Dimbi and into the Wahgi valley (Nilles 1987a:10–18). They returned by the same route and followed the Simbu River and Mondia pass back to Bundi.

A Lutheran reconnaissance plane with Rev. Bergmann aboard traversed the area in October 1933. On 22 May 1934 Bergmann crossed the Simbu River with Revs. Vicedom and Foege (Folge) going west (Bergmann n.d.). He founded Ega on 13 September 1934, and went on to found the Kerowagi and Ogelbeng missions with sixty evangelist carriers (Bergmann 1971, 1:15ff.). In their travels they met with Fr. Ross and other Catholic missionaries. Neither of them wanted to disclose their plans to the others, and each group attempted to steer the other into a different area; however, both Lutherans and Catholics built stations in the Wahgi valley, and each made some contact with Simbu and other groups at many highland locations.

Air contact with coastal stations was crucial to both government and mission, and the larger stations sprung up close to the airstrips. The Simbu, in their stories, often condense flights and meetings into a single surprising experience. In 1933 and 1934, most of the planes flew past Simbu. Mirani airstrip was used by Catholic, Lutheran, and government planes after September 1934, and the Mingende airstrip was built in 1935. The Kundiawa airstrip replaced Mirani after the Lutherans were established at Ega. It was only then that Simbu could observe planes landing on the ground (see Chap. 6). Nothing so big had ever been seen before, and as late as 1960 people gathered to gawk at planes as they landed in Kundiawa.[13] Leahy's diary recounts the masses of people who came to view planes at Hagen landing field and bring offerings to the great bird. It was from the beginning a source of cargo, the supplies and trade goods brought to the white man, and a demonstration of his association with the origin of these goods beyond the horizon.

The route taken by Taylor crossing the Simbu River near Mirani and following the Wahgi valley was generally followed on three more trips, when the passage through Kuman Simbu was made in two or three days: Taylor and Spinks returned to Bena in August 1933; Taylor went again to Hagen in September and returned with the Leahy brothers in October. Stories of the strange otherworldly spirits circulated among many Simbu without firsthand contact for months or years. For others, a first experience of gifts and exchange was followed by attempted (or successful) theft of white man's goods, shootings, arrests, and stories of death and retaliation. Both airplanes and travelers became fairly common in the subsequent years, and after the Chimbu-Wahgi post became a regular patrol post in 1935, patrols by kiaps were common. Goglme was a police post. Mission stations at Kerowagi and Denglagu followed.

Simbu See the Airplane

This has become a lively theme which my assistants heard from their elders and recorded many times. The first airplane was an astonishing sight to Simbu: a great spirit-bird, a magic bee from Bundi (Upper Simbu), a poison bird from Bomai (Dom), or a great mother bee (Simbu valley, east of Kundiawa). In some cases, it was attributed to the dangerous magic of peoples living in the direction from which the plane came. The plane, now known as *balus* (P.) was first called *kua kande* (S. big bird), a visible substantiation of the great mystical bird, a way of fitting new experience into traditional spirit belief. Its sudden appearance from the north or east, land of strangers, was a manifestation of danger. People were forbidden to look upon it and fled into the bush for safety. In some areas, when planes landed, quantities of food were presented to it. The sight of a pilot, the riches brought in the plane, and the behavior of Jim Taylor when he informed the people, in sign language, that he was responsible for the airplane, bolstered the fear of this great magical creature. Later flights, and bombs dropped in World War II, reinforced the idea of danger. The stories of the first impressions of airplanes are important memories that portray dismayed Simbu speculating about the source and meaning of the flights. They reflect local concerns: sorcery and the retaliation of enemies, as well as attempts to protect women and children against attacks.

Young Simbu collected many details of the stories from their elders. Kee Wemin of Genabona, Dom, told interviewer Joe Gelua:

> One day I heard some noise above the cloud which made me frightened. That same afternoon people gathered at the mens house and discussed the matter.

We don't know the noise, and blamed Bomai poison, the mother bees, sun noise, dead body spirits. The next day the same noise again, father and I saw it just like the birds but it is much bigger than the bird. We went to the nearest village to find out. We came home and killed 50 pigs because that is the first thing in our life. After that when we heard the noise above the air we ran inside the house or in the bush. Now we know the aeroplane. First aeroplane believed: 1. Poison from Bomai. 2. Mother bees. 3. The sun sent the mother birds to kill us.

Kua Bogia of Kangrie, Simbu valley (interviewer Joseph Mando):

As it was related to me, an extraordinary white bird making thunderous and booming sounds suddenly appeared over the eastern horizon disappearing into the west. The strange bird went so fast and flew so high that everyone was baffled.

I thought that the Gende people of Bundi were about to perform one of their famous magic spells [S. *kimagl*] on the Mitnande people. The fearsome Geril or Gende people over the other side of Mondia were notorious for their *kimagl*. The rumours were spreading everywhere. The people did not venture far from home, for it was also said that the predicted catastrophe would fall on them in the form of floods or landslides.

Kugame Tange, Endugwa (interviewer Lawrence Gigmai):

People thought the first plane was a flying man with stretched hands (wings) with his smoke pipe (wheels) and folded legs (tail). They blamed Tangigl Endepinge for stealing kina shells from a Geregl so he killed his pigs to drive the magic away. The plane we called *mu-ta-yagl* (S. sound-making man) and later when seen landed called it *kua kande* (S. big bird).

Guwand Kombugun of Gena (interviewer Harry Godfrid):

Then came the first plane. We were having a gathering at that time and we at first thought it was a big mother bee so we searched. But then all of a sudden "it" was above us. We dived into the nearby bushes. We thought it was a big mother bee out to take revenge for what our children did (that is, damaging the bee's nest for honey). Some people started belting up their children.

Gull Kumugl of Gou, Endugwa (interviewer Harry Godfrid):

The first airplane was thought to be a big angry bird who made a frightening noise. One crazy man said he could fight the airplane. His name was Keregil.

Some said that their death relatives were back to take them back. In general, it was a frightening scene.

Kiugl Waguo of Endugwa (interviewer Lawrence Gigmai):

The first airplane flew over and circled but our people thought it was a death magic from the Geregl people at Bundi and is sent to kill us all in the form of a hornbill bird (S. *kua kauga*) so the people fired their arrows simultaneously when the plane was circling above us but didn't hit the plane. Before the plane there were some Kamanekus in our area and one of my fathers called Tangigl Kumugl stole one of their conch shells and the owners [we thought] have contacted Geregl to kill us all. After a while the airstrip was built by Rev Berchman's [Bergmann] boys and plane landed finally at the strip.[14]

Guri of Endugwa (interviewer Harry Godfrid):

The first airplane came before the kiaps came. We were dead scared at the sight but many people said that Mondo Kama (the man I killed earlier) is back for us. So one of our witch doctors made some magic and fired two shots towards the airplane but nothing happened after all. The plane circled our area and went back. Some thought our dead ancestors had come back to help us because we were under heavy attack from six different tribes. Many of our people were killed but we fought bravely and killed quite a number of our enemies from each tribe.

Anton Wuka of Upper Simbu valley (interviewer John Karl):

The first airplane was like a monster buzzing around in the sky like a praying mantis. We think that it is the mother of the pandanus or *amul ma* [S.]. We were scared to see it because some people say you will die if you watch and some say it is *gerel kimagl* [S.] meaning magic bird from Bundi.

The White Man

Another popular subject in the interviews with elders was the first view of and ideas about the white man, the patrol, and the goods they had. The interests of Simbu storytellers emerge in their concentration on goods and trade and the shooting of Simbu. Dogs and, later, horses appear in many of the stories, being the largest animals in their experience. Clothing was seen as part of the body, and concealment of body parts was another matter for speculation.

Gando of Nek village, Kerowagi (interviewer Jenny):

The missionaries came first into Sime, from Madang, on the Bundi road. Some people helped to carry their belongings mainly suitcases and they settled at Womatne. The suitcase was full of shell money. When a man helped the missionary they gave him that shell money as a reward. People had very big interest in that shell money so they helped the missionaries very much. When they first came to Gembogl, people thought that they were the spirit of their dead ancestors but the missionaries explained to them and the villagers understood them.

Witne and Mondia, Siambugla men of Dimbi,[15] tell the traditional story of origin at Womkama and the traditional history of the Siambugla. Siambugla were at Kogai and found unused bush at Dimbi, between the Wauga and the Naregu, and men took over the land. Stories indicate very unsettled times, describing Siambugla settlement as an intrusion between groups already in the area. The fights and shifting alliances when they were young men involved Wauga, Naregu, Kombuku, and Siambugla. They had friends in the Simbu valley and went up the Mondia road to Bundi with Kawagl, where they found Fr. Schäfer. Visits to Bundi were to trade plumes, and their sisters were married there.

At Bundi there was taro and pandanus, and they told Fr. Schäfer that they had food and pandanus at Dimbi. Since Fr. Schäfer could speak Gende (the Bundi language) and Witni of Dimbi knew that language, they could talk. They went through Toromambuno and slept there. They were given *girigiri* (P. cowrie shell) for food and recalled that two pigs were shot by a Brother. After they saw what the priests would give them, they visited Bundi to get shells and steel axes. Later, when they built a house of *kunai* (P. grass) for Fr. Schäfer, he gave them shells, rings, and axes for the work. It was in this way that the exchange of food and labor for shells began. The men described the route taken by the Fathers through the Gena country, stopping at Kogai and then continuing to Dimbi. The Fathers went on to Nondugl on the first trip.

Fighting among these groups continued. One element in the invitation to the whites to settle was that they might protect their settlement at Dimbi, and another was to obtain shells and axes.

Guri of Endugwa (interviewer Harry Godfrid):

I was at Agemake when the first kiaps arrived. They had a dog called Dikirwagele. As they were there their dog died and was buried near Agemake. Today that place is called Dikirwagele. The kiaps came with some police men in short *laplaps* [P. loincloths]. They threatened us with their "sticks of fire" (guns) and showed us they could be dangerous if we resist their visit by killing some pigs. We were dead scared and followed what they said.

Kee Wemin of Dom (interviewer Joe Gelua):

Here in Kundiawa there was another news around the village. I came to see because the white man supplied salt, axes. He called out for all the leaders to come to Kundiawa so I came with them. The white man was to shake hands with us. I felt very happy. We stayed two days; later went back home with some kina shell, salt and one axe. My people and the nearest clan they were very frightened of the story I had told.

Ulka Baglau of the Simbu valley (interviewer John Karl):

We heard of a white at Bundi. Went to see what they would be like. Some say devil or *masalai* [P. spirit], one who died, or what. Men of my own tribe said not an enemy or devil but just like us and has many good things for us; we'll take him down to Kangre and he'll camp down there. He has been teasing us with salt, paint for our faces, pearlshells, axe and so many things. We started blocking the road and we do not want anybody outside us to split all these things.

Kugame Tange, Endugwa (interviewer Lawrence Gigmai):

One afternoon we heard a distant call that a dead ancestor has returned to make us rich. That was Jim Taylor and he camped at Mirani. I walked there myself with other small boys. They gave us salt and other stuff to attract our attention and finally we befriended the new party. Taylor moved around the highlands many times and settled at Mirani. The name Simbu is derived from "Sipu" the word used to express thanks and praise during Taylor's arrival and wherever he goes same response so he called us Chimbus from there.

Angil, Endugwa (interviewer Michael Mugua):

I heard that white men came to Kundiawa. People said they were spirits or *gigl golka* [S. dead spirit] or dead men who died long time ago coming out of the grave. Might be ancestor. White men and native men came passed through our village, went through Narku clan. The Narku sent a message that this white man and his men had kill a lot of men from Wauga clan so when they come to your place keep away from them. A message was sent down from Kamaneku clan there was another ghost or spirit coming from Sumbugu clan. They went to Irpui then to Dimbi and later on to Mingende.

Kuglbo, Endugwa (interviewer Michael Mugua):

People did not know signs of white men so they said they were spirits of dead men coming out of the grave. Passed through. On way back I heard message that they kill a lot of people of Kunabau. Then a message coming from Guye that there is another ghost or devil coming down with three men from Sumbul tribe. People thought they came with their relatives who died a long time ago.

Lan, a woman of Naregu (interviewer Michael Mugua):

My people have never seen the whites before so they thought they were devil or spirit or their ancestors who died long time ago came out of the grave to life. So they cried bring in food to give them. The people of Kamaneku sent a message to my clan Narku that another *gigl golka* come down from Gembogl with these fellows from Siambugla clan their names are Witne, Mondia, Kawagl. It was Father Schäfer but we did not know it at the time. People from my village went to work for the missionary and bring back kina shells and I saw them. Came down to Mingende, built an air port there. They build house, schools, and aid post and church. At that time there was lots of fighting and it was very hard for girls and their mothers to get there.

When I interviewed Kamanau at Ega in 1987, he said he was about twelve years old when Rev. Bergmann came. Then his family went to live at Ega.

There were large gardens where the airstrip is now. We were afraid to let him leave the land, and gave it to Rev. Bergmann. He bought our trees and gardens for axes and bush knives, so we brought kunai grass and wood to build a house. He brought workers from Finschhafen to build the house. Bergmann was just a newcomer. He couldn't speak our language. He used hand gestures. I taught him to speak Kuman, after I learned Kate.[16] At the school Bergmann gave laplap, biscuit, soap and knives when we worked for him cutting grass.

Guwand Kombugun of Gena (interviewer Harry Godfrid):

Jim Taylor came with his police men from easterly direction down from Konoma, crossed the *wara* [P. water, river] Simbu to Endugwa land at Mirani. As soon as he arrived at Mirani the Endugwas gathered and welcomed the party by saying "Sipu" meaning welcome or thank you. Jim Taylor got the impression that they were welcoming him to Sipu tribe but wherever he goes it was the same word Sipu he heard so he finally named the province Chimbu. I was at Goglme when the first kiaps and the missionaries came. I was living with my sister. Generally our reactions at that time could be described as frightened and furious. We had the guts to start attacking them but to our dismay we found they had the so called "gun" which blasted and tore everything it passed through. It made us scared and we later gave in to their orders but there was still some resistance. Others thought they were our dead ancestors. Some thought they were those who died recently who came back to seek revenge. Each time we saw a white man we were given special treatment called *gene kar* [S. ginger]. It consisted of ground ginger and casuarina leaves. This was believed to protect us from any magic or spell cast upon us by the white man. Missionaries called themselves patre and burter.

Taylor then killed pigs that were given to him [with a] pistol and the people were scared but he gestured that it won't affect them so we became friendly with the party. When Taylor left for Hagen he brought with him two of my brothers namely Kawagle Kinawia and Kura Siune and came back. When he came back he appointed the boys as interpreters.

Kiugl Waguo of Endugwa (interviewer Lawrence Gigmai):

When the first kiaps came we fought with the Kamanegus and the Kamanegus were fierce enough to drive us out of Dirimaundo and Mirani Bindai. When Taylor came down from Konome, he crossed Simbu River and settled at Mirani. People reckon Mr Taylor as one of their tribal warriors who died has returned to save us from tribal warfare and finally make us the richest tribe our of all tribes. During that time my father a bald headed man was with his younger brother and my father had with him a tomahawk [stone axe]. Mr. Taylor grabbed it from him, tried it on a tree but it didn't cut deep so he threw it away and gave my father the first white man's axe. To his brother Mr Taylor gave a large conch shell known in Kuman as *guglumbo* and they took off to nearby bushes and disappeared fearing that the gifts may be taken back. Very primitive that time so we had to collect droppings from Taylor believing that *konia taglimbo* has left us magic spell for us to fight. When we go for tribal fights we fought courageously and in fact won few tribal fights.

That time I was a small boy but when Jim Taylor picked me to be an interpreter and I finally joined police force and retired quite recently and am living on pension.

Mondo Ola of Ombondo, Simbu valley (interviewer Paul San):

When the first kiaps and policemen came they did shoot people and animals and I saw them. They shot one of our leaders by the name of Kapaki, Degba Mondia and from my clan they shot a man named Waugla Sungwa. They were shot by the kiaps and police men because they were trying to keep peace among those people. We were all scared to attack them so we all run off into the bush. The missionaries came later.

Interviews by Moro in 1985 included some with women from eastern Simbu. Mrs. Nukama of Womai (interviewer Moro):

Some said the dead were coming back to join us, or come back to life. When first white men came, his mother took him to nearby village. Kiaps were there near Chuave. Kiaps got people together to show them things like axes, bush knife. People tried to attack the kiaps in the night with bows and arrows to get the axes and knives, but the kiaps get their guns and fire one of their leader through the leg and all the people run away; the leader Okoro Bal dead. The first kiaps were so rough that the natives were very scared of them and they never came close to hear what they were saying. The first kiaps did their best to tame them by showing them axes and salt. Some of the villagers tried to steal the things which the white man showed them so that's how the shooting starts. There were about five people killed at that time.

Mrs. Maldoa (interviewer Moro):

First patrol officers and missionaries came. The people of Yobakogl believed them as dead people coming down from heaven. One gave her some shells and paint. She went to show parents. They thought of getting some more so they killed their pigs and brought food from their gardens and gave it to the white-man and the whiteman gave them kina shell, tambu shell and paint and they became friends.

Mrs. Mandango, a woman of Masai village (interviewer Moro):

When the white man asked them about their house the people didn't know what they were talking about so they just made signs with their hands. They thought the white man would kill them and eat them. Gave salt, paint, shells, showed to relatives hiding in bush and told them they were friends not enemies so they came out of their hiding places, Smoking pipe, they said something burning inside their body. Belts were thought to be penis. Girls and women were not allowed to look at white man's waist.

Mrs. Yaumau of Masul (interviewer Moro):

Missionary was thought a dead relative. A few months later I heard a white man was here in Kundiawa and there was another news around the village, I came to see him because white man supplied salt, spade, axes. He called out all the leaders to come to Kundiawa so I came with them. The white man was to shake hand with us, I felt very happy. Later I went back home with some kina shell, salt and one axe. My people and the nearest clan they were very frightened of the story I had told.

These many personal stories, collected from Simbu of different areas, repeat some themes: the surprise at the airplane, its size and noise, and fear of its power; the unfamiliar clothing, appearance, shells, and goods of the white man and his superior tools and weapons—axes, guns. The whole experience was attributed to the magical power of returning spirits of ancestors.

When I collate and compare the records in my notebooks and the records of interviews by many others, I can see how local experience, discussion at the time, storytelling and retelling over the years, have built a wealth of local legend for the Simbu. The sighting of the first airplane has become a favorite entertainment, now interpreted as "see how ignorant and fearful we were," a look back at the credulity of the elders. Several of the stories are much elaborated in retrospect, quoting the contemporary views of people in their community and speculating about the precise reason for sending a giant instrument of sorcery.

Places and neighbors, the route through the valley, and gifts or exchanges have been preserved in retelling. They have a specific local meaning about the relations of the storyteller's group with some enemies or strangers. The appearance, clothing, food, and goods of the patrol party were the objects of much comment and conjecture. When the newcomers were thought to be dead ancestors returning, their equipment, personal possessions, and goods offered for trade signaled that they had acquired unfamiliar objects of great value. This wealth was greatly desired by Simbu, and they sought ways to obtain it. People collected discarded matches, food containers, and excrement for their magical value. When the newcomers refused gifts and exchanges and moved on to other places, attacks and thefts were attempted. It was then that guns were used against them. Simbu wondered whether they and their goods could be captured or used to protect against or drive away enemies.

The Intruding Bena-Hagen Patrol

The joint exploratory party of the Australian New Guinea administration, represented by James L. Taylor, gold prospectors employed by New Guinea Goldfields Ltd., the brothers Michael and Dan Leahy, and Ken Spinks, a surveyor, with seven police constables, a medical orderly, two native headmen, thirty carriers, and two personal servants, is recorded in Taylor's patrol diary. M. Leahy had twenty-six carriers from Waria; four local carriers, and ten Bena youths joined the group. A total of eighty-two were on the expedition; two died (Taylor 1933:22). The reconnaissance flight had marked the general area to be traversed, and arrangements were made for supply-plane landings in April in the Wahgi valley. At each camp the group traded shell, salt, and some other goods for vegetables and large shells or steel knives or axes for pigs. Some people of the Simbu valley said that women and children were forbidden to look upon the newcomers, but this was not Taylor's observation in the Wahgi valley, where, rather, large crowds of men, women, and children gathered to look at the patrol at each stopping place. Communication was of necessity in a kind of sign language, and local place-names were elicited when possible. A rope circle was often placed around the campsite and tents, and a watch was set every night at 6 P.M. to secure the patrol. In 1935 Leahy states, in a summarized diary for 4 April 1933: "A thousand or so natives met us and cried Chimbu Chimbu in welcome" (1935b:15). However, this shout, which is said to be the basis of the naming of the Simbu River and people by the expedition and accepted by the people, is not mentioned in the original diaries of either Leahy or Taylor.

In the preface to his report of the 1933 Mount Hagen patrol, Taylor states:

> The objects of this patrol were:
> (1) To examine the headwaters of the Purari River within the territory of New Guinea.
> (2) To make contact with the native inhabitants and so prepare them for the advent of the white man.
> (3) To protect Europeans and their employees who might be operating or travelling in the area.

and the results:

> (1) A large area of country has been examined and a new mountain range and several valleys discovered.
> (2) Many thousands of natives whose existence was previously unknown have been visited and the way paved for their Christianisation and development.
> (3) The Europeans operating in the area carried out their work without trouble or disturbance.

A few observations of Taylor's 1933 patrol are pertinent to the first views. The following quotations are from his diary.

> Throughout all of this country we were, of course, without interpreters, and all communications were by signs. This was satisfactory in most cases, but occasionally the people were so astonished they stood with staring eyes and gaping mouths.

Eventually we obtained sufficient sweet potatoes and three pigs. After the pigs had been shot, the local people became very interested in the new weapon, digging up the ground to discover the bullet. I took advantage of a service rifle to demonstrate to them the effect of a service rifle on a hardwood tree. The small annulus cowrie shell was most appreciated here. (1 April 1933, east of the Simbu River)

A few natives had followed us through the bush, some carrying cargo, but many more came running up when we reached the open country . . . natives, although very excited, did not hinder our progress, as they were able to run alongside the track over the open grass. . . . Reached a large village . . . native headdress which included the King of Saxony's bird.

The people of this village begged us to remain and one old fellow threw himself across the track and lay there to prevent us passing . . . I made a gift of a knife and he was very pleased. . . . The natives nearby seemed a passive and stupid lot, and very few women were seen. We had some difficulty in getting them to understand that we wanted food (2 April).

Leahy's diary[17] on 2 April 1933 notes that the houses were long rather than round, that dollar-bird wings and skulls, red and white bird-of-paradise feathers were worn, and the men were "fairly big and the marys are good looking wenches. Country is limestone. Not too much native foods about."

Taylor in his report states that they made secure a native bridge with rope, crossed the Simbu River on 3 April, and camped at Mirani. The reaction of native peoples to the visit seemed to be incomprehension:

The natives were somewhat of a similar nature to those at camp 6, and seemed dazed and I had to take some boys with bags and go down to gardens where the women were working to buy food. Later on after the men had satisfied their curiosity to some extent they brought along four pigs which we bought. The natives of this locality favoured the wings of dollar birds as headdresses, and the men seemed the most decorated of any we had met. They are of small stature, but well proportioned.

Leahy, in his diary of 3 April, calls them a "very quiet people." He sees the Wahgi valley gardens made in checkerboard squares with small sticks to prevent erosion on slopes. He observes:

no barricades houses long oblong shape built not in a clump but here and there and anywhere no provision for a fence of protection from night raids. The axes very little steel about tambus mother of pearl best trade . . . native gardens planted on terraces in 10 ft squares with drainage channels about 6 ft around the squares.

On the next day, Taylor continues:

Many natives followed us, carrying bows and arrows, but with bowstrings loosened, a practice which we had insisted upon from the beginning, and one with which the natives have readily agreed. The presence of some of the boys' wives in our party helps to give them confidence, and the fact that local native women become very curious and follow the line as well as the men, should make for peace. . . . We passed well laid out gardens in which pieces of limestone were plentiful.

On the track on 4 April, both Taylor and, in his diary, Michael Leahy observe some few objects and decorations of western manufacture—shells, belt buckles, worn steel blades—and speculate that there is trade with the Madang area. Goldlip shells were greatly prized, and small shells were also used in trade. Stone axes were better in quality.

The Koronigl River was crossed on 5 April. Taylor found large, well-laid-out gardens. In the Wahgi valley goldlip and other shells were in demand. Mirrors and tomahawks were also used in trade. The first observation that the natives were boisterous was in the Wahgi valley, west of Simbu. On 6 April they encountered natives in a threatening attitude with spears.

Leahy's diary for that day reads:

Almost got into a fight with a tribe of spearmen they were very frightened and at first would not let us pass. A bit of diplomacy on Jim Taylor's part squared it for us and we got in touch with them and camped in their locality. They are OK now having brought along plenty of native foods and explained to us that they would like us to stop for about a week. We will look about for an aerodrome and put in a couple of days here. The plane is due on Monday. The natives are big physically.

On that day they felt that good relations were established when food was brought. The patrol group explored, prospected, and made a landing field on land that Taylor reports he purchased from a native named Paraiyer. The first landing in the Wahgi valley was on 10 April 1933, at a site near Nangamp; it was a Fox Moth plane piloted by I. Grabowsky of New Guinea Airways, with H. M. Kingsbury of the New Guinea Goldfields Company as a passenger.

The group made contact with the people of the upper Wahgi and Mount Hagen area, constructing another landing field and receiving further supplies and visits by air for some months. During these travels, some incidents of theft and demonstration of gunpower are mentioned in the diaries and reports. Every night an armed guard of police was set.

The Leahy brothers remained in the western Wahgi area exploring the region until October. As they returned to Bena, Michael noted: "Oct 12 Friendly mob. Plenty of food, pigs. Fowls bought for a sea shell." On 13–14 October they were at Simbu, and then on to Mariefuteger where they witnessed a fight between local groups.

Dan and Michael Leahy established permanent camps and began gold-mining operations in 1934, with air contact, visits, and deliveries of supplies. The people who worked on a regular basis for several months at the Leahy brothers' first mining operations were paid in goldlip shell or tomahawks. In 1987 a man at Mount Hagen told me, "We liked everything the white man brought." The friendly and submissive relations that generally characterized the visits of patrols differed greatly from the difficulties and hostility that met Hides and O'Malley in their Strickland-Purari patrol in the southern highlands of Papua in 1935 (Hides 1936; Schieffelin and Crittenden 1991). Highlanders collected discarded matches, tins, paper, and excrement from the patrol route.

Taylor (1933:216–223) wrote:

> Generally we were received well and without hostility, weapons were seldom seen, and we were regarded in awe as something ghostly or supernatural. In some parts we were regarded as people returned from the dead, some of the party actually recognized as ones who had died in recent years. Scenes of great emotion and enthusiasm were witnessed as we passed through the villages, laughing or crying people rushing to caress or kiss, or even touch the members of our party. The recognized ones were asked to stay and take their old place in the community. . . . When I removed my hat they would gasp "oh" and talk excitedly, and hold their children up to get a good look at us . . . [on return]. The attitude of the natives through whose territory we passed was, with certain exceptions, entirely different from that on our first trip; then they imagined us as gods or spirits, but on reflection they must have realized their mistake, as a revulsion of feeling had taken place throughout the people. . . . Our peaceful behavior they regarded as being merely due to us not being warriors, and to an absence of weapons. Rifles they appeared to imagine were sticks . . . day after day we encountered large numbers of hostile or contemptuous people . . . with their natural avariciousness aroused, here was a chance to raid the line and plunder our cargo. Twice . . . bows were drawn and spears raised . . . it became necessary to use firearms to protect the party . . . It now remains for us to bring to the inhabitants the Pax Britannica.

Taylor attributes the attitudes and emotions of Simbu and Wahgi people to a belief that the patrol personnel were spirits, which then turned to belligerence, avariciousness, and attempts to plunder. The Simbu statements put a somewhat different interpretation on the behavior.

Dage described an incident that may have occurred on 19 August 1933 (interviewer, Paula Brown 1987):

> When the Europeans came we thought they were *gigl* (S. spirits). They came to the Koronigl River, I saw them; they went to Hagen. As children we went to see the big men who were spirits or children of *Ande*, the sun. We stayed in the grass. The headmen went to see them. There were two whites and some blacks. They had cargo and tents. We thought the tents were their wives tied up. Headmen were given girigiri. Then went inside. Said the spirits would come at night. Some were told to go to the cemetery and watch. But they didn't come and they weren't spirits. They stopped, made house Kerowagi. We brought food and got girigiri, salt and beads. Then we heard that some were coming from Hagen. Some said they would kill them and take their cargo and their women tied up in the tents. They were going to attack Jim Taylor. People of Siku, Kamanegu and Dage put on grass, black paint [as warriors' decoration], and took spears. Taylor shot three of Dage Duglkane—blew off their heads. We were afraid; didn't know about guns. This was down at the Kerowagi bridge where a Siku had a garden and was shot and killed.
>
> People thought they would all be shot. We didn't fight the white man again. Missionaries made a place at Mingende and Kerowagi, and the Lutherans were at Kerowagi.

At Kunabau August 1933

> They shot a lot up because a bush knife was stolen at Kunabau.[18]
> We tried to kill the kiap with our spears, but he shot his rifle at us.[19]

In August 1933, Taylor and Spinks returned eastward with two policemen and carriers from the Markham area who had completed their contracts. Taylor observed on 17 August that there was a "marked difference in the atmosphere from the time of our earlier trips—then we were welcomed as something supernatural, spears were immediately concealed and groups of people welcomed us." West of the Koronigl River, Taylor found the natives "boisterous" and "hostile." When he stole a pack, the thief was stopped and the pack recovered; and when a group rushed the line, he fired a volley over their heads.

This became a memorable incident in the area from Kunabau to Mintima, repeated in many stories. Taya, an elder of Gamgani, Naregu tribe (Paula Brown interview, 1958), said:

> Taylor stopped at Kunabau, went to the west and returned. Dege took a bushknife. The policemen and kiap shot many Wauga. Then they came down to the Wahgi and up to Pinga [Taya's home place].

Going through Simbu, Taylor and Spinks stopped at Kunabau on 20 August to purchase pigs and food, requesting these in sign language, and paying in shells. They found the people "very troublesome." At Kunabau the Wauga wanted to take the cargo and men were shot.

Wena, a former Wauga tultul, at Kunabau (interviewer Paula Brown, 1987):

Wena was a boy at Yage, then after a fight his family went to Kunabau. Saw Schäfer and Taylor when a young unmarried man. Saw Fr. Schäfer at Dimbi house. Remembers that one Muguabu named Gege took a bush knife to steal and ran away. All the police went after him.

Kiap Taylor came to Mingende, then to the Koronigl. On his return, police asked for food and gave girigiri and salt. Called for people to bring the food. I brought wood and grass to help to build a house for Taylor, then for his police. There was a fence and we stayed outside of the house. Jim Taylor took me in his house, while the others ran away. He said wait until tomorrow, so we stayed. I held his hand. He made a noise like a pig um, um. We ran and got a big pig. But I was not afraid. I fastened the pig and got five kina shells. Some Wauga thought this was good, and brought pigs. But Taylor was leaving; he did not want the food and pigs. He slept up here and then left. In the morning he would not pay for other foods. Those with weapons wanted to kill the police and the kiap. When the kiap saw this, he shot at the men and many were killed. Other Wauga took bow and arrow and spear and went to Taylor's place. Gege[20] wanted tomahawk and bush knife. He took a bush knife and ran away. Next day, when Taylor was leaving without buying more food, some Wauga took their bow and arrow and spears to kill him and the police. I was on the mountain and watched with four men while the kiap looked through his glass and saw them, and shot his gun and killed one man. We carried this man, put the body in the bush. We ran to dodge the bullets but we were not killed. All the people were afraid of the stick—the gun. But Taylor was ready to go; spent one day, slept, and didn't want that food and pig. We thought kiap Taylor would shoot us all. Then Taylor went to Kundiawa.

Kum of Mintima was a boy at the time and remembered, in 1987:

When I was a little boy the balus came. We thought it was the men of Bundi making sangguma [P. magic]. I saw kiap Taylor when he came. We said Papa and tumbuna [P. ancestors] died. We thought they had come back. They came to Damar. There was no road then. They came on a little road. Built a house at Damar. Cut banana leaves and pitpit for the house.

Karkugo, an old man, fastened a pig. Came to give it to kiap Taylor. Taylor took a tomahawk, girigiri shell and red paint to give to Karkugo. Karkugo didn't want it and took his pig back. We all ran away to hide from him. I went into a ditch and stayed there overnight. Taylor slept one night at Damar and left in the morning. We wondered. The cargo men went up to Iwagl, Nokun, to Ganba and built another house. They got some food from us—banana, *kaukau* [P. sweet potato], sugar; we got salt, beads and girigiri for it. We gave them a pig, Kama's pig. They gave us the head, *bel* [P. intestines, stomach] and liver. We were afraid we would die if we ate it so men threw it away. Thought he was a ghost that had died and came back. Next morning he went to Kugame. I was a child and didn't go. Then he went to Hagen and came back, slept at Kunabau. Gege of Kunabau said to kill him and take his cargo. He was a Wauga boss, said we can kill this white skin. Took a bow and arrow and shot him. Taylor took his gun and killed plenty of men at Kunabau. Some were afraid. Then he returned on the same road through Nandi, Keramugl, Mintimanigl, Pinga. Some Sungwakani said we will kill them; we can get their shells, bush knives, tomahawk. Some thought the bow and arrow would be enough. They didn't know about white skin. They were told that he had killed some men at Kunabau with his gun. Taylor said he could not be killed. We heard him and went away. They were told that he had killed some men at Kunabau with his gun. Then he went on to Kundiawa. We had fought with the Endugwa and Kamanegu and did not go there. The mission was later. Fr Schäfer and Bergmann came. The Gembogl people killed a father. When Fr Schäfer worked a house at Komugl we took feathers and food, got salt and beads and girigiri.

Kum was not a witness at Kunabau. He told the story to me at a Mintima roadside shop in a lively fashion and took great pleasure in the group that gathered to hear it and applauded his recitation. People of Mintima, recalling the time, say that they were preparing to attack and steal goods, but when they heard of the shooting of "many" Wauga, they allowed the party to pass through.

An interview by Francis Kombugun in 1987 of Mondia of Dimbi (pp. 235–236ff), a Siambugla who had known Fr. Schäfer in 1933, tells a different tale.

Jim Taylor went to Mt Hagen and came back to Kunabau near Mingende and a person stole a axe from Jim Taylor. There Mr. Jim Taylor asked the people to return the axe. But the one who stole the axe didn't return it to him. So Jim Taylor was getting very angry that time when he did not return the axe so he told his police men to shoot the Siambugla Wauga people they killed them about two or three hundred people there at Kunabau.

Naregu, Wauga, and Siambugla people tell of the theft and retaliation at Kunabau. Yet the stories are not identical. They differ in the name of the culprit, the object stolen, and the identity and numbers of people shot. Some of the stories include eyewitness accounts of incidents or the movements, camping spots, and dogs of the travelers. However, only one person mentions any other white man on the trip. The retelling keeps the essential elements of each teller, while some particulars differ. This single incident has become, for the local people of Kunabau, Wauga, Siambugla, and Naregu, and for many others of the central Simbu area, their first and fearful experience of the kiap.

Taylor's report for 21 August reads:

> Soon after daylight crowds of natives gathered round the camp, and it soon appeared that they were only waiting their opportunity to destroy us and plunder our cargo. One old fellow actually brought a rope to tie up his share of the loot, or so it seemed. They refused to put down their weapons, and just before we were due to leave one fellow raised a spear to throw. I thought things had gone far enough and fired, killing him. We then fired several volleys over their heads, and put the rest to flight. We departed, firing into the air as we went, and passed through this thickly populated area without casualty. We took a more southerly track than that which we had used on the way in, travelling over grass spurs and ridges most of the way. We were followed by hundreds of natives, many of whom were boisterous and turbulent, but by continually stopping and addressing them we reached the Chimbu [River] area without serious incident. There were thousands of people about, but they seemed pleasant and the atmosphere was much better.

After crossing the Simbu River on 22 August, he noted: "The people were extraordinarily numerous, well over a thousand people being around the camp. There was great excitement, and they were not unfriendly, but inclined to be boisterous."

On 23 August the patrol halted and were surrounded by a thousand people when

> a determined attempt was made to plunder the line. One of the leading men of the tribe drew his bow on Spinks. I called out to him and warned him to desist. He then relaxed for a few moments, but someone shouted something to him from behind (that is one of his own people,) and he immediately refitted his arrow and prepared to shoot Spinks. I then fired a shot and he fell to the ground. The remainder of the local people then withdrew a short distance, and by firing over their heads we were able to pass on without further trouble. The adjoining people of Karinori were very pleasant, and we moved on to the Mairi-futeikar at 2 P.M. We had with us one Heruku, who belonged to one of the villages a day further along this stream. He was able to talk to the people here, and so we made contact without hostility, even though the local natives were infected with the same truculent spirit as those whom we had met this morning.

Stories of conflicts with the intruding kiaps and police and shooting and killing in eastern Simbu are reported by Warry (1987) and Hatanaka (1972:26) for Simbu groups east of the Simbu River. The official report recognizes fewer casualties than do the Simbu, but in an interview years later Taylor admitted that his figures were "modified" (Connolly and Anderson 1987:154).

In 1934 the Chimbu-Wahgi post, the first outstation west of Bena, was set up in Kundiawa. A.D.O. R. Melrose and J. L. Taylor were the officers but were not in permanent residence there. At the time of the killings of Fr. Morschheuser and Br. Eugene, they were in other parts of the large and heavily populated Morobe District. The Hagen post was first established in 1938 by George Greathead. Between 1934 and 1937 officers of the Chimbu post Kyle and Bates occasionally visited the Wahgi valley area.

Officer Black reported in September 1934, upon meeting Taylor in Simbu:

> A feature of this patrol were the large numbers of friendly natives who thronged every camping place, keen to trade. No shortage of foods and pork was experienced at any stage of the journey. . . . Because of the great purchasing power of gold lip, small cowrie and tambu shells, their country would be opened up very cheaply, and the country is densely populated, and the natives have good and extensive gardens and innumerable pigs.[21]

Taylor made another trip to Mount Hagen through the area of Wandi, Kenenunambro, Ona, Mindima, and Kargil on 23–24 September 1933, when he commented: "The people on the day's route were very friendly, and very few weapons were seen, but they were all dressed in their war paint. Those near the camp were quite friendly, and there was no sign of the previous attitude which had been one of truculence." On return trip 12–14 October with the Leahy brothers, the natives are reported to have been friendly.

4

Discovering the Gun

They killed to get the cargo. . . . Then the kiap came up and
shot many people, pigs and burnt houses
—KIAGL OF KAMANEGU
  (interviewer Paula Brown, 1958)

Their death also made clear to us that those white
men we thought were gods and can not die were just like us.
They were real men like us and can die like us.
—MONDO GUNAMA OF DENGLAGU
  (interviewer John Karl)

Deaths in the Simbu Valley, 1934–1935

The deaths of Fr. C. Morschheuser in December 1934 and Br. Eugene Frank
in January 1935, and the patrol, arrests, and first steps toward Australian
control of Simbu, were all outstanding events in the early history of Simbu
and stranger. They have often been described by witnesses, historians, and
writers. The incidents and their aftermath remain significant in the history
of the Catholic mission; in the Simbu valley they have been retold and
reinterpreted many times. I shall attempt to summarize, clarify, and examine the data from many sources. This section is based on personal documents, government reports, and mission sources; the next will tell the
Simbu story.

Before the arrival of these strangers, few Simbu ventured beyond their
tribal territory for fear of enemy attack. Thus their experiences and knowledge of these visitors differed from place to place. Simbu were much engaged
in intertribal warfare, and permanent enmities separated the large Upper
Simbu valley tribes. Kukane and Inau both fought against Denglagu; long-
distance trade and outside contact were rare.

The first European visitors surely knew of tribal warfare, but their rapid
movement through the highlands precluded involvement in hostilities. Australian government officers, New Guinea police, native Lutheran evange-

lists, missionaries, and prospectors traversed the area in patrols and small parties in 1933 and 1934. The return and subsequent passages of white men in the area found Simbu now eager to acquire the goods they carried. Every Simbu spoke about the goods, mentioning one or more of the things they carried: salt, knives, tomahawks, beads, tambu and other small shells, kina and other large shells, laplap, mirrors, and face paint. Some of these were given to providers of vegetable food; a pig brought the owner a large shell, many small shells, or a steel knife or tomahawk. Later, when Simbu worked for the mission by providing building materials or building houses, they were paid in these goods. Retail stores did not exist, and money had no use.

In New Guinea, formerly a German possession, both the Catholic and the Lutheran missions had many German missionaries through the 1930s. Lutheran practice was to place native evangelists, most of whom were coastal natives who spoke and taught the Kate mission language, in native villages. White missionaries usually established larger posts at places where there was some other white settlement and an airstrip where they could receive supplies and set up communications with other mission stations. In 1934 both Catholic and Lutheran missionaries made plans to establish stations in many places in the Simbu, Wahgi, and Hagen areas. Both Lutheran and Catholic missionaries wanted to exclude each other. The Catholics reached the central section of Simbu from the Simbu valley. Rev. Bergmann,[1] with other missionaries, went from the eastern highland areas to found a station at Ega, and then into the Wahgi valley. They met with Fr. Ross, who attempted to dissuade them from establishing a station there (Bergmann n.d., vol. 4).

Catholic posts to the east of Mingende were short-lived. At Mount Hagen a Lutheran post at Ogelbeng quickly followed the Catholic establishment of Fr. Ross at Wilya. The Catholics at Guyebi (Bundi) believed that the Lutheran native evangelists were disturbing the peace and stirring up people against them. In 1935 Fr. Cransen ordered a Lutheran evangelist to leave, and when this was reported to the Australian authorities, the priest was arrested, convicted, and then sent to another mission field.

The reports of missionaries, government officers, and private prospectors show their personal attitudes toward natives and one another in these encounters. Their competition and differing views of one another underlay some conflicts involving natives.

Catholic Mission Movements and Posts

Fr. Schäfer, Fr. Cransen, and Br. Anton of the Catholic Society of the Divine Word (SVD) mission established a post and airstrip at Bundi (Guyebi) in the Madang District in February 1932. Kawagl, a Simbu from Dimbi who had married a Bundi woman, was visiting with his fellow clansmen Witne and Mondia and trading there when Fr. Schäfer met him in 1933. A big man who played an important role in the entry of Catholics into the Simbu and Wahgi valleys, Kawagl invited Fr. Schäfer to come to his home area at Dimbi. In November 1933 Fr. Cransen, Fr. Schäfer, Br. Anton, and their mission servants accompanied Kawagl and some 350 Simbu (at that time called Korugu or Arawa by the mission). They went over the Mondia pass and camped at Kangrie among Denglagu clansmen in the Simbu valley. Fr. Schäfer noted their feather decorations and stone axes, their shouting and friendly greetings (Ulbrich 1960:30). The missionaries bought food for shells and salt, and a pig for an axe. They traveled down the Simbu valley to Womkama, through Kukane and Kogai to Dimbi. Fr. Schäfer noted possible future locations for mission posts in the Simbu valley at Keglsugl and Denglagu, planning an airfield. They walked into the Wahgi valley as far as Kerowagi and Nondugl before they returned to Bundi (Nilles 1987a).

Finding a large population, the Catholics obtained permission from their parent body in January 1934 to establish a Simbu mission post at Dimbi. Plans were made to extend mission activities into the Wahgi valley. During 1934 some houses and stations were begun in other parts of Simbu. In March 1934 an expedition of Frs. Ross, Schäfer, Aufenanger, and Tropper and Br. Eugene, with forty-five boys, went to Wilya. They met the Leahy brothers, Mick and Dan, who were beginning to mine gold in the area. Br. Eugene and Fr. Ross, both Americans, arrived at Wilya on 28 March 1934 and began building.

In Simbu Frs. Tropper and Schäfer and Br. Anton, supported by seventy or eighty carriers with supplies, established a station at Dimbi, Kawagl's home area. Kawagl was given a large axe head. It would seem that such a gift was considered by the mission to be payment for the land. Mission contact with the Simbu included work with the language and training interpreters and teachers. Simbu were employed as carriers and carpenters. The priests and brothers brought in dogs, traveled between their main stations, and built houses on native land at various places in the highlands area. In 1934 houses were built, but not continuously occupied, at Goglme, Denglagu, Kangrie, and Womkama; the mission also had some land at Mirani (Ulbrich 1960; Nilles 1987a). Mingende, below Dimbi on a large area of relatively flat land of the Wauga, a group allied with Kawagl's Siambugla, was to become the major Catholic station in Simbu. In 1934 Fr. Schäfer began to build an airstrip, school, clinic, church, and residence houses.

In October 1934, M. Leahy met Frs. Ross, Morschheuser, Schäfer, van Baar, and Br. Anton and mentions thefts from the mission at Kuruguru (or Korugu, in the Dimbi area). Fr. Schäfer sensed hostility and noted thefts from the mission at Dimbi.[2] Among his reports (Ulbrich 1960) is a description of his demonstration of the power of guns in killing a pig purchased from people in the valley, showing also how bullets can penetrate Simbu shields (also described in Nilles 1987a:31). However, this did not seem to deter the Simbu, who stole nails, shells, knives, and other trade goods when the opportunity arose. Simbu carriers ran away with rucksacks and their valuable contents; storerooms were looted and houses burnt or destroyed when the missionaries left. In incidents in the Simbu valley and at Dimbi, some Simbu pigs were shot after goods were taken. However, Fr. Schäfer realized how highly pigs were valued and cautioned against retaliating for thefts by shooting pigs.

The Catholic priests prepared for a Christmas gathering at Denglagu in 1934. Priests and Brothers were in the area, building mission houses and establishing posts. Fr. Schäfer sensed a change in peoples' attitudes. Mission workers carrying supplies were attacked in the Simbu valley at Womkama and Goglme and in the Dimbi area. On 11 November four mission boys were threatened with bows and arrows at Womkama. On 28 November 1934, Fr. C. van Baar found one of the mission's houses, near Womkama, burned down. He ordered the local people to rebuild it and threatened to kill pigs if this was not done. Then he continued to Dimbi. Frs. van Baar and Mor-schheuser then went to Koge, east of the Simbu River, for a few days to begin building a mission station. According to Fr. Nilles, the mission bought land for an airstrip and a house from the local people (1987a:33–34).

The Killing of Father Morschheuser

An account of these incidents was made by Fr. Schäfer to Acting A.D.O. McCarthy on 2 January 1935. To summarize, on 16 December 1934 Frs. Morschheuser and van Baar, with a line of carriers, went into the Simbu val-ley to join the priests' Christmas gathering at Denglagu.[3] Van Baar found that the orders to rebuild their house at Womkama had not been followed.

> No work had been done on the house and after a discussion Father van Baar decided to carry out his threat of shooting the pigs. The natives (except for some old men) were not present in the village. They were probably hiding in ambush waiting to attack the party. Father van Baar considered it would be a dangerous sign of weakness if he failed to carry out the shooting. This is what every man who has experience in the country says. (Schäfer 1935:1)

Two pigs were shot and one ran away.

> I think the natives intended to attack the party in any case and the killing of the pigs did not cause the attack which followed. The men in hiding now com-

menced to shout and dance while the party commenced to get out of the village. Van Baar was leading about twenty carriers which they had with them while Father Morschheuser carried up the rear. The party was armed with seven shotguns and two .44 Winchester rifles. . . . During the attack shots had been fired in self-defense by the Fathers' party but there is no means of telling if any of the attackers were hit. (Schäfer 1935:2)

Fr. Morschheuser was struck by two arrows, one of which killed him in a few minutes. A carrier who was accompanying him was injured. Going to the rear to see to Fr. Morschheuser, van Baar and the carriers were shot with arrows but not seriously injured. "The shooting stopped when the news of the Father's death was shouted to the attackers" (Schäfer 1935). After Fr. Morschheuser had died a stretcher was made; Womkama men helped to carry the body to the Denglagu border. They stole four knives and two axes. When van Baar asked them why they had attacked, they said it was to get the cargo, and did not mention the shooting of the pigs. The attack was planned beforehand. At Denglagu there were further plans to attack the priests, until Fr. Tropper arrived on the nineteenth, Fr. Cransen on the twenty-first, Fr. Schäfer and Br. Anton on the twenty-fourth.

At Madang on 28 December 1934, Acting A.D.O. McCarthy reported an interview with five Madang natives who had accompanied the priests on this trip. They said that when Fr. van Baar found the new house had not been built, he carried out his threat, killing one pig; and two other pigs were killed by his carriers. The carriers expected an attack because there were no villagers there.

Immediately the pigs were killed waiting natives attacked the party. Arrows began to fall and Father Van Baar set out at the head of the line leaving Father Mosschheuser [sic] and his carriers to bring up the rear. The arrows were being fired from some distance and Father Mosschheuser [sic] opened fire and killed two natives. One of his carriers killed another and then a falling arrow struck Father Mosschheuser [sic] in the neck. It apparently pierced the jugular vein for the Father began bleeding from the mouth and in a short time died. The carriers called to Father Van Baar but he did not believe them and threatened to punish the carriers for telling lies. The five men stayed with Father Mosschheuser [sic] and succeeded in carrying the body to Dengaragu where it was buried on the 17th inst. (McCarthy 1934)

These five men had been attached to Fr. Morschheuser and went to Alexishafen, then reported to the government at Madang. McCarthy comments: "On the face of it the action of Father Van Baar in shooting the pigs seems to be extremely unwise and if the foregoing statements are substantiated I would recommend due consideration be given to the cancellation of his Uncontrolled Area permit" (1934).

Fr. Nilles' account, which is based upon Fr. Schäfer's writings and the statements of other priests, states that two pigs were killed and that Fr. Morschheuser fired shots into the air, killing nobody (1987a:36).

The fighting between Simbu valley tribes at this time was exacerbated by competition for mission favors and trade goods. People of the Denglagu tribe friendly to the mission carried Fr. Morschheuser's body for burial at Kangrie, a mission center. The grave still stands by the roadside. Fr. van Baar offered shells to compensate for the pigs killed. He asked why they had attacked and was told that it was to get the cargo. Because they took only four knives and one axe, Fr. Nilles does not believe that this was the only reason for the attack. Word of this reached Kundiawa and Mingende. When Fr. Schäfer and Br. Anton came into the area from Mingende, they were met by Inau tribesmen smeared in mourning clay. They continued to Kangrie and met with the priests there.

When Fr. Schäfer asked the Denglagu why the Womkama people had burnt the house down and attacked the party,

> They said that although the first payment made by the Mission for the ground was satisfactory and that the owners were satisfied now, six months later, quarrels had broken out amongst the natives and that in consequence the house had been burnt. A second reply was also given; that the fire was an accident. Their reason for the attacks was that they were filled with the bloodlust and that to fight is natural to them. (1935:3)

In his investigation he knew that there were more plans by the natives of the upper valley, including the Denglagu, to attack the priests. Fr. Schäfer stated: "The natives of Womkama and the surrounding villages appear to fight for the love of it and they are always willing to attack for the chance of robbing the cargo."

When he returned to Womkama, at first the people would not speak with him, but later he was able to make contact. "Father Schäfer visited Womkama on 26th December, a fight ensued, and three Womkama natives were killed" (Taylor 1935a:1). Schäfer was not satisfied with the answers given him by the Denglagu and went to Womkama with Frs. van Baar and Cransen and Br. Anthony to hear explanations. According to his report (1935:4), he found ten pigs fastened at the outskirts of the village and a crowd called to take the pigs. Schäfer replied that he did not want to fight but to hear explanations. He asked that the knives and axes be returned, but only one axe was brought. Schäfer was determined to shoot only in self-defense, but when they were in danger he ordered his carriers to shoot. He then went to Bundi and Madang to report. "Fr. Schäfer himself told me that the missionaries were attacked and killed 3 natives" (Nilles 1990). Schäfer reported to his mission leader at Madang (Nilles 1987a). When Fr. Cransen and Br. Anton attempted to return to Dimbi, they were stopped by an attack. Some report of the incident was made to the Chimbu post, but Melrose and Taylor were elsewhere on patrol at this time, returning in January.

Fr. Nilles writes:

> Fr. Schäfer heard after his return to Kangrie that the Denglagu clan, possibly the whole Denglamagu, the four clans of the Upper Simbu, had attacked the Kulkane early in January. Twice they were successful, but the third time the Kulkanes together with their historic friends, the Inaus, ambushed the Denglamagus and inflicted some losses on them.
>
> The Denglamagu asked Fr. Schäfer for the mission to enter the war on their side. Father refused to do so and assured them that the Kiap, i.e., the government officer, would soon be up and restore order. This promise satisfied nobody and on the following Sunday the Fathers and Brothers were threatened with bows and arrows. But there was no real attack. (Nilles 1987a:39)

In the mission accounts of both incidents, Simbu motives were considered to be the desire for goods and involvement in intertribal competitions.

Brother Eugene in the Middle Simbu Valley

In early January 1935, Br. Eugene and a line of fifteen carriers left Wilya. They went up the Simbu valley on 8 January, as Br. Eugene was on his way to a retreat with the priests in the upper valley. He heard of the death of Fr. Morschheuser while at Dimbi, but this did not prevent him from traveling. He first followed the east bank of the Simbu River and later crossed it, going through Barengigl. Crossing again into Goglme, the party was attacked, apparently for cargo, and some of their goods were stolen. Br. Eugene did not shoot or attempt to prevent or retaliate for the thefts. He recrossed the river then returned. The attack intensified, and Br. Eugene was seriously injured by arrows and then by a spear. Two of his carriers were also wounded. It was said by the people after he fell, "he bled like a man." He and two native carriers were carried by friendly men across the river to Barengigl and treated there by Kewandegu Simbu tribesmen. Br. Eugene remained in a native house, his wounds increasingly painful and infected, eating only a few green bananas for a week. Carriers who had escaped reported that he had been killed. Pilot Gurney of Guinea Airways Ltd. was told at the airstrip on 10 January that Br. Eugene had been killed. The information reached D.O. Melrose; then Melrose, A.D.O. Taylor, and three police flew in to Ega airstrip. They were told by Rev. Helbig that some natives had reported that Br. Eugene had not been killed, but on the twelfth at Pari they were again informed that he was dead.

The news of Br. Eugene's death reached the Leahy and Fox brothers at Kuta via pilot Bob Gurney, who had been at Simbu the day before. Mick Leahy said, in an interview with T. Morpeth in 1970, that they were afraid these killings and lootings

> would start some sort of an uprising in the valley, and we wouldn't have enough ammunition to get out of it. So we decided, with the Fox brothers, to go straight down in the morning and go up the Chimbu and as another white party and a lot of boys we were hoping that we, also, would be attacked, which would have been the case. I have no doubt whatever about that. Tom Fox and I flew down with Bob Gurney in the Junker in the morning and landed on the Chimbu 'drome. There was no European there at all and no word whatever from the Administration. Bob flew on to Lae to report.

Leahy elaborates (1991:237–238): "Dan and I realized that the end result would be a general attack to sack and loot all white stations as the word trickled down from the Chimbu.... The locals' confidence had been boosted by two successful sorties...."

On 12 January Tom Fox and Mick Leahy met their brothers and carriers who had walked from Hagen: "We camped in isolation—no friendly bartering for food and pigs, no flirting girls. It was imperative that we resolve this unfortunate misunderstanding, for no white man could hope to have much influence in the future control and development of these people and these fabulous highland valleys" (Leahy 1991:238).

Dan and Mick Leahy, Tom and Jack Fox, with over one hundred carriers, started toward the Simbu valley when they received a note (carried in a forked stick by a native) from Melrose, who had just arrived at Simbu, ordering them out of the area. Reports of the death of Br. Eugene and two natives on 8 January 1935 had been made by Melrose and then telegraphed by the Administrator, McNicoll, to the prime minister and the apostolic delegate. In a letter of 3 February 1935, to Leo Tracey, M. Leahy is more outspoken.

> We decided to do what we could to murder a few of these murderers ... Tom Fox and I flew to Chimbu with Bob [Gurney] and Father MacEncroe, where we thought the kanakas may get nasty and have a go at the Lutherans and the next day walked back 3 hours to Kuruguru Mission Stn to wait for Dan and Jack Fox who were coming as fast as they could down the [Wahgi] valley with the boys. Saturday, 12th about 8.30 Dan and Jack got in a hell of a good walk from Mogai

and after they had a feed we pushed right on over into the Chimbu fall to get as near to the murderers as we could before we camped that night and also to get as far away from the Chimbu Drome as we could, knowing that if the D.O. heard of our free lance justice effort he would have to order us out as is done in any area where a murder has been committed. . . . Melrose . . . ordered us back to the drome.

They continued to Bena. On his way back to Hagen, Dan Leahy was appointed special constable and joined the Taylor patrol, accompanied by his carriers.

Only when a government patrol to investigate the death of Fr. Morschheuser reached the area on 16 January and Br. Eugene had his assistants fire a gun to attract attention, was Br. Eugene discovered to be alive and rescued. He was carried to Kundiawa on 17 January and nursed overnight by the Lutheran Reverend and Mrs. W. Bergmann. Bergmann (who had some medical training in Germany) found that Br. Eugene had a high fever of 40°, a pulse rate of 145, and sepsis in his wounds. He attended the wounds and tried to give him food, liquids, and rest (Bergmann n.d., 5:22–24). Br. Eugene was flown to the Salamaua hospital on 18 January where he died on 23 January 1935.

The Patrol and Arrests of A.D.O. J. Taylor

When the killings occurred, in December 1934 and January 1935, Taylor was patroling in the Waria area south of Salamaua. His was a "roving assignment" at that time, and he was then sent to Simbu. However, there were delays in preparing a force under Taylor to inquire into the killings and make arrests. He believed that the natives of the Simbu valley, who had no experience of the government, were capable of overwhelming a small government force, and additional Australian officers, police, and carriers were brought in.

Taylor's investigation began on 18 January 1935 with Acting A.D.O. Roberts going first up the valley to Dengaragu, where he told the missionaries about the death of Br. Eugene and closed the road to travelers. The patrol found so much turmoil in the area, with crowds of heavily armed men and fighting between Denglagu and Inau, that they returned to Kundiawa. On 22 January 1935, reinforced by Special Constable D. Leahy, A.P.O. Black, Roberts, 12 policemen and 130 native carriers, Taylor reached Dengaragu. He spoke with mission employees who had been with Fr. Morschheuser and located the attackers.

From local inquiry, and from what the mission "boys" told me, I was now able to form a pretty good idea of who the offenders were, and where they lived—that is collectively, not individually. That the arrests could be made I was perfectly confident, but the problem that would soon arise was what to do with them when we got them. So the next day Roberts went off to EGA to build a station on a site nearby which was previously marked, and put up a prison large enough to accommodate fifty persons and hold them securely. This he did and it speaks volumes for his ingenuity that he did it without a nail!(1935a:7)

Then, with Dan Leahy, Black, 12 policemen, and 120 "boys," Taylor left for Womkama and Denglagu. "I decided to pass through WOMKAMA, visit DENGARAGU, and attempt to effect the arrests on the return journey. TINEI and MERUWO were said to be those who actually killed Father Morschheuser, though most of the WOMKAMA men of fighting age were sure to have been involved" (1935a:7). He spoke with the mission people. On 11 February they went to the Inau-Dengaragu border area at Mondia battleground.

A party of between twenty and thirty armed men rose to attack from both sides of the road. They were driven off, three being killed. Twenty-one shields were taken by us, with many bows and arrows and spears, a bonfire was made to impress upon the people what we had already told them—that the plunder was not for us, and that we came to bring peace, not war.

Whilst this was going on several hundred INAUHU people were looking on. Seeing us depart, the INAUHU rushed down to attack the DENGARAGU, who had returned for their dead. I then turned back with a small party and forced these people back to their own territory, two being killed. The party then continued on to WOMKAMA. Arrived there we made camp.

The problem which confronted us now was this—what would be the effect on the WOMKAMA people when they learned we had shot the INAUHU people, their allies? Would they be openly hostile or return to their hilltops? As it happened, neither of these things occurred; the people were quieter than usual, so our task was made easier.

The next morning, at a given signal the suspects, forty all told, were seized and fettered. A terrific struggle took place but our numbers overwhelmed them. (Taylor 1935a:8)

In 1987 I was told by Fr. Nilles and Simbu valley people that about twenty known persons were killed. Black states in his diary that he stitched up the wounded prisoners, who had head wounds from rifle butts, knives, and tomahawks. In his diary written at Goglme, Black (1935, 5 February) comments: "All mission parties are invariably poorly armed. . . . There is not the slightest shadow of doubt that if Bro Eugene had taken a firm stand and shot only one or two men it would never have occurred. . . . A fight, some rifle wounds and the lesson on the spot would be far more effective."

After the arrests at Womkama for the killing of Fr. Morschheuser, Taylor went to the Goglme area to arrest those responsible for attacking Br. Eugene. Black had found much evidence of the looting of Br. Eugene's goods, including a man and a woman who were wearing parts of a watch acquired in trade from those who had taken them.

While at Goglme base camp, on 7 February, Black disarmed fighting Simbu and destroyed their weapons. Taylor had shot a man who came to the post with weapons and was "truculent." After this they came unarmed to trade:

> They began to have doubts about us being quite as harmless as missionaries. "The clean shaven blokes are another kind; the bearded ones are easy." . . . The missionaries they regarded as only being in the territory on sufferance. Now the unpleasant surprise of the kiap and his police stopping where he wanted and when he wanted . . . brought home to them the tales of the power of the white man they had heard were true. (Black 1935, 10 February)

On 15 February, Black was asked to help one group of Simbu and retaliate for their deaths in a fight by shooting some of the enemy; pigs were offered as payment. Although he did not become a partisan in intertribal fighting, he did offer support: "I told them if they behaved themselves they would be assisted against tribal attacks. They were told to come down in force and visit the camp with food as soon as Taylor arrived back from Chimbu" (Black 1935, 15 February).

Three days later, traveling through Pari to Kundiawa, Black was attacked. "I don't know how many were killed but the members of our small party escaped without any wounded" (Black 1935, 18 February). The prisoners were held in the jail built by Roberts. Soon Melrose, the District Officer, Medical Assistant Walsh, and acting P.O. Greathead arrived; Black departed with Melrose. Then Taylor and Roberts went back up the valley to arrest forty-one at Goglme. They had to use dog chains and padlocks to secure them all. Taylor's report states that he explained to people why arrests had to be made, and they appeared to understand: "Object of the arrests was to secure as many as possible of those implicated in attacks and to discover the true story of the murders. . . . Too early to expect a reliable story" (1935a:11).

Taylor had received information that the men whose arrows had struck Fr. Morschheuser were Tinei, Meruwo, and perhaps Kindeikwa; the first two were arrested and Meruwo was in hiding. In Goglme, "Mondu, who is said to have actually struck Br. Eugene with an arrow; is now in custody with others. Kwambongerineim and Ego of Nunu-maina, who also shot him, are still at large" (Taylor 1935a:11).

Fr. Nilles' account of the arrests, based upon Fr. Schäfer's diary and talks with Taylor, Fr. Schäfer, and Fr. Tropper, supplements and differs in some ways. In his account the Taylor party came to Kangrie from Madang via Bundi to investigate and arrest Womkama men on 21 January 1935. Their plan was to form a circle, throw cowrie shells out to the people, and seize the men as they picked up the shells. This would suggest that they would be pleased to take any members of the group prisoner, and not to identify those who were responsible for killing Fr. Morschheuser. Fr. Nilles continues by stating that near Gembogl a group of Denglagu appeared.

> On the way from Kangrie to Womkama when the party approached Gembogl, a group of Denglagu men sprang up out of the kunai. Mr. Taylor did not know that the Denglagu-Komkane and Siagu clans were at war with their traditional enemies, the Inaus. He thought they were attacking him, so he ordered his police to fire. Several men were killed and the rest ran away. When the Inaus saw the Denglagu-Komkanes and Siagus run uphill and heard the shots, they thought the government officer had come to fight on their side. They ran down the hill toward the government party. Mr Taylor thought he was being attacked on this side too, so he ordered a volley of shots. Some Inaus were killed and the rest ran away. (Nilles 1987a:45)

Fr. Nilles told me in 1987 that when Taylor thought he was being attacked he shot twenty or twenty-five at Gembogl. The Inau thought he was supporting them by shooting the Denglagu, so they massed, jumped in, and Taylor shot again.

When Taylor proceeded to Womkama no one would meet him for several days. Finally, when they came he trapped them by throwing the cowries and arrested forty men.

> It must have been a tremendous strain on those men of the Kulkane clan to walk along a track in one line with their hands in chains, policemen at the front, behind and along the line. They had never been bereft of their freedom in this way. The women and children had probably not been on the spot when their husbands and fathers were handcuffed. But they would have been hiding in the kunai and behind shrubs nearby. When they saw their men moving away with their hands fettered, they must have set up the death wails. (Nilles 1987a:45)

Taylor and Leahy then continued to Dengaragu to inform and check on missionaries, who were safe, and reported that they found the people friendly. However, at Goglme Roberts and his guard had been attacked, for which two were shot attempting to overwhelm police and release prisoners. There were some further attacks on the government patrols, and on 7 March the party took prisoners to Kundiawa. D. Leahy left for Mount Hagen on 10 March 1935.

Some of the prisoners were released because it was thought that they were not responsible or were unable to endure the trip, and some escaped. On 18 March, with ten police and sixty-seven prisoners, Taylor left Kundiawa for Salamaua. Five prisoners escaped that night. The party proceeded, reaching Salamaua on 14 April.

> When they reached the Markham valley, so Jim Taylor told me, they had all behaved in an orderly way and none had tried to escape. He, therefore, told the police to take their handcuffs off and allow the Simbus to walk into Salamaua as free men.
>
> Twelve years later, 1947, the war was over and we built a church at Womkama. At that time, I met a man who had been among the forty prisoners taken to Salamaua. He said only three of them made it back home. (Nilles 1987a:46)

Fr. Nilles was told that the man who shot Fr. Morschheuser was not taken prisoner and was still alive years later. The prisoners were detained for about six months and were to be brought back to the Simbu area in small groups. However, the first group of twenty died of malaria on the way, and the others were held at Kainantu for medical treatment (Taylor interview with P. Munster, April 1983). I was told in 1987 by Simbu valley people that few survived the trip, exposure to malaria and other diseases, or imprisonment to return to Simbu. I have not met any survivors.

Taylor made a general statement:

> The natives of Womkama and Gorime [Goglme] and the rest of the Arawa people welcomed with great enthusiasm and awe the first missionaries—they were the first white men to visit the Upper Chimbu.
>
> As the natives got to know them better, through parties travelling to and fro, the strangeness wore off and native self-confidence reasserted itself. This later became truculence and, coupled with the desire for the white man's goods (particularly his fabulous wealth in shell money) they became bolder and bolder. That this boldness and many more or less serious acts of hostility went unpunished, as it did, caused them to believe that the white man's weapons were powerless. Of arrest and imprisonment they had naturally never heard. . . . The fact that we have weapons and do not use them makes us appear to the natives as unarmed people.
>
> The extremely friendly attitude in the first instance, followed by over-confidence and later hostility, is characteristic . . . of the highland people. . . .

What must be recognised is that native law is the law of the spear, and if there is no Government to enforce a new code, the native will settle his disputes with arms. . . .

The murder of Father Mosscheuser [sic] was obviously due to his shooting of the natives' pigs. This was an act of war and brought about war's consequences. . . . The white man (the natives did not know who the missionaries were) passed continually through their country on sufferance, and in their mind he was only entitled to that sufferance as long as he was strong enough to command it.

In Brother Eugene's case the underlying cause was the same. Hearing of the first murder, the whole Chimbu people realised that the white man could be killed, just as a native. This, together with a desire for plunder and the native's delight in battle, made the tragedy almost inevitable. (Taylor 1935a:2–3)

Other writings on these deaths have been published, either taken from the reports or letters of the time or from later conversations and experiences reported to the writers (Simpson 1964; Ross 1968; Mennis 1982). Although they mostly repeat or confirm the statements quoted above, some also add to the discrepancies or create new versions of the events. Both mission and government writers were concerned to defend their actions, and some later commentators also had a position to maintain. These comments reflect a later view of the events and did not contribute to the outcome.

The most notable difference between the mission view and the government view (Schäfer versus Taylor) is found in the reason given for the attack and killing of Fr. Morschheuser: Schäfer believed that the killing of the pigs was not the reason, whereas Taylor believed that it was. However, both agreed that the Simbu were inclined to steal and fight.

What the Simbu Say about the Deaths

The deaths of the missionaries hold a particularly important place in the contemporary Simbu understanding of their relations with the white man, mission, and government. Many of the men interviewed say that the first white men were thought to be spirits of dead ancestors, and some that they did not expect them to be mortal. But few of them thought that the attack could test their mortality. Some stories do not name Fr. van Baar but attribute the pig shooting to Fr. Morschheuser. Many state that there was tribal fighting at the time, and few mention a desire for cargo. Only one or two speak of the arrests and imprisonment. In one story, where Gando says that the missionary gave shells as a reward, the implication is that this was not a payment; thus land and houses for mission use did not, in Simbu eyes, become the property of the mission.

Simbu began to discover that the mission had come to settle among them and bring Christianity; the kiap was there to arrest and shoot them, and to make roads. Simbu valley stories observe that the padres came first, and the kiaps came when this killing of the padre was reported to them. The kiaps and police are given a punitive role, whereas missionaries in only a few stories are blamed for violence toward pigs or Simbu. Simbu stories attribute their knowledge of gun power to these incidents and the killing of men and pigs to the government kiaps and police.

My first recording of the killing of a priest was on 19 May 1958, shortly after my arrival, and told to me by Kiagl, a Simbaigu Kamanegu at Umbundo. After telling a story about the origin of Simbaigu clan, their movements and wars, he said:

> fighting stopped after Fr. Schäfer came. The priest killed at Simboro—Mitnande happened when people had been fighting. The Pater broke up the fight. The people talked: priests have salt, shells, and if we kill them we can get it. They thought the guns were nothing. Thought the whiteman had plenty of cargo, they were marsalai [P. spirits] with a lot of goods. They killed to get the cargo. At that time there was no kiap at Kundiawa and they sent a message to Goroka.[4] Then the kiap came up and shot many people, pigs and burnt houses. They stopped the fight between Simbaigu and Umbanegu and settled fights at Umbundo. The kiap has put an end to these fights. Before they tied the arms, legs, and so on of the men.

Mondo Gunama of Denglagu, Upper Simbu valley (interviewer John Karl):

> During tribal fighting he went with mother to Bundi. Houses, pigs and gardens destroyed. Men came and fought enemies. Some of our people who were left behind came and told us that they say the red spirit of our ancestors who died before is coming back to us with many things we haven't seen before. They brought magic things so my father and the other men went down to Bundi to see the magic goods they brought. They saw the first white men who waved at them to come close but they were scared. Some of their brothers who were down there before were used to the white men pulling their hands close. The white men supplied them with salt, kina shells, axe, and so on. My father told the white man that I have a son at home so they gave him a laplap that was around 50 cm and it was thin. The white men were so kind to my people and they asked where they come from. They told the whites they are from Denglagu. My father brought them to Kangre, gave them land to stay. There

was a priest and a brother. They build some sort of school where they teach us how to polish shoes, cook, wash clothes, and sweep the house and learn pidgin. Some students called *sumatin* [P. Catholic pupil]. Fr. Tropper went to Mingende, and also Fr. Morschheuser, who returned, saw fighting and shot pigs. People got angry and shot him dead. The people of Denglagu heard the story of his death and went and brought him to Kangrie where they buried him. That was when I was still a student of him. Fr. Schäfer or the Brother sent message to Jim Taylor. He brought carriers, cook boys, and many police men and told our fathers not to fight. Some who heard the message did not go to fight. The others who didn't listen went to Gembogl to fight. They hid their selves in the bushes waiting for their enemies. During the same day Jim Taylor with his police men wanted to see the people who had shot Fr. Morschheuser and accidently saw the people hiding and told his police men who shot all our men who went to fight. Jim Taylor went all the way to Womatne and gathered all the head men and ask them who shot Fr. Morschheuser. He captured some of them and took them all the way to Goroka. Fr. wanted me and the other students to be carpenters so he taught us about carpentering.

Mondo Ola of Ombondo, Simbu valley (interviewer Paul San):

When the first missionaries came I was still up at Kupau when I saw them. They came about the same time as the kiaps did. With the kiaps came Rev. Bergmann of the Lutheran Mission. He settled down in Kundiawa. Coming from Mondia down were the first Catholic missionaries. They were Fr. Morschheuser and some others which I don't know of. Fr. Morschheuser was a huge masculine man with a big beard and he was wearing an army helmet when I saw him. At first I thought they were our dead ancestors coming back to life. We also thought they were the God of the thunder and lightning coming to us.

We were all scared.

Yes I can remember their deaths because we all mourned for them. I don't really know the cause of the death. Their death also made clear to us that those white men we thought were gods and can not die were just like us. They were real men like us and can die like us.

Kua Bogia of Kangrie, Upper Simbu valley (interviewer Joseph Mondo):

Kiaps came after the first missionary. First missionaries were Fr. Hoopernanga[5] and Fr. Morschheuser and another white man also, at Kangrie. Heard of death of Fr. Morschheuser. Kiaps came because of his death. The Kulkane people killed him. I think the Kulkane people killed him for two reasons (their own thoughts): A. Killed him to rob his belongings. B. Shoot him just to see whether white people might die or not. Because at that time we said these white skinned people are ghosts or spirits of our ancestors who died before—

and they won't die. The late-comers were called kiaps and the former ones were called *batres* (P. priests).

Dama Caspar Daka of Bogo, Kerowagi (interviewer Naur Awi Philip):

The first kiap came to our area through the request of the first missionaries. Their request was due to the attack and shooting of the first missionaries. The first kiap . . . came with a big patrolling team. It was that time when Dama and all the villagers first saw the gun, when the kiap shot the pig. The firing of the gun frightened the people, and many ran away. For the celebration of the kiap's arrival, the villagers slaughtered many pigs and collected many foods. In return, the kiap delivered salt, laplap, kina shell and rice. Rice at that time was said to be the earthworm's eggs. Also during that time, the kiap was believed to be the spirit of the dead ancestor. They remember the time when they first saw the native policemen. They were so active in the work. They followed every instructions from the kiap. Policemen were specially chosen, and many people feared them, even though they were from this country. They also said that pigs were just taken away by the policemen without the owners' permission, whenever problems or disputes arose in that particular area.

These quotations show the isolation of the Simbu valley. There is limited knowledge of places outside Simbu: some saw the government as centered at Goroka, which was the Eastern Highlands headquarters years later. In the last account the kiap is the one who shot pigs. Also, the people celebrate the arrival of a kiap with a great feast presentation. In this account, and in others, the police are blamed for taking pigs.

The killings, the significance of written communications, the reasons for these actions, the shooting of pigs, the way in which the arresting patrol arrived in the midst of tribal warfare, and the punishment, all seen in the light of intertribal relations, put quite a different face upon those events from the views of the government or the missionaries. The belief that the missionaries summoned the kiap to help them, and then the government began to shoot pigs and people, is widespread among Simbu.

What Simbu Have Written

Simbu have contributed to a body of oral history and fictional writings that tell the stories of their people. Three of these have particular relevance to the story of the missionaries and these killings. They offer insights and attest to the continuing attention paid to these events by the people of several tribes in the Simbu valley. The written accounts of educated Simbu are mainly by young men who attended mission schools in the 1950s, 1960s, and later, reporting what they have learned from teachers and villagers. The accounts are interesting in their view of the proceedings, but also show how events of different times and persons are conflated. Labor recruiting (which actually began in 1951), is said by one author immediately to have followed these deaths.

Ignatius Kilage's book, *My Mother Calls Me Yaltep* (n.d.), is in the form of a semifictional autobiography told in the first person and recounting many of the historical incidents in the upper and middle Simbu valley. Kilage had a distinguished career (see Chap. 8). The novel dates his birth from the time of the

> sudden appearance of an extraordinary white bird, making thunderous sounds over the Eastern Horizon and disappearing into the West . . . rumours of the Gende people of Bundi were about to perform one of their famous Magic Spells on the Mitnandi people. (p. 1)
>
> Fresh rumours . . . from the lower Simbu, the Nigl Kande, that strange ghost man *(Gigl Yomba)* was seen walking into Simbu and doing strange things.
>
> People were casting counter spells. . . . Sudden arrivals of white men . . . trying to communicate. . . . White people who arrived from Upper Simbu were a gentle crowd, our people took them to be the spirits of their ancestors, and treated them with respect.
>
> But there was a misunderstanding at Womatne. A Kulkane man shot one of those men, then suddenly a much tougher and dangerous looking white man and his black men arrived on the scene. These late comers were called Kiaps and the former ones were called Batres (Fathers or Priests). . . .
>
> The usual tribal wars fought with bows and arrows, sharp spears and blackened shields were suddenly halted by these "good spirits" with the help of their polished sticks. These magic sticks of the Whites were so powerful that the people came to fear them more than anything else. . . .
>
> That stick spoke like thunder and spat fire and smoke when it was pointed at something . . . even one of these sticks was capable of wiping out the entire tribe.
>
> The kiaps, with their sharp headed black-men from the Coast, were always on the move, ready to go wherever there was trouble. With the aid of their thundering sticks, they could put fighting warriors to flight.

Kilage recounts that his mother took him to be named by the priests, for she wanted him to wear one

> of those shining things that the children named by the batres wore around their necks. These she took as charms to ward off evil spirits, for batres were considered good spirits. (p. 2)
>
> When the census was taken, some people believed that their names would be

given to the ancestors who would then send them cargo. They saw that the black fellows with polished magic sticks . . . would handle people most roughly. When a shining object—an empty tobacco tin—was thrown from the white man's house, it was taken as a sign of cargo. (p. 5)

We young people hated and feared the kiaps and their black-boys. The most effective tool used to silence us in those days, was the mere mention of the word "kiap" or "*kimbri nem*" (meaning the father of the polished stick, or Policeman). . . . We hated them for their intrusions. (p. 6)

In telling of the killing of Fr. Morschheuser, Kilage mentions his uncle:

In the prime of his manhood there came the batres, one of whom shot a pig belonging to his people, because the people did not fulfil their part of a deal. . . . Uncle became involved in a conspiracy against the batres and . . . shot one of them. . . . The kiap came with his policemen, terrified the people . . . captured the young and strong men of the clan . . . took them off in bonds to the unknown. . . . (p. 10)

The batre had come to stay with the Mitnande people and had made friends with them, but one of our men killed a batre and some of our warriors wounded some black men from the Coast. However, people as a whole, were not perturbed because when the Mitnande people asked the batre to declare war against the Kulkane tribe, he advised against it and warned them that if they did any such thing the kiap would come with greater force and take them off to the unknown, like some of the people who had killed the batre.

The people were at variance—some thought that the whites were men because some of them had been killed, but others thought that they were not men at all . . . —if they were men, then they would be sons of women, but we never saw a white woman among the batres nor the kiaps—therefore it followed these whites were not born of women.

Scouts were sent to find out, and found very large, dog-like creatures . . . these monsters were called 'hos' (horse) while the other kind . . . were called 'Bulmakau.' Some called them '*Bugla Kauo*,' meaning huge pig. (p. 11)

Kilage speaks of the appointment of *bosbois* (P. headman) who were given a white ring by the kiaps and police and seen as very powerful. They provided the kiaps and police with girls when they visited the village (p. 13).

This story and those written by Toby Waim Kagl and Benjamin Umba attest to the lasting significance of the killings, how the gun was seen by Simbu, and a mounting fear of kiap and police as compared to the milder and kindly priests. Fr. Nilles insisted that the missionaries always fired above the heads of Simbu, whereas kiaps and police shot people and pigs. Only the later bean-stealing incident suggests that the priests might kill Simbu for theft. None of these written accounts mentions arrest and imprisonment of

Simbu. Any stories of prisoners who were taken to Salamaua and returned to Simbu seem to have been lost and the prisoners disappeared.

The Power of Guns Was Feared

The information and quotations presented provide a rich set of statements and many viewpoints about the early relations and impressions of Simbu and strangers. Simbu in these areas, and the several groups of whites and New Guineans from other areas, had different concerns, goals, motives, and interpretations of their actions and those of others. These unforgotten incidents in 1933–1935 that involved deaths and arrests had a lasting impact on the relations between the Simbu and government kiaps, police, missionaries, mission assistants of other areas, prospectors, settlers, and other visitors. The incidents were seen differently by the several parties, and the events were probed for many years, analyzed in reports, and retold in gatherings with ever new and varied interpretations. The many accounts, stated and reported days, months, and even years after the events, show how varied the experiences and impressions were. However, from the point of view of each teller, and in some cases of several related tellers, there are consistencies and positions that indicate shared impressions and memories.

For all the Europeans and police—but not, I think, for the Simbu— what happened in Simbu followed, and was seen in the light of, other fighting incidents and attacks (see Chap. 3 and Radford 1987). Whereas Simbu people had no direct knowledge of these, they were well known to the missionaries, prospectors, and kiaps. The Australian government was called upon to protect white men in its territories and responded officially to questions about these deaths.

In his report of the Hagen-Sepik patrol of 1938–1939, Taylor, more experienced and less pressed to present his final report, expresses some of his concerns very clearly. Particularly in the remote areas of the western highlands and Sepik, where population numbers and distribution were not known, his greatest concern was food supplies for his large party. Thus he was quick to take and offer the goods he thought would be acceptable in quantities to assure adequate food. We have little direct information about the expectations and satisfactions of the newly contacted people. However, a comparison of their welcomes and acceptance of the patrol's offerings with the hard efforts made to obtain food supplies and the privations of the Hides-O'Malley expedition into Papua in 1935 (cf. Hides 1936; Schieffelin and Crittenden 1991), where their trade goods were unacceptable, shows up the differences and the rewards of Taylor's concern. The 1933 Bena-Hagen expedition was never far from native settlements and food was adequate nearly everywhere. They also had arranged for air contact, supplies, and visits by officials.

The first Simbu reaction to the entrance into the area of these strangers was surprise, awe, and fear. The airplane, seen as an extraordinarily large bird, could be identified with Simbu mystical birds and flutes. The white skin, clothing, shoes, and goods marked the strangers as otherworldly. The appearance of white strangers and their accompanying black carriers, helpers, and police challenged the existing social categories. Simbu thought the white men might be spirits, and immortal. Black police and carriers were seen by some as deceased relatives and by others as possibly dangerous cannibals who spit blood from mouths colored red (from chewing betel).

My reading of Simbu statements and reactions to this new relationship is that they were very willing to accept the newcomers for what they had to offer. As Simbu had no knowledge or previous experience of metal, cloth, manufactured goods, or shells of this quantity and variety, the goods of the white man seemed miraculous, and the newcomers amazingly rich. The goods they carried were desirable and were given in return for food and pigs, thus introducing new values into the exchange system. After the first startling view of the white strangers, black policemen, carriers, and their goods, the highlanders wanted these goods and attempted in different ways to get them. Their ideas of the interdependence of the exchanging of goods and friendly alliance were adapted to making ready offerings of food and pigs for the shells and other goods they received in return. This immediate exchange of valuables for goods and services was a wonderful new form of intergroup relations. But it was not beyond Simbu experience. The exchange was not unlike the trading and bartering that took place at the border of Simbu and Bundi, using cowrie and tambu shells and trade for salt. Nilles also notes that lending, borrowing, and the return of goods was practiced (Nilles 1944:12–23).

The new goods were incorporated into the Simbu exchange system as valuables. For white men, the purchasing power of shell was enormous; to the Simbu and highlanders, the shells were of great value.[6] The Simbu placed the newcomers in their traditional context of friends, allies, or enemies, who might change their allegiance; the exchange of foods, pigs, and valuables would confirm the relationship. The Simbu had always been wary of outsiders, and their expectations in these encounters ranged from hope for alliance to fear of attack. They were engrossed in intertribal relations and conflicts. Each Simbu group hoped that the newcomers would take their side in these. The Simbu might compete for favorable treatment and engage the newcomers in their local intertribal conflicts. Each group offered land, frequently on the border of enemy territory, to the white newcomers in the hope that they would become long-term friends, providing shells, steel, and other wonderful things to them and refusing such goods to their enemies, protecting them by their presence and with their guns, and joining in their attacks against enemies. To the Simbu, the payments were friendly gifts cementing alliance; they were not a transfer of land to the outsiders.

Thus, when the mission built houses on tribal land and then left them untenanted, as had been done by Fr. van Baar at Womkama, the advantages of mission alliance evaporated. The local Simbu considered the building abandoned, to be dismantled for firewood. Fr. Schäfer observed that the Simbu did not think of the land and house as a final sale, and I do not believe that Simbu at that time had such a concept. Contracts for land sale, transfer of rights to another, and the maintenance of a foreigner's property were unknown to them.

The strangers were mysterious, magical creatures who did not know their route or destination, and their intentions were incomprehensible. They had wealth in goods never before seen, yet they were few, evidently defenseless, often trusting. The origin and materials of their goods, their appearance, and their motives were unfathomable. A small force, their apparent vulnerability was tested in later encounters. The "sticks," which in fact were guns, did not at first reveal their lethal power.

The response of parties of armed whites, police, and helpers killing attackers and arresting warriors was unprecedented. The Kunabau thefts, attacks on the patrol, and deaths occurred a long way from the Simbu valley, and given the general state of hostilities and lack of communication among distant tribes in 1933, the news may not have spread to the Simbu valley. Although Fr. Schäfer states that he demonstrated guns, none of the Simbu stories from the valley mention this.

After some months in the Simbu area, mission posts and traveling parties of missionaries and their helpers began to see the Simbu as thieves. The Fathers may have expected that their property would be respected and orders obeyed, but they found that houses were broken into and traveling carriers were robbed. In the Simbu valley the traveling party came on the scene during tribal hostilities; they interrupted an excited warrior force and presented them with an opportunity for obtaining coveted goods to the exclusion of the enemy. The prizes could be a proof of victory, an advantage over the tribal enemy, and perhaps the gain of an ally in future tribal conflicts. In both of these attacks in the Simbu valley, there were people who had been friendly to the mission and could hope for continued alliance and gifts, and others who knew less about the newcomers and could only attempt to take their cargo.

Those who carried Fr. Morschheuser to a burial place and Br. Eugene to be nursed at Barengigl were demonstrating their special relationship with the newly arrived white missionaries. At Kangrie, where missionaries had been established for some months, alliance with the Dengla-Maguagu in their fight against those enemies who had murdered Fr. Morschheuser placed the relationship on a Simbu-defined footing as allies. The Dengaragu people asked the mission to join them in an attack upon Womkama.

We can see discrepancies in the stories of the killings of Fr. Morsch-heuser and Br. Eugene,[7] in the inquiries made by Fr. Schäfer and Jim Taylor, and the subsequent telling of the stories that concern the events, the sequence of events, the movements and location of the white people in time and place. These varying interpretations influenced attitudes and decisions of both government and mission in the years to follow, and also the way in which the story was told to young Simbu who later wrote the semifictional tales and those who answered my questions. Some confusion of motive and action can now be attributed to Simbu tribal hostilities and their expecta-tion of retaliation; some must be the perceptions of those who wrote about the events from a different viewpoint.

The most important difference between the two attacks on missionaries is that the first may have been provoked by, if not a direct response to, the killing of the pigs by Fr. van Baar, whereas the second was incidental to theft from Br. Eugene. The attack on the priests in the Simbu valley was thought by the government to be a retaliation for killing pigs. However, Fr. Schäfer reports that when Fr. van Baar, and later he himself, inquired at Womkama, they were told that the attacks were for cargo. One man of the Kukani told Fr. Nilles that Fr. Morschheuser was shot in order to ascertain if an arrow could kill a white man (Nilles 1987a:17).

The attack on Br. Eugene was clearly for the purpose of getting his goods, and then to test his vulnerability. When the Nunu-Yomani tried to obtain his cargo, and he failed to defend himself, the result was attack and fatal wounding. It would appear that the Goglme people thought the white men were defenseless prey, and perhaps were also testing the theory that they were spirits and could not be killed. The rescue and caring for Br. Eugene by the people of Barengigl was motivated, it has been said, by the desire to keep him as a valuable ally and giver of wealth. Some Simbu thought that the white man might be immortal, and that his immortality might be put to the test. If he was truly a spirit he would live on as a friend.

Fr. Nilles (1987a:44 and 1987b) suggests one motive mentioned by no one else: that the killers of Br. Eugene did it for prestige among Simbu. This shows his deep understanding of Simbu motives in warfare. To Simbu, it is a special achievement to kill an important man in war, or in any other way; big men of size and courage are bold, placed in the forefront of battle and exposed to enemy attack. Their power is in their invulnerability to physical and magical dangers (see Chap. 2).

If the people of Goglme knew of the killing at Womkama, which is likely as the distance was not great and two weeks had gone by since Fr. Morschheuser was killed, they might have been emboldened to try to take the goods of Br. Eugene. And when these goods were given up with scarcely any resistance (as reported by the carriers who accompanied him and then escaped), the attack might well have intensified. Then, with the resistance of Br. Eugene's party and shots fired in defense, Br. Eugene and his helpers were wounded in the fray. This course of events was then followed by the enemies of the Goglme group coming back into the fight, carrying off the wounded to Barengigl, and attempting to treat them there. Saving Br. Eugene would give prestige and future alliance to this group.

In a commentary on mission activities, Taylor observes that both Catholic and Lutheran missions are established in the Simbu area.

> The Catholic priests move about amongst the people endeavouring to make friends and gain the people's confidence, and at convenient spots erect houses which they then leave untenanted. This practice appears to be unsatisfactory and is inviting trouble. . . . The shooting of pigs has been instituted . . . as a punitive measure. . . . The Lutheran mission places natives or "helpers" . . . in villages and native settlements and leaves them there to learn the language and bring the people under influence. . . . It would appear that the intention of the Lutheran Mission society is to flood the area with native helpers. . . . In the race for ground what is probably not realised is the almost irreparable damage that is done by such occurrences as the recent murders. It should be possible to bring these inland people under control without the loss of one European life or many native lives. Though it is difficult to see how such calamities can be avoided unless missionaries are prevented from operating in remote places, or unless police control of new areas is established before or side by side with missionary settlement. Otherwise missionaries are compelled to introduce penal measures . . . for their own safety. . . . That some government control of mission activities is necessary becomes apparent from the arrogant attitude of missionaries, European and native, among these new people. . . . What the native requires in his early contact with Europeans is firmness so that he will respect white lives and property, and friendship so that the racial clash will be softened. (1935b:1)

He advises the District Officer and the government not to permit inexperienced men to work except in company with others accustomed to natives in a new country, not to build houses that are untenanted, not to shoot pigs as punishment or thrash natives, and not to establish native stations without first referring to the District Officer (Taylor 1935b:2).

Today, Simbu valley people remember their first experience of the white man as the kindly priests and the kiap who came to avenge the (accidental or unintentional) killing of the missionaries, initiating an era of fear of guns and retaliation. Simbu of today believe that the missionaries had not used their guns before this. Catholic priests carried guns only in self-defense. In his discussion of the early days of the mission, Fr. Nilles describes Fr. Schäfer's efforts to secure the return of stolen goods. This included taking pigs as hostages and returning them when the goods were brought to him. Fr. Nilles says that killing pigs was soon regarded as poor policy. Settling in the rural areas and inviting people to attend their services required good and peaceful relations with the surrounding people. Mission workers, schoolchildren, and teachers were given cloth, soap, salt, shells, mirrors, beads, and small trade goods. Fr. Ross noted that "the Administration was under fire from southern papers. The question was pointedly put; 'why does the Administration in New Guinea permit missionaries to go into uncontrolled areas where their lives are in danger and where there is no government protection?' " (1968:62).

New restrictions applied in 1935 refused highlands area permits to new missionaries and kept missionaries already in residence at their main stations. White people could not enter the highlands or travel there without government permission. In January 1936, the restrictions were somewhat modified to allow missionaries with four years' experience on the coast to go to the highlands, requiring them to carry rifles when traveling. Missionaries were restricted to a radius of five miles from their stations until 1947. Fr. Ross comments that the benefit of these restrictions was that language learning was intensified and good houses were built (1968:62).

Taylor's attitude seems to have derived from his opinion of the necessity of force in administrative control of the highlanders. He advocates stopping and punishing acts of hostility or theft and demonstrating the power of weapons. In a comment to the District Officer Morobe on 27 April 1935, when he reported the patrol and arrests in the Simbu valley, he said: "Robbery is in native eyes an act of war akin to murder, and if not resisted and overcome by force, murder will almost surely follow. . . . War is to them . . . a blood sport . . . native law is the law of the spear" (Taylor 1935a:3).

The effect of Taylor's shootings and arrests was to make Simbu afraid to steal from police and kiaps. Some stories told to me or my researchers go on to say that they expected Australian kiaps to shoot pigs and men, and to take women, from that time onward. The Simbu began to distinguish between white men—harsh kiap from kindly missionary—after these events. Jim Taylor's name is symbolic of the beginning of Australian rule; he is known throughout the highlands to natives and Australians as the first Australian kiap who discovered the million people of the highlands and enforced peace.

The actions of Taylor in the Simbu valley were taken by the local people to indicate alliance with one or another side of a tribal fight, whereas Taylor believed that he was being attacked. After the arrests and establishment of the Simbu post, the kiap was asked to intervene with powerful guns on the behalf of their friends. The Simbu asked for alliance, and they were told that the kiap was there to stop attacks and warfare.

To Simbu today, stories of the first patrol, the arrival of Fr. Schäfer, the killings of Fr. Morschheuser and Br. Eugene, the Taylor patrol, arrests, and establishment of Australian administration are often repeated, both in the community and to interested visitors. After these deaths the white man was known to be mortal, not a spirit. The main actors are huge figures, symbolic of the meeting, the surprises, and the consequences. These particular incidents are legendary: the Kunabau theft and killings, the Womkama and Goglme killings and arrests, are most often repeated for a particular place or group. After becoming the first Kundiawa kiap, Taylor is credited with stopping fights, bringing peace and roads, showing the power of guns, and punishing thefts.[8]

Commentary on and reactions to the incidents in Australia, Papua New Guinea, and internationally have taken many positions and shown great differences in understanding and aims. The writings and statements of Leahy and some other white settlers, miners, prospectors, and a few government workers, proclaim the opinion that these newly contacted natives must be shown that the white man and his weapons represent strength, might, and right. Any attempts at theft, injury, or resistance must be immediately punished. The power of guns should be demonstrated in action, by shooting pigs and men.

Popular reports and memoirs of these incidents by Australians claim that penetration of the highlands was peaceful and understate the use and threat of force by government officers and police (Simpson 1964). This legend of the benign kiap is shared by many Australian writers and Simbu who experienced the impact and hopes of the postwar period from 1945 to 1965.

5

Establishing Control

Then more white men came and we knew that they were not
devil or spirit but real men.
—MOA OF NAREGU
  (interviewer Michael Mugua)

This chapter describes the first years of administrative control following the deaths and arrests, and the new regulations of 1935 and 1936. It is in this period that the events of 1933–1935 were perceived and their impact was felt. The comments of Sahlins are pertinent: "From the perspective of many colonized people, it is the moment of domination and transformation, the assumption of subaltern status, that is most marked in historical consciousness rather than the period of early contacts that preceded it." Speaking of the imposition of an alien power, he continued:

"This is the B.C. and A.D. of *their* world history, Before Colonization and After Domination, and it entails a different sense of the cultural qualities of time and change" (1992:3–4).

Simbu Acceptance of Government Control: Pacification, Road Making, Native Headmen, Payments, Exchange and Gifts

In one of my first interviews in 1958, Luluai Kiagenem of Kamanegu proclaimed his support and appreciation of the kiap and the white man's government:

> Then Kiap Taylor came through the wilderness, gave us schooling, talk, and now we live well. Before we did not live well. After Kiap Taylor came, he put me in jail, took me to Salamaua to see what the white man did. His good food and things. I came back and told everyone, and they listened and did not fight. Now we live well. The government brought good things to us. The kiap told us to take our sticks and spears, and burn them all up.

When they finished their investigations and arrests, Dan Leahy and officers Taylor, Melrose, and Greathead left the area. Roberts wrote a description of the Simbu people in 1935, with a map of the valley (dated 22 March 1935) showing rivers, tribal locations (with some names that can no longer be identified), and posts of police, government, and missions. Black reports a patrol throughout the highlands in 1935. The highlands area was divided between Morobe and Madang Districts in 1937.

The Chimbu-Wahgi post was staffed almost continuously by experienced officers from 1935 to 1941, and police officers were posted at Chuave and Goglme most of the time. Contact with Bena post began with regular runners. The airstrip built by the Lutheran mission at Ega in 1934 was used by government and mission planes. Several of the officers —Melrose, Taylor, Bates, Kyle, Greathead, Roberts, Black, Vial—were shifted among highlands posts. They investigated attacks and conflicts involving white miners and missionaries, police and employees, and highlands natives, as well as tribal warfare and killings. Pacification and the construction of roads for better access to populated areas were the first tasks in administration.

Many of the first officers at Chimbu post had served at Upper Ramu post during some turbulent times (see Chap. 3). A kind of peace ceremony in which native weapons were stacked and burned, and food and pigs were shared, was instituted to establish administrative control. Kyle and Bates had been engaged in pacification and early census taking in the eastern highlands before they were assigned to Chimbu post.

Patrol reports, an incomplete record, give some impression of the problems and actions seen from the viewpoint of Australian officers in this period. Simbu views of these pacification moves are discussed later. The recommendations of Taylor for restricting missionaries from travel in the area and from building houses for occasional occupation in native communities were in force. In 1936 an amendment to the Native Affairs Regulations made Lutherans remove their native evangelists from villages and restrict them to the main stations. Both Lutheran and Catholic missions had two main stations in Simbu: the Lutherans at Kerowagi and Ega under Revs. Bergmann, Hanneman, and Folge (German: Foege); and the Catholics at Mingende and Denglagu, under Frs. Schäfer, Meiser, and Tropper, and Brs. Lucidius and Markolinus. A set of distinct spheres of influence began to develop around the mission and government posts that were later to become contentious. Catholic schools prepared young Simbu as teachers (catechists) and for baptism.

The Chimbu post was in charge of P.O. C. D. Bates in the first part of 1936, then J. L. Taylor for some months, A.D.O. A. F. Kyle from October 1936 through 1937, and Acting A.D.O. L. G. Vial in 1938–1939. They were assisted for parts of this period by Cadet or Patrol Officers Grant, Murphy, Skinner, Wedd, and Noakes.[1] Vial made maps showing tribal boundaries and took census counts in the tribes near the station. Most of the government patrols were in a limited area: between the Chimbu-Wahgi post and a police post at Goglme; to the head of the Simbu valley; east of the station to Chuave, constructing a road connection to Bena, the other highlands post; and west to Kerowagi and Arave in the Wahgi valley. Vial reports one journey south of the Chimbu-Wahgi post and describes salt making (1941).

John Murphy was a cadet in 1936; his photographs show an aid post, the first public building in Kundiawa, and a market where vegetable foods were sold for the use of government personnel. In Murphy's and Vial's photographs, Simbu men and women are shown wearing strings of shells and large mother-of-pearl (P. *kina*) shells with woven belts and armbands, net skirts, and feather ornaments; men carry bow and arrow, shield, spear, rarely a knife.

Taylor and Murphy were in the Wahgi valley and Mount Hagen in September–October, 1936. Kyle made one extended patrol to Hagen, where fighting in the Nangamp area was stopped and many weapons burnt.

The reports describe experienced administration officers' activities and impressions of native Simbu and mission conditions at the time. They look over conditions of mission employees and recount investigations of problems between natives and missionaries involving theft, trespass, imprisonment, and homicide. Government consolidation efforts were directed toward peaceful relations, respect for the administration, and maintaining communications.

Supplies on these patrols were many pounds of girigiri shells, dispensed for food and other services, a few kina to reward special services, and various patrol items including kerosene, tent flys, marmite, biscuits, salt, sugar, soap, tobacco. Steel axes and knives were rare gifts, especially valued.

Reports of P.O. C. D. Bates

The first serious case reported by P.O. Bates in February 1936 was the "deprivation of liberty" of a native by Rev. Folge of Kerowagi. To summarize the investigations, which required several visits and interviews: on receiving a report from his mission helpers (who were coastal natives) that goods had been stolen by Danga natives, Rev. Folge took ten armed helpers to the scene. He took hostage a native and demanded four pigs in compensation. The stolen goods consisted of two blankets, two rucksacks, a knife, a spoon, a singlet, and some small shells and beads. Bates found that Pobara, the native who had been captured, had not been involved in the theft. It also appeared that Rev. Folge had disregarded administration orders in sending mission helpers to the Danga area and in traveling there himself.

On 21–24 April Bates revisited Kerowagi and Dagl mission station, identified the spot where the native was captured and held, inspected and noted the arms at the mission, and inspected laborers. He found a feeling of unrest and intertribal raiding among the native groups in the Wahgi area west of Kerowagi. Bates reported that the mission had little influence on the natives. He also advised that more patrols be deployed in this area, citing the success of consolidation through effective patrolling in the Simbu valley. On this occasion he was not able to persuade the native captive, Pobara, to accompany the patrol to the post.

Statements were obtained from the mission helpers who had been the victims of the theft. They said that Rev. Folge went to Dagl mission station to meet the mission helpers, and then he and his helpers went to Danga settlement to ask for the return of the property and found that most of the men were away. The natives were called, and one captured, tied up at Rev. Folge's orders, taken to Dagl, and kept overnight. Then they returned to Danga. Rev. Folge asked for four pigs and the stolen property; some of the goods were returned and four pigs brought. One pig was killed, and half was given to the Danga people; the captive Pobara was released and a few girigiri shells given. Three pigs were kept by Rev. Folge. The investigation interviewed Pobara, who denied that he was implicated in the theft. Folge was later sentenced to two years for this deprivation of Pobara's liberty (Mennis 1982:75).

Bates reports patrols in the Simbu valley and east of Kundiawa for consolidation, inspections of Goglme post and Denglagu, and road inspections. A road from the Chimbu post up the valley was under construction. Bates writes:

Numerous Gogol [Goglme] natives joined the Patrol. In reaching Pari and point where road gang had reached it was observed that all manner of wooden implements were engaged in road-making helping the road-gang under the Police. The road was under rapid construction. The air was filled with the yells of the natives as they tore into the ground and stones. Quite an impressive sight, and very heartening to think that these yet savage natives, of their own volition were helping the road gang without expecting any reward . . . it was a pleasurable sign of their attitude of willingness to assist. (p. 11, 19 February)

Next day at Goglme, hundreds of natives visited the station. Continuing to Denglagu on 21 February, the patrol was given large supplies of native foods and many pigs. On the twenty-second, they were visited by Chiagu (Siaku) natives. Bates spoke to them of "the evils of tribal fighting" and advised them, "if they were going to continue it, that very drastic measures to stop it would be taken in the immediate future" (p. 13). He comments, "[T]hey nevertheless still retain their early insatiable curiosity for the Patrol and also an increasing desire to accompany the Patrol on its trip"; "The natives mix quite freely with the personnel of the Patrol" (p. 14). The road would make movement and patrolling much easier. "I have not previously in my seven years in New Guinea seen such enthusiasm amongst natives as that portrayed by these people making the road" (p. 15). Then, "with the exception of the Inau and Denglagu phratries, the Simbu valley is quite quiet"; these two "spasmodically continue to have fights." "When a Patrol is sighted in the valley these natives if fighting at the time, immediately cease fire, and in turns bring large supplies of native foods to the Patrol, and remain on the friendliest of terms with the patrol, until it leaves" (pp. 15–16). He notes of Denglagu mission that "numerous young natives are attached to the station for schooling purposes" (p. 17).

One incident reported was that, during fighting between Inau and Denglagu, a native, Anduwang of Denglagu, led a party of armed men to a bridge built by the mission. Told to go back by Br. Lucidius, he refused. Others of his party left, and when he began to break the barricade, Br. Lucidius fired and killed Anduwang. Bates questioned Denglagu natives, who said the killing was deserved.

In March another patrol went up the valley to Goglme and Denglagu. Bates was aware of the boundaries and relations of the several tribes (which he called phratries) along the route and sensed that conflicts might occur between road workers and visitors to the sites from different tribes. "Besides a more close and friendly contact obtained with the people by the Administration Official, there was a satisfactory mixing of natives from different parts of the Chimbu area which will do a great deal towards the forming of friendship of these natives amongst themselves, which hitherto was practically nonexistent" (p. 23).

Eight hundred natives worked the road daily; the trip from the Chimbu-Wahgi post to Goglme was reduced from eight hours to four and a half. The little progress of the road from Denglagu toward Goglme was attributed by the mission to fighting between Denglagu and Inau, and each promised to work for the administration. Bates next inspected road making east from Chimbu-Wahgi post among Yongamul, China siva (Sinasina), and Dinga. Rapid progress was reported.

Bates led a patrol up the Simbu valley to investigate the killing by Br. Lucidius. Enroute 1 April, they encountered a party of armed Kokane, who appeared to be attempting to ambush, and spoke to them. "Patrol opened fire—natives dispersed—no casualties." Stopping to speak with Kokane, "at first they were afraid, but later quite friendly" (p. 30). In the investigation of Br. Lucidius' killing Andawang, a case of unlawful killing was made. (These papers are not included.) Fr. Nilles (1987:63) writes from the court record translated by Fr. Schäfer, "In his statement, Br. Lucidius said he did not aim at the man." Br. Marcolinus was present as a witness and testified, "we gave a consolation present to the wife of the dead man: a pig, a small knife and some smaller shells" (Nilles 1987:63). There is no confirming evidence from Simbu statements that they saw this as a suitable compensation. The case was considered by the government as a criminal offense. Br. Lucidius' sentence of six years was reduced and then annulled; he returned to New Guinea.

Another incident noted by Bates on this patrol was the alleged attack on a Goglme native, Bage, wearing a lavalava (cloth wrap), by a party of Kokane. Evidently, Bage

> had boasted to the Kokane natives of his friendship with the Administration and made some insulting remarks to the Kokane native on the strength of this. He was rewarded with an arrow which entered his breast, in a superficial wound, he deserved it, as on numerous occasions Gorgme [Goglme] native had been warned about using the Administration as a lever in any matter. (Pp. 31–32)

The injured native was Bage, a recognized big man, who claimed that Bates was coming to fight the Kokane. Observing that the Kokane had little contact with the administration, Bates visited them, was at first met with hostility, and later spoke to them about the shooting of Bage. He then returned to Goglme to warn the people there against further such incidents: "[W]e must be constantly on the alert that an injustice is not done to other natives, irreparable harm may be done by a false move" (p. 33). Bage is mentioned as a big man and, later, a most powerful and respected luluai for twenty years (see Chap. 6).

A special patrol was undertaken on 28 April to prevent hostility toward Pari people by Gena. In their attack, Gena were burning houses and destroying gardens. Bates found three hundred armed men approaching Pari. After the patrol shouted, the Gena began to retreat, so the patrol continued into Gena country. Many Gena shouted "kill the kiap, he is of no account" (p. 48). Then they found themselves surrounded. "I gave the order to open fire, the Patrol fired into the tall grass, and up came about fifty Gena natives" (p. 48). When they fired again, four Gena were killed. Shouting ceased. The patrol continued and "found about 50 very frightened Gena women hiding in two houses" (p. 49). When they could not get in touch with the men, the patrol began to move off, a large party of armed natives appeared, and then another armed group was encountered. "I gave the order to fire. Three men were wounded, and this dispersed all hostile natives" (p. 50). They then had to dissuade the Pari people from attacking the Gena. Bates comments that the Gena had practically no contact with the administration, whereas the Pari were on the main route up the valley. The Gena had killed a native constable some months earlier, and by this were encouraged to continue their intertribal hostilities. When they found that the Pari people had gone to the Lutheran mission at Ega, they burned four Pari houses and destroyed gardens. Bates remarks that the Pari people felt safe in the presence of the government official and did not expect an attack from Gena. He understood that the Gena expected the patrol to destroy them fully, as they would have destroyed the patrol and the community at Pari.

In May, on another patrol up the Simbu valley to inspect the Goglme post and visit Denglagu, native girls requested and were granted permission to accompany the patrol. The girls, with their parents, were frequent visitors to the posts and promised good behavior. Bates regarded this as confidence placed in him by the people. Crowds of natives gathered to meet them. For the first time, the former enemies Kokane and Denglagu gathered together in friendship at the posts.

On this patrol Bates investigated a report that Br. Lucidius, in the presence of Fr. Tropper, had beaten an indentured laborer for theft (p. 61). There was another report that Brs. Lucidius and Markolinus had assaulted a laborer for stealing.

Bates' next patrol took the road east, with Sinasina natives to accompany and work on the road to Marifuteka. He found six to seven hundred natives at work, the people singing (p. 64) and dispersing pigs. Quantities of native foods were purchased. "Yesterday two villages were fighting with each other, today most men from these villages were working together on the road" (p. 67). The road work continued to the east, reaching Siane. People on the road east were familiar with Taylor, calling him "kiap." "This is already a byword, and those who had been with Taylor could converse in Pidgin English" (p. 73).

In June, he investigated complaints against one of his police, Sgt. Aiwai: the deprivation of liberty of natives of Dinga and Mirani. It was learned that Aiwai wanted Wonumba as his mistress. When she refused, he gave an order to fire on natives. Local natives attacked the post. Aiwai made Wonumba come and sleep with him and threatened her with his gun. She ran away. Then Aiwai caught her brother Gawagl and tied him up. Bates reported this as deprivation of the liberty of Gawagl and Wonumba, and as rape of Wonumba (pp. 76–79).[2]

Bates departed from the post and J. Taylor took over from about July to October 1936. He found the native situation "excellent: probably no part of New Guinea has come under government influence so quickly. . . . They appear to have perfect and complete confidence in us."[3] Taylor completed the investigation of Folge, investigated tribal fights and murders, reviewed road and bridge building, and conducted an inquest concerning Br. Lucidius, who was committed to trial for a killing. He advised the withdrawal of native missionaries.

C.P.O. John Murphy

Cadet John Murphy arrived at Chimbu post on 8 August 1936.[4] This was his first New Guinea posting, following a year of medical school. His personal diary recounts his observations and reactions and his decision to remain in the service. He later published a pidgin dictionary (Murphy 1949). At first Taylor was his superior officer and Murphy held the station at Kundiawa, in daily contact with Morobe District headquarters Salamaua, except when the wireless broke down; then he spent his time fixing it. Taylor's main activity as observed by Murphy was to go out after murderers, usually on raids that started in darkness. He acted on reports brought in by natives for fighting or troubled areas. He mentions visits with missionaries in the area at this time: Fr. Schäfer, Br. Markolinus, Revs. Bergmann, Goetzelman, Harold, and Hannemann. Chinnery, the government anthropologist, visited in December 1936, and Grant relieved Murphy at end of his tour. Medical Assistant Ewing arrived in November, observed venereal diseases and malaria, and stayed through to the end of Murphy's tour. A.D.O. Kyle arrived in October 1936, and Taylor departed. The period does not correspond to that covered in the reports of Kyle taken from the McCarthy papers, discussed in the next section.

There were planes every few days: Catholic and Lutheran mission planes bringing supplies to the missions and government or private planes with passengers and supplies for the station. Pigs were purchased from local sources and were shot every few days to supply the station with fresh meat. Pigs and fowls raised at the station were sometimes stolen, attacked by dogs, or got away. Murphy remarks about the locally available fresh food. When he left, he took bags of vegetables to the coast.

Murphy supervised the building of houses, fowl yards and houses, a school for pidgin interpreters brought in from the highlands and Purari areas, roads and bridges, and building maintenance. He set up a pitsaw (a site for preparing lumber), dug a well, built a stable when Kyle brought a horse from Bena, and was building a timber house for Kyle. Other duties were buying food and supervising workers at Kundiawa, reviewing laborers on contract with missions, taking inventory of equipment and personnel (about one hundred workers), paying workers. He seemed to enjoy cooking, taking photos and developing them, shooting ducks and other birds, making a Simbu word list. He noted that all the women on the station had venereal disease.

Groups from all areas—China Sina, Dom, Yonggamugl, Mirani, and Ku—came in to trade food and pigs. He made contact with nearby native groups, visited and observed singsings, and describes a large vegetable and game food distribution at Dirimandin when Pari and Mirani people brought food. It included richly decorated people dancing, singing, and drumming. "Monkeys" (P. *manki*, native boys) at Kundiawa did some work. Murphy noted many fights and stories of fights. He observed dress, decorations, arched gateways, burials, took down myths and legends and accounts of customs, and described many dances. Stone pestles were found and sold to officers. Murphy took notes on sorcery and divination at Hagen, and saw a Kanana courtship singsing. The government officers investigated fighting between Nanga and Iramdi in Wahgi and set up a peacemaking ceremony at Kilewa where former fighters broke and burnt spears and shields. They took some police recruits from the Wahgi valley to send to Rabaul. I quote from some pages of Murphy's diary for 15 August 1936: "A crowd of young Maris [P. native women] have been haunting the house all day. They are very coy but not a bit shy. Two younguns of about 12 summers are my friends for life. They are rather pretty too—Tick and Tootsie are their names."

16 August:

> There are about twenty villages around here and a few thousand natives and about half hang round the house all day staring and smelling like Dantes inferno in a lavatory. They are very friendly. . . . The old birds look particularly stupid too when one looks at them. They give a sheepish grin and murmer in a self-conscious tone—"Wahgai" [S.] meaning "gudfella".

20 August:

> Couple of fights around the joint today. Some Kanakas sneaked into Dom and did a bit of a massacre last night and a bit of a fight started. Also another on the N.W. side of the station. Gathered a host of young Maris about me this after-noon and acquired quite a comprehensive vocabulary in the Chimbu dialect.

21 August:

> Police boy arrived from Gorgume today for fresh supplies. Thousands of young Maris swamped the house today. They are rather entertaining and some are quite pretty. Played the gramophone to about 100 coons on the back porch today. They thought it was hot dog. . . . Had another look at the house-sick today and the VD cases. I'll have to do something for them I think.

22 August:

> Fires all round the joint in the Kunai today. Kanakas set them. A few fights going on too round the joint.

23 August:

> Had another look at the new house and it looks O.K. I shall move in during the coming week. . . . Everything is progressing favourably. A couple of bags of peanuts were planted today. They will do well here as most vegetables do.

24 August:

> Today a mob from Yogume made raids on China-sina wounded a man with an arrow and stole a pig. The man with the wound in his leg came in this afternoon. The raiders took a pig to Pari and sold it.

27 August:

> All the police boys were walking about with their rifles today in view of the threatened trouble. . . . One of the police boys—BUBU—went off to a sing sing at MIRANI tonight. I gave him the automatic, just in case. Everything OK.

3 September:

> Mr Taylor went out this morning to settle a few disputes. He broke the stock of his rifle across a native's head. Two were shot and two prisoners brought in. . . . Mr Taylor gave two natives an N.A.B. injection this afternoon. They have a wonderful confidence in our medicines. I have quite a reputation as a dentist and many of the natives bring their toothaches to me. I syringe the tooth out with iodine solution in hot water, with a hypodermic syringe. It seems to be effective.

7 September:

> Mr Taylor out last night and caught a couple of the murderers. Heard report of a murder today. A woman committed adultery. Her husband cut off her hands and feet, called his other wives together and warned them of a similar fate. He then killed the erring wife in front of them, with his stone axe.

11 September:

> Mr Taylor left this morning for another shot at the murderers at large.

12 September:

> Shot six pigs this afternoon but was a bit off in the shooting and took eight
> shots. Printed some photos.

18 September:

> The China Sina natives were bringing in some pigs when the Yogume natives
> swooped on them and tried to rob them. They socked one bird with a stone axe
> and threw him into the river but he was only stunned. I took two police boys
> and hurried to the scene but the Yogume mob did a bunk before we got there.
> The China Sina mob arrived OK.

24 September, en route to Hagen:

> The natives about here are extremely skilled agriculturalists. They don't live in
> villages but in scattered houses about 3 1/2' high.

In Hagen in October, Murphy saw Fr. Ross, M. Leahy, and Taylor apprehend
murderers. Taylor's patrol to Hagen included his staying with Mick Leahy
and investigating some killings in which Leahy was involved in 1934. This
inquiry was requested by the Aboriginals Protection Society in London after
reading Leahy's account.[5] They asked the League of Nations to make inquiries. Murphy comments: "Really a case of backseat driving. If Leahy
hadn't shot he would have been killed."

27 October [returning to Kundiawa]:

> Off at a little after 4 A.M. with a line of 303 persons counting carriers, police,
> personal boys, prisoners, mission boys and women.

31 October:

> We got in to find Kyle the ADO here to relieve Taylor, has been here a fort-
> night.

15 November:

> Put three coons onto a well yesterday they are down about 12 feet now. Mr Kyle
> set out for Dom on the other side of the Wahgi today to collect a bunch of
> natives. Be away about 3 days. The Dom mob cleaned up the Dinga crowd who
> were bringing us food.

16 November:

Added a goodly number of words to my Dictionary of Chimbu dialect today. Had a couple of monkeys in listening to the wireless today. They reckoned it was hot dog.

17 November:

Well down about 16 feet now and prospering. Started on a brick fireplace inside this afternoon. Have about 450 bricks made now. Some native women hopped into our peanut patch today. I just gave them a friendly warning.

18 November:

Mr Kyle back this afternoon. His party tanned the backsides of 530 coons who had been fighting. Suffered no casualties. . . . Well is finished down 30 feet.

2 January 1937:

The Lutheran mission boys came with information that in pursuance of a vendetta, the natives of Kou had attacked the people of GIWI on the road to TEMA and killed one man.

3 January:

Sent BAITA and SEOGO for the GIWI people this morning and they arrived with them this afternoon. I interrogated them and found that the KOU people —two only—UMBA and KORULOMA had gone to TERAUKUOWA's house and shot him with arrows.

4 January:

Saw a funeral procession today. The people here bury their dead in a sitting position in a shallow hole about 2 feet deep with the sides staked with wood. The corpse is covered with banana leaves and then a thin covering of earth.

5 January:

A big crowd of DOM, KOGO, PARI, CHINA SINA people came with food today. A pig got away today and I was obliged to shoot it as it was pretty savage. The China Sina work boys were looking after it, so they get no pig on Saturday. Arranging for all our Chimbu monkeys to have a Sing Sing on Sunday next.

22 January:

Broke camp Pari at 7 A.M. climbed a steep stretch of road to 6450 feet and then along a mountain side. The Kanakas here have cut a fair road. I told them if the horse hurt his leg on the road he would blame them for not repairing the road, and would eat them and rape the women. This, to ensure they keep the road in a state of repair. We passed two steep narrow holes in the mountain side. They are about 4 feet in diameter and one is 500 and the other 700 feet deep. I sounded them. If a Kanaka dies without next of kin to bury him, the men are thrown down one hole and the women down the other. Also diseased people are thrown down.

23 January [In the lower/mid Simbu valley]:

This is a very rich and fertile part and large native gardens abound, growing beans, New Guinea peas, cucumbers, pumpkins, native edible leaves, sweet potato, sugar, tomatoes, bananas, pitpit, edible shoots, taro, mareta [P. pandanus fruit], figs and other native vegetables. We are surrounded by steep limestone mountains of which every available scrap of land is utilized for gardens. There are also many pine trees growing in the ravines. There are hundreds of natives about here and so far all friendly. A large number are helping us on the road. . . . I was surprised to find some of the young girls here can talk pidgin.

26 January:

All the Police boys got an intravenous injection of T.A.B. for V.D.

31 January:

Got all of the work boys to store their effects in my room in case any should run away. All of the Siane bunked last night.

4 February:

Mission boys questioned re alleged slander against police boys. Police very hostile.

10 February:

> Fr Schäfer passed through today to have a look at his old stn at Mirane.

11 February:

> Mob still going strong on A.D.O.'s house site. Getting a wooded house soon.

15 February:

> Mirani people had a free for all with Wammies over a stolen pig. Fired two shots over the village but they apparently thought I was shooting pigs at the stn. so sent Sgt. Lepangum and cpl SEOGO [sic] who succeeded in quieting them. Big SingSing nearby.

22 February:

> Leprosy in 8 cases revealed.

1 March;

> Issued monks [P. *manki*, boy] with laplap and singlets.

2 March:

> Sent all the monks in their new singlets and laplaps to be photographed. They looked pretty good and thought so too.

In a letter Murphy writes:

> One day an irate husband lugged his wife into the station to me. She had a cut on her head (bleeding) and pushed me a sock, a singlet and a couple of hand-kerchiefs which, out of step with the communal policy, she had filched from my clothesline. The husband spoke appropriate words of undying honesty amd high regard and lugged her off.
> "What an honest, loyal chap!" I thought. It was a long time before I realized that he was terrified; feared I would wreak vengeance upon him. How could he avoid 10,000 implacable police hurling pellets of vengeance? (Murphy 1992)

A.D.O. A. F. Kyle

The detailed observations in the reports of Kyle present the views of an experienced officer and the flow of information from post to District Office. His administrative goals are clear, and his actions justified, in detailed reporting. I have no direct information from other participants and can only attempt to interpret some Simbu reasons and actions. The persistent attacks on patrols by the Inau tribe stand out in his reports; they may have been lingering attempts to retaliate for the losses they suffered during the Taylor patrol and arrests in 1935. The available reports of Bates' patrols the year before do not identify Inau as attackers.

When Kyle took charge of the Chimbu-Wahgi post, he continued the policy of regular patrols, supervising road construction and investigating reports of fighting and other disturbances. Compensation payments were arranged for deaths, and when a tribe or group agreed to stop fighting there would be a ceremony of burning weapons and sharing food. Kyle's reports include an account of goods expended, in which mirrors, small knives, and salt begin to appear along with shells. These goods were paid to Simbu for food supplies and other services to patrols.

In July 1937 Kyle reported a patrol to Dengaragu mission and the Iwam area "for the purpose of (1) escorting missionaries with horses and cattle from Iwam to Dimbi. However, the animals were found unfit to travel. (2) investigating feasibility of short mule train to Madang."

The Inau tribe, which includes some subgroups whose members were originally migrants from the eastern highlands, maintained these ties. Kyle's report of the an Inau attack on 22 July 1937 states:

> On the main bridle path from Gorgme to Denglagu while passing through Gire-tamagh the natives met us on the road, crying, and informed me that in the early morning they had been attacked by Inau people, attempts made to kill them and their pigs stolen. Later blood was seen on the road where the pigs were cut up. Nearing the first Inau group men were noticed on the mountain top at the road but on arrival had disappeared. I called out without result. Leaving the cargo & carriers I walked down the mountain to a garden accompanied by a police boy and an interpreter to try and speak to the men. Some men were seen hiding but refused to answer. I called to them that I was going to Denglagu and before my return they must return the stolen pigs. No reply and I arrived further down the garden towards a house where I had seen some men. Almost simultaneously there were shouts of *suo-suo* (a war cry) and arrows were fired at us from ambush. A "big man" then jumped on the house, fired at me, landed down again and shouted "who killed the Mission? I did. I will break the white

man's jawbones and kill him." The attack was so unexpected that the youth carrying my rifle was at the top of the garden and the police boy looking for the other natives some 200 yards away . . . police with the cargo had heard the war cries, which were quite unusual . . . , and ran down the hill through the cane grass and casuarinas to my assistance. I had opened fire and on their arrival told them to do the same. After the natives had been dispersed, attempts were made to arrest the man who appeared to be the ringleader, and during the attempt Constable Tokeruru was shot at close range from ambush and slightly wounded in the armpit. . . . Later Inau natives gathered on mountain tops and shouted "Where will you sleep? we will come and kill you." We learned then from friendly natives that the attack had been pre-arranged. All women, children and pigs had been sent away to hiding in the early morning and the warriors waited for the Patrol. The main ambush had been made ready in the bed of a stream in a deep ravine, some distance further, but the fortunate accident of my trying to get in touch with natives in the garden had precipitated an attack some distance from the main body. Next morning [p. 5] another ambush was prepared but on our arrival their courage failed, and they ran away without attacking. All attempts to get in touch with them failed. While I was in Iwam I asked Father Meiser to have messages conveyed to the Inau, saying that the fight was of their choosing and if they were now satisfied to meet me on my return I would make peace. In reply they shouted and made indecent gestures and said that they would kill me and my horse and afterwards kill the two mis-sionaries. They reiterated that they had killed whites before and could do it again.

On my return to Inau . . . contact could not be made. I have not sufficient police ammunition or stores, nor were the police and myself sufficiently fit to begin a probably protracted campaign against from 3000 to 5000 people, assisted as they are by the Womkama and Kukane groups, some thousands of people more. . . .

Although, as previously reported, I have studiously avoided taking any action which might conceivably lead to a brush with natives, in this case the trouble was of their own making, was quite unexpected and casualties could not be avoided if my own life and that of others were to be preserved.

It is interesting to note that last time I passed through the Inau group 3 weeks ago, fighting and killings had taken place, but in pursuance of present policy I took no action. It is possible that inaction was mistaken for weakness with the usual aftermath. All now agree to finish fighting. Couple of arrows fired at police purely from nervousness. No action taken on return—only arrests. Arrested natives released after payment made. . . .

Kyle also comments:

Chuave post is in very good condition. School children are healthy, and show marked improvement in physique, and knowledge of "pidgin" etc. Very large gardens have been made and planted. Native food is becoming short at Chuave, and the school [children] will soon have to return [home].

General The visit to new people at Erembali [Elimbari] was made for a number of reasons. In the first place, they are comparatively close to the station, and will form a further and valuable source of food supplies. In the second, particularly as regards Darma and Eri, they continually harass our natives nearer Chuave, who are more or less under control, and daily visit the station. Third, people have disarmed at our request, and it happens frequently that when they visit us, either their villages are attacked in their absence, and people killed and pigs stolen, or the unarmed visitors are ambushed while returning to their villages. It is hoped that as a [p. 8] result of the patrol these attacks will cease. The Erembali, or Magankane, people are very numerous, I should guess at least 3000, are very warlike, and cannibals. Two local chiefs were selected during the patrol, accompanied me back to Chuave, and were of great assistance. They were returned under escort, and should later prove valuable in their areas.

After visiting the Magankane people, he wrote:

Two very intelligent seeming youths volunteered to accompany me and enter the school. These people speak a language for which as yet we have no interpreters, although most understand the languages spoken at Chuave and China Sina.

Natives in the vicinity of Chuave are becoming more and more under influence. Two arrests were made of murderers and fight leaders and in each case without difficulty, or resistance from the people. This is an excellent sign, and greatly to the credit of [policeman] Buasi, who is doing very good work there. No trouble was experienced on the patrol, and it was not necessary to fire a shot. [p. 8]

A report of A.P.O. J. A. Grant (Patrol Report 29/9/37):

The groups visited are on either side of the Chimbu River 4 hours away from this station. For some time sporadic tribal fighting has been taking place in these groups, culminating in a fairly serious outbreak some weeks ago. This fight was stopped and with some difficulty a number of the people persuaded to come to Kundiawa. Influential chiefs were found and appointed "bossboys" and the people promised to live in peace. I promised them that they would shortly be visited, at which time they undertook to destroy their weapons. The patrol was in fulfilment of the promise made. The natives, with the exception of some members of the KO group, carried out their promises, and the position was now much more satisfactory.

The whole upper Chimbu position is now greatly improved and only the Kukane group being a bit reluctant to accept control. A number of groups in the higher ranges have never yet been visited, but are now beginning to send representatives with friendly messages. The whole tone of the people is in marked contrast to that prevailing a few months ago. A great deal of the improvement is due to NC Balama, constable in charge of Gorgme post, who works continuously, tactfully and well amongst the people. Natives now come to him from all the upper Chimbu to settle their disputes.

No trouble was encountered on the patrol. The effect should be valuable.

Kyle returned to the Inau in October 1937 for the purpose of investigating killings and attempting to establish friendly relations with exchanges of gifts. The officers attempted to arrange payment of compensation for injuries and killings to enemy groups. As I have noted, this had not been a Simbu practice.

Gorgme was reached the first day. Messengers were sent to Inau, the station inspected. Next morning an early start was made for Inau. On arrival the nearer group were deserted. After much calling 2 men came in. The party ascended to a hamlet of the main group by 2 P.M., after the usual fears wore off large numbers assembled. The people expressed contrition for ambushing and attempting to kill me, declared their intention of living in peace in future. As an earnest, they presented me with 2 pigs, a baby hornbill, brought from Iwam, numerous plumes other ornaments and two young women. For the former I exchanged gifts; had to refuse the latter as tactfully as possible.

After investigations it was found that their killing of Kamenkane was brought about by the latter stealing. Payment is being made for the dead and peace made. Many shields, spears and bows were brought in and burnt. . . .

The main feature—that the road to Dengaragu is now clear and safe.

There is now no place in any part of the District where I have had trouble with natives that have not been revisited until the natives are completely friendly, under at least partial control.

In December 1937, Kyle and eight policemen patrolled to Kerowagi and Gena for the purpose of bringing the areas under administrative influence.

At Dimbi, Dagl and Kamenegu, many natives were present. After discussion, all agreed to assemble at Kerowagi for peace ceremonies, to include the Pagau and upper Dagl people. The position was uncertain, but with nearly 1000 people present, and after much talk all agreed to cease fighting, & ceremonially burnt huge pile of weapons and shields. Many troubles were finalized. . . . Proceeding Dec 8 to old mission station they encountered large crowds from Wauga and Siambuga, Kunambau, Koraguru, Narugu assembled. All declared peace finally burnt weapons. On to Gena, where the people were very nervous & difficult. No native food with gardens destroyed fighting. However by 5:30 P.M. some hundred assembled agreed to peace, burnt weapons. Next day back to Dimbi, accompanied by chiefs, station women, pigs, cassowary. Gena Winba assembled also stolen goods were returned, peace finally made. Many payments were exchanged.

10 December, returned to Kundiawa:

General In many ways this can be considered the most satisfactory patrol yet carried out. The groups dealt with have been outstanding in their determination to keep fighting, and in their hostility to me. Djiku [Siku] Kamanegu and Pagau have been fighting since our occupation, & the mission have for 3 years tried vainly to control them. Visits to the same end have been made by officers without success. In the latest big fight, some months ago, 9 or 10 were killed, and the Djiku driven from their grounds, their houses and gardens destroyed. They are still living scattered about in the lower Dagl country. Upper and lower Dagl have also continually fought. In this case work was done on the last Hagen patrol, and this time after considerable difficulty all met on neutral ground at Kerowagi aerodrome. After much talk from myself with chiefs, all decided to live in peace. Djiku may return to their ground, and hundreds of weapons were burnt to show sincerity. Probably 1000 people were present (the mission has seen no such crowd before) including the following groups—Pagau, upper Dagl, Dagl-Muguagu, Djiku, Kamanegu, Siambuga, Gena Wimba, Waura, and other smaller groups. 19 chiefs were present, and all spoke for their people, promising future peace. Probably in all 5000 people were represented. It can now be hoped that tribal fighting on a large scale is finished there, although no doubt there will be killings—such long continued enmity cannot be expected to finish in a day. The Pagau people near the Mission were particularly nervous and their confidence hard to obtain. There is no doubt that the mission have continuously threatened them with drastic action by the kiap, and they expected the worst. The crowd and ceremonies at Dimbi were quite unexpected, and not required, as the people have been [p. 23] at peace for the last 6 months, and under our control. However they insisted on burning their weapons as a sign of good will, to emphasize that fighting is really finished. As regards Gena, these have been the outstandingly recalcitrant people in the district, and I have repeatedly promised to visit them, and have been told by them each time that they would kill me as soon as I arrived. They have continually fought, & a few weeks ago a very large fight resulted in the Gena-Wimba being driven out altogether, and scattered amongst the Dimbi, Koro river people, and where continual fighting was disrupting the whole of our peaceful people. The Gena position was discussed with the Assistant Director on his visit. He counselled even further patience, and eventually with the help of boys employed by Fr. Schaefer, and Mr. Catter, Gena agreed to meet me on this patrol. On arrival very few could be persuaded near; but at length some hundreds of the Nokun, Kegagu, Toagu & Koimande groups [clans] came. Gogomba & Bondugu did not come, & may cause trouble later. After much discussion, there being many contentious matters, peace was agreed upon, ceremonial burning of weapons took place. They agreed to accompany me next day to Dimbi, & return to Gena Wimba women, pigs, and cassowary stolen from the Wimba. I understood that Wimba would return the captives. All outstanding troubles were adjusted & all parted friends. The Gena being sent back under escort for safety. The outlook is hopeful but uncertain. The Gena, who number about 2500 to 3000, live in high country surrounded by forest, and are a highly excitable and impulsive people. This is the first contact made with them, and I am at least confident that if future trouble arises, some of their [p. 24] chiefs—Pugaragla & Diluamande, will tell me, and I can prevent it becoming widespread as before. The Gena people can hardly be blamed . . . they have been visited on 3 occasions before. The first, a constable went apparently to help his wife's relatives in a fight. He was killed & the interpreter with him killed a Gena with a rifle. A patrol then visited the fringe of Gena some mornings later, some natives were killed, and the patrol returned to Pare to sleep. No return visit was made. Some time later the Patrol officer at Kundiawa got word that Pare and Gena were fighting. The patrol left Kundiawa, reached Gena in the late morning, were attacked at the border, some 6 or 7 natives killed, and the patrol returned to Kundiawa that evening. No return visit was made. It is difficult to conceive how such patrols could possibly result in the ultimate pacification of the people, as no contact was made within during or after the patrol. Under the circumstances, it is surprising that the Gena agreed to meet me but after their initial fears wore off then became very friendly and relieved, while later some came and showed me bullet wounds formerly received. It was particularly impressed upon them that in the event of one man killing another he would certainly be arrested, but that innocent people were quite safe, & should neither attack me or run away (p.25).

No hostility was shown to the Patrol anywhere, and no shots were fired.

Kyle continued at the Chimbu-Wahgi post until 1938. Southeast of Elimbali (Elimbari) he investigated an incident of pig stealing and rape by a mission "boy," and tribal fighting on the Kuinigl. Another fight involving Gena and Kamanegu involved the arrest of hundreds of fighting men: "I think that every native within a radius of 10 miles has been in to explain that he had nothing to do with the fight, and has no intention of ever fighting again." In October 1938 he investigated fighting within Nauru in which houses were burnt and arrow wounds reported. He "told them to bring disputes to government."

Kyle's patrols and actions were chiefly directed at pacification, arrests for fighting and killing, supervision of peace payments and exchanges, and the ceremonial burning of weapons. He reports success in road maintenance and construction, and in the Simbu's proclaiming that peace will endure.

Grant and Vial

After Kyle, whose term was partly assisted by cadets Grant and Skinner, each for a short period, Acting A.D.O. L. G. Vial was stationed at Chimbu-Wahgi post.[6] On one patrol to the upper Chimbu (1938) Grant states that luluais from the Iwam (Gende people) wear hats,[7] come over the pass and make trouble. This is another indication that natives recognized as headmen by government officers sometimes tried to obtain payments or services from natives less familiar with administration officers. Grant's patrol was attacked by Kukane and killed eight of the attackers. The pig-killing feasts were held in several places, and he notes that groups of girls, escorted by men, go to dance, sing, and feast in other tribes. This custom was described by Fr. Nilles as *ambu ingu bekwa* (S. women break into the house), which he considered something of an orgy, and the mission asked Simbu to discontinue. Several officers observe that unmarried girls have leisure to pay visits and entertain guests (Vial 1939:21).

Grant and, later, Vial (1938–1939) conducted some census and mapping in the area near the post. Vial observes that some of the Kewandegu at Goglme visit the upper valley and demand pigs, saying that the police will punish them if they are not given. They continue to encourage wrongdoers to bring disputes to the post or patrols and recognize "headmen" as responsible group leaders, or "bossbois." They note that some few have wide influence, to be later nominated as luluais—that is, an appointed native official —usually the head of a clan or tribe as selected by the kiap.

Exchange and Administrative Control

These patrols and the comments of the officers set the stage for administrative control: road construction, pacification, seeking responsible leaders, and resolving troubles involving mission personnel and government police.

During the 1930s exchange of native food for shells became commonplace in the areas and routes frequented by patrols, in their consolidation and road-building work. As Salisbury noted in the Siane area to the east as well (1956; 1962:112ff.), this created new centers of wealth and discrepancies in wealth among tribes and groups, affecting the flow of valuables and marriage. It was evident in the western highlands, around the mining works of the Leahy brothers, too. There was thus some competition to obtain these new valuables from the white man. A rare token of white man's friendship and esteem was a greater valuable, given to leading big men and those who presented the patrol with pigs or other special gifts. Goldlip and other large shells, cloth, knives, and axes were such exceptional gifts, which not only rewarded the recipient for his loyalty or service but, in Simbu eyes, made the recipient a special friend, ally, and partner of the white donor. Both missions and kiaps sometimes made such gifts. In the case of Bage, receiving a laplap cloth marked him as a favorite, and he exploited this by claiming special treatment and bragging to others.

The favored leaders and their constituent clans and tribes saw themselves as special allies of the kiap who would provide more gifts and protect them against enemy tribes. This expectation of alliance also led to inviting white men to settle on tribal land in many highland areas. The farm at Korgua, near Mount Hagen, was also a battleground and was offered to Dan Leahy (Leahy 1987) as a buffer. In this case a considerable area was involved.

The missions also had their favorites; however, this began to irk some government officers (cf. Downs chap. 6). In 1937 Kyle mentions appointing some men as headmen in recognition of leadership and support of the administration. The appointee, who was sometimes given a hat and later a porcelain ring as a sign of office, was responsible for keeping peace with other groups and reporting fights or killing within his group. The formal appointments of luluai and tultul (government titles) were a later phase, designated with an official badge. Men who could claim that they were friends of the kiap and the police attempted to extort pigs and other goods from inexperienced and credulous Simbu. The practice created a government-sponsored position of power, which was exploited by some bossbois.

Patrols attracted a crowd of followers of all ages, including girls, which officers found surprising. Travel outside Simbu tribal boundaries had always required exceptional courage and the protection of a friend or relative in the host group. Thus only the big men (as we have seen of Kawagl) and their retinue traveled far beyond tribal boundaries to visit kinsmen, arrange marriages, or trade. Until administrative control was established, an undefended stranger was vulnerable to robbery, rape, and death. When the kiap traveled, his police and carriers could be friends; hangers-on grasped the chance to visit under the protection of such powerful friends and allies. They sought opportunities for entering the web of trade and exchange, stimulated by the infusion of shells and other valuables. These travels were concentrated within the Simbu- and Kuman-speaking area. The coming of administration made trade and visits, access to other goods, and marriage possible; the new friends and relatives shared a common cultural understanding and gift-exchange patterns.

The relations of opposition and competition between tribes continued despite the kiap's ban on tribal warfare. Some tribes that had begun to depend upon their alliances with the kiap were attacked by tribal enemies who had no such ties to the administration. Thus when the Kamanegu of Pari attended church services at Ega under the protection of both Lutheran mission and kiap, they were invaded by Gena who destroyed houses and gardens. In the Upper Simbu, the Denglagu were linked to the Catholic mission and attacked by Inau. When patrols went to the scene, the Gena and the Inau attacked them and suffered from gunfire. The lesson was hard learned, as each group discovered the power of the white man's gun in a separate demonstration.

Some incidents were regarded by the administration as minor internal and local disputes between normally friendly groups. The kiap supervised peacemaking and agreement for compensation payments of shells, including the newly acquired large shells and strings of small shells, stone axes, and pigs. Since that time compensation payments for a death (S. *yomba yagl*) have become common practice when tribal fighting was suppressed. In recent years the inflation of compensation payments for road accidents and other deaths has become a matter of concern. Compensation now is intended to satisfy the relatives of the dead person and forestall retaliation.

A frequent feature of these patrols, throughout the highlands, was the destruction of weapons as a "peace ceremony."[8] The shields, bows, arrows, spears, and clubs of both parties to a war were brought to a bonfire in celebration of the *pax Australiana*. This ceremonial gesture impressed all parties.[9] The manufacture of weapons continued, of course, for birds were still game, and the ceremonial entry of a clan dancing troupe includes a display of spears and bows and arrows.

In the early years of administration, Australian officers, German missionaries, New Guinea police and employees, and Simbu each held different views and expectations of the others; each saw the acts of others in their own light. Some Simbu at first tried to destroy the kiap and police. To others a white man's settlement might be a buffer and protector against enemies. Many Simbu made friendly overtures to the white man in order to acquire his magic and wealth through gifts, services, or theft. When the relationship was established, some flaunted their advantage before others, suggesting that the power was transferable. Some of these beliefs have new forms in present-day politics, as we shall see.

6

Securing Control

Chimbu men used to be fighters.
Now we are like women and children
—KAGLWAIM OF MINTIMA, NAREGU
(interviewer Paula Brown, 1958)

Because policemen and kiaps were strongly using guns and
whips there is less trouble. . . . I changed my whole being to be
a good Christian in 1985
—KAGLWAIM
(interviewer Bruce Kair, 1987)

Missions and Simbu Life

Many writers have commented upon the rapid spread of Christianity in the Pacific. D. Whiteman (1983:188–189) explains the spread of Christianity in 1900–1942 in Melanesia in terms of a number of motivating factors that make up a total package of European influence. Whiteman sees conversion as a positive emotional experience for Melanesians. The factors apply to Simbu as well as to the Solomon and Vanuatu island areas with which he is specifically concerned: (1) the explicit linkage between Christianity and schools, education as the passport for entry into the white man's world; (2) the desire for material objects of European origin; (3) the desire for peace; (4) connection to the outside world; (5) the Christianity adopted because it is the white man's religion; (6) the influence and force of individual mission-ary personalities.

D. Langmore (1989) defined the threefold task of Papuan missions as: winning the confidence of the people, establishing themselves among them, and learning the language. The mission organizations in New Guinea under the German administration followed similar rules and prepared to use local languages. In Simbu the SVD (Society of the Divine Word) Catholic priests, like the Papuan missions, would live among the people, but the restrictions on movement and travel imposed after the deaths of Fr. Morschheuser and

Br. Eugene confined missionary personnel to their main stations for some years. Thus restricted in their movements and prevented from building houses at which personnel could not be permanently posted, the missions proceeded to build up their main stations, airstrips, and schools. They were most influential in those localities where priests and ministers, church services and schools were placed. For some years the spheres of activity and influence of Lutherans and Catholics were distinct. The Catholic mission had Brothers to build and maintain their houses and lands, employing Simbu laborers and carpenters. The Lutheran church used both coastal natives trained as evangelists and teachers and local Simbu natives.

The Catholic Missions at Mingende and Toromambuno

Theft, trespass, and threat of attack were persistent worries; missionary persons and property were defended by firearms. Yet the Simbu most often link guns to the kiap and police, rarely to missionaries. Serious actions, such as mission personnel ordering work and punishment or retaliating for offenses by taking captives or killing natives, were breaches of government rules to be investigated and reported by local officers and perhaps tried by the administration. A number of incidents and conflicts between missionaries and local Simbu were investigated by government officers and recorded in reports in the 1930s and 1940s. As compared to kiap pacification patrols, the incidents with missionaries usually involved only a few people. In this account the kiap and police do the shooting.

Anton Wuka of the Upper Simbu valley (interviewer John Karl):

> The missionaries planted some beans and the outside people admired the beans. They start stealing them. The missionaries tried to find out but could not, so later a man from my clan stole some, cooked them and ate it. He hid the skins in a wooden dish which belong to the old man I am interviewing. Some sumatin or students of Fr. Troppa found the skins and report to him. He told the kiaps. The kiap came with some black police man and shot six of my people dead because of the bean that was stolen.

At this time the Lutherans employed mission helpers, mostly from the north coast of New Guinea, where they had long been established. The sixty who accompanied Bergmann acted as carriers, workers, and evangelists. Catholic schools used pidgin and the Simbu language, and Lutherans taught Kate, as the medium of instruction. In 1987 I was told by Kamanau, an early convert, that the Kamanegu at Ega allowed Rev. Bergmann, the Lutheran missionary, to build an airstrip and a church (see Chap. 3). The airstrip at Ega, now the main airport for Simbu Province, was built next to the Lutheran station at Ega in 1934 (Bergmann 1971, vol. 1). Kamanau said (interviewer Paula Brown): "We had a school in 1936. The church did not come yet—only the Kate school. Did not speak of God. At the school Bergmann gave laplap, biscuit, soap, knife when we worked for him cutting grass." As he tells it, Bergmann paid for the gardens and trees, but nothing is said about how the payment was distributed. Land and territory are traditionally tribal rights. Ega was disputed territory between the Kamanegu and the Endugwa: the question of payment for the land has been revived in recent years.

Fr. Schäfer made up primers, vernacular prayers and hymns, and texts for use in the Catholic catechumen schools and services. Several priests and brothers were stationed at Mingende, Gembogl, and Denglagu, and building proceeded while the missionaries were under a curfew and not permitted outside the mission residence (Nilles 1987a). Catholic mission schools took in fifty boys for a class and were intended to train teachers as catechists in religion for adults and some pidgin school subjects for children. The men trained would then teach in mission village schools. The government pidgin school at Kundiawa was mainly to train interpreters. In late 1938 Fr. Schäfer moved his mission from the small Dimbi ceremonial ground to the larger area of Mingende on Wauga clan land near the airstrip. Mingende became a center for school, church, and residence. Bandiyagl of Naregu said that Fr. Schäfer gave shells and axes to those who helped build his house. These Catholic centers and the Lutheran centers west of Kundiawa built, held services, and taught in areas where there were no kiaps.

Fr. Schäfer's letters and diaries (Ulbrich 1960) portray his life and Simbu incidents, ceremonies, and relations with the people. The Mingende airstrip was built by three to four hundred workers. In 1936, alone at the station, he buys a bag of sweet potato for a small shell, a pig for a large one, and begins a school. Br. Markolinus arrives for building; Schäfer remarks that he has no nails. They plant many varieties of European vegetables and beans. The airstrip and mission airplanes permit visits to the priest, and he travels to other mission stations. Horses and cows arrive in 1937. He observes injuries to women (see also Schäfer 1938), preaches against wife beating, and administers some medicine for illness. He is joined at the main Catholic station at Mingende by Fr. Küppers and Br. Symachus. The arrival of the first plane, *Paulus*, is greeted with great jubilation, and it is an even greater event when the larger *Petrus* lands. They make a garden with students and workers, hold services, and bring people in for a singsing at Christmas. Fr. Schäfer reports a pandanus festival in 1937 and a pig feast in 1938 when one thousand pigs are slaughtered. The boarding school grows to two hundred children in 1938, and Fr. Schäfer has a new house. Soon some Simbu ask to be baptized, and the church is filled to overflowing, with 1,650 inside and 780 outside. Songs are translated and introduced into the service. Fr. Schäfer goes on leave in 1940, is interned in Australia during World War II, and returns to Mingende in 1947 for another long stay. The first girls are taken into the school in 1949. Nilles reports that Mingende has baptized 1,282 in 1943; at Denglagu, 900 are baptized (Nilles 1987a).

Two Brothers, Lucidius and Markolinus, worked at building in Dimbi, Kangrie, Gembogl, and Denglagu. In 1987 I was told by a man in the Upper Simbu that he learned carpentry from the first missionaries. When I asked him why, he said, "They were building houses; that's what they wanted us to do."

Mondo Gunama (interviewer John Karl) said: "Fr. wants me and the other students to be carpenters so he taught us about carpenting. During this I was thinking a lot and worrying. I gave up school and I got married."

After the killing at Denglagu and the sentencing of Br. Lucidius (reported above; see Bates), Fr. Meiser, Fr. Tropper, and later Fr. Nilles lived at Gembogl and supervised the construction of church and school buildings at Keglsugl, which were occupied in 1939. Then a priest and brothers lived there, with boys as boarding students.

A fictional/historical account of mission–Simbu relations in the middle valley is the basis of a novel (Umba 1976). In it the Kukani resolve to kill the white man at the school and the students who follow him, blaming the missionary for the deaths of people. The people resent the great wealth of the white man and blame him for their misfortunes. At the story's climax, the warriors are slaughtered by the white man's guns.

Fr. Nilles also describes his life and observations from the time of his arrival in 1937. He was escorted to Gembogl by police and lived there with Fr. Wilhelm Tropper while the station and airstrip at Keglsugl was being built. They planted gardens with European vegetables, and whenever a mission plane came to the airstrip they sent food to the mission at Alexishafen. They ran a small clinic, opened schools, and held services. He recalled that the Simbu thought that the white man's smell of soap showed that they were spirits, and that he felt rather sick when he first held mass in a church filled with the scent of Simbu, pandanus oil, and pig grease.

Outstations in the Simbu valley, built at the request of the people for churches and schools at Pompameri, Sitnig, Womkama, Giraitamagl, Kuragl, Gunguglme, Kalauingu, and Goglme, were opened between 1938 and 1941, and catechists taught there.

> His [the catechist's] first job was to form a catechumen class of men, women, and teenagers. If he got too many, he was to divide them into two classes. He was also to enroll boys and girls in the school to which I would send a teacher

later. . . . After two and a half or three years in our own schools, the best students were employed as catechists and teachers. (Nilles 1987a:79–80)

In December 1942, my last Christmas season in Denglagu before being evacuated, I baptised 250 men, women and teenagers in groups of fifty at a time . . . the ninth of January 1943 . . . ANGAU[1] suddenly appeared and ordered us to be ready to move out early next morning. And then there were no Catholic missionaries, as Father Ross said, in the whole Highlands, from February 1943 till the eighth September 1944. (Nilles 1987a:81)

In 1941 the Australians ordered the Keglsugl airstrip closed. When German residents were evacuated in 1943, missions were abandoned or staff replaced or reduced. Thus, at Mingende in 1945, Frs. Labor and Bernarding, both Americans, were stationed.

Rev. Hannemann (an American Lutheran) at Kewamugl said that native fighting at Kerowagi ended about 1939, when World War II began (Paula Brown interview 1959).

Karigl Bongere (interviewer Apa Tobias):

Karigl was about 10 years old when the first missionaries came. . . . He was so curious about the white man that sometimes he hid in the nearby bushes to see what was going on . . . Karigl started primary [school] at Gembogl, a school built by the Catholic mission, then transferred up to Denglagu community school to do grades three and four there. Being a very bright student in class, he was sent by the missionaries to be trained as a Catechist at Kumb [Kondiu], a kilometer down from present Mingende station. He was there for a year.

Then the priest in charge asked each Catechist if he could take the Good News to the people of Goglme but all of them refused, frightened that they'll be martyred like the two missionaries earlier. Saw no one was going to Goglme, Karigl volunteered, keen confident that some of his relatives were living there. He worked there for a year, then a priest was called in to confirm his work and Karigl became the head catechist. He travelled to Madang, Hagen, Kavieng and Goroka for conference and other missionary work.

Karigl Bongere became a prominent businessman and member of parliament in later years (see also his life story, Chap. 9)

Joseph Teine, a former catechist and Member of the House of Assembly 1968–1972 (interviewed by Lawrence Gigmai and Paula Brown 1987; see also his life story Chap. 9):

I was about 7 years old when I was enrolled to a mission school at Kumbu where I was taught basic alphabets and arithmatics in pidgin which I don't fully understand but picked up quick enough that I was selected to be a mission teacher (catechist) in 1947–62.

For many years the missions dominated schooling in Simbu. Political leaders and teachers from the 1940s on had their first lessons at mission schools. However, as late as 1951, a patrol officer, D. Kelaart, observed in his report that the educational value of these mission schools was negligible. In the 1950s, Mingende and Kondiu had classes for the upper grades, extending to high school, with a staff composed of De La Salle teaching Brothers and missionary Sisters.

Fr. Schäfer at Mingende mission recognized the leaders of the Siam-bugla-Wauga and Naregu, and made them responsible for bringing their group to work on church projects and buildings. The porcelain rings distributed to these leaders were the same as those "bossboy rings" the New Guinea administration awarded in the 1940s. The government's recognition of boss-boys was rescinded when they were found going to *karim leg* courtship parties (P. carry-leg: young people sit and sing in a circle, with boys' legs crossed over those of girls); and then tultuls were recognized with proper badges, according to Kaglwaim (interviewed by Bruce Mondo Kair, 1987). This is an instance of conflict on the part of mission and government over loyalties and leaders.

Fr. Schäfer described how he gave the Simbu pig-killing feast a new Christian meaning. When he learned that the parish (in about 1948) was planning a pig festival, he spoke with his Legion of Mary leaders and members of the congregation to discover its meanings and then told the congregation how he thought they should Christianize the festival. He would stop sorcerers from making magical incantations, remove *gerua* boards representing Simbu spirits, and bring Christian blessing and prayer to the festival. The pigs were not to be killed at cemeteries or sacrificed to the ancestors. He also modified the sacrificial altar aspect of the central house or *ingu bolum* by placing a large cross at its center. The priest blessed the dancing ground, preventing fights and brawls. At the time of writing, the "new ritual was observed on thirteen dancing arenas" (1981:222), and Schäfer says: "Around Mingende Christ has conquered the gods and spirits. The former pagan festival has been turned into a blessing for the people" (1981:222). Nowadays all over the Simbu and middle Wahgi the priest is invited to visit each festival ground "to bless its cross, people, pigs, sweet potato vines, seedlings, and tools used in gardening or pig herding" (1981:223).

Fr. Nilles, in several thoughtful discussions of the mission and its role in Simbu, evaluated the influence and meaning of Christianity to the Simbu. He believed that traditional and Christian belief were compatible, and wished to combine them, giving a place to traditional belief in Christian liturgy. Deploring the Lutherans' denigration of traditional beliefs and practices as *pasin bilong Satan* (P. satanic rites), he would have rather included the *gerua* and flutes in church. He proposed the inclusion of ancestors in burial ceremonies, the recognition of native name-giving ceremonies in baptism, and the addition of prayers to the ancestors in baptism and marriage rituals. These incorporations, whether taken up generally by priests or not, must produce new syncretisms and practices. When observing that people volunteered to burn *gerua* boards, he felt that although this might indicate a true conversion, perhaps the children had influenced their parents, or the people hoped that the mission could combat anthrax (an epidemic of the 1950s) with *ka nimbine* (S. medicine and prayers) (1987a:69). Fr. Nilles described how the churches have modified the *bugla gende* festivals and have brought *gerua* into the church for decoration. He noted that Fr. Schäfer in 1958 broke the mythical power of the *bolum* houses, central icons of the pig cult, by placing a cross on top of the ancestral pole. Thus the church blessed the house and the pigs (see Schäfer 1981).

When I saw *bugla gende* rituals in 1959 and 1960, there were crosses on the *bolum* houses. Rather than being thatched, as was customary, some houses were unfinished and only the cross stood in the center of the grounds. Catholic prayers were chanted over sweet potato vines at the climax of the rite. For Lutherans, in one ceremony in 1960, there was a separate small group of houses and no cross or religious symbolism; only the killing and distributing of pigs was allowed. In this way the Catholics have incorporated Christian symbols into Simbu festivals, whereas the Lutherans have in most respects condemned traditional rites, beliefs, and practices.

The Lutheran Mission

Rev. W. Bergmann founded Ega in September 1934. In traveling through the area east and south of there he found many Catholic establishments (Bergmann n.d.). He was interned during World War II and returned in late 1947 (Wagner et al., n.d.).

Lutheran missions at Ega and Mu became important centers for teaching and conversion. The first baptisms were in 1948, and religious training centers for hundreds of people preparing for baptism were set up in 1949. My interviews with Lutheran elders at the church sites in 1987 include strong assertions of the importance of the word of God and the transformation of the Simbu through the church. They tell much the same story of early visits, the theft of knives and goods, shootings by kiap and police of those who stole cargo, the collecting of discarded goods—tins, paper, matches, excrement—because it was thought that they gave strength and power.

Agl Gandi, a Pagau of Kerowagi (interviewer Jenny), said:

. . . went to Lutheran school, worked as missionary. Married 2 [wives], then sent a wife away on missionary's advice so she could be baptised. After baptism they gave me a laplap to wear. I was so happy then because before we never had any clothes.

The combination of traditional belief and practice with mission teaching is evident in the actions and statements of dedicated churchmen. Many enjoy describing the life of their youth while praising the benefits of the church and new worship. For instance, Rev. Bob Hueter (an American Lutheran): "It is a rare life that could see and experience all that we did . . . to see these people accept values that a Christian civilization has to offer" (1990); and a Lutheran elder at Mu (interviewer Paula Brown 1987): "The white man brought good things, good laws. The spirit of God is now here. The first kiaps were good, but later some were bad." He went on to tell a version of well-known incidents in 1946–1948 when a named kiap (Costello) and police shot people. They took over a large church building and had the young women brought there at night. This practice was stopped by another kiap and the culprits sent away. The people of this church ask God for guidance in new ways. The white man is seen as the bringer of good things.

Ilia, a Lutheran elder at Ega (interviewer Paula Brown, 1987), said:

He has been a church elder for many years and now as Lutheran church president lives with his family at Ega, mission site. Came to the school from Du in 1949 at age of 12. Spent many years in schools at Kewamugl, Finschafen, Ega; a teacher in Simbu area since 1957. Many in the family are teachers, seminarians. Tells me the story of power of magical stone sorcery (S. *de koga*) and curing (S. *gilgiai*), and says he forgot this when he went to the mission. Differentiates Sinasina belief in the high power of sky (S. Yani) and earth (S. Gela) from the Kuman powers, sun (S. *ande*) and moon (S. *ba*). These make food and pigs grow; prayers were said to them.

Another Sinasina, Talaba Sinne (interviewed by Fred Eremuge), likens Yani-Gela to God, who helps the people. When asked for stories of sun, moon, animals, and origins, he says he knew nothing about them in the past but now he realizes that these things were created by God.

Okuk Palma (interviewer Lawrence Gigmai):

At that time Rev Bergmann has many boys working for him so he asked us to clear up a place and flatten it. We did as we were told and when weeds started to grow Rev Bergmann called on all mission boys one bright sunny morning to wait at the head of the long flattened area. All of a sudden in the clear blue sky

we heard a thundering roar or a big bird from the easterly direction. Suddenly
Rev. Bergmann pointed to where the noise came from and there we saw to our
amazement a huge bird coming towards us. Circled overhead and came in to
land so everybody dashed into the bushes for cover and I was just about to
follow when Rev. Bergmann seized my hand and gestured to wait beside him
with few shivering and nervous but pretended to be brave boy missionaries.
The *kua kande* (S. big bird) finally landed. I saw in Bergmann's eyes that tears of
joy rolled down his pale cheeks and we cried as well. Dropped off some cargo
and after a while the *kua kande* took off to the direction where it came from.
The mission helpers came from around the bushes and helped carry the stuff to
Bergmann's place. The government plane was called "Giniava" and the mission
plane was called "Papua." After the Papua left Bergmann gave us colored beads,
salt and other good things as payment for the airstrip (S. *barsu makan*) that we
built. After learning that the whites were friendly both old and young
befriended them and missionaries started building schools for us and lessons
were taught in pidgin which we understood now.

The Lutheran mission brought Kate-speaking Finschhafen area pastors
and teachers into Simbu for many years. The schools, often reported by
patrol officers as providing primarily religious training and little basic education, used Kate as the medium of instruction in the 1950s. A government
regulation of about 1954 required that the first two years of schooling be in
the vernacular and that thereafter English be taught. The debate over the
value of pidgin as a language for instruction continued for many years. One
result of this was that Kate was no longer taught to children in school. However, it is still a preferred language among older Lutherans and is used by
European missionaries in conversation with them. In 1953:

> At PARI in the Kamanegu Area the Lutheran Mission is building a settle-
> ment for the purpose of preparing natives for baptism. To date a church has
> been completed and various houses for the native are being built. The owners
> of the land have been given presents for the use of the land.
> I was informed that as soon as the settlement was built the first group of
> potential converts would be received and that after their baptism several weeks
> later another group would come for indoctrination.
> However it is not definitely known how long the conversion course will last.
> By the size of the settlement already built it should house about two hundred
> without any difficulty whatsoever. (Pegg 1953:6)

This settlement and a number of others were a matter of discussion and
contention between the mission and the government for a time. Here it is
said that the mission pays for the use of the land, with no statement of length
of time. Some disputes with the local landowners arose when demands were

made for them to provide food for the residents. Patrol reports on these Lutheran communities discussed the problems for a period of the 1950s, and the practice seems to have been short-lived, except perhaps at the main mission settlements at Ega and Mu.

By the 1950s the Lutheran and Catholic church missions had spread to most parts of the subdistrict, and Seventh-Day Adventists were also widely established. All had schools for children and religious instruction in many rural locations. In the areas where they had been established for a generation or longer, their influence was considerable. In the Chuave area and some other places many other missions began work, including Baptist, Anglican, New Tribes, Church of Christ, Four Square, and Ba'hai (Warry 1987:80ff.).

In the 1950s the sexual segregation that led young boys to the men's house might be delayed, and Simbu male initiation, which was discouraged by missions, was no longer performed. Mission schools occupied children and adults at times when they might otherwise have been engaged in subsistence and community activities. One of the most significant effects of conversion, which was most remarked upon by officers in Lutheran areas, was the insistence that only monogamists could join the church and be baptized. Because a distinguishing mark of an important man had been to attract and support many wives, who in turn bore many children and provided food and pigs to their distributions and enterprises, this was particularly difficult for "big men" and their wives. Polygynists might attend church, but they could not be baptized. Among Lutherans, some problems arose when polygynists were converted: the second wife was taken from her children and sent away to her kinsmen. Furthermore, her relatives were expected to repay the bride-price. Officers saw this as disruption of family and community life, and a particularly severe treatment of women. "If the convert has more than one wife he must choose one of them permanently. The others are discarded. The male convert seldom makes any provision for these discarded wives" (Kelly 1955:2).

The effects have been long-standing. In 1984 I was told in Ku, a Lutheran area, that an important purpose of the women's club is to provide assistance to widowed, divorced, and disabled older women. Lutheran practice established communities at mission stations for residence while they received intensive instruction preparing for admission into the church. These were critically viewed by the officers as possibly infringing upon land-use rights and displacing families from their home communities. Other criticism of officers about missions included the poor quality of education, the destruction of ancestral relics, the interference of mission teachers in local affairs, and the dirty clothing worn by Lutherans in settlements.

In the 1980s, both Catholic and Lutheran missions had many adherents, and some other Christian groups had small congregations, meet-inghouses, and services in the area. The two main churches continued to dominate, with their schools, adult groups, and many activities. The large Catholic establishment at Mingende maintained a hospital run by nuns, much used by local families, where many women bore their children. There was a vocational school for girls that taught sewing, cooking, hygiene, and home arts to girls who were not continuing in an academic program. The technical program for boys was in manual-arts subjects, carpentry, mechan-ics, and so on. The mission maintained automotive repair and agricultural and building units under the direction of mission Brothers and skilled native workers.

The Catholic mission had developed Rosary High School at Kondiu before government high schools began in the province, and graduates go on to mission and government schools throughout Papua New Guinea, where they are trained to be teachers, health workers, professional workers of all kinds, and public servants. A high proportion of leaders and political candi-dates are members of the two largest church groups (Brown 1987a).

The missions have influenced all generations of Simbu through schools and mission teaching. Their chosen sites for stations have been areas of fairly level land suitable for airstrips, permanent buildings, and large group gather-ings. To the Simbu, such places formerly had often been battlegrounds, inde-fensible no-man's-lands. Simbu believed that the mission could serve to separate enemy garden and settlement areas. The schools and churches became a meeting place of former enemies, and many Simbu experienced the missionaries as kindly friends and teachers.

Kiaps and Police

Amero of Talasea, constable at Kundiawa under Taylor (interviewer August Kituai, 1985), said, "I felt big and strong because I knew what damage the rifle was capable of causing." Simbu response to administration and police in the 1930s, following the missionaries' deaths and Simbu arrests, can be told through their recollections and some reports of their actions. Gifts made to police and patrol officers were attempts to establish and confirm a friendly exchange. To the Simbu they were placatory, as well as first counters to a return gift. In the first years valuable mother-of-pearl and green snail shells were given for pigs and special services, while small cowries were used in small transactions. Simbu close to stations had considerable stores of wealth. Steel axes, tomahawks, bushknives, and shovels were given as special payments; some of these were incorporated into marriage exchanges in the 1950s.

The government and mission encouraged compensation payments for death and injury in warfare, and the missionaries entered into these exchanges, as we have seen.[2] This later developed into demands for large compensation payments in the cases of accidents and threats against the clan or tribe alleged to be responsible for a death. Payments for land use by government and mission were introduced as well. In the Simbu valley in 1934, the dismantling of Fr. van Baar's house indicates that the Simbu did not consider the gifts made by the mission for the house and land as cementing a permanent land transfer; the mission built and then evidently abandoned a structure. The present-day practice of payments in money and pigs for land rights, injury, and personal obligations as part of exchange relations suggests that Simbu do not fully share western ideas of commodities, sale, and transfer of rights (Brown, n.d.b).

Many patrols were run into the area between the Mai River and the Simbu, up the Simbu valley, and westward into the Wahgi valley. Perceiving a perpetual shortage of officers and police, the administration restricted contact to the area of the Simbu valley and the east–west route of travel, where roads were built by the local people. Areas south of the Wahgi and its lower reaches were not regularly patrolled until the 1950s. Local contact continued to be by foot and horse, and with the coast by radio and plane, after landing strips were constructed.

In the later 1930s, Officer Vial directed a mapping program to establish and clarify tribal boundaries in the Simbu valley and central Simbu area. These became the authority for dealing with intertribal land disputes. Vial began appointing headmen or bossboys and delegating responsibility to local leaders.

Patrol reports mention shooting and injuring or killing one or two natives; in telling of such incidents, Simbu may state that a hundred or, in native count, *merekinde* (S. very many) were killed. The mounting fear of guns is amply demonstrated in their accounts. The knowledge of the power of guns, and fear of them, had reached all over Simbu within a short time of the first violent incidents in the Simbu and Wahgi valleys.

The Simbu's first view of New Guineans from outside the highlands was as police and carriers with the white man's patrol or mission travelers. These Melanesians resembled highlanders, having black skin, but they were wearing western cloth. They were seen by many as relatives, and by some as specific relatives returning from the world of the dead. New Guinean police who were stationed at government posts and went on patrols took on a special role in contact relations. The firearms they carried and used, their capacity to injure and kill, were an important part of their image, both to themselves and to the Simbu. A number of reports state that the government officer gave the order to fire or fired over the heads of the natives; most of the shooting was done by police.

From the early days of contact young highlanders accompanied patrols as carriers and worked at mission stations, learned pidgin, and were given shells, cloth, and metal. A few were employed on government stations as interpreters, domestic servants, and laborers; police and medical assistants received training and salaries. Some government officers encouraged the recruitment of local highlands men, who would live with their families in close contact with the government and accompanied patrols, serving as translators and intermediaries in contact. Many of the New Guinea police and employees took highlands wives to live on the stations.

Simbu Statements about Kiaps and Police

These accounts by witnesses and stories written by young Simbu about the statements of their elders describe punitive actions taken by police and kiaps that rarely appear in the official writings or those of Australian writers. Furthermore, I do not find instances of brutality, whipping, shooting pigs, and killing Simbu in my early field notes. At this time adult and older Simbu expressed gratitude to the kiap and the mission for the good things they had brought. The period corresponds to Sahlins' "A.D.—after domination" (1992). These interviews of the 1980s, after independence, paint a picture of fear and violence that contradicts the Australian contention that their colonial administration was a benign blessing to highlanders. Many people described confusion about the administration's intentions due to whippings and shootings of people and pigs by kiap and police.

Guwand Kombugun of Endugwa and Gena (interviewer Harry Godfrid, 1987):

> The policemen who came with them frighten us with their "sticks of fire" (meaning guns). Worse still they eat betel nuts and when they spit out we thought they had spit out blood: the blood of the people they had killed with their sticks of fire.

Gull kumugl of Endugwa (interviewer Harry Godfrid):

> The first kiaps with their policemen were rough and tough. We tried at first to fight them because of the rough treatment they imposed on us. All our attempts failed because they had the "sticks of fire" [guns]. They threatened us and shot

our pigs and dogs. Those who rebelled were shot and wounded. We had no alternative but to follow them.

Mondo Ola of the Simbu valley (interviewer Paul San):

Yes when the first kiaps and policemen came they did shoot people and animals and I saw them. They shot some of our leaders by the name of Kapaki, Degba Mondia and from my clan they shot a man called Waugla Sungwa. They were shot by the kiaps because they were trying to keep peace among all those people. We were all scared to attack them so we run off into the bush.

My people were surprised to see that the kiaps, with their sharp headed black men from the Coast, were always on the move, ready to go wherever there was trouble. With the aid of their thundering sticks, they could put fighting warriors to flight. That stick spoke like thunder and spat fire and smoke when it was pointed at something. Even the birds in flight were brought low by it.

August Kituai, a Bundi, writes:

History . . . was a series of collections of past events. . . . The events which followed the arrival of the foreigners have become part of the history of the village. The cruel activities of some of the first patrol officers are often retold.

and after they found a man who had been missing,

The patrol's policemen beat him up and his wife and brought them to the village in handcuffs. . . . Once there the patrol officer ordered his police to strip the couple and hang them on two poles stark naked facing each other in the village square. . . . The type of treatment they received from the patrol officer quickly reversed their earlier evaluation of the foreigner as being some ancestral spirits to that of identifying them with devils. (Kituai 1974:8–15)

Igobuno Bi Gertrude, a woman of Bogo, upper Koronigl, Kerowagi, was interviewed by Naur Awi Phillip. She was a girl when the first missionaries arrived, and older when the first kiap, Jim Taylor, came to Kundiawa. Kundiawa then was bush and pitpit. She went to visit her brother Siune Kunma, an interpreter at Kundiawa, and then she married a policeman from Wewak; she was later divorced. In Kundiawa, "The prison was not a building, but a deep dug moist hole. Prisoners were just thrown down and told to wait until their sentence was over. Prisoners were made to carry heavy objects and fettered to a big log. Their severe punishment was to make the offenders realize their faults and learn from it."

Police Statements of Early Contact Relations

Amero of Talasea, a policeman in Simbu under Taylor in the 1930s, was interviewed by August Kituai on 2 March 1985. This is a summary including excerpts from the manuscript of the tape:

> The government's ultimate aim was to bring peace to the community, and he felt that his power was given him by the government. Guns and target practice were given during training. The guns were loaded when they went to quell disturbances in villages, such as tribal fighting or attacks against government officials. When an incident was reported, they would go to the village, surround it and catch the culprits if possible, then bring them to the station jail. When the culprits resisted or tried to escape, they might be shot. The kiap ordered the police to shoot in these circumstances, when the police were attacked or the culprit escaped. Police were encouraged by the kiap to get involved with unmarried girls, teach them pidgin English, and help to spread the word of the government to the people.
>
> I did a lot of patrolling while I was stationed in Simbu. Most of the patrols were done to bring people under government control. I cannot remember a patrol where it did not involve fighting between the people and ourselves. When we first came upon these communities we would first indicate that we were there as friends. If they did not react in an unfriendly manner, we would distribute presents—salt, beads, knives etc.
>
> Whenever and wherever I said something, the people [P. kanaka] would listen to me. If any one of them failed to listen to me and bighet [P. were arrogant] it would be like refusing to listen to the government—it was our task to fight them and bring them to jail if necessary only for the purpose of educating them. The stern measures were only corrective and not punitive for punishment's sake. The government's aim was to bring peace to the community.
>
> In going to arrest a renegade sergeant who had stolen from the station and then became a bush kanaka like his wife: The kiap commanded me to shoot him.
>
> The first step was always to establish communication between the people and ourselves. We would call the leaders of the communities together and have a dialogue with them in an attempt to correct the tense situation with no or little bloodshed. Usually we would distribute gifts to them first and then instruct them in the nupela pasin [P. new ways], gutpela pasin [P. good ways] and try and reach some form of understanding with them. If they did not understand, or continued to be belligerent, we would be patient but at the same time nervous but always hoping they would understand our peaceful intentions. We would attempt to pacify them three times and if by then they still refused to accept the presence of the kiap and ourselves, the kiap would order us to either frighten them away with rifle shots, round them up, especially the instigators,

for imprisonment, or shoot them if the situation was thought bad enough to threaten our own lives.

I followed the kiap's instructions most of the time but there were times when I acted without them. For instance, I would be walking through an area and I was attacked by the people. I would shoot at them if I thought the situation warranted such an action. I was well-versed, however, in government regulations regarding such situations. Patrol work was good. We were rewarded if we did a good job—pacified people, brought people to jail if they had committed any offences, stopped people from fighting etc. We were rewarded with money, tobacco, laplap etc. The kiaps that I worked with had a lot of pride in my performance.

Kituai's interview of Tawi, an elder from Bundi, describes the community's view of the first white men, missionaries, and kiaps, and the police. To summarize and excerpt:

Of the killing of missionaries in the Simbu valley, he says that government officials "just about wiped out the population of those responsible for the missionaries' murder." The missionaries warned people who refused to work for them that a stronger force, the government, would come and use force to make them do what they wanted them to do. "This proved to be true—their predictions were correct, the government came and forced us to do a lot of things—build roads, carry cargoes, build airstrips, maintain roads, etc." When the people gave the missionaries food and pigs they got very little in return, but if they complained, pigs were shot, and the people would run into the bush at the sound of the rifle. The rifle was seen as powerful: "I thought now I have seen the source of what makes lightning and thunder." "We thought they were going to kill the whole lot of us." The people were caned and handcuffed, and women were taken for sexual use, for which they were given small gifts. (Kituai MS from tape 1985)

Tawi described the jail at Kundiawa to Kituai in much the same terms as did Igobuno Bi Gertrude, as a deep hole that was cold, wet, filthy with excrement, and crawling with rats. The prisoners were forced to work hard at hauling logs, building, and fencing, and were poorly fed and teased by their guards. Kituai writes: "Police . . . were innovators as agents of the publicly proclaimed policy of the colonial government to pacify and civilize. And they were both aggressive intruders and innovators in the way that they ensured compliance with their demands" (Kituai 1988:166).

In 1986 Paul Dage interviewed Geregl Gande, a Kerowagi Simbu man who became an interpreter and later a policeman. I summarize and in part quote the interview record:

Learning pidgin was a preparation for government service. Because he held power given to him by the kiap he became aggressive. He was a good policeman to the kiap but bad to the people because he beat them with a cane whip all the time. Policemen solved the smaller crimes by beating them and putting them into prison camp. He loved his job as policeman and interpreter because he got goods from the government that other people did not have. He believed that the kiap government was better for the people. On patrol with the kiap, the kiap would point to the rifle and make a big "boom" sound, then signed that this would kill. The important cases were brought before the kiap. Following his police service, Geregl became a medical orderly, agricultural officer, elected councillor and magistrate. (Dage MS, 1986)

Diunde Koma and Kugame Amugl, two policemen of Endugwa, were interviewed by Philip Kai Moore in 1984. They had attended the first pidgin school in Kundiawa, which trained them for police and interpretive work, which became the life career for each of them. Both have stopped tribal fights, heard court cases, and report that in the early days police shot pigs and fighting tribesmen. Kugame said, "out of fear people started obeying government rules and stopped fighting."

The Simbu had little experience of white settlers until they began to travel and work outside the Simbu area. I am unable to find reports of their attitudes toward these settlers in the 1930s. Work opportunities with miners in the eastern and western highlands were few, and no Simbu were involved until World War II or later.

Ian Downs: Stabilizing Administrative Control from Kundiawa

Ian Downs says in a preface:

I belonged to that last wave of white men, who, with extraordinary didactic arrogance, went out to colonies to make other people do things they would not have done for themselves. I had my share of ambition and greed occasionally tempered with compassion and altruism. But I never pretended that I really "understood" Papua New Guineans. (Downs 1986)

The Hagen-Sepik patrol of 1938, led by Taylor and Black, which located many new peoples of the western highlands, Enga, and Sepik areas, was another landmark in highlands exploration. The Hagen post formed the link from Simbu into this new administrative region. Ian Downs joined the patrol, which had already recruited the other experienced officers, Walsh and Greathead. Downs' illness forced him to withdraw from that enterprise, and when he recovered, a man in his early twenties, he was posted as officer in charge of the Chimbu post in September 1939, when Vial left. His time in Simbu was devoted to the vigorous pursuit of control, road improvement, and establishment of communications through patrols and at Kundiawa. Downs' reporting style and discursive discussions of action and personal policy are of special interest as the culmination of relations between Simbu and kiap in the 1930s.

Downs briefly recounts his experiences in Simbu (1986:119–121). In 1939 his total police force numbered seventeen, and he made up a force of Simbu from tribes near Kundiawa regarded as pacified and under administrative control. At the beginning of his tenure in September 1939 to stop a Yonggamugl tribal war, he advanced with some two thousand men from Kamanegu and Siambugla-Wauga to the fighting area. While the Yonggamugl people withdrew, the government force took many pigs hostage[3] and demanded the surrender of fighting leaders. He marks this action as the end of tribal fighting and adds, "Peace was maintained by the people themselves because they discovered the freedom of movement this gave them" (1978:238). Few of these pigs were returned to the owners, but many were given as payment to the war victims, used to pay helpers, and taken to begin a pig farm. Downs introduced European Berkshire boars to breed with the native varieties, resulting in improved stock. But the Yonggamugl fighters were surely punished. When collecting a record of pig feasts in this area some twenty years later, Brookfield and I noted a long delay in the feast sequence, attributed to inadequate numbers of pigs. However, we could not be sure that the shortage of pigs was due to this capture or to an anthrax epidemic.

In discussing tribal land, Downs says:

> Fighting over land rights . . . had to be treated arbitrarily. Where agreement could not be reached by an exchange of some kind, we froze the ownership: the group who possessed the land when the first patrol intervened was allowed permanent possession. These were final orders. They were respected and observed in the Chimbu without demur until 1968. (Downs 1986:124)[4]

Downs also remarks (1986) on the prevalence of venereal disease in Simbu at this time, which he attempted to control by requiring the then unmarried police to marry one woman only. He recommended that the "beach boy" mission helpers be sent home and tried to restrict the sexual activities of mission helpers. A medical assistant was posted for a time in Simbu, and a hospital area set aside. In April 1940 the hospital treated a serious influenza epidemic.

Downs' patrol, monthly, and annual reports are especially direct and outspoken, sometimes in reaction against administrative regulations or orders and his District Officer, Oakley, in Madang. He favored tight discipline of police and native employees. Communications and movement were improved by the roads, now used by mission and administration. Downs was proud to report that a horse track up the Simbu valley made it possible to reach Denglagu from Kundiawa in one day. He was zealous in upgrading paths to horse tracks, fencing the road against pigs, and with Greathead instituted regular runner communications to Hagen. "The road from Hagen to Benabena must become vehicular. It can be done."[5] When Downs was District Commissioner of the Eastern Highlands District in 1952, it was done (Downs 1986:230–251).

Because the administration favored the consolidation of control over expanding contact with new areas, "inner Chimbu" was defined as the area accessible in short patrols from posts. Downs saw this as a "ribbon of control" that followed the highlands road; "inner Chimbu" was a triangle around Kundiawa, whose points were police posts at Chuave, Goglme, and Awagl, on or close to the highway. Oakely thought that Downs was doing too much and counseled him to reduce his contact with the outer groups. The Wahgi River was a significant boundary, and administration did not extend south of the river in Simbu, although it did in Hagen. The road on the south bank of the Wahgi, recommended by several highlands officers in the 1930s, was not built as a stretch of the highlands highway until the 1970s, and then remained the only unpaved section for many years.

In 1938–1940, when Vial and Downs were posted at Simbu, administration patrols began to outline the clan organization and territories of Simbu tribes, identify tribal leaders, and take a census of tribes in the area near the Chimbu post. Under Ian Downs and his small police force, "inner Chimbu" groups began to provide a mobile support force to intervene in tribal fighting: they would make surprise visits, confiscate weapons, take livestock hostage, and arrest war leaders. The New Guinea police force was then supported by Simbu tribesmen, who assumed the new role of intervening in tribal warfare. Downs was resolute in putting down fighting and attacks on patrols. He believed that the previous officers at Chimbu post had prepared the ground for the strong reactions of his administration to fighting. The serious incidents in this period were mostly in the western area and at some distance from Chimbu post. He defended his actions against criticism by his superiors.

Downs' analysis of tribal warfare is insightful. He distinguished vendetta from other wars and arranged a payment for a killing: "In these cases it is not sufficient to settle payments merely of the current killing but it is necessary to adjust the original injury which caused the vendetta to commence . . . no matter how many years ago." He takes a western legal position in saying, "When this is done the native groups concerned cannot have any moral excuse for continuing the vendetta." One incident was in the eastern Simbu area beyond Chuave, and he said: "All the natives in all the groups concerned were caned as this part is not under the the same control as the areas within the base camp. The next offense will invoke the N.A.R."[6]

The Native Affairs Regulations of 1939 made some differences to administrative policy. When an area was considered under control, the officer in charge would hold court for offenses against the regulations and could imprison natives. In newly contacted areas not yet under control, natives could be whipped. Disliking the term "bossboy," Downs suggested using the local term *yombopondo* (S. big man) (November 1939, p. 3); in his reports, "headman" is used. Of three hundred headmen, twenty were recommended for appointment as luluais. His selected luluais, "all capable of dominating the other headmen within the same clans as themselves . . . are constantly drawn in for talks and conferences. . . . They go on tours to other areas" (Annual Report 1940, p. 2). But luluai badges were in short supply, and the white rings supplied to headmen were the same as those for sale in mission trade stores. Downs comments on his efforts to instruct tribal leaders in administrative expectations for peace and order. Appointing and confirming the appointment of headmen, praising many by name, his ardent report states that they must be treated with dignity and respect to make them responsible. He details his own analysis of behavior and motives of individual leaders and his methods of instilling loyalty and control. The Annual Report stressed that chiefs must be treated with respect by the police and by himself, "taught to be fearless and loyal in the face of other influence" (p. 3). Later, as he prepares to leave the post, he says: "the organization of luluais and headmen is on a firm and established basis. . . . They definitely have great authority and regularly apprehend thieves, vandals, murderers, and natives who start or wish to start fights. If fights occur they proceed to any area within their influence and bring all those who fight to the station (Patrol Report, October, p. 2).

Downs names Ambagarawari, a man with authority over all of Kewandegu, and Bage of the middle Simbu valley at Goglme as outstanding leaders; both were sons of former powerful fight leaders and had influence over large groups of people. They were taken to visit Madang District Office in 1940. There is no suggestion of despotism (cf. Brown 1990b:99), and it may be concluded that as early as 1939 luluais held authority through recognition and support of the kiap (Brown 1963). In August, Downs says: "Both Bage and Ambagarawari are beginning to handle their own courts and the situation is most satisfactory. . . . In fact the Middle Chimbu is so good that it is almost boring" (Patrol Report, 6 August: 1). These two men are named and commented upon in reports throughout the 1940s and into the 1950s. Downs promoted a marriage of Ambagarawari to the daughter of a Minj valley luluai, commenting, "Do not be surprised if luluais only marry daughters of other headmen or luluais in future" (Patrol Report, 21 October 1940:3). He is skeptical of some pacification techniques that had become popular with officers: "The lack of success attendant upon 'a burning of spears' is well known. The natives just make new ones" (Monthly Report, February 1940: 2). Among his projects was reforestation; planting ten trees for every tree cut down. A report (18 March 1940) reviews several species found in the area and their uses.

Administration from 1939 continued in the shadow of World War II. The Australian government and the New Guinea administration feared that German influence would cause anti-Australian disaffection among the natives, and required a monthly check on aliens. Members of a Nazi group attached to the Lutheran headquarters in Finschhafen were interned in 1939; later, many German Lutheran ministers and Catholic priests and Brothers were interned or evacuated to religious houses in Australia. Downs, awaiting a call to service, "looked forward to being subjected to navy discipline" (1986:127).

Downs was sensitive to the potential competition between mission and administration for loyalty and prestige. He noted that the government gave just 12 pounds[7] for entertainment and the celebration of Christmas–New Year, while the missions provided a grander feast, with foods from their own gardens and livestock herds. When mission employees attempted to punish theft and trespass by Simbu, the administration reacted with inquiries and arrests. Seeing that the Catholics held Gembogl, the only level site in the densely populated upper Simbu valley, as a post for church and school, Downs advised acquiring it for the administration. With reference to mission sites, he said, "The chief reason the mission want to have the Gembogl site . . . is the fact that the mission wants to keep the Administration out of the upper Chimbu" (Patrol Report, 3 September 1940:3). He requests permission to have the mission withdraw from Gembogl, and the administration take it over for a station. There was a police post at Gembogl in the 1940s, under ANGAU; the government's administrative post was built in 1959–1960.

The influence of Rev. Bergmann and mission evangelists from Finschhafen made people at Yonggamugl believe that the administration punished what the mission forgave, Downs felt.

In this way feeling grows that Yonggamugl belongs to the Lutherans, Kamanegu to the administration and Naragu to the Catholics . . . I am jealous on the Administration's behalf . . . we do not need the interference of these alien missionaries to control and properly administer our territory."[8]

Then, in August:

It is with satisfaction that I record the departure early in the month of 12 mission teachers from Ega and one from Kerowagi. The natives themselves forced the position.[9]

And later:

The matter of the missionaries settling disputes and courts has been done away with owing to the fact that headmen now know that what they are headmen for and the natives as a whole can now distinguish between the Administration and the mission. . . . Twelve months ago they called the government officer Father and regarded him as a branch of the mission who did not interfere at all in upper Chimbu affairs . . . the upper Chimbu problem . . . is one of controlling the mission at Toromambuno . . . the same situation was present in Naragu and Siambuga-Waugwa as relative to the Mingende mission. But here it was simplified because the Chimbu Post was so close that I could give those tribes a greater amount of attention. The departure of Father Schafer clinched the matter.[10]

According to Fr. Nilles, Downs had Fr. Schäfer deported because he did not observe the curfew regulations imposed on enemy aliens (Nilles 1987a:57).

New regulations (N.A.R.) of 1939 made some differences to administrative policy. In Downs' annual report of June 1940 he reports on success:

The early contact and exploration, the efficient and utterly essential punitive and police action which followed it along the most humane lines, and the mapping and tribalisation of the area had all played their part in forming a basic platform for the present development and progress which cannot be attributed to any particular thing but rather to the continual and combined force of continuity operating through a policy which has actually not differed although it may have been applied in a different manner by different officers to meet the degree of development they found. The credit for this belongs entirely to the Administration and the Officers it appointed to Chimbu and it can be clearly shown that the work of the Alien Mission societies, whatever influence it exerted has nothing to do with progress; and without their presence the area would probably be more advanced than it is at present. On the other hand a non alien mission body could perform useful work, so that would not conflict with British ideas.

To maintain order Downs urged the appointment of local police. The "lockup" held up to sixty men, and he proudly announced toward the end of his term that the number in lockup had dropped to seven. He states that the introduction of the N.A.R. has brought results and safeguards the native in hearing the case, finding that:

1. The natives regard imprisonment, regulation prison routine, head-shaving, striped lavalava, and indeed the whole precision and legal internment as THE MOST SEVERE PUNISHMENT EVER INTRODUCED AT CHIMBU.
2. They are learning the native administration regulations and the educational value of the procedure cannot be overestimated.
3. The officer in charge is on firmer ground and the punishment of natives loses in this new legality the distastefulness of the former methods.
4. The lock-up constructed has been built by headmen only; but although every care was taken to build a solid structure, there have been attempts to escape from Chimbu.
5. I have been impressed by the fact that the natives obviously appreciate the system is a fair one. (February 1940 Monthly Report, p. 3)

In March: "It will then be obvious that if we can substitute litigation for the settlement of individual's disputes by violence we will also eradicate group and tribal fighting" (p. 3). In the Annual Report: "The last months of 1939 were all spent in educating the natives up to the Regulations, in beginning the new methods of developing headmen, and in planting food for the prisoners to eat and in erecting the lock-up. Whipping is gone from the inner area" (p. 9). The lock-up "is used . . . to prevent murderers from going unpunished and it is particularly useful in checking men who are constantly getting into trouble. These men are educated in the lock up and at the end of their term are reformed natives" (p. 10). Of Kagun he says: "He confessed to me that the reason he was such a nuisance was because he could not understand what we aimed at. Now he knows and is telling other people west of the Ad Nigl" (p. 10).

Reporting on the native situation Downs says that there has been no group fighting in a long list of tribes of "inner Chimbu" since January: "It should be noted that the areas now giving the least trouble are areas that have indeed been firmly dealt with even to the extent of rifles having to be used in the past" (p. 11). Air supplies then included knives and axes. A native wireless operator is requested. Police range from good through reliable to useless. He wanted to recruit local men for police and warders, wants a bugler badly. Downs' attitude toward women and sexual activities is hinted at when he says: "adultery will not often be dealt with under the N.A.R. on account of the difficulties presented by certain classes of women who are often more to blame than males. I cannot cope with women prisoners of course."[11]

Downs returned from naval service to play an important role in postwar Papua New Guinea, first in the administration, where he served as District Commissioner of the Eastern Highlands from 1952 to 1955, then in coffee development and in government, but not at Simbu.

The next officer, F. N. Warner Shand (1940–January 1942) continued these policies. He, too, was especially active in the Simbu valley and said in 1941, "Tribal fighting I believe in the main Simbu valley area is at an end." The Inau, who had caused much trouble to earlier officers, were found to be friendly. Luluai Ambagawari, who had been a favorite of several previous officers, was found to be misusing his authority, attempting to exert his influence to his advantage in bringing to light old disputes, so was severely spoken to and told the proper extent of his authority. Shand conducted a census in the valley and extended roads connecting to east and west. Rest houses were built. Simbu kiaps had reason to be satisfied with the progress in pacification and administration at the beginning of the Pacific War. But this rate of progress did not continue.

7

Simbu Dependence

> Those who hold that we should have left the primitive mountain tribes of New
> Guinea to their innocent, idyllic existence would possibly change their views
> had they have been able to see the fear, superstition and pain that dominated
> the lives of these people before the government stopped tribal fighting, bound
> their wounds, and broke open the prison of their fearful isolation. (Sinclair
> 1981:89)

Sinclair, a former kiap, here voices the Australian conviction that their
administration, particularly in the highlands, was welcomed by the natives
and rescued the people from a terrible war-torn existence. His comments
reflect a common Australian view of the 1950s through the 1970s. The
Simbu today, in retrospect, do not all agree. Nevertheless, violent opposition
to the newcomers was very rare; mission and government representatives
were peacefully met, and patrols after these first intrusions often reported an
enthusiastic welcome. After friendly overtures and the kiap's insistence on
pacification, most Simbu did not rebel against colonial rule.

Simpson, a careful observer who met the anthropologist K. E. Read in
Goroka in 1952, wrote: "The Administration has stopped their fighting.
They are at peace with each other.... They are at peace with other tribes.
... However, they did not stop fighting from any sudden change of heart but
because it was in their general interest to co-operate with the Government
and against their interests to incur its displeasure" (Simpson 1964:208).

In the middle period of colonial rule, around 1958–1963, subordinate
relations with Australian officials were accepted, and Australian development programs—local government, cash cropping, labor migration, schools,
health, and welfare programs—were eagerly accepted. I was a frequent visitor
to Simbu, and it seems to me that after twenty-five years of contact and pacification, there was an episode of willing colonial dependence.

When I arrived I was brought to Mintima by the kiap to live for some
months in a government rest house, which the local people repaired and
expanded for my use. I paid local people for work, firewood, and food sup-

plies, and contributed to group payments. I was transported and had supplies delivered by the kiap. The only white women known in the area were attached to the Catholic mission, and I was greeted with "God bless" at first. Later, I made my role separate from that of the mission and the government and was known to be resident at Mintima.

In their way the Simbu attempted to make the most of modernizing opportunities. New goals and high expectations of wealth through coffee growing and local resources were proclaimed by Kondom (see Chap. 9) and other leaders who encouraged their people to support government programs presented to them by the kiap. Government officers on patrol were welcomed with lavish presentations of food, including store-purchased foods by some people close to commercial shops. Attendance at the Catholic mission schools and services at Mingende, which I had the opportunity to observe on many occasions, was high. Government schools were supported by community contributions of labor, building materials, and food for the students.

In the 1950s there were many loyal luluais, some of whom were noted as former leading warriors who had earlier been jailed for their fighting; impressed in jail by the power and values of the government, they became strong progovernment leaders. When I met them in the field in 1958 their authority was well established; they took a prominent position at every meeting.

The Simbu View of Pacification and Colonial Changes

This was a typical statement made to me: "I was a great warrior. Then the government came and I heard the words of the kiap. I now am a luluai, I stop fights and do the work of the government. We are glad that there is no more warfare, and good things have come from the white man."

In my fieldwork of 1958–1959, interviews with men who remembered the early days of contact contained elements of heroic war experience and the lost status of a leading warrior. A few deplored the suppression of fighting and the prevention of violent retaliation against enemies and witches. Lost land and territory were regretted; discussion and litigation attempted to regain these; and, locally, land disputes were confrontations between persons and small groups.

For some, the thrill of battle and memory of bravery remained; they made good stories. Some of these stories are still told to youngsters and visitors by the participants. Heroic stories are the genius of the men's house, the arena for indoctrinating youth in tribal lore, loyalty, and pride. The change is noted in stories:

Kaglwaim, Naregu, in 1959 said:

I killed the Endugwa, the kinsmen of Kugame. Killed many when I was young. Now whiteman comes and takes away the weapons. Then I got brass [tultul badge]. I killed plenty. (interviewer Paula Brown)

Kamanegu tultul Tagai, in 1959:

Before we Kamanegu pushed the Simbaigu, the Gena, the Endugwa out. They wanted to kill us and take our ground. We fought the Kewandegu, Naregu, and Yonggamugl. We made shields, carried them with the stone axe and bow and arrow. We stopped them all. My ancestors were here. I killed a cassowary, pig, took and gave to Simbaigu, because we are all Kamanegu and I thought we should stay together. We fought the Gena and took some of their land. We didn't pay when we killed a Gena. We did not pay when we killed Ogondie and when they killed us. We took a girl, and she went to the Ogondie; we were angry and killed in revenge. We did not take ground from other Kamanegu. Before the white man came we fought, now we are like brothers and do not fight. (interviewer Paula Brown)

This statement seems to confirm that the payment of compensation to enemies was not a precontact way of settling wars, but was instituted by the early kiaps in their efforts toward pacification.

Luluai Kwatinem of Kamanegu said, in 1959: "Our ancestors did not know about God. Now we know. So we stay together like brothers. Now that we have the Council we do not have weapons. Have no trouble here" (interviewer Paula Brown).

At Inau, Upper Simbu valley, in 1959 (interviewer Paula Brown):

We made a low house because we had no blankets or clothes. We put the woman's house a long way away, so the enemies would not see them. There was a small door to the house for escape. At that time we had bush between Denglagu Wandigl and Inaugl. When we fought, we burnt *pitpit* (P. canes) and *yar* (P. casuarina trees). Then a mark was made and we began gardening there at Minmogl 1953. Now that it is peaceful we are settled and we have good food.

The heroic time of tribal warfare, of ancient enmities and alliances, is the lore of Simbu men; the memory of wrongs and unsuccessful retaliations becomes the justification for new tribal fights. This was stopped by the colonial administration, through the arrest and imprisonment of fighting men. It has been only since independence that I have heard older men state their resentment or bitterness, notably those who lost land when pacification policy fixed boundaries to take land recently conquered by an enemy. Simbu continue to point to burial grounds, trees, and ceremonial grounds as claims to land and territory, and many wish for more land for cash crops.

Colonial Life and Administration

The mood of acceptance was dominated by the Australian officers' appointment of Simbu officials, who were instructed and indoctrinated by kiaps and became models of the new way. The early reports mention loyal headmen who received gifts and assumed that their friendship with the kiap gave them special privileges, as did Bage and Ambagawari (see Chap. 4: Kyle). The officers saw them as strong leaders on whom they could rely to keep peaceful control over a wide area. These men assumed power with the support of the kiap (see Brown 1963) and as powerful men became the first luluais. Their success spurred the search for the same type of leaders throughout, and their appointments lasted until the institution of elected local government councils, when men with some schooling, fluent in pidgin, and active in new cash-earning activities were favored. Within a few years these leaders were effective spokesmen for the Australian administration program of pacification and development, brought out their people for roadwork and censuses, took disputes to the government office for settlement, and lectured the people about the new life under the white man.

One difficulty encountered by Downs and some other officers was competing loyalties to mission and government.[1] These were especially problematic in the areas around the Catholic centers, where the first government-appointed headmen and luluais were often also mission adherents. Fr. Nilles describes early mission activities as including the establishment of friendly relations with the natives who visited the mission to barter and receive medical aid. Young boys were taken in as boarders and trained to be teachers, and the missionaries learned to speak Kuman. "It was not until the missions began to build schools and called the natives together for instruction that they began to realize the distinction between missions and government and their respective aims" (Nilles 1953:15).

Simbu began to distinguish mission from government, and found different ways of rewarding support, obedience, and loyalty. The missions produced food and bred livestock, and built and paid for the construction of houses, schools, and churches. Their favored followers were rewarded for helping the mission cause by increasing adherents and attendance at church. Mission-appointed leaders received gifts of goods and livestock, which were often considered more attractive than the rewards of government appointment.

The government demands were political and developmental. Road building and communications were major endeavors; as reported, the Simbu became enthusiastic road builders, using steel tools provided by the government. Ian Downs wrote: "Although the response of the Highland people to our road construction was magnificent, it was never undertaken without payments of some kind" (1986:233).

Other rewards were given to those who provided a force to stop warfare among other tribes. A few Simbu were employed as police and interpreters and served to defuse fights and conflicts. In their efforts to prevent disputes and homicides from becoming tribal wars the kiaps introduced and reinforced peace ceremonies, burning of weapons, and compensation payments.

The Simbu traditional form of exchange was fed by new ties to the mission and the kiap, in which there were some attempts to control access to shells and metal goods. Simbu expanded their practice of beginning and confirming relationships with the transaction of gifts. Exchange and *yomba yagl* (S. payment for a man) persist because they are open, negotiable, innovative, and can resolve immediate obligations.

There was often a different understanding and expectation of the meaning of these gifts for Simbu and for missionary, kiap, or visitors. Women, marriage, headmanship, jobs, and rewards were all commercialized through the introduction of trade items into Simbu society. The white man's goods carried a magical value for many Simbu well into the 1950s. My friend and interpreter in 1958, Wagai of Naregu, had a precious cigar box that contained a toothbrush given him by a *masta* (P. white man), some broken and discarded parts of my primus stove, and other such objects. When the toothbrush broke in half, he was heartbroken and unconsoled when I told him he could buy one at the Kundiawa store with the money I paid him. Small trinkets, beads, tin pieces, lids, and rubber rings were greatly prized, and some have continued as decorative objects.

Appointments of Native Officials

In New Guinea the system created by the German administration, in which officials were called "luluai" and "tultul" (terms taken and redefined by the German authorities from terms in use among the Tolai people in New Britain), was in use by Australian administration until local government councils were established in each area. The patrol officer and officer in charge of each station on patrol recommended the appointment or removal of officials.

In the first efforts toward administrative control, 1930s officers recognized local leaders and referred to them as "bossboys" (P. and English) or "headmen." Evidently the Australians assumed that every community had some form of chieftainship. They looked for the leader, endowed him with administration-sanctioned office, and assigned to him the responsibility of keeping law and order and conveying the orders of the administration. The arrest and imprisonment of war leaders, fighters, and killers who were thought to be community leaders was the first step in instilling in them a respect for the new kiap's rules. Six powerful tribal leaders in the Simbu valley were appointed luluais by 1940; there were nine in 1946. Appointments were made throughout the Simbu area. They then (see Downs, chap. 6) could be made native officials responsible for establishing a volunteer labor force for roadwork, stopping tribal fighting in their own tribe, and assembling the whole community for patrol visits, census, and instruction. Downs engaged these leaders to provide a peacekeeping force and stop fighting in other areas. A loyal and hardworking headman was rewarded with gifts of shells, knives, and axes, and the people close to him would sell food to the patrol on its visits. These informal appointments were confirmed by giving a white porcelain ring, when these were available; but officers saw that these rings were on sale at mission trade stores and not suitable as distinctive badges of office for government appointees. It was not until after World War II that luluai badges or pendants, hung from the neck or head, became official "brass" to the Australians—"namba," "batch," or "metal" (P.) to the Simbu.

In practice officers in charge of a post or station recognized and selected leading men, recommending them for positions of luluai or tultul. This was seen by the Simbu as a momentous recognition of individuals; in their eyes, they were given new powers. I found Simbu quick to accept new titles and to endow them with authority. Downs grasped the highlanders' practice in which an esteemed person stood for a group and represented group values as a basis for the development of leadership. He cultivated the authority and confidence of such persons by assigning them responsibility and rewarding them. When they failed to meet expectations, they were jailed for retraining or dismissed with recommendations for replacement. The few men selected as officials were recognized as leaders and empowered to take offenders and problem cases to the kiap and court, made responsible for stopping fights, maintaining roads, and bringing out their tribesmen for census and service. In the 1940s some were praised for ably settling disputes in their areas.

Patrol reports for the 1930s and early 1940s[2] often mention these headmen by name, commenting on their authority and occasionally on their failings. The two most impressive men of the Simbu valley, Bage (sometimes spelt Baka) of Goglme (see Bates 1936) and Ambagarawari (or Apa, Aba, and other spellings) of the Kewandegu, had demanded gifts and services from people in their area. They were reprimanded by kiaps. In 1941, Warner Shand reported that he gave a long instructive talk to Ambagarawagi, who had been attempting to use his influence to his own advantage, bringing to light old disputes. These two leaders were renowned and favored for many years, until a local government council was set up in 1960.

Arime, a Naregu luluai and convert to the Catholic mission at Mingende, suffered from the competing ambition of Kondom, finally losing his post of luluai to the younger man by what some of Arime's clansmen consider deceit. Kondom, a polygynist and never a Catholic, after his appointment in 1942 or 1943 remained fiercely loyal to the government and became a leading spokesman for progress throughout the highlands (Brown 1963, 1967, 1990b).

World War II: The Australian New Guinea Administrative Unit

The Australian involvement in World War II took precedence over the program of exploration and control of the Australian administration. For the mandated territory of New Guinea, as for Papua, the Australian New Guinea Administrative Unit (ANGAU) had administrative, operational, and production responsibilities in the unified territory. While the Australian officers were concerned about the pro-German sympathies and possible espionage of Germans in New Guinea, including the missionaries in the highlands, it was the Japanese who threatened New Guinea after the declaration of the Pacific war in 1941. Japan bombed and invaded the coasts of Papua and New Guinea.

ANGAU had urgent military priorities and administrative requirements. Some officers—for example, G. Greathead, J. L. Taylor, and F. N. Warner Shand—took army rank and continued to work in administration and control. Some kiaps were recruited into the ANGAU military administration and continued in Papua and New Guinea, with different duties. Vial, for example, became a coast watcher observing Japanese fleet movements, a very hazardous activity; he was killed in the war (Manning 1959). The New Guinea police force continued. ANGAU activities involved Papuans and New Guineans in the armed forces and as laborers. Production of copra and rubber increased the labor force on plantations, but this little affected the highlands. Only a few laborers were recruited in the highlands to become road and airstrip workers and carriers.

German Catholic mission priests, nuns, brothers and German Lutheran ministers and laymen were regarded by Australians as possible Nazi propagandists and spies. Several were interned early in the war. The missions continued their work for a time, but in January 1943 military officers supervised the removal of enemy aliens. Foreign missionaries were rounded up and escorted to embarkation points (Leahy 1987); all persons of German nationality were evacuated, mostly to Australia. Many mission posts were abandoned or left to native and non-German assistants (Nilles 1987a).

Military officers, many of them inexperienced in dealing with natives, were given responsibility for the control and maintenance of Australian administrative posts. They are hardly distinguished from kiaps in native memory, yet the priorities shifted to military needs. The Japanese occupied parts of New Guinea, and American forces joined Australian and allied forces to retake the area. Land, sea, and air battles were fought near many coastal settlements, but no Japanese penetrated the highlands.

The war required construction of roads, bridges, and airstrips. At Goroka, in the eastern highlands, in seven days from 29 June 1943, an airfield was built by the work of one thousand Simbu.[3] Some Simbu who served as police or laborers during the war later joined civilian police and other work units. It was the beginning of Simbu men's experience of Papua New Guinea outside their district and home area. Some men who became local leaders and elected officials had their first work and official experience in World War II.

Many of the Simbu interviewed had as their only memory of the war the planes that flew over, a plane crash on the slopes of Mount Wilhelm, and the bomb dropped at Mingende. Several local people knew that a girl from Nandi had been killed by the bomb.

Mondo Ola of Ombondo, Simbu valley (interviewer Paul San):

> I can remember the second World War because I was taken as a carrier. By then I was married. The only thing I saw of the war was the plane which came in numbers circle around the Waghi valley and bombed Mingende.

Porongo Kunma of Bogo, Graiku, Kerowagi (interviewer Naur Awi Philip):

> Porongo left his beloved family to join the Allied Soldiers to fight in World War II. He remembers very well the time when he first used the gun. He also remembers the time when the Allied Soldiers dug deep holes at Kerowagi [airstrip] to prevent the Japanese war plane from landing.

Kua Bogia, Simbu valley (interviewer Joseph Mondo):

> The kiap said that the Japanese will come high like that (making action with his hands) and kill us all. They will come on planes. He told us to dig many big holes at Mondia. The holes are still there today.

Geregl Gande of Kerowagi (as reported by Paul Dage, 1986):

In the second world war, Geregl was taken to join the Australian troop, stationed in the highlands to fight the Japanese. They were taken to Eastern
Highlands towards the coast in Morobe province. The Japanese were based in
Nadzab area overlooking the countryside of the coast to their main base in
Buna in Northern Province where they attempt to head into the Australian
base Port Moresby. There was the famous Kokoda trail where the bloody dig
and hit battle resulted for the Japanese and the Australian great numbers of
soldiers died. . . . Geregl says he did not get involved in the real battle with the
Japanese but was patrolling while the war went on in the air with the Australian and Japanese planes.

Wamugl of Mintima described his experiences working for the Australians in World War II. For Wamugl, and a few others we met, World War II
was a life-altering experience, in its way comparable to those of some Americans who were interviewed on television during the fiftieth anniversary of
D-Day celebrations in June 1994. Along with a number of Simbu men,
Wamugl worked on roads, constructed airstrips, and was a carrier in the
highlands. They were taken to work in Rabaul on New Britain. When the
Japanese came, Wamugl and the other policemen buried guns and cargo in
the ground to hide them. Wamugl was shot at and ran away, forced to walk
in the bush without food for a long time. Then he found a house where a Japanese officer was living. When others ran away, Wamugl and some highlanders worked for the Japanese. They went to Rabaul during the bombing when
the Americans were coming. When the Australians took over again, they
were at first treated as traitors for helping the Japanese and jailed. After
Wamugl was recognized as Simbu and given some food and medicine, he
grew stronger and was allowed to return to Mintima, where he became a pidgin-speaking local leader until his death in 1990.[4]

A shift to military objectives and control is evident from the surviving
ANGAU reports of officers stationed in Kundiawa in 1943–1945. Whereas
concern for native development and peaceful penetration dominated the
interests of prewar Australian officers, reports of patrols conducted by the
ANGAU officers stationed in the highlands indicate that controlling the
spread of a dysentery epidemic was a major concern in 1944. The officers visited villages, instructed people in the proper construction of latrines,
reported on the state of houses, hygiene, health, and food supplies. Control
of the epidemic included a ban on native travel to other areas and forbade
participation in festivals as well as fighting.

The administration approved the building of rest houses in the rural areas for the assembly of local people and census-taking points where kiaps, police, and Simbu could meet. Tracks between them on the routes used by patrol officers were maintained by the local people. The system was used regularly until vehicles were commonly available to officers.[5] During World War II rest houses in the rural area were built, and some new ones established; roads were maintained and sometimes extended. Most officers included maps and census figures in reports.

The comments of G. Greathead, then an ANGAU officer overseeing the highlands, reflect prewar priorities. The area to be patrolled was that which had been under administrative supervision at the time of suspension of civil administration in 1942. This was a continuation of prewar policy that emphasized the pacification and control of tribal groups accessible to the main roads. Little could be known of the spread of dysentery into the unpatrolled areas. Greathead criticized the manner in which patrols were undertaken, advising the military officers to patrol less, and better control the patrolled areas. On these patrols all of the population were called to the rest house, lined up, and counted. But without earlier records no demographic information could result.[6] Some patrols investigated disturbances and dealt with disputes.

Some military officers were shocked by the behavior and living conditions of Simbu. In an attempt to improve hygiene and the standard of living they instructed the people to redesign houses so they would be higher, admit fresh air, and have a pitpit (P. cane) floor. They evidently did not realize that in the highlands low night temperatures, the fires, thick walls, and low roofs maintain warmth without clothing and blankets. One officer advised making an effort to get women to "refrain from sleeping with their livestock." There was some encouragement of concentrated settlement also.[7] In their census work some officers commented on changes in the birth rate and sex ratio, and lectured the inhabitants (through interpreters) on hygiene, architecture, and reproduction. It is hard to guess how this advice might have been taken. Officers stationed there later remarked upon the new house style that was promoted and followed in some areas. In the 1960s, misin ingu (S. mission-style houses) became popular when blankets were available.

Lt. Winterford noted in the Simbu valley (in May 1945)[8] that people were rebuilding. The patrol was given great quantities of food, which they were only able to compensate "frugally." When he found a low birth rate while conducting a census, he gave individual talks to women, telling them that the fighting was over and they had enough land and could now raise families. He reported that men said women were using contraceptives.[9]

In his patrol report on SinaSina and Dinga, Dennis (1945) observed that food was plentiful, gardens being built on 45–60-degree slopes with pitpit stakes. Latrines, he said, lacked covers. Another ANGAU officer observed that the whole area of Simbu was intensively cultivated and terraced. He thought the people were natural-born road builders: roads and bridges were well maintained and everyone was happy. In the Simbu valley, luluais Baka and Ambagawari were noted as being particularly good officials. One officer observed that the people were rebuilding and was given quantities of food. Health inspections found few cases of dysentery, but noted meningitis, frambesia, *kaskas* (P. scabies), leprosy, and venereal disease.

Certain Simbu behavior was objectionable to the military officers. The greetings of Ikedi and surrounding villages were rather embarrassing to Warrant Officer Dennis. The patrol was rushed by hordes of females and "leg hugging was freely given. . . . Advise anyone patrolling to wear long trousers . . . to combat the very intimate gestures." The officers found some villages dirty and commented that Danga and Dagl men continue to cover their bodies with pig grease and charcoal; houses were also filthy. When an officer found some bossboy "numbers" handed out by police and luluai, he demoted and removed officials.

In 1945 a government station was built at Minj in the Wahgi valley, and for a time an officer stationed there was responsible for the Simbu, with no officer at Kundiawa. The Simbu considered this a sign of lack of interest and reacted with tribal fights and neglect of roadwork. In 1946 the eastern highlands area was part of Morobe District; soon after, Simbu became a subdistrict of the newly created Eastern Highlands District, and Minj of Western Highlands District.

For some years after the end of World War II, Australian officers on patrol mentioned payments for war damage and losses; little was needed in Simbu. Among the Simbu, the lasting effect of the war appears to have been some recollection of preparations for invasion, bombing, and the employment of Simbu men as laborers. Postwar patrols attempted to continue prewar policies and expand the area of control, but in some areas the lack of continuous contact with patrols made the reestablishment of practices difficult; they found a very mixed group of unofficial and officially appointed luluais and bossboys, with some unrecorded and doubtful claims. These problems of continuity and control were to be confronted by the postwar Papua New Guinea administration.

Missions returned in force after 1946 and began to build stations, schools, and church buildings. The Lutheran practice of placing a mission teacher, now often a Simbu, in a settlement produced some difficulties observed by patrol officers. They encouraged the construction of village communities to enforce their instruction in proper Christian behavior. Lutherans asked their converts to wear clothing—laplap and "Mother Hubbard" blouses (which the patrol officers invariably found dirty)—to discard traditional ornaments, and to stop *carry-leg singsings* (P. courtship parties) and other traditional entertainments and rituals. The appropriation of land for mission bible schools and gardens took over scarce clan and privately held agricultural land, with little or no compensation. Some were said to spread antiadministration propaganda, calling the government satanic. The situation was investigated by C. Julius, a government anthropologist in the early 1950s, and conversion villages were soon restricted to designated mission lands.

Luluais and Tultuls

Tultuls in Simbu were headmen of groups of 150 to 250 people, usually corresponding to a subclan (Brown 1960); the census book confirmed the appointment and listed the families and individuals in the group. These census groups often combined or divided traditional clan segments and became effective units through the administration's assignments of responsibility. In 1958–1960 we heard contradictory statements of Naregu clan segmentation, because some informants followed the census units and others told us about traditional units and relationships.

Luluais were appointed for a large group, usually a tribe (sometimes called clan or phratry by the kiap and mission) of 1,200 to 3,500 people. Some of these officials appointed others (Warry 1987:70). In the 1940s and 1950s administration policy approved the appointment of paramount luluais for larger areas, and some were suggested for Simbu.

Comments from patrol reports for 1946–1948 show that the postwar government officials found a confused system and great differences in effectiveness and understanding. Patrols into little-contacted areas on the fringe of the area of control observed men eager for recognition but uninformed of the responsibilities of village officials, as these notes from patrol reports of 1946 show.

H. L. Williams Acting A.D.O.:

> Village officials—not clear what system adopted, not approved. Boss boys porcelain rings were sold by the Catholic and Lutheran missions; what is now worn as a badge of office often came to bearer in return for a bag of sweet potato and not as recognition of outstanding service or high status. These officials have never been competently appointed.
>
> Majority of bossboys appreciate their rights and duties, enthusiastic in work. New badge of office recommended; select most suitable natives.
>
> Approximately nine powerful and influential men have been properly appointed as luluais, mainly in eastern section.

Village officials system of "bossboys" not approved by DDS; not clear if pre-war or wartime measure. Bossboys claim legal redress for disobedience of their "legal" orders.

Because he wears the porcelain badge of office, he is automatically a power in his group, his original status within the group notwithstanding and it may be said of the majority of "boss-boys" that they have a better appreciation of their rights and duties and far more enthusiasm for their work than have their counterparts in controlled areas.

Suggest setting Village Official system on proper legal lines with new badge of office. Select suitable natives without regard for past "appointments." It would take seniority over present one. (Williams 1946)

V. F. Reitano, in the Upper Simbu:

Native officials: may be trouble. LL Baka of Goglme brought an offender of Nunu Yomani to justice, and he died in gaol. His people want payment from Baka; he refuses, is told to keep this. People and bossboys have threatened; they said they would go to Kundiawa. Baka is outstanding. Abakarowagi has been in prison twice, while he has a strong hold over his people he does not appear to be anxious to help the Govt. In fact he attempted to try-out the writer, asking him to bring three wives back, while husbands could not appear; tries to alter decisions on disputes. Bossboys satisfactory. (Reitano 1946)

There is a distinct difference in the role definition of luluai and tultul when the kiap and Simbu views are compared. The kiap regarded them as minor officials whose job was to accept orders and assist the administration as required; Simbu saw them as important new positions of authority. They were not in agreement on the responsibilities and success of the officials.

Simbu Statements about the First Luluais and Tultuls

Kutne Kura of Wandi, Naregu (interviewer Dilu Siune Robert):

The first headman, tultul, luluai were people who could talk out, were well built or were physically fit. Their wealth which includes many pigs, wives, many gardens etc was also counted. Generally speaking a person who was wealthy and who could talk was respected and that was how a big man came to being. Kutne said the tultuls and the luluai's role was to assist the kiaps and the police. They made sure there was no trouble in the village. They made sure everybody in a village respected and obeyed the kiap and the police.

Kutne appears to believe that the appointment was crucial in creating authority for officials and obedience by the people.

Gull of Endugwa (interviewer Harry Godfrid):

The kiaps appointed in each village tultul and luluais. I was a tultul then. Our job was to organize people to build roads, bridges, air strips, government posts, aid posts, etc. We also round up law breakers to face justice and so on.

Kua Bogia of Simbu valley (interviewer Joseph Mando):

I saw with my own eyes when the kiap appointed Kindua and Kangwa from the Siako clan to become tultuls. These two were leading men and fearless men of the clan. The two men were to assist the police and also the kiap. The kiap appointed well-known leadermen of the clans to become tultuls and luluais.

Observations in the 1950s

As administrative control and regular patrols extended throughout Simbu, the authority of luluais and tultuls increased. Some were very active in arbitrating disputes. Simbu responded to the suppression of warfare by turning to unofficial and local courts. The disputing parties or complainant and accused were brought to *kot* (P. a hearing, court) by their relatives and associates. Then they would speak of their dispute, with witnesses or others allowed to comment. Following this hearing, with general agreement as pronounced by the luluai, there might be a decision that the offender must make payments to the injured. Other luluai kot consisted in a first hearing prior to taking disputes to the kiap. Because tribal fighting or any kind of self-help was forbidden, and the native officials were responsible for bringing fights and killings to the attention of the police or kiap, their positions depended on their adherence to this rule. If the luluai really held the respect of his people, he succeeded, and it seems that disputes were referred to native officials quite often.

In practice, police and interpreters (P. *turnim tok*) often served as a second hearing. At patrol posts and in the forecourt of the government office, tultuls, luluais and the disputing parties discussed the case with them. They might either discourage (in effect, dismiss) a case or bring it to the kiap. The interpreters and Simbu police thus became mediators and legal advisors to the villagers, recommending compensation and ways to present cases to the kiap. They were rewarded for their advice by the people. The same police were local big men, who were expected to return these gifts when ceremonial distributions were held and might disappoint men who expected repayment in pork.

I found in the field that the very act of public discussion of a dispute or complaint was satisfying to the participants, and that in fact the kot system as it developed in Simbu was more a venue for public discussion than a legal procedure.[10] The public airing of complaints has continued in local disputes with elected councillors (P. *konsel*), ward committeemen (P. *komdi*) and (since 1976) local magistrates, as a first hearing, while the official court system and the established local magistrates' courts deal with the cases referred to them.

A luluai was usually the leading man of a large clan or tribe and a tultul the head of a segment of a clan. The chosen man continued as an official until death, retirement, or dismissal. After some years, an aged official could retire and might be replaced on his own recommendation, preferably by a pidgin-speaker. This was often a son of the official who had taken an opportunity to attend school and learn pidgin in order to take a job or a local leadership role. The privilege was clear, and the acceptance of sons as replacements for retiring officials implied that leadership positions were hereditary in Simbu. This became a belief in succession to office among Simbu, and now extends to elective office as well.

Tultuls would appear with members of their group for any hearings or service with the kiap, such as reporting for census, roadwork, and other administration business. In Simbu they did not always speak pidgin, but the men I knew were respected senior members of their groups. Comparing the style and activities of tultuls in the Mintima area in 1958, I found each to be a distinct personality (Brown 1974). If they had been given any specific instruction as to their duties, they saw them somewhat differently and pursued somewhat different goals. Tultuls would accompany the parties engaged in disputes to the luluai, police interpreter, or kiap and act as a sort of intermediary whether the case was within their group or, as was more common, involved another group. Each subclan at Mintima had an assigned segment of the highway or a side road to keep in order. Every Monday each tultul called his constituents to work cleaning drains and scraping the surface or, when necessary, repairing and helping with bridge replacement, on their section of the road. When roadwork pay was handed over by the kiap, the tultul received and distributed it to his group. Tultuls would sometimes accompany ailing members of their group to the medical-aid post or Kundiawa hospital.

In 1956, under Luluai Kondom's direction and the local supervision of tultuls, Naregu made communal coffee plots on each subclan's land, to be subdivided for individuals. Also at that time, when a school was being built at Wandi, school "councillors" assembled men to work cutting logs and sawing planks. Soon afterward, building of the local government council house and preparing the site at Wandi was also a matter of assembling a work force, as was Kondom's big project of clearing land for a massive tribal cash-crop

venture. During my first years at Mintima the men of Naregu seemed perpet-
ually on call for labor, and we wondered if they had time to prepare gardens
and replace houses. At that time some young men were away as migrant
laborers, and many were reprimanded for evading responsibilities, while the
dedicated few seemed always to be at work. Naregu caught gambling or
breaking the councillor's curfew were made to carry rocks and work at the
local government council site.

These new responsibilities and official recognition were unprecedented
in the traditional Simbu pattern of leadership (Brown 1974, 1979). Warry
observes: "The Duma paramount luluai was Mama, who people today say
ruled like a king: a leader whose power has never been equalled and against
whom men measure the authority of all subsequent leaders" (1987:72).

Backed by police rifles and kiap courts and jails, the native officials performed their duties and promoted the new rules of community pacification.
Their power rested mainly on the fear of administration sanctions (see Warry
1987:73–75). The defined realm and scope of authority, tribe, or subclan,
was unprecedented. At the time of my first field visit, most of the tultul units
were recognized as community groups, especially where they corresponded to
subclans. However, where they cut across traditional units there was much
confusion; the "book" (census book in which the names of persons of each
tultul group were listed) became an authority for membership, and was later
used as the list of electors and tax record. New wives and children were
entered into the books, and deceased members excised, when the kiap came
to take a new census. An officer patrolled each area, stopping in rest houses
each night on annual census patrols in the 1950s and 1960s.

The names of luluais and tultuls appear in patrol reports of the 1950s,
with comments on their performance and recommendations for dismissal or
replacement as the patrolling officer saw the situation. This of course meant
that an ambitious man did what he could to impress the officer with his
eagerness to follow directions and his abilities to bring out the people to
work on roads and other projects, to attend census and other meetings, to
settle disputes, to bring offenders to court, and to inform or persuade his
people to pursue whatever plan or program the government might be pro-
moting, such as health inspections, schools, labor recruitment, cash cropping, taxation, and so on. Big men had important functions in ritual,
intertribal relations, and ceremonial distributions. Many luluais and tultuls
were recognized as big men for community activities, and the ceremonial distributions at death and marriage were often directed by native officials.

The Catholic mission also appointed local leaders who would call
people to work on mission school or hospital buildings and attend services.
Leaders recognized by the mission were sometimes also called bossboys, and

as we have seen, some of these seemed to the kiap to have divided loyalties or to favor the mission and fail to obey the kiap. Mission appointees took some disputes, often marital quarrels, to the mission, and a division of loyalty arose when the problem lay properly under the jurisdiction of the government. Many natives and their leaders were confused about which issues should be considered by mission and which by the government. The areas with mission stations but no permanent kiap or police post often seemed to resist the kiap's orders, and people did not travel to the government post to report problems. There were many complaints that the mission teachers and police, as well as their superior officers and qualified mission representatives, interfered in local affairs and preached against the other. Mission rules concerning marriage, divorce, polygyny, and schooling affected everyone.

The luluai and tultul ranks in the 1950s were composed of ageing traditional leaders who had proved loyal to and supportive of the administration and a younger generation of "progressive" men with some knowledge of the world beyond Simbu. Recorded patrol officers' reports on individual native officials ranged from "excellent," efficient," "satisfactory," and "average," to "old and inefficient" and "useless." "Young, good worker, one of the few who can speak 'pidgin' " (Colman 1954) is a typical comment. This mix was balanced toward the younger men with each new appointment, and when local government councils were introduced in 1959 and later, knowledge of pidgin and a progressive outlook were essential to election. Their advancement was evident in their use of money, clothing, house styles, interest in coffee and cash crops, playing lucky (a card game), and later (when the law permitted the sale of liquor and beer to natives), drinking beer.

Some officers commented:

> As might be expected, considering that only two patrols have so far visited the area, the officials, with one or two notable exceptions, have little idea of what is required of them, or have any visible influence over their people, and remain more or less nonentities. (Keogh 1953:6)

> Four of the village officials in this census area were abusing their powers, while other officials were somewhat at a loss when it came to asserting their proper authority. (Mellor 1953:7)

> There were only two really outstanding luluais in both census areas. They are luluai Bage, of Gogme, and luluai Abakarawagi of Kangere. Both are officials of long standing, and are real powers of leadership, and are also loyal servants of the administration. Their authority is not confined to their own tribal groups, indeed, it has extended throughout the entire Chimbu valley. It would be hard to find any official in the Chimbu Sub-district who could match either of these luluais. (Mellor 1953:12)

Luluais appear to be doing their job well. Head and shoulders above the rest is ENDIMONGO of ENDUGA. He is very much liked and extremely respected by everyone. His success can be attributed largely to an objective approach and obvious fairness. He can certainly talk a great deal but does so intelligently. (Gauci 1954:4)

In the Maril, Salt, Nomani, and Upper Bomai in the mid-1950s, there were many bossboys remaining from previous official and unofficial appointments who were being weeded out; officers recommended appointments of tultuls and luluais to regularize administration by approved officials. Officers often commented on individual officials in the area: "Speaks pidgin and has plenty of authority, however, does not take enough interest in affairs." "Has the hereditary standing." "He is the only one with any real authority but his past doings are very questionable. Under supervision it is felt that SIBA would be all right." "Speaks pidgin. Was of great assistance. Is the most outstanding person in the SALT" (Haywood: 1955a:10 appendix).

Here are some remarks on officials in Dom and Sinasina:

Will soon need to be replaced; old and reformed now; inclined to be argumentative; does not impress; not good enough; good; well above average; suspended for one month; failed to appear on call; in gaol for fighting; absent on a buying spree; fair. (Haywood 1955b: appendix)

Village Officials: Most of these gentlemen can be grouped together and labelled "unimpressive and lacking in initiative." There are a few outstanding officials, notably luluai Kondom, who has received mention in previous patrol reports. Admittedly he is inclined to allow his authority to run wild on occasions, but there is no lack of enthusiasm on his part and many of the other officials could do worse than follow his example. I feel that it is an easier task to curb someone who is a little over zealous, than to try to whip up interest and enthusiasm in someone who lacks these requisite basic characteristics. . . . Coffee land surveyed on this patrol. Kondom built a "haus kibung" [P. meetinghouse] at Wandi and road meetings were conducted there in 1955 (see books). Great pig feast end of 1956. (Seefeld 1956:5–6)

The responsibilities and official recognition were unprecedented in the traditional Simbu pattern of leadership. Backed by police rifles and kiap courts and jails, luluais and tultuls performed their duties and promoted the new rules of community pacification. The tribe, clan, or subclan had never been a seat of authority, but Simbu quickly accepted the census unit as a basis of group definition.

In the 1950s people in central Simbu were familiar with and accepted the authority of the Australian administration, but they continued to fear kiaps and police. For example, in my first days at Mintima I found climbing up a steep slope difficult and suggested that the people accompanying me to a gathering go on ahead. They said they dared not: if anything happened to me the police and kiap would kill them. My daily food requirements were shouted to the neighborhood by one of the leading men, and foods were were usually paid for in spoonfuls of salt. Sticks of trade tobacco and sheets of newspaper were used for gifts and some payments, such as house repairs. Only a full-time worker or a large quantity of firewood was paid for in money. This practice was replaced by small money payments in the 1960s, as there were local trade stores selling tools, clothing, kerosene, foods, and tobacco. There was a passionate rush for any of my broken or discarded goods, furnishings, containers, metal, or clothing.

In this period, 1946–1960, everything belonging to the white man (P. *masta*) was desirable and the kiap's orders were paramount; this lent authority to native officials. Kondom was an exceptional case who conveyed his interpretation of the *govman* (P. government) to all Simbu (Brown 1963).

Medical Training and Service in the Community

A special category of "medical tultuls" was developed by the German administration of New Guinea prior to World War I and then renamed "aid post orderlies" by the Australian administration. After World War II a two-year training course was given to medical workers in government schools, and some mission-trained orderlies also were employed. The program was developed to place aid posts in rural areas where first aid and some medication for common diseases were dispensed and, when possible, to arrange for the transport of serious cases to hospitals for treatment. The orderlies were not usually called "tultul" and the health service was separated from civil administration. The first aim was to have immediately available health workers in rural areas where they could speak the local language and provide immediate service and contact with medical professionals in hospitals (Radford and Speer 1986).

At the time of my first visit the local aid post was popularly used; the favorite treatment was a "shoot" (shot of penicillin), and injuries and malaria were often taken there for bandaging and medication. Women in labor were taken to nearby mission or government hospitals, while more distant communities continued to build birth huts for parturition. Medical orderlies stationed in rural areas were in charge of aid posts or attached to station hospitals. Some accompanied patrols and examined the ill, treating some cases and sending others to station hospitals. Serious cases had to be carried to a hospital.

Paraka Kombugu of Kup (interviewer Moses Parkay):

> After the war I was enlisted to become a medical orderly. Those of us who were enlisted did our basic training in Goroka. After our basic training we were posted all over the highlands provinces. No roads, no means of transportation we had to walk to where we were posted to. Life was very difficult.

Patrols

In 1941 a vehicular road was built from Chimbu post to the Mingende mission and then to the Wahgi river crossing, where a bridge was built and the track from Chimbu to Hagen was maintained. The highway was not constructed for many years, and only in the 1950s were four-wheel-drive vehicles in common use by government and mission. Many areas could only be reached by foot tracks, improved over the years.

Eastern Highlands District headquarters were in Goroka, a hub of business activity for government, air service, and developing agriculture and coffee plantations, and a center for schools, health services, and missions. In the 1950s Kundiawa, headquarters of Chimbu Subdistrict, was served by a small airstrip and a dirt highway: landslides and bridge washouts interrupted traffic frequently. An Assistant District Officer was posted there, with a varying support staff. Although the Simbu might recognize the authority of the officer in charge, all were kiaps. Young men were recruited in Australia and given a short course at the Australian School of Pacific Administration (ASOPA). They served a term as cadet patrol officers in the field and then returned to a long course, after which they would become patrol officers and were given greater responsibilities.

Substations or patrol posts were established at Chuave (1953), Kerowagi (1954), Gumine (1955), Gembogl (1959), and Karimui (1960); these, some police posts and base camps, schools, medical and other facilities were not fully or continuously staffed. Elementary and religious education and some medical services were provided by missions. Patrols were irregular in the large and little populated southern area (Hide et al. 1984). Some people of the Bomai division saw their first patrols in the 1950s, and just as the northern Simbu people in the 1930s and 1940s had, held them in awe, lavished gifts on them, or ran away. Great differences in attitude and expectations were noted in the patrol reports of the 1960s in these areas, which

were to become districts of Simbu Province in the 1980s. For some highlanders, then, there were very few years before independence.

By the early 1950s a characteristic form of colonial dependence was
established in the northern and central Simbu area. Both missions and the
government had greatly influenced the behavior and attitudes of the people.
Simbu continued to seek gifts and payments through many means—
exchange for native foods and products, offers of work, labor on roads,
employment as domestics or laborers—and asked for gifts as reward for
friendship and good behavior. The dominance of western institutions and
culture was evident in their acceptance of church and schools. Mission-educated natives were most often chosen for official positions and for employment. Gifts and payments were usually given to men, except when women
sold foodstuffs. Generally, where records are available, about one-quarter of
the pupils in school are girls. The mission welcomed women and many children were baptized at Mingende.

Patrols into the hinterlands of Chimbu Subdistrict (South Simbu) often
found groups with little experience of native administration. They endeav-
ored to bring these groups under control as it was regularized in the 1950s.
Building, planning, and maintaining roads were discussed by every officer in
patrol reports. Natives were asked to work one day each week for a small payment. Road-making machinery, experienced supervisors, and modern materials were only rarely available in the 1950s and 1960s. The highlands
highway from Kainantu to Hagen was vehicular by 1952–1953; government
and mission jeeps and landrovers were soon in use. Side roads were mostly
tracks of varying width and navigability. Horses were used by some missionaries, and motorbikes by some government officers on patrol. Few Simbu had
an opportunity to ride; this was a rare privilege sometimes granted to officials
and employees. I often saw men frantically waving at the roadside, hoping
that a driver would assume an emergency and offer a ride.

Although Goroka and Mount Hagen were relatively well supplied with
special services and officers, it was some years before an agricultural extension officer was posted to Chimbu Subdistrict to direct crop improvement,
cash-crop establishment, coffee planting, care, and marketing. Simbu was
always a densely populated native area with no surplus land that could be
allocated for settlement and development by expatriate enterprise.

Patrol officers had a wide range of routine responsibilities, conducted
patrols throughout the subdistrict, and were often given special assignments
by their superior officers. Administrative priorities of the day might be war
reparations (in the 1940s), boundary marking, afforestation, political instruction, cash-crop development, inspection of mission schools and leases,
roads and bridges, the condition of rest houses, resolution of disputes, review

of native officials, or health; each patrol is preceded by letters of instruction from headquarters and district officers.

A patrol diary noted the location and movements of each day, and sections reported local conditions and observations about schools, missions, attitudes, roads, and other matters. Simbu of the "inner area" had seen many patrols since first contact in 1933. By 1950 there was a standardized pattern in which luluais and tultuls were informed that a patrol would be coming and be instructed to meet it. They were required to assemble their entire constituency of subclan or clan at the appropriate rest house. Village official appointments were regularized: the village book became an official document as it recorded the families' and members' names, estimated ages, population counts, and any special notes made by the patrol officers concerning roads, food and water supplies, and advice given officials.

The luluais and tultuls at each stop brought the persons whose disputes (for example, over marriage, debts, divorce, fighting, insults, land, livestock) were unresolved to the patrol officer for arbitration by the officer and eventual agreement by the parties. Serious cases of assault, fighting, major theft, and homicide were to be taken to the appropriate court.

The patrol officer and his retinue stopped at each rest house for one or more nights. Besides taking an annual census according to the village books, they lectured the people on government affairs and policy, election procedures, regulations and responsibilities; urged peace and good behavior; introduced any medical or other attached personnel; proposed new projects for development and cash crops; and distributed seeds of European fruits and vegetables. They often stated, "The Blue Ensign[11] was flown at all rest houses visited, and each evening the village officials were invited to take part in the ceremony of lowering the flag, with the patrol party" (Fowler 1952:11).

Some kiaps inspected villages, houses, latrines, and sanitary facilities; they commented upon village affairs, health, and hygiene. In the 1950s officers often questioned the natives about practices and customs, composing an "anthropological" section of the report devoted to myths of origin, group structure, housing, succession, kinship terms, marriage practices, and observations of any ceremonies in progress at the time. Only a few of the later patrol reports on little-known areas contain this section. Such inquiries might be the subject of assignments made to junior officers in the correspondence courses for native administration. The condition of roads and bridges was observed and reported, with some discussion of the payment which should be given for roadwork, and recommendations made. The officers reported on agriculture, crops, food supplies, the missions and their schools. Native officials and the native situation were evaluated. The report contained remarks about the patrol's reception by local people and comments—for example, "proadministration," "filthy," "litigious," or "indolent."

The government sponsored particular projects from time to time. For example, reafforestation (sic) was urged upon all Eastern Highlands people in the 1950s, despite the many Simbu areas where consideration of land shortage would raise doubts of the appropriateness of this policy. Often the patrol had a special assignment to check on land-lease applications, mission activities, and schools. Some officers presented their opinions on problems and proposed solutions, such as teaching people sounder methods of cultivation, crop rotation, and a better land-use system. These reports were read and commented upon by the Subdistrict Officer (A.D.O.), the District Officer (D.O.) and/or District Commissioner (D.C.), and the Director of District Services and Native Administration. Comments ranged from approval of the conduct and writing to criticism of the patrol as not having devoted adequate time to the native situation or expression of the need for the writer to improve his spelling. Suggestions and recommendations of the officer who wrote the report and/or one of the superior officers might be approved by a higher authority.

Administration sometimes made specific rules for an area. For example, in 1957 a three-year ban on the burning of kunai grass in preparing gardens was imposed, and Patrol Officers were required to announce it. The Acting District Officer commented on a report, "Burning is bad." Later the same officer commented that "native agriculture is not improved by agricultural officers," and the Director of District Services and Native Affairs retorted that native practice is the product of long experience in their area.

Every patrol was accompanied by an interpreter, native constables, and sometimes a native noncommissioned officer. Each of these was named, and his conduct evaluated, in the report. For example, a constable might be said to be good at controlling natives, getting things done, or to lack initiative or perform adequately; their informal power or alliances in communities were not usually a subject for comment. Police constables or officers were sometimes put in charge of a police post or base camp where their contacts with natives might develop further. Native attitudes toward these policemen are not often known, but several of my interviews suggest that they were wary of them after their first experiences of punishment for fighting and using guns. In a report on one official interpreter, it was said: "TONGIA ... accompanied the patrol. . . . He is an experienced and capable native. TONGIA'S best asset is the ability to understand how a European looks at a problem" (Haywood 1955c:14).

The Simbu had great interest in and desire for shells and western manufactured goods, especially cloth and steel. Trade and use of parrot and cassowary feathers, and plumes and feathers of birds of paradise did not depend directly upon patrol visits. However, the opening of roads and freedom of movement that followed pacification and administrative control made the travel of small trading parties possible. Migrant laborers found that plumes highly valued in the highlands were far cheaper on the coast and used their money for such purchases. Simbu traders were known widely in the highlands and surrounding forest areas, trading plumes for money or pigs (Bulmer 1962). The Simbu and Wahgi areas maintained a demand for exchange goods into the 1960s.

A great contrast was observed by officers when the formerly "outer" Simbu, little patrolled and restricted areas to the south of the longer contacted tribes, was visited in the 1950s. By this time many men of the "inner" group had contracted with the Highlands Labour Scheme as migrant laborers to other parts of the island, and all had long experience of patrols, missions, and the rule of the kiaps. Natives outside this area knew of most of these things only by hearsay, and some were wary of or resistant to the first patrols. Visits to South Simbu in the 1950s found that trade and the influence of returned laborers and other Simbu were exploiting some of the Bomai people. On subsequent visits, officers often noted the same sort of enthusiastic welcome and presentation of food that had greeted officers fifteen or twenty years earlier in the Simbu valley. This time lag in experience is in some ways still evident; for schools, medical facilities, cash crops, roads, and communications are relatively less developed in South Simbu (Hide 1984), cash crops and money are scarce, and more people migrate to work in towns outside their home area: "The Maril River natives have not had the close contact with the Administration as enjoyed by other areas. This patrol found them to be rather stubborn, argumentative, and slightly unwilling to co-operate. Whilst it is a natural Chimbu custom to be argumentative and roudy [sic] this lack of co-operation should be overcome" (Haywood 1955d:3).

Maps drawn by Vial in 1938–1939 were interpreted by the government as fixed tribal areas. The principle followed was that the lands occupied at the time of first contact should be permanent tribal territories. Ian Downs, as District Commissioner, would not consider modifying these lines of demarcation. In fact, Simbu land has long been densely populated; intertribal boundaries and frontiers were contested; intertribal relations often involved unoccupied battlegrounds and boundary wars. Since the imposition of Vial's marks, boundary disputes among tribes have not ceased. One of the tasks of patrol officers in the 1950s was to inspect and encourage the planting of rows of trees to mark these boundaries. Thus tribal territory was fixed by the administration. Patrol reports in the 1950s deplored the failure to plant trees as required; however, few officers seemed to take this to be native resistance

to the government's defining of tribal boundaries as at the time of first contact, or as opposition to the boundary placement. Rather, they redoubled
their efforts to enforce conformity by repeating patrols and lecturing. Every
kiap had some training in map drawing, and every patrol report was accompanied by a map based on the current government base map. Land disputes
were noted by patrol officers, who attempted to resolve some of them (Hide
1973:11–28).

A long-term tribal land dispute was the subject of comment:

> Some dissatisfaction still exists amongst the people of the section of the GENA
> Group, living in the Koronigl valley, over three land boundaries to the North
> with the SIAMBUGA-WAUKU Group, to the West with the SIKU Group
> and to the South with the SIAMBUGA-WAUGA Group. This section of the
> GENA Group originally lived higher in the hills to the West and during the
> days when they were a war-like people they descended into the areas of the
> three before mentioned Groups and forced the people to flee. After the advent
> of the Government the three Groups gradually returned to their former lands
> though the GENAS still retained a large section of them. The land boundaries
> were marked several years ago and at the time the GENAS were dissatisfied
> with the decisions because they considered that they did not give them suffi-
> cient land on which to live; the SIKUS were dissatisfied partly because some of
> the land which originally belonged to them was given to the GENAS and
> partly because they considered the decision did not give them sufficient land to
> live on; the SIAMBUGA-WAUGAS were dissatisfied mainly because some of
> the ground which originally belonged to them was given to to the GENAS.
> (Bailey 1954a:7)

The Eastern Highlands Land Titles Commissioner was rarely able to
visit Simbu and examine conflicting claims. Native land committees established some years later failed to resolve many disputes (Hide 1973). Many
Australian officers and the several land courts and Lands Commissioners'
investigations on these and other similar conflicting claims to land and territory show them to be a continuing source of intergroup tension. When land
decisions transferred land from one group to another, the former occupiers
were compensated for trees and crops by the government, but not for the
land itself. Today Simbu continue to fight over land; land disputes combine
with other sources of intergroup conflict. Dense population and unavailabil-
ity of new areas for expansion within Simbu are permanent restrictions on
growth, development, and rural enterprise. Many Simbu land conflicts have
proven to be unresolvable, frequently renewed, underlying grievances in disputes between members of the several groups, and an element in many fights.

Several wars can be partly attributed to these continuing disagreements, and the modern state system has been unable to prevent intertribal fighting.

In the 1950s the dependence of Simbu was well established, a product of local conditions and general policy. Both Simbu and I see this period as one of great moves toward self-government and economic development. The dependent phase was, and still is, a time of important achievements through the white man's introduction of goods and activities. The paternalism of mission and government was approved by almost everyone in the rural areas.

The introduction of schools, health services, and agricultural development depended upon government and mission, and the Simbu had little opportunity to observe the effects of private enterprise in the European centers of Goroka and Mount Hagen. The difference in economic development was most striking. Because of the dense population, the government ruled that there should be no land alienation, no European entrepreneurs, and it followed that there were no advanced economic or technological models for Simbu. To the east, expatriate Australians began to develop businesses and acquire large tracts of land for coffee and cattle, using western techniques of stocking and marketing. These have developed into large commercial building complexes and ownership by joint partnerships of Goroka businessmen and highlands entrepreneurs (Finney 1973, 1986). In the early years there was only small-scale commercial business based on community, clan, or contract. Government policy in 1950s did not allow sizeable loans to native business development, withholding opportunity. Native land had no mortgage value.[12] It is only recently that the Simbu of Mintima have transferred land for money, and this has usually been for government roads and roadside sites for shops.

From 1950, in order to get support for secular teaching, mission schools were required to follow an approved curriculum and teach in English. Most of the early Simbu leaders learnt pidgin and received elementary schooling in mission schools. Patrol officers in the 1950s often commented that school attendance was poor, and the standard of education also poor. Some told parents to encourage their children to attend, but at that time many parents did not see the value of education. In 1955 it was observed that the Lutheran Rev. Hueter (an American) of Monono mission was in control of schools and "is doing excellent work in trying to overcome some of the more obvious weaknesses in the schooling system of the Mission, and has introduced some secular subjects into the school curricula. He is also keeping a close watch on the activities of his evangelists, which is already paying dividends" (Mellor 1955:5).

Simbu Initiatives in 1958–1960

In 1959–1960 a new government initiative brought primary schools to rural areas. The program was accelerated through recruitment of expatriate teachers often unfamiliar with Pidgin English. In rural areas some were housed in furnished prefabricated aluminum houses supplied with electric generators and other modern conveniences. English was taught and there were new opportunities for Simbu to gain further education for employment, not only as religious teachers. Government high schools as well as the Catholic Rosary High School at Kondiu were boarding schools in several locations. In the first years these schools were the entrée to further job training, but in the 1970s and later only a small proportion of high-school students could continue on to occupational training and jobs. Simbu today see schools as their route to success in every field, but this has not often been attained (Brown 1987a). School "dropouts" are common and underemployed (Rambo 1993).

The relationships between individual Simbu leaders, luluais, tultuls, and others and the kiaps, police, and missionaries, could make for complex interpretations of rules and practices. For example, marital conflicts and divorces are viewed differently by a mission that prohibits divorce, a government that seeks to avoid intergroup conflict, and the Simbu concern for the return of bride-price payments. Interpreters, and a few police, were Simbu, with friends and relatives in the area often being parties to cases in which the interpreter or policeman might hope to influence the decision. The police gained great power over the local people.

When I observed the leadership and entrepreneurship of Kondom in Simbu in 1958–1965, he was taken on visits and had opportunities to see and copy development projects elsewhere. Kondom often said that he waited for the government to tell him what to do and that it showed him what he could do and have. When some successful Simbu entrepreneurs were buying cars, a very high-prestige item, Kondom said he waited for the administration to permit him to do so. He built a stone house and used finished timber in another as models for the Simbu. The Kondom legend today (Brown 1990) cites him as a great leader who in his work and demonstrations showed the Simbu the way to progress and business, developed roads, and introduced coffee.

White residents took on assistants and employees on the advice of established trusted native favorites. For example, my first house servant turned out to be a totally inept relative of the chief interpreter, a member of a traditional enemy tribe of my hosts. I soon became aware of the problem— my health suffered—but could not easily replace him with a better-trained local helper.[13]

There arose in Simbu some new forms and practices of gift exchange and compensation payment that monetized and applied in cases of accidental death in highway accidents, drunken fights, injuries in brawls, and property damage (see Podolefsky 1987).

In Simbu thinking, gifts establish a reciprocal exchange relationship that should be honored on appropriate occasions. By 1958 some precontact valuables such as dog's-teeth necklaces were no longer accepted in marriage payments. Steel knives and axes were popular marriage gifts as substitutes for stone axes in the 1950s, then were disdained as gifts and became ordinary household tools. Later, when money became the main item, only a few types of plumes were acceptable and also used in dance festivals. Plastic jewelry, beads, and decorated belts were worn by many Simbu but not used in payments. The value of pigs has grown greatly, and pigs are essential in most ceremonial payments, as well as being the center of the large *bugla ingu* festival. Shovels, which had no precontact equivalent in the exchange system, were to my knowledge never used as gifts. Shells, too, were of decreasing acceptability; first the tambu-shell headbands were refused, and then goldlip and bailer declined. Increasingly, money took the place of all other goods, and the amount of money demanded by a bride's family has soared. Today the families, when friendly, exchange pigs and feast together on purchased foods; all-important is the money payment.

Funeral payments, too, had been lavish in local produce—vegetable foods and pigs—with some valuables being given to relatives of the deceased person (Brown 1961). But elaborate funeral exchanges have become rare. The large-scale food exchanges, *mogena biri*, between tribes have increasingly required money gift displays and the purchase of imported foods, beef, and beer. The tribal *bugla gende* feasts, which require the building of many men's houses at ceremonial grounds and huge houses for guests, have become infrequent. These traditional exchange activities are now of little interest to Simbu, while those which are enjoyed today are increasingly monetized with cash payments, the purchase of goods, imported foods, frozen meat, and beer.

The image of colonial benevolence was fostered by Australian administrators, reporters, and historians (McCarthy 1963; Simpson 1964; Sinclair 1981). United Nations investigating teams generally made favorable reports of colonial relations and development, and before 1965 there were few Papua New Guineans who were sufficiently educated and familiar with other colonial situations to respond differently. The advances enabled by the colonial introduction of western-manufactured goods, cash, agriculture, and medical services were enjoyed by highlanders, and they perpetuated the image of benevolence. Furthermore, they saw the government as having ended tribal warfare, with its feared dangers, insecurity, and erosion of community life. It was not until the 1970s and later, when educated Papua New Guinea people learned about anticolonial movements in third world countries, that a different viewpoint developed among younger people. Most of the generation of highlanders who were born before 1950 and never attended school became loyal colonial supporters. When independence was first discussed, in the 1960s, few highlanders could advocate it. Many accepted their subaltern, dependent status for they saw (and for the most part correctly) that they were unprepared for the responsibilities of self-government, and they feared that the more advanced peoples of the coastal areas, who had longer experience of education and administrative responsibility, would reap all the jobs and benefits of independence. Several important developments—the Highlands Labour Scheme, cash crops, and local government councils—began in the 1950s.

Buga Ambukwa, Simbu Valley headman. This important fight leader (also called Ambagara) became one of the first government-appointed Luluais. In 1935 he wore a headdress of cassowary and other feathers, a net cap, woven armbands, and many varieties of shell in necklaces, head and nose ornaments. Photo C. B. (Pat) Walsh 1935, by permission of Bob Ennor, Brisbane; copies courtesy of Bill Gammage, Adelaide.

Girl at Chimbu-Wahgi police post, 1935. She is wearing mother of pearl shells and cowries, a decorated net bag, and woven armbands. Photo C. B. (Pat) Walsh, by permission of Bob Ennor, Brisbane, copy courtesy of Bill Gammage, Adelaide.

Man in cassowary headdress decorated in shells, with shield, bow, and arrows. The shields were carried by men in open battle to deflect arrows, as this man demonstrates in 1935. In the background, a fence of vertical stakes joined by horizontal pieces that are tied to the stakes with strips of bamboo and reed. Photo C. B. (Pat) Walsh, by permission of Bob Ennor, Brisbane; copy courtesy of Bill Gammage, Adelaide.

Fr. Morschheuser's grave, 1935. This grave has been maintained and decorated with flowers continuously since 1935. Photo C. B. (Pat) Walsh, by permission of Bob Ennor, Brisbane; copy courtesy of Bill Gammage, Adelaide.

Father Ross with C.P.O. John Murphy at Mount Hagen, October 1936. Photo from Murphy files, Fryer Library, University of Queensland.

Boys at school for interpreters, Chimbu-Wahgi post, 1936. This was the first school for interpreters and brought its students from several areas and language groups to prepare them for interpreting between their home language and Pidgin. Murphy was a gifted linguist who wrote a dictionary of Pidgin English. Photo from Murphy files, Fryer Library, University of Queensland.

Market at Kundiawa, 1936. Vegetable foods and sugar cane stalks were brought to the Chimbu post and sold as food supplies for station personnel. Photo John Murphy.

Man dressed in netted apron and cap and woman dressed in string skirt with shell bands. Large terraced gardens stretch up the mountainside behind them. Simbu valley, 1936. Photo E. W. P. Chinnery collection, Museum of Victoria, Melbourne.

Group of Simbu of Goglme highly decorated wearing goldlip mother of pearl, nassa and cowrie shell necklaces, headbands, and nose decorations, woven rattan armbands, woven rattan belts, string skirts, netbags, feathers, bangle headbands. Women carry many goods in netbags suspended from their foreheads: babies, food, garden implements, firewood. 1936. Photo E. W. P. Chinnery collection, Museum of Victoria, Melbourne.

Kaglwaim tultul in 1958. Kaglwaim had been a leading warrior and had several wives in 1958, when he was tultul for two subclans in Naregu tribe. In the 1980s, with only one surviving wife, he became a devout member of the Catholic church at Mingende. Photo Paula Brown.

A marriage payment in the 1960s. Large wooden display boards are decorated with shells and feathers and carried by the groom's clansmen to the bride's home. In the 1960s traditional marriage payments of dog's teeth necklaces were replaced with shells and stone axes had been displaced by steel axes. Money is increasingly important, while plumes and shells have declined and disappeared from marriage payments. Pork and live pigs are part of the marriage exchange. Pork is carried separately and laid on leaves at the base. Photo Paula Brown.

Young divorcée insists on keeping her pigs, 1962. The marriage was made by the elders of two clans in Naregu tribe while the husband was away at work. The wife did not work for his parents, as she was expected to, and on his return the husband demanded a divorce. The marriage payment had been dispersed long ago and could not be recalled, but there was a continued dispute over the pigs given to the wife to raise, and she wanted to keep them. The men of her subclan could not persuade her to give them back. Photo Paula Brown.

Voting, 1963. A tent is set up for privacy. A woman voter tells her choice to an interpreter and it is recorded by Australian officer in a "whisper" ballot. This woman is carrying several netbags on her daily rounds of gardening and harvesting. Photo Paula Brown.

Kondom addressing a crowd, 1964. He is a member of the Legislative Council and tells about his visit to Australia, describing the streets and buildings in an Australian city. He said of elevators: "you go into a little room and the doors close. When the doors open you are in a different place." Photo Paula Brown.

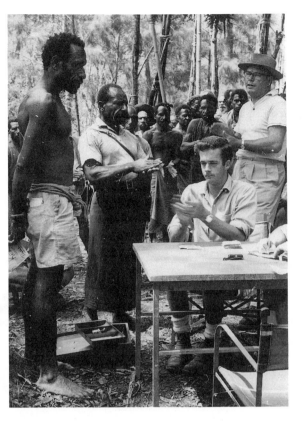

Kondom and Australian officers collecting subscriptions to the Kundiawa Coffee Society cooperative, 1964. As each subscriber joins, the crowd applauds. Photo Paula Brown.

Ninmongo, one of the Catholic church's leading women members of the Legion of Mary, leads a prayer in her home area for people in the locality, 1984. Photo Paula Brown.

Wamugl and Chimbu Players dividing up their payment for tourist entertainment, 1984. Wamugl was among the first men to speak Pidgin and joined government forces in World War II. After the war he was a prominent local leader and entrepreneur, coffee grower, shopkeeper, councillor, and manager of the Chimbu Players, staging performances for visiting groups of tourists at Iwagl. Photo Paula Brown.

Peter Kuman, politician, Member of Parliament 1984. Became Member of Parliament (Regional) for Simbu Province 1987. After provoking violence in his home area he became a fugitive. Photo Paula Brown.

Iambakey Okuk addressing crowd after 1984 Provincial Assembly elections. He spoke in favor of making the newly elected members to join his National Party and make it the leader in Provincial Assembly. Photo Paula Brown.

Paula Brown with Bomaiambo Clara and daughter Rose, Maria and daughter Paula Brown Witni, and other people in a farewell party at Bamugl, 1984. Photo Harold Brookfield.

A woman receives gifts for her family at a distribution of feast foods. These were purchased for this occasion and include many tins of fish and meat, packages of biscuits, cartons of food. 1964. Photo Paula Brown.

8

Old Ways to New

"When you first came to Mintima we had nothing; now everyone has clothes and goods. Next time you come, everyone will wear shoes." These words were spoken to me by Francis Nokuk when I returned to Mintima in 1984, eight years after my previous visit.

This chapter will be a general overview of changes in Simbu life after World War II: the influences of mission, schools, and government-sponsored programs upon political institutions, economic and technological developments, labor, training, and cash crops.[1] It combines my observations at Mintima and throughout Simbu, archival records, interviews, and other reports.

Downs (1980) divides postwar Australian colonial government in Papua New Guinea into three eras. The first is postwar reconstruction, 1945–1951, in which war reparations were paid and administration reestablished. In the highlands, patrols penetrated areas that had been rarely contacted before 1942. The Menzies government and Hasluck as Minister for Territories in 1951–1963 promoted economic development and cash crops, elected local government councils, and extended the Legislative Council to include some elected members and native representatives. The following period, with Barnes as minister, established the House of Assembly and increased elected representation in preparation for self-government and independence in the 1970s.

My field research in the years 1958–1965, and later visits, is amplified by the reports of government officers and other observers. I lived at the Mintima rest house, and later Wandi and Bamugl in the Naregu tribe, and paid short visits to other Simbu and highlands sites. Mission and government influence and control in various parts of the highlands, and within Simbu Province, are of uneven intensity and length of time. Some areas had missions and/or prospectors before government posts; access to health services, schools, roads, agricultural extension officers, courts, job opportunities, missionaries of various denominations, and other kinds of outside influence and contact differ for areas, tribes, and individuals. The memories and experiences reported by Simbu add another dimension to my account of change. From the Naregu standpoint of my fieldwork, this is the era of Kondom, who is responsible for coffee as the chief business of Simbu and for elected government.

Family and Domestic Life

The Simbu family and community center around patrilineal local groups. Land is the most important value and source of group identity; tribal and family history are linked to places and the defense of territory. The land of a family lies in several parcels within clan territory, and houses may be scattered in this territory. Often a house where pigs stay at night is adjacent to pig-browsing bushland. Each family has several active gardens in which they cultivate a subsistence crop of sweet potatoes and grow a variety of fruits and vegetables. The sexual division of labor and activity makes men responsible for land ownership and garden preparation, house and fence building, and most tool making. Women's main tasks are child rearing, food growing and preparation, pig care and feeding, and the making of most fiber materials and clothing. Adults and children may gather and carry firewood, water, and other materials within the communal territory.

The separate men's house is a social center where Simbu men meet, sleep, and plan to pursue group goals. The men's groups, ordered into tribe, clan, subclan, and smaller segments, are arenas of exchange, competition, and big-man prestige. Simbu wives, born into one clan and married to men of the local group, rarely participate in men's discussions, and live separately; they are family producers who join the local group to celebrate their relationships to kin and affines during visits and exchanges. Their independence is expressed in personal and private affairs, not as directors in group exchanges.

These basic conditions persist in new contexts. Modernization in Papua New Guinea owes most of its impetus to western colonial and introduced economic, educational, governmental, and legal institutions. Simbu have known missionaries, government administrators, traders, and employers. They attend schools and hospitals, vote in local, provincial, and national elections, grow coffee for export and cash crops to sell at markets, and migrate to work outside Simbu Province. Many of the rules of behavior and belief that elders recall are no longer binding on young Simbu, who quote school and mission as their authorities. The impact of these modernizing forces is strongest near mission and government headquarters and along main roads; traditional ways persist in remote rural sections of the province.

In the 1980s I could distinguish three generations or cohorts. The oldest was born before contact, whether this was in 1933 or years later. These men and women were raised as Simbu, and most have childhood memories of periods of hunger, fear of enemy attack, personal and community insecurity, and tribal warfare. Girls were controlled by parents and taught formal courtship behavior by older girls. The oldest Simbu, especially women, have had little opportunity to travel and little contact with foreigners. Some, close to missions, have become adherents and are greatly influenced by the church (see Ninmongo life story in Chap. 9; Christie 1980).

Kaglwaim, a renowned former warrior, was a respected elder and long-standing tultul when I first met him in 1958 at Mintima, Naregu. His statements over the years reveal changing views of the past and new values. Interviewed by Bruce Mondo Kair in 1987, he said: "My first and second wives died and my third wife is with me now. I got baptised to be fully a Christian and so am living like a Christian as what I've promised in Baptism. Hence, I don't know when I'll finish or die but am trying my very best to live like a devoted Christian."

Members of this older generation made a great transition in the colonial period and have now for the most part retired from political activity. The cohort includes the first government interpreters and police, and some of the first mission adherents. Although very few of them had any schooling, their children had some opportunities through the mission. Young and middle-aged Simbu men and women have not experienced tribal warfare, hunger, and fear of enemies as did this older generation.

A second, colonially raised generation of men may have had some mission education and work experience on roads as contract laborers or as migrants on plantations and spoke pidgin in 1958. Several were our close associates at Mintima. From among these middle-aged and young married men the councillors and local leaders were selected by their constituents in the 1960s. Women of this age group rarely went to school: their social life is limited to their home groups, husbands' groups, and church. However, some exceptional women (cf. Kal Mondo life story in Chap. 9) have entered political and community leadership. Mintima women and men regularly attend church, have coffee gardens, sell produce, spend money, wear clothes, vote in elections, and (at least until recently) hold traditional ceremonial exchanges for their families and tribes.

The generation of men and women who were youths at the time of independence, and those born since 1975, have often been to government or mission school and speak pidgin, but not many in the rural areas have gone beyond one or two grades. Young people travel to towns in motor vehicles, and they are familiar with money, shops, lamps, writing, radios, and many items of modern life. Some of the comments and ways of recording of the

younger literate interviewers in this book show these generational differences in outlook.

Youth and Marriage

Traditionally, and still in the 1980s, most girls are secluded and under ritual
taboos for a few days or weeks at first menstruation (Nilles 1939). This event
announces a woman's puberty and readiness for marriage; the instructions
and songs prepare her for marriage and adulthood, when she leaves her birth-
place for that of her husband. In their life stories, many older women
describe childhood fears of warfare and loss of parents; and some were
required to care for younger siblings while still children themselves. Girls
have a brief period of freedom and leisure when they can choose and invite
young men to visit and sing with them, hold courting parties, and visit relatives and boy friends outside their home localities. Traditionally, marriage
was permitted only by the agreement and marriage payment arrangements of
the families and kin groups concerned. Women are sometimes portrayed as
eager to marry, whereas young men are reluctant to be married, arguing their
youth and the dangers of close association with women. Men continue to
dominate in public life, holding most of the professional positions and all of
the elective offices in the province.

Whereas a man may spend his life in the locality and with the male relatives of his birth, a young woman must leave her childhood home to join
her husband. The first months of marriage, when a bride lives with her husband's older female relatives, can be very trying. A bride is expected to have
domestic skills in food preparation, housekeeping, gardening, and pig care
even before she begins sexual relations with her new husband and has a
house of her own. Wives of a community are of different local origins; some
may come from unfriendly and distant tribes, but friendship with those of the
same birth group is common. Women's garden work and pig raising are
essential to men's success in exchange, as childbearing and child care are to
the continuity of the patrilineal group. Women are divorced or punished for
barrenness and neglect of children and gardens. Independent life as a wife
and mother, with a separate house and gardens, sets each woman apart.

Men, in contrast, in their house building, garden preparation, planning
of festivities, fighting, ceremonies, and residence, are with other men. Men
and women are further differentiated by colonial experience. Today, political, occupational, and rural–urban differentiation in village and town, so
basic to class formation in Simbu, is affecting gender relations. Men's education, travel, and new occupational and political roles reinforce and provide
new outlets for the traditional male dominance in highland Papua New

Guinea public affairs (Brown 1987a). New status positions for men and women have different effects on gender relations. Whereas men magnify and consolidate the hierarchy in pursuing new opportunities for wealth, high prestige, and renown in professions, business, and political activities, the achievement of professional status for women removes them from rural home and community roles. Young men and boys who are the first to attend government and mission schools, or to work in close association with the representatives of colonial society, acquire some skills different from those of their rural peers.

Among Simbu men of an older generation, the first step in contact was a job as policeman, laborer, or domestic servant. When men migrate to work, the women at home take on some of the men's responsibilities in garden production, land preparation, and house building. Coffee, the major cash crop, was first planted by men on land allocated by the subclan. Women have learned to pick and process coffee beans. As described in other parts of the highlands, too (Hayano 1979; Boyd 1981), communities adapt to cash cropping with some new work demands upon women. However, at least in the early days, women keep little of the cash proceeds. Simbu men spend money on tools, household supplies, and clothing for the family, all of which have largely replaced home craft work. Money is now needed for ceremonial exchange, marriage payments, and political contributions; it is often used for gambling, food, and beer.

Ordinarily, the wives of the first educated and employed men do not share the husbands' direct experience in contact. The children, however, have opportunities for schooling, and some have formed a new Simbu elite. Schooling has become increasingly available, up to the level of a full National High School at Kondiu in 1995, and Simbu have studied in universities and professional schools in Papua New Guinea and abroad. Nevertheless, they still lag behind many coastal groups whose contact began generations earlier.

Men and Women

The whole Australian colonial period of social and cultural change was marked by the introduction of new educational, training, job, and travel opportunities for men. Through training and contact experience men are prepared to take charge of introduced political and legal institutions. The Australian administration, missions, job recruiters, and commercial representatives hardly considered girls or women as candidates for any training, jobs, or travel. In the 1960s at Mintima, there were occasional visits of infant-welfare nurses and short-lived projects for women's and children's health and family life. The disadvantaging of women prevailed through the colonial period into the establishment of self-government in 1975, and then in national and provincial governments.

The educational and contact experiences of men make them leaders and intermediaries when government- and mission-sponsored development projects and women's clubs are established. The effect of colonialism and modernization has been to introduce new western institutions and to reduce traditional taboos and ritual fears. The past fifty years of Australian administration, mission activities, schools, self-government, and economic change have had important effects upon gender relations. Compared to the 1960s, rural women today are more outspoken and aware of their rights in local affairs. Since the institution of local courts and magistrates elected by the tribe, minor local cases are heard and decided by adjudication. Now women take a prominent part as litigants able to respond to questions and argue their cases effectively. They are involved as complainants, victims, and defendants in marital disputes, theft, property damage suits, beating, rape, and other sexual offense cases. They both receive and pay damages. However, my suggestion that women might be given a role as magistrates in these courts or in separate family courts met with no interest from the legal officers, all of whom were men. Women's demands for recognition and legal rights are postcolonial developments.

Women have sold vegetables at the roadside and town markets for many years. With increased road traffic and economic specialization, local food marketing has expanded. Market selling gives women some independent income and contact with the mobile town milieu. Many use this income to help educate and support children at school.

Contemporary Simbu women have considerable control over their lives. Marriage and the establishment of a home, family, and adult responsibilities are no longer dictated, arranged, and forced upon women by men. School, highway, and market have expanded social contacts, especially for those young people who live near the towns and highway. Even more significant, the decline of taboos and fears that once controlled sexual relations among young people, the availability of beer, the frequent commercial parties at taverns and village centers, highway public motor vehicles, and the visits of young people from distant communities, all make social life freer and widen the choice of partners. Quite a few Mintima women had defied their parents' wishes and gone to live with men of their choice; some returned with children to live with their brothers or marry locally. Nuns at the clinic noted the increase in sexually transmitted diseases and tuberculosis.

Two generations of colonial and western influence, and the attendance of Simbu at missions and schools, have profoundly changed both behavior, reducing sexual segregation, and attitudes, so that fear of sexual contact has greatly declined. Young people have a sexual freedom that amazes their elders. The reduction in the intensity of taboos concerning sexual contact and segregation also affects family life and residence. Women often go to clinics for childbirth, and menstrual huts are not seen. Men's houses are not used exclusively by men: they have become group gathering places, and a family house becomes its social center. Family roles and mother–child relations have been modified: birth spacing is reduced, children begin to eat solid food[2] at a younger age, and a father is closer to his children of both sexes when they are very young. Children at school form peer groups and learn nontraditional subjects and games. Schoolgirls do not follow their mothers as much as in the past, although those I questioned at the university said they knew how to do gardening and traditional crafts such as bag netting.

Education and Change

Education here, as in so many developing countries, is seen as the key to advancement. Indeed, it is particularly true where dense population and land shortage have limited agricultural expansion and industry is undeveloped. Simbu Province has no large landholdings or coffee plantations, as are found in the Eastern and Western Highlands Provinces and have become a basis of rural economic differentiation. Commercial and professional occupations and politics are favored. For many years highlanders watched the coastal people, whose contact and access to education began two or more generations earlier, take the administrative and technical jobs of Papua New Guinea; now the Simbu attempt to control political and economic rewards and jobs. They realize that land shortage is a limiting factor in development, and by many whose land is located at high altitudes or is adequate only for family food supply, cash crops cannot be grown. Subsistence land was formerly reallocated by *magan nim* (S. land fathers) who acted as trustees for family and local group land; now coffee trees and other improvements are kept by men and shared with their sons and some close relatives. Our long-term study of land tenure in the Mintima area (Brown, Brookfield, and Grau 1990) reveals different patterns of utilization and allocation in the territory of one subclan. Although much land in the central area remains in the hands of the 1958 owner and his immediate successors, fringe areas held collectively at the beginning of our study were subdivided and transferred to individual tenure over a generation in which the population grew and demand for both subsistence and coffee land increased. Many critical problems of subsistence agriculture have been noted (Wohlt and Goie 1986).

Education is seen by many as offering the best, or only, opportunity for advancement through jobs in the public or private sector. However, in Simbu Province, 74 percent of children aged seven to twelve were not in school in 1980 (Townsend 1985). Although education does not automatically award jobs and prestige, no one with a good job or a flourishing business is uneducated. Educated men are most often elected to office in provincial and national government, and achieve employment and professional standing in Simbu and in Papua New Guinea. Some have international school or work experience. Their social life includes playing in and leading sports groups, travel to other towns, drinking and attending sophisticated social gatherings in hotels, active participation in election planning, and running for office.

High-school boys, responding to a questionnaire about career goals in 1984, said they consider a wide range of technical and professional occupations. The opportunity for girls to take courses preparing for jobs in health, social work, teaching, government administrative work, and clerical work as typists, bank tellers, or bookkeepers is very recent.

The churches and the national government of Papua New Guinea have now introduced programs for women, family, and community welfare. In a province of nearly two hundred thousand people, fewer than one hundred women in the 1980s had skills to lead village club groups or engage in business full time. Most women aged about thirty to forty-five attended only a year or two of community or mission school. By special circumstance—for example, having fathers who were employed close to mission or government, or through marriage and residence near a government or mission post—some women, though little schooled, have had special opportunites, mentors, and more contact with the agencies of change. An important result was learning pidgin. Present leaders in mission and women's club groups are women with this background.

Coffee in bean or cherry is now sold by both men and women. As compared to the few men who bake scones or sell tobacco and some other products in the markets, many women sell food, household goods, handicrafts, and cooked foods at roadsides, in villages, or in the towns. A very few full-time businesswomen own shops in town and at roadside centers. Full-time market sellers, mostly in the thirty to forty-five age group, supply major provincial markets, and provide their own transport in cars they own or share with others. Some supplies—such as betel nut, coconut, second-hand clothes, nylon string for making *bilums* (P. string bags), and peanuts—are purchased in coastal towns, which involves at least two days of travel and the costs of transport, as well as larger outlays and greater profits.

Simbu High-School Students' Career Goals in 1984
Q-4: What kind of work would you like to get?

	GIRLS		BOYS		TOTALS	
	No.	%	No.	%	No.	%
Teacher	2	8	14	18.2	16	15.7
Health officer (doctor, nurse)	11	44	2	2.6	13	12.7
Clerical (typist, switchboard operator)	5	20			5	4.9
Gov't. officer/development officer	2	8	6	7.8	8	7.8
Agriculture/forestry/livestock officer			3	3.9	3	2.9
Army, navy, police			2	2.6	2	2
Banker/teller/accountant	2	8	1	1.3	3	2.9
Mechanic/electrician/sawing/ draftsman			17	22	17	16.7
Professional (geologist, economist)			4	5.2	4	3.9
Butcher/carpenter			4	5.2	4	3.9
Engineer			4	5.2	4	3.9
Businessman			1	1.3	1	1
Other (boatbuilder, driver)			2	2.6	2	2
Double choices (various)	2	8	10	13	12	11.8
Triple choices	1	4			1	1
Unspecified			6	7.8	6	5.9
Unanswered			1	1.3	1	1
	25	100	77	100	102	100

The women who hold full-time professional positions in government employ, and successful independent businesswomen with shops selling food, clothing, and household goods, are often active in clubs, churches, sports, and social groups. A few have considered becoming candidates for political office. They can select their friends, participate in church and social events, and choose to make financial contributions to family or community affairs. They are aware of the difference between themselves and their rural relatives.

One professional woman, Theresa Simon (interviewer Paula Brown, 1987) said:

Women have always been looked on as inferior. That was the concept. Women were brought up to believe it. We, in our women's group, tell them they should not be treated as inferior. Some things women can do that men cannot do: take care of themselves, survive on their own, garden work, look after a family. They've always had these abilities. We try to change women's concept of them- selves. Men's domination is in their blood. We've had our revolution for women—quietly.

A prominent businesswoman, Judy Tokam (interviewer Paula Brown, 1987) said:

> The problem of Simbu women is that they don't think for themselves. In the villages women are frightened of their husbands. They vote and do what their husbands tell them to do. I do things on my own. If women stand on their own feet they are stronger than men. We have to help develop programs for women and youth.

The new Simbu elite is composed of twenty- to forty-year-old, educated, professional men and a few exceptional women. Education is seen as the key to success today—as entrance into a career in business, government and politics, work and travel in Papua New Guinea and overseas. Because land and rural economic activities are restricted by the very dense population of North Simbu Province, education for an urban professional occupation is the goal of many young Simbu today.

These first-generation educated Simbu, both men and women, mark the beginning of class differentiation. The competition among men for provincial and national elective office is intense. Men have found new rural arenas for political action and hierarchic relations that exclude women. Success in elections depends on rural support; money is essential for campaigns and gifts. Rural women can hardly join in or compete in the men's barroom discussions and distributions, which are an essential part of electioneering in the province. Political goals and candidacy are rare among women, and none has been successful.

Western forms of health care, primary schools, household equipment, churches, and other innovations have a profound impact upon village life. Many home crafts have been discarded. As new ideas and economic goals have come to be important, women have made their children's education a special point of concern. Schooling and the many forces of westernization have familiarized the younger generation with some urban western values as well as technology.

The social roles of men and women in the rural and urban context of Simbu have responded to stratification and differentiation in various ways. Urban men's roles are continuations and adaptations of traditional men's competition and dominance as leading warriors and orators. Rural and town support groups are essential to political ambition and election to national or provincial office. Successful men distribute favors to their rural kin and district. Women, however, have not as yet involved their rural relatives in support of political ambitions. The virilocal residence pattern would make this difficult.

Urban women discard many aspects of the traditional wife/mother role in exchange for wage earning, household management (rather than housework), and independence. They maintain close family ties through visits and often incorporate rural relatives into their urban households. The emerging class structure and urbanization retain links to rural society: there is a continuity running through men's political and economic activities, but for women urban life is quite unlike that of their rural relatives. In the absence of the domestic role of wife, their individuality and independence is striking.

Although there is a rising class structure in Simbu, there is not yet a permanent class stratification or rural–urban division of the society. Though this may be a transitional generation, divided between rural and family ties and urban, elite attachments to a multiethnic society, it is not yet possible to predict whether this new urban elite will abandon ties to family and rural community and identify itself wholly with its urban multiethnic affiliation. I have met many men who, after advanced education and employment in urban occupations or election to office, have had a career abruptly ended by a personal crisis, dismissal, or electoral defeat, after which they returned home to become an "ordinary villager."

Simbu find that elective office, careers, and employment are highly unstable, having high turnover, uncertainties in opportunity for advancement, and job stress. The majority of young Simbu have had at most a few years of schooling, with no preparation for clerical, administrative, skilled, or commercial employment. Rural community schools are often criticized for their high rate of teacher absenteeism and low level of instruction. Papua New Guinea "school leavers" are often discouraged, unwilling rural dwellers drifting to towns. Some of these unemployable youths steal goods or money, participate in criminal activities, and a few even join gangs. *Raskol* (P. rascal; a euphemism for gangs that stop vehicles to attack and rob travelers, sometimes seriously injuring their victims) gangs are believed to be composed of school leavers, partially educated and disgruntled young men, both in towns and on the roads. Many raskol gangs are composed of Simbu; but they are by no means the only ones.

Economic Change in Simbu

The first jobs available to Simbu were as laborers and carriers for the missions and government. In the Eastern and Western Highlands areas, employment with miners was another possibility. One advantage of being employed was learning pidgin, for police and interpreters were needed and missions trained teachers and catechists for work in the area. Domestic service for government and station personnel was available in a few years, and these contacts with the white man were valued for the experience and gifts as well as the income. During World War II the Australians recruited men from the highlands to work on roads and airstrips and as carriers. For many, the experience was memorable as the first glimpse of the world beyond their valley.

Paraka Kombukun of Kup, Kerowagi (interviewer Moses Parkay), recalls that, when he was about twelve years old:

> The white man was based at Banz. The second world war was about to come so the whiteman decided to recruit people as carriers and interpreters . . . I was chosen to go and see the white man. Even though I was scared I had to go through the force of the village elder. We had to walk to Banz . . . [met the white man at Banz] . . . we were told that we had to be his carriers. [They were afraid and some ran away.] Others said that if we ran away the whiteman will catch us because he is a deadly ghost from our great grandfather. [They stayed; the white man was Jim Taylor]. . . . Carried patrol box to Simbu . . . given rations of tinned meat and flour . . . reached Mingende . . . Catholic missionaries . . . next day heard sound of war planes . . . scared . . . threw bombs in Mingende. . . .
>
> I have served with the health department for nearly 30 years. I am now in the village. I have retired. I am about 50 years old. I have one son and one daughter. My daughter is married with five children. She only reached grade six. My son has reached up to grade 10 and he is a professional salesman. He has been working all over Papua New Guinea. After all I am a happy old man in the village.

Mondo Alfred Tangil, Endugwa councillor (interviewer Paul Ambani):

> Went Catekist training school and graduated was about to be married when war came. Was taken to Bena Bena as carrier, and later was told to look after the airstrip. But injured from some shots and bomb blast. Later after was good paid 2 kina shell an axe and a bush knife.

Another opportunity was in local employment, usually as a station laborer or domestic servant for government officers and families. This too required speaking pidgin and involved learning many skills—cooking, washing and ironing, house cleaning, and child care. When a young man had learned the skills, he often recruited a young relative as apprentice and became *manki masta* (P. master of boys) to the *manki* (P. boy).

Kutne Kura of Wandi, Naregu (interviewer Dilu Siune Robert):

> Kutne told me he worked as a cook when he was young for a priest at Wabag. He said before he became a cook he usually sweep and usually does the cleaning

up. While doing that he could observe other cooks doing the cooking. He said he became a cook just by observation. He couldn't recall the date when he worked but it could be in the early 1940s.

Harold Brookfield and I employed one or two local men with long experience in working for white men as domestic servants. They maintained and guarded our houses, purchased food, cooked, laundered, and at times one of them accompanied us on our local walks, assisting in interviews on land and family studies.[3]

Deglba Mathias of Naregu (interviewer Bruce Mondo Kair):

He was a first Christian and knew how to speak pidgin when school started at Mindima village. . . . After World War II he left for Omura and work for a white Mr. Sura as *cook boi*. After leaving Omura he came back to Mingende and worked there as cook boi again with Fr. Schäfer. . . . He went to Port Moresby Aprarie Rubber Plantation and worked as a rubber boi. Then he come back to Chimbu and to Goroka, and worked for Mr. Ron as cook boi again. One day during lunch time I interview with a kiap Mr. Bang who was in charge of Police College at Goroka where I recieved [sic] my training for 6 months, and monthly pay 10 shilling. After the training I was posted to Kainantu . . . monthly pay was 7 dollars. But however government supplies like rice and meat etc. was given to me. I was dropped to Opura and started off a kiap station and Kasam Pass with prisons and policeman. During the term of 5 years in police force he came home for his first leave and got married. It was a forced marriage and the bride was paid. [He names children and places of birth.]

All new stations were started by his hard work with prisons. . . . Before it was a hard time because we police had to look after roads, bridges, prisons, etc. We were very strict because we had guns and whips so there was less trouble. The wages were still low. . . .

He retired [in 1975] because he got tired of the life and situation in the Police Force by the trouble makers and also tired of the foot patrol. After he left the force he stayed as a simple villager in the village. . . . I really appreciate my pension because I am old and just sit back and depend on my pension.

The Highlands Labour Scheme

In the 1940s the Australians began supervised recruitment of workers on contract. Brookfield (1960) observes that the Simbu area was known in the 1950s to have a very high population concentration and thus be of singular interest to labor recruiters. At first the danger of exposure to tuberculosis and malaria was a deterrent to sending laborers out of the highlands. Labor migration in 1949 was to the goldmines at Wau, and then to other areas in 1950.

The Highlands Labour Scheme was established in 1951 to control the numbers of men absent from villages and the working conditions of contract laborers from the highlands. It required health examinations, malaria control, and repatriation after the completion of contract. The scheme allowed government officers to accept as volunteers men aged sixteen to forty-five for eighteen-month labor contracts. A maximum of 25 percent of men from this age group, in any census unit, was considered acceptable by the administration. When the men reached their place of work, they were assigned unskilled or low-skill work activities. They worked on roads, as carriers, and on coastal plantations where they were assigned to such work as land clearing, copra picking, and rubber tapping. During this time they were clothed, housed, and fed by the employer, and were given some cash. At the end of the contract they were given the main part of their earnings, to purchase what they wished, and returned home with the money and goods.

This was the first cohort of Simbu to travel outside their home areas. The census of each group contained a report on the numbers and percentages of absent migrant laborers, and this varied in 1951–1954 from a low of 5 percent to a high of 60 percent of the men in eligible age groups. The program was intended to be limited to unmarried men, but many married men were attracted to the opportunity and volunteered. Kuman Simbu were willing recruits for a few years, 1950–1955, and longer in the densely populated areas that had little cash-crop potential.

While the men were away, families had to cope with a reduced male labor force, placing greater demands upon the women and old people. Traditional male tasks such as house building, fencing, and garden clearing might be delayed or become makeshift repairs, and women had a heavier burden in garden preparation, firewood collection, livestock care, and food production.

Mondo Ola of Simbu valley (interviewer Paul San):

Yes I was once a carrier and a worker out at at the goldfields in Lae (Wau-Bulolo). We were collected by the company as contract workers. I was appointed by the company bosses to look after the group of men from my area. I worked there until the death of my father.

Ulka Baglau of Upper Simbu (interviewer Michael Gandi):

The kiaps called for contract and so I was one of the people who went to Madang for work. I liked it very much because I was told to work at the missionaries house sweep clean the flower bed and also cut grass around the house and the church too. The rest of our people worked in the plantation while I had a good time. I liked the job very much because they used to give me pearlshells, salt, meat, rice, laplap, and so many things.

Kutne Kura of Naregu (interviewer Dilu Siune Robert):

Kutne said he did work contract. He said he heard that some people from Kundiawa wanted people to go and work on the coast. With great interest he went to Kundiawa and got his name written down. They flew him from Kerowagi down to Goroka then to Madang where he worked at a coconut plantation. He said he was flown back due to his misbehaving attitude.

Kua Bogia of Simbu valley (interviewer Joseph Mando):

I do work contract at Kokopo copra plantation. My mates and I were marching over Mondia pass and down all the way to Madang. In Madang we had our first taste of rice and meat, but for some of us it did not look too inviting, for we had heard disagreeable stories about these things. The kiap told us one day to get ready for the *balus* (P. plane) would come on the next day to take us to the unknown. Early the next morning we were forced to hop onto a huge monster called "truck" which took us to a place called *ples balus* (P. airstrip) where our balus was waiting. From there we marched into the balus belly. It looked exactly like our limestone caves which were numerous in the middle Simbu River. We were seated on both walls of the plane and were instructed to put big belts over ourselves. I did not see the reason behind it, but as everybody did it I don't worry. Then two dangerous looking things in front went into action and they spun like mad and produced a mighty roar. The whole body of the plane shook and after a while we were up in the air. What made me speechless with wonder was that we were flying between two blues—that of the ocean and that of the sky. It was the first experience for me to see so great a body of water with seemingly no limits.

We landed at Kokopo airstrip. We were sent to a plantation some miles out of Kokopo township.

Early the next morning the employer came and give us our appointments of various duties. I worked as cook at the copra plantation. I learned to cook rice mixed with meat and sometimes rice with fish. I worked as cook for seven months at the Kokopo copra plantation four weeks after my arrival and work as *big lain* (P. big work line) men. I was appointed to the big lain. I and others from the big lain were given bushknives each and were told to cut grass and copra. So that's where I worked two full solid years contract at Kokopo copra plantation, Rabaul.

On my first visit to Mintima in 1958 there were many young men recently returned from laboring at coastal plantations. They had gone to many different places—Madang, Rabaul, Wau. For these young men, it was a first experience in many things. Years later they remembered that they were given blankets, towels, laplap, and food; then, at the end of the contract, they were paid a sum of money and sent home. Some liked it enough to sign on for a second tour, but others found the coastal climate hot and the work unpleasant. My first observation of returned laborers was that most of them spoke pidgin; they were the first generation to travel to the coast and get to know white men, working conditions, and people from other places. Permanent additions to the local language included vocabulary designating time: *belo* (P. the lunchtime bell) and *belo bak* (P. time to return to work).

A few told lurid tales of wild cannibals and weird customs. Wagai, for example, said that he had asked the local people where their cemetery was, and on being told there was none, concluded that they were man-eaters. He was afraid of them.

Their store-bought clothing and household goods, plumes and shells to be used as gifts, and cash, made the returned laborers a new young elite. Upon their arrival home they were welcomed with a celebration.

Waine of Bamugl, Naregu, was one of the first men I knew who had finished contract. He was a boy when the first government officers came, had little schooling, and became a contract worker along with many men of Mintima in 1951. They were taken by plane from Kerowagi to Madang and then to Karkar Island to work on a coconut plantation. Some cut grass, others made copra. He said: "I was a bosboi. We got 1 kina per month. At the end were taken to Goroka and got five kina and had to walk with our money to Kundiawa. Bought some things in Goroka—there were no shops in Kundiawa then. We bought shirts, tomahawk, paint" (interviewer Paula Brown).[4]

Patrol Officers' Observations on Laborers in the 1950s

One defect of the system was noted by J. A. Gauci: the government transport of workers was to and from Goroka. The recruits had to walk from their homes and take the highlands highway to Goroka; people along the road found an opportunity to exploit these travelers.

> These labourers inspected by the Patrol said that they did not mind working on the coast rather they enjoyed it. They voiced however a very general grievance. This concerns their travelling to Goroka and back on their way to and from the coast. They request that they do this by Air. Apparently on the road they have to pay for food, for shelter, firewood and water. . . . The demanding suppliers are natives; and the particular road complained of is the stretch between Goroka and the Chimbu sub-district boundary. (Gauci 1955b:4)

The several officers whose patrol reports discuss migrant laborers clearly differed in their observations and in their view of the benefits of the labor program.

Very obviously the better off amongst these natives are those that have gone to work on the coast. In fact many are of the opinion that betterment and becoming richer is best achieved not by staying at home and rearing more pigs but by working for money and with it buying riches. They are becoming more and more money concious [sic] and indeed cash transactions often settle disputes. Coastal labour has introduced higher prices generally and in particular a higher bride price. A headman at Kalingu complained that too many of his line were away at work. Upon investigation the writer discovered that a number having been accepted for work on the coast the line was still above the overrecruited mark. Later however quite a few more decided to set off and find work here in the highlands as casuals. (Gauci 1955c:3–4)

Returned labourers were questioned about their stay on the coast. Most enjoyed themselves and thought the experience well worth while. Of the 393 labourers on the coast at the time of the patrol, 107 (26.7%) of them are serving a second term and 6 (1.5%) are serving their third term. This is a very healthy situation and augurs well for a future labour supply for the coast. (Hibbard 1954:3)

Hibbard notes that people buy clothes and plumes for adornment.

Probably the most obvious [effect] brought to bear on these people, has been from returned labourers of the adjoining Maril River and Salt who, in their newly-found affluence and sophistication, make regular trips to the Bomai for the purpose of buying pigs, bird of paradise plumes and other finery, and sometimes wives, all of which are cheaper and more plentiful in the Bomai than in their own areas. (Keogh 1953:6)

Officers in the 1950s were instructed to take note of the behavior of returned laborers, to see if they were reintegrated into village life. Some were observed to gain attention and prestige from their command of money and knowledge of the outside world, and to threaten the authority of the native officials, who were mostly older and unworldly. Speaking pidgin, for most laborers, was an entrée to communication and an opportunity to see the outside world. Some patrols reported that returned laborers were fitting back into their communities, but by the mid-fifties a change seemed to be taking place. The returnees, who were the main source of money and manufactured goods at that time, were dissatisfied with their status at home and with the traditional leaders who held office.

In transactions, there was a growing demand for money rather than trade goods. Marriages had been arranged for many of the men while they were absent, and some of them refused to accept the wife and obligations thrust upon them. The young women married in this way often refused to work for their new in-laws and ran away. Some returned laborers defied their elders; some spread dissatisfaction among their fellows; and some went into remote uncontacted areas to sell goods at high prices. "Bossboy rings" were sold to unsuspecting natives, who then claimed authority when the patrol officer arrived. Stimulated by the influx of money and goods from laborers, bride-price and other payments were greatly inflated, and elders were unable to maintain their dominance in transactions.

> Labourers returning from the coast appear to be resettling without trouble. A fair minor proportion of these natives do not like coastal labour. The general reason given is that it is too hot on the coast. Some are afraid that they might get sick and die there. Those giving such a reason had invariably lost relatives in this way. (Gauci 1954:2)

> These people were some of the first to volunteer for work on the coast and the fact that so many are now working within the District seems to point to the fact that the glamour of working on the coast is wearing off and the natives now prefer to work within the District, as casuals, where the working conditions are much more congenial and they can return home to visit their relatives much more frequently. (Bailey 1954b:3)

> In the GENA group ex Constable SIWI is certainly a force to be reckoned with. He commands considerable respect and influence and although initially it was thought that he might be anti Administration all indications now are that he is exactly the opposite. He is a strong supporter of the government school at Kundiawa, he is leading everyone in the size and care of his coffee plot and in talks the writer had with the assembled natives his good sense was very much apparent. (Gauci 1955a:3)

Patrol officers counted the numbers of absentees in every census and inquired about the care of their families and how the returned laborers fit into communities. It was observed that bride-price was sometimes now made up by the returned laborer himself, thus freeing him from the obligations and debts to which traditionally new grooms were bound.

In his novel *Kallan* (1984), Toby Waim Kagl tells of recruitment to the *mundinigl* (S. saltwater coast). His story includes trade relations between highlands plantation laborers and villagers, tensions between the groups, and a welcoming party on their return. In the story, recruitment to coastal labor contracts immediately followed the killings of missionaries in the Simbu valley and subsequent arrests. Although the author was a young man who did not witness the events of 1935 or the recruitment of 1950, this juxtaposition suggests that these occasions of exodus of young men from the valley to the coast have some common meaning in the stories of older people. In fact the Simbu valley, densely populated and lacking resources for commercial development, has been and continues to be one of Papua New Guinea's greatest sources of emigrées to coastal urban and rural places of employment and squatter settlement.

Coffee on Plantations and at Home

Coffee is a suitable crop for the highlands, and beginning around 1950 plantations owned by white men were established in the Eastern and Western Highlands but were not permitted in Simbu because of the high density of the population. Although their interest and ambition may match that of Eastern Highlands people, the Simbu did not have the models or the opportunity to develop entrepreneurial skills like the Goroka business leaders (Finney 1973, 1987).

It was noted in the Simbu central area in 1954 that many men were absent at work on coffee plantations near Goroka and Kainantu, not on contract. For these men, the experience could be put to advantage in growing coffee at home. Volunteering for contract work was discouraged by Kondom and senior men once coffee growing was introduced: they wanted the young men to plant and tend coffee at home. However, it soon became clear that the highest densities of population in Simbu are in high-altitude sites where coffee cannot thrive. Recruitment to the Highlands Labour Scheme declined except in areas such as the Upper Simbu valley whose altitude is too high for coffee, and in inaccessible places without roads such as Gumine and the lower Wahgi valley. Migration for resettlement on land where cash crops can be grown and to the coast and cities for employment continues today.

The economic development of Papua New Guinea depended upon establishing cash crops and marketing procedures. For many years seeds of European vegetables were distributed by patrol officers, so that the grown vegetables could be sold to missions, settlers, and government families: "The only cash income received by the inhabitants of the area at present is derived from the sale of vegetables and pitsawn timber to the Government and Missions, and money paid for road and airstrip maintenance work" (Bailey 1954a:8).

After the Chuave patrol post was established, officers observed that there was a greater spirit of cooperation in the area, as the people were receiving pay for their roadwork, food, building materials, and pit-sawn timber; and they expected this would improve even more when cash crops were brought in. Peanuts were to be both a cash crop and a valuable addition to the native diet. Passion fruit seed was distributed to be a cash crop in 1952–1953, and intermittently fruit was purchased, but the expected processing plant was never built at Kundiawa. Pyrethrum at high altitudes proved unattractive as a cash crop. Both passion fruit and pyrethrum came to little, tea is grown as a separate and controlled plantation crop in the Wahgi valley, and the hopes for cardamom in the 1980s have hardly been realized. The primary highlands cash crop remains coffee.

Coffee planting had begun as an experiment by missions and others years earlier, was greatly expanded with the plantations on land acquired by Australians (often former government officers) in the Eastern and Western Highlands, and then was extended to natives in the 1950s. Kundiawa had a demonstration coffee plot in 1952 and a coffee nursery in 1953, with plans to make this a major cash crop.

Simbu soon began to set out areas for planting and received nursery plants; there was an agricultural extension officer in Kundiawa in 1954. Coffee was planted and beginning to bear at Masul in 1954 (Bailey 1954c:7), when the only coffee planted at Kerowagi was by Siwi (Bailey 1954a:6). The interest in the central area was "quite high" (Kelly 1954b: 2). Within a few years the plants matured to bear fruit so that there was some coffee produced, and in the subsequent years coffee became the only significant cash crop in the area. The demand for labor and the intensity of establishing coffee plantings discouraged volunteers to contract labor in the later 1950s. Local leaders, and particularly Kondom in Naregu, discouraged labor migration and urged all the people to make their business planting coffee. After coffee was established, individual Simbu casual labor migrants preferred walking the highlands highway to plantations to working on contract.

The hero image of Kondom centers on his enthusiasm and drive to bring coffee as a cash crop to Simbu (see Brown 1990b). Kondom said that, for Simbu, coffee was their gold, their cocoa, their only source of money. He made the first coffee garden and showed the people how to grow and process coffee. The prevailing attitude, stated often to me between 1958 and 1965, and frequently by Kondom in his lectures, was that he listens to the kiap: the govman (P. government) gives, takes, and shows him what to do. Kondom had extensive coffee plantings, a coffee-hulling machine, a horse, a timber-frame house, and a restaurant (P. *haus kaikai*) at Wandi.

Moa of Naregu (interviewer Mugua Michael):

> Coffee was brought by Kondom. He bring development to our people like coffee, schools, aid post. And know everybody's problem, correct them in the right way, and live with people. Talk kindly.

Agricultural officers supervised land preparation, planting of shade trees, and spacing of coffee plants. Individual householders owned plots and their trees. When the first coffee berries appeared after several years, Simbu were told how to pick, hull by hand, wash, lay out in the sun, and dry the beans. Very few coffee-hulling machines or washing tubs were available. The dried beans were sold by the owners.

Then people began to plant their own separate coffee plots, often without the spacing and shading of plants recommended. During the early 1960s, coffee was of great interest in Naregu, and Kondom, as president of the Waiye Local Government Council and member of the Legislative Council, promoted it throughout the highlands. In 1964 the Kundiawa Coffee Society cooperative was launched with Kondom's strong support, and each subclan in Naregu had a coffee weighing, pulping, washing, and drying plant, with periodic pickup from the cooperative and income divided among members according to the amount of coffee they had brought. Production in Simbu rose from 378 tons in 1963 to 2,700 tons in 1965 (Cochrane 1966). Leading Simbu coffee growers made up the district-wide board. Falling coffee prices, financial and management difficulties, and growing competition from private traders operating from other areas brought mounting problems to the renamed Chimbu Coffee Cooperative after 1969 (Singh 1974). Fiscal and managerial problems eventually defeated the cooperative, and since the 1970s coffee production has returned to individual and family work, and sale at the roadside for immediate payment by private coffee buyers. Prices fluctuate with the international market: high expectations and satisfying payments in the mid-1970s were followed by lower prices; then people picked and sold less.

Coffee has continued as a main source of cash income for Simbu except in the high-altitude area. For several months each year coffee picking and processing absorb Simbu labor and interest; payments and debts depend upon the coffee harvest, and payday is an occasion for beer drinking, food buying, and other celebrations. More recently, some buyers purchase newly picked coffee, and hulling machines are used by many. Truck ownership and coffee buying are now an entrepreneurial opportunity. Rural wives and family members sometimes process the beans they pick and sell separately.

Compared to the large plantations of the Eastern and Western Highlands areas, Simbu remains a region of smallholders. The Highlands Farmers and Settlers' Association was founded by Australian expatriates in 1955, but did not invite Simbu to join until 1965. The natives had little opportunity to benefit from their counsel. In the Eastern and Western Highlands provinces, many formerly European-owned plantations are now owned by native syndicates.[5] Simbu has none of these, and Finney's observations in the Eastern Highlands (1973, 1987) do not apply.

Both the government and the Simbu have had many ideas for new crops and agricultural projects, both practical and unsuitable: among them apples, sericulture, oranges, passion fruit, pyrethrum, tobacco, European vegetables, beekeeping, cardomom, forestry, livestock, hide curing, and brick making (Economic Consultants 1979). Simbu recognize their limited land resources and often favor commercial and manufacturing projects (Howlett et al., 1976). Technical and vocational training schools have made a small contribution to the skill pool. There were short-lived projects of wool weaving, brick making, and clothes manufacturing. Many Simbu have built community shops selling foods, clothing, and household goods; few of these are long-lived or expanding. Some Simbu wanted a "money factory," or mint, for themselves. There have been several groups that perform dances and plays for tourists. In the 1980s there was a disco at the Chimbu Lodge, canteens and restaurants on the highway and in Kundiawa, doll making and a craft shop. In 1991, a casino was proposed and approved by the national legislature. Marijuana is grown in the province as a cash crop (Phillip Kai Moore 1992). Most potential cash crops were abandoned because of failure of labor, supply of raw materials, marketing, or management. Rural, family, women's, and youth training and development projects continue to be advanced by economic and welfare officers in many formats. There are a few Simbu businessmen and businesswomen who successfully manage rural and town commercial enterprises (Brown 1987a). Commercial land and shops are now bought and sold.

The Simbu economy is not truly diversified, but subsistence farming is mixed with cash crops nearly everywhere. Coffee, cardomom, vegetables, and occasionally other crops are grown for sale where conditions are favorable, and Simbu have migrated to new agricultural and work places. Simbu own trucks, passenger motor vehicles, shops, and business enterprises. They work at many occupations throughout Papua New Guinea. But Simbu remains an overpopulated and poorly developed province of Papua New Guinea.

Money is now essential to everyday life, needed for clothing and household supplies. During the period when coffee is productive, there is a sharp increase in money spent on food, beer, and gambling. Money is the major or only component of fines, compensations, and payments at marriage; every ceremonial display and intertribal *mogenabiri* (S. food distribution) includes money displayed on a ceremonial board, canned food, beer, and other purchases. The measure of a big man and a family is their goods, cars, trucks, travel, modern house, and largesse in the distribution of purchased food and beer. Political candidacy and success depend on it, and the successful candidate then must use his power to obtain services and gifts to his constituency. In Papua New Guinea, land planted in long-term cash crops, Australian concepts of land ownership, money in payments, and political expenditure have had a great impact on local exchanges and transactions; the distinctions between gift and commodity, valuables and money have blurred, if not disappeared (cf. McKellin 1991; Carrier 1992).

Since the colonial period in which the kiap initiated peace ceremonies and payments to end hostilities, there has been a great inflation of payments to institute new relationships and restore relations after a conflict. At the beginning of my fieldwork in 1958, the traditional practice of death payments to the kin of the deceased, including exchanges of foods, pigs, and shell valuables, was usual practice (Brown 1961). Soon afterward, these exchanges ceased. The pig feast, discouraged by Kondom, was held less frequently and abandoned by some groups, whereas money payments at marriage and intertribal festivities increased.

The institution of *yomba yagl* (S. people/man, compensation for the death or injury to a person) has come to be an important Simbu practice, requiring the assemblage of large sums of money by a clan and tribe. Death in a motor accident or fight, or any killing of a person of a different clan or tribe is followed by the demand of the victim's group for compensation, up to 50,000 kina in some cases. War and retaliation is threatened if the group does not comply. Paul Dage (1985) explains that making a very large compensatory payment is the pride and demonstration of wealth of a killer's tribe and clan, and that the victim's community status, physical build, education, and potential earnings are taken into account in making the demand. Payment (S. *topo*) for children and women victims would not require such large sums, except for unmarried educated women, whose group would expect a large bride-price at her marriage. Dage considers *yomba yagl* a moral precept accepted by Simbu's educated men and politicians. Although the former practice of retaliation against enemies for killing in war is now condemned, a killer is now punished in court and is also required to make a large compensation payment. As intertribal fights continue in the postcolonial period, deaths in battle are also the subject of compensation demands; this compensation to an enemy group was not a precolonial practice but follows from the colonial imposition of peace ceremonies and exchanges. The Simbu see this, not as an equivalence of a life for money, but as a restoration of peaceful relations between groups.

The Political Transition to Independence

Papua New Guinea introduced elective office and localized officers in a series of stages. The process was stimulated by United Nations reviews, the advancement of education and specialized training, and international pressures. Many Australian residents continued to believe that Papua New Guinea could not be successful as an independent nation (Leahy 1991).

Local Government Councils

Elected local government councils were introduced into Papua New Guinea beginning in 1950. The first in the highlands, in 1958, was Waiye Council, combining four tribes near Kundiawa. It was chosen as a venue for the enthusiastic leadership of Kondom of Naregu tribe, renowned as a strong supporter of the administration and as a great orator and prophet of the new way of *bisnis* (P. commercial enterprise). His own enterprises in coffee, cash crops, and support of roads, schools, and health facilities became a model for the highlands. Soon Kondom would be the first elected highlands member of the Legislative Council.

Councils were established in Chimbu Subdistrict for each area, usually a population of about nine to twenty thousand, composed of one large group of clans and subtribes (Yonggamugl, Dom) or several tribes (Waiye, Sinasina, Kerowagi). The innovations were: the election of a councillor from each unit of about two to three hundred, usually a clan segment; election of a president and other officers from this group; selection or election of *komdi* (P. ward committeemen and committeewomen) to assemble local groups and supervise activities; and collection of taxes from each adult male and female, a reserve fund. A council clerk, usually a young educated man of the area, kept minutes and records under the direction and supervision of district administration officers. Each council built a meetinghouse, and many had a vehicle, engaged in economic activities, and voted to support health facilities, schools, and development projects. Waiye council policemen kept order and brought disputes to Kundiawa. The dispute settlement activities of councillors, komdi, and council policemen were not a recognized part of the judicial system, as patrol officers instructed them in their duties.[6]

Preliminary meetings of the four Waiye tribes were celebrations of enthusiastic speeches and plans. They were proud to be chosen as the first highlands council. From the beginning most of the men elected were relatively young pidgin speakers dedicated to the new goals of peaceful intertribal relations, cash crops, and business. Through experience in meetings of the council appropriate procedures were learned. Voting for national elections was instituted soon after.

As luluais and tultuls of the 1940s and 1950s had aged, officers sought young leaders, pidgin speakers with some familiarity with police, courts, and government methods. Some sons of native officials succeeded their fathers; these men had often been among the first to attend local schools. The council marked a new phase of administration, for councillors were elected by the people, often had some experience with government or employment, and participated in meetings where formal democratic procedures were followed. In monthly meetings the budget and other matters were debated and voted upon. The council was to pursue modernizing goals, adding to and improving cash crops, schools, aid posts, roads, and communications, and to follow the new procedures to maintain law and order. It was expected that councillors could speak pidgin and become familiar with these new forms. Though a few elders were elected to the first council, a younger group predominated. The council was made up of men who had been in the first wave of youths to attend mission schools and be employed by Europeans. From that time onward, elected officials were predominantly among the educated men with experience in both work and administration (Brown 1979b, 1987a). Simbu views of the duties and activities of the council varied greatly. To all it was a new phase of political participation.

Anton Wuka, elder of Simbu valley (interviewer John Karl):

> The people of each clan vote for their own councils. They look at the person who can talk strongly, solve disputes. Sometimes the councils tell their people to work on the road . . . or do other jobs that the kiaps want them to do.

Martin Nombri of Naregu (story collected by Paul San, written by M. Nombri):

> I was never a councillor or committee but I can still remember the beginning of council. They did tremendous work. They collected taxes, they built schools, roads, health centers and many other things. I can remember the first election because I took part in voting and educating people on how to vote and what elections was for.

Guwand Kombugun, Endugwa (interviewer Harry Godfrid):

> I was only a tultul but my son Pek was a councillor . . . I can remember the council system. The councillors would go around and inform us about new coming changes, council taxes, council election. They organise things like aid post, schools, meetings, solve conflicts and disputes between families, tribes and clans. More recently, they base themselves in towns, and look after the toilet system, rubbish dumps, the town area.

Hatanaka describes the first years of the Sinasina council from 1964: "the establishment of the local government council was the first step toward political development" (1972:49). There was opposition to the council by

older big men "because they felt that councillors would have even more difficulty organizing people to work on community projects" (1972:50), and they
feared that the tax rate would rise. Within three years the council had a firm
foundation and the people participated in local politics; development projects
moved hand in hand with cash crops. Reelected and experienced Sinasina
council members were influential and promoted public services and roads.

In the 1960s councils were firmly institutionalized, and councillors and
committee members were the local authorities on projects, disputes, and
council decisions. The optimism and progress of the council's first enthusiastic years did not last. Soon councillors and elders alike complained that
young Simbu did not *harim tok* (P. heed the leaders); they were *bikhet*
(P. arrogant, disobedient), disobeyed their elders, did not work on council
projects or for the group goals, avoided taxes, ran away to work outside the
area, and in general lacked respect for the kiap and council, making trouble.
Evasion of council tax by leaving the area was common. In the end the government found tax collecting more costly to pursue than its benefit and
abandoned local government tax. This harsh judgment of elders of their
children continued through the 1970s, as council and economy failed to
accomplish early promises, Australian kiaps were replaced by indigenous
officers, and the focus of decisions and investment shifted to the new central
and provincial government bodies. This brought new problems of authority
and administration.

Area Authorities, Provincial and Central Government

In a series of steps, local government councils were amalgamated into larger
councils and Area Authorities. Following independence in 1975, districts
became provinces and Area Authorities were replaced by provincial government. This was intended as a move towards decentralization. In the 1980s
provincial government became Simbu's main administrative, budget, and
planning body. The provincial budget depends upon central government:
elected officials and ministers disburse funds and contracts. Standish recognizes the centrality of the state in the economy (1992:253). Local government councils have become ineffective, and many disbanded; only the
titles of "konsel" and "komdi" remain as tokens of local esteem. Tribal bodies
of magistrates meet weekly in a tribal courthouse to hear disputes. Local-
trouble case discussions often involve the former officials, magistrates, and
other important men. In many parts of Simbu the local rural community has
become a backwater: the activities of elders hold little interest or respect for
the young, who cluster near the highway in Kundiawa and travel to other
centers when they can.

Provincial administration in Simbu, as in some other provinces, has been found to be corrupt. The election of provincial government representatives in 1984 was quickly followed by suspensions and placing an administrator in charge of Simbu Province. Fraudulent use of funds and favoritism are common occurrences in Papua New Guinea, and Simbu seem to excel at it. Nor is discovery, conviction, and imprisonment a disgrace or deterrent to political ambition. Elected members of the Simbu Provincial Assembly returned in 1985 and again took up their positions in provincial government. Several of the suspended and convicted members of provincial government were candidates for the National Parliament in 1987.

The Papua New Guinea administration established an elected central government, first in the Legislative Council, then in the House of Assembly in 1964, 1968, and 1972. In the 1968 House of Assembly, Eric Pyne, of the Kundiawa Coffee Society, was elected to the Simbu-wide regional seat, and five Simbu in subareas were elected to open seats.

Many Simbu statesmen have been prominent in provincial and national affairs for many years.[7] For example, Yauwe Moses of Chuave (interviewed by me in 1987) said that he had carried cargo for Jim Taylor when he was a child. As a young man he went to the mission and became a fluent pidgin speaker. He was a luluai, served on the Kundiawa Coffee Society Board, and was elected to the House of Assembly in 1964. Public works were brought into the area. Then, in the 1970s and 1980s, he joined the provincial government and became speaker in 1984. At that time he was one of very few men in his age group to be reelected and prominent in government. He is proud of the roads, beer, and improvements brought to Simbu during his time in office.

Siwi Kurondo, who served as a constable in the 1940s, and for a time as a gold miner, returned to Simbu to plant coffee and encourage development in his home tribe, Gena, in the 1950s. I recall that he set aside land for a university on a Gena mountaintop in the 1960s. He was elected to the Legislative Council in 1964, appointed as Minister of Forests, and carried out international trade negotiations. Within the province, he was a leader in the Area Authority and the Provincial Assembly, continuing to stand for office. In 1984 Siwi stood for the Provincial Assembly, and in 1987 for Parliament, when he told me that he expected to be made Minister of Agriculture; however, the time of electing ageing statesmen had passed and he received few votes. Both Yauwe and Siwi have been honored by Queen Elizabeth II. Many senior statesmen, like them, had long political careers and retain the respect of their constituents, while many younger and better-educated men are elected to office only once and are not reelected.

Simbu have held ministries, led the opposition, been headlined in the national press, established political parties, and taken a very prominent part in Papua New Guinea government since Kondom first took office in 1961. In each election dozens of men are candidates for every seat. If defeated in one election, a man often stands again. But, as we shall see, politicians are not admired by all, and there is deep dissatisfaction with the national government. Many of the elders interviewed in 1987 by their educated tribesmen expressed their distaste for the corruption.

Ulka Baglau of Toromambuno, Upper Simbu valley (interviewer Michael Gande):

> I remember the first national elections. . . . We voted for Karigl Bongere because the councillor told me that we've got to vote for this man because he is going to build big school big hospitals and also maintain our road. I told all the villagers that we've got to vote for Karigl Bongere so we voted him and he won the seat. The 1987 election is not going to be like my times because I heard that they are buying people with money not like before. I do not know who is the good candidates I am going to vote for because I never saw one in my house so I'll wait till my son who is now a teacher will come and tell me who to vote for.

Several elders said that they would take their educated sons' advice on voting, as they were confused and undecided about contemporary political issues. Few women had political views and preferences, and it was generally thought that local groups voted as a unit, as the leading senior men directed. Furthermore, the belief that votes were sold by these men was widespread. When I observed voting in the 1980s I saw many teenaged youths claiming adult rights and placing votes, with the approval of the electoral officers. Many middle-aged and young men voiced their mistrust of politicians who sought personal gain and thought that government was corrupt throughout in the 1980s. But few were as bitter as the next man quoted.

Kua Bogia of Kangrie, Simbu valley (interviewer Joseph Mando, 1987):

> The Government is out to create an economic empire for itself at the expense of the people back home.
>
> Independence was a personal gift for Michael Somare and a few select elite. Independence was NEVER meant to you and me and our people until a REVOLUTION determine our true Independence.
>
> The 1987 election will be the last Democratic Election. Future Election will be cleverly guided Democracy and may lead to Anarchy or Revolution. This Election is the one from which people must choose their rightful leaders. Otherwise this country is heading for an internal revolution or an ethical or moral chaos.[8]

Simbu Leaders and the Politics of Independence

A 1984 study of leaders and stratification involved an interview questionnaire on Simbu leaders (Brown 1987a), including 177 male candidates for
the Provincial Assembly and 166 other leaders selected by myself and a
group of literate Simbu assistants. Of these 312 leading men, over half of
those aged forty and older had no schooling, while over half of those aged
thirty to thirty-nine, and over 70 percent of those under thirty had high
school or advanced schooling. Most of the candidates for the Provincial
Assembly in 1984 were under forty years of age. A significant 119 of 312
leading men, and 57 percent of the winning candidates, had some advanced
schooling.

Although Simbu has remained primarily rural, the occupations of leaders
include elective office, civil service employment, police and army service,
teaching, and business. The diverse occupations of leaders, as compared to
the rural majority, indicates the beginning of a stratification in which an
educated, urbanized elite is emerging in the province as well as in Papua
New Guinea. For this elite, education is the key to higher income, government employment, and political office. They are professionals with business
interests; their living standards are modern and western. At the same time
they depend upon their rural home base of friends and relatives for support
and votes; they participate in festivities, payments, and projects of their
clansmen. The drive to education is intensified because population density
and limited opportunity for rural development put exceptional pressure on
government sources of money and investment, and politics is known to be
the avenue to access to government funds.

David Mai's education in politics, economics, and finance includes
a course at the Administrative College in Port Moresby, a B.A. from
the University of Papua New Guinea, and a graduate course in economics in
Australia. After serving as provincial planner for Simbu he was elected to
the provincial government in 1984. His interest, training, and service as
Simbu minister of finance and planning was the key to his becoming premier
in the 1988 provincial government. He was determined to make Simbu a
more developed province, with free education for all. The Simbu provincial
government voted in 1990 to provide free education to all Simbu, and to
support secondary schools and students attending institutions of higher
education. Simbu Province finances were increased by a retail sales tax,
liquor tax, and license fees. However, the education policy was found to be
costly, and high-school students who were absent for two days were expelled
(Gigmai 1993); later, the policy was withdrawn by the education minister
(Gigmai 1994). In 1987 David Mai told me that his next step would be to

stand for the National Parliament. The results confirm this: he succeeded and was elected to the regional seat in Parliament in 1992 and made minister for labour and employment under the Wingti government (Dilu Deck 1992).

Ignatius Kilage, born in 1940, Chimbu's first priest educated at Holy Spirit Seminary, Papua New Guinea ombudsman 1975–1984, and provincial administrator in 1985, was a candidate for the Simbu regional seat in 1987. When he lost the parliamentary election, he was honored as Governor-General until his death.

John Nilkare was "Australian schooled and university trained, very well dressed and westernized in manner, Nilkare was a former magistrate and footballer in Simbu, whose father had been Gumine council president" (Standish 1983:91). He was chief liquor licensing commissioner. After losing in 1977, his first parliamentary attempt, Nilkare was the elected regional member and a minister from 1982 to 1987. He was known to be a rich man with many profitable business interests, and distributed thousands of school notebooks with his picture and name on the back cover. He was one of the founders of the League for National Advancement party and lost the regional seat in 1987. Nilkare gained the Gumine open seat in 1992. As minister for provincial affairs and village development he proposed to abolish provincial government and replace it with village services (Deck 1992). In the change of government of 1994, he lost his ministerial post.

It has long been usual in Simbu to have very many candidates for every elective office, each with a small local support group. With so many candidates, no majorities are ever achieved, and the person elected often polls less than 10 percent of the total vote. In a move to restrict this large pool of candidates, the registration fee was raised from K100 to K1,000 (Kinas) in 1992; however, there were still 224 candidates for the six open and one regional seat in Simbu Province. Simbu disaffection with elected members of Parliament who have used their official privileges for personal gain was again confirmed.

> The election result in Simbu is very good. In that none of the seating members retained their seat. All new persons were voted in . . . there were 224 candidates stood for election this year. Only 7 won while the rest loose. . . . None of the seating members were voted in because the Simbu people believe that they were not faithful in their work. (Deck 1992)

The many independent candidates who join party coalitions, mainly after elections, cannot result in party alignment and policy formation. In fact, there are hardly any differences in candidates' political stance. Each candidate declares himself in favor of good government and better social and economic conditions, and hopes that he can benefit his constituents with roads, health facilities, economic growth, and schools, using government funds to invest in local activities. Party splits, new beginnings, and realignments are common throughout Papua New Guinea.[9]

Political hopefuls aspire to renown and esteem as big men. Seen as grand orators and generous feast givers, they dispense beer by the carton and tour the district. Many speak of buying votes and access to huge government gifts and contracts for development. Many people said that Peter Kuman won his support and election in 1987 from the money he dispersed as minister for local work on roads and the large beer parties he gave to voters. In 1991 he was said to have used a high-powered gun (AR15) and was sought for his part in a tribal fight (Gigmai 1991).

The apparent contradiction between a national electoral system, unstable political parties and membership, and the large numbers of independent individual candidates (whose chances are nearly hopeless) is, I think, a result of different meanings placed on the election process. Though national government must rest upon the party alignments of those elected to office, resources are allocated through ministries and regional competition, and there are prizes that those elected may gain by aligning themselves with a winning party. These associations are made after the successful candidates come together. But election campaigning among candidates is a stage for local rivalries: competition is with one's tribesmen and neighbors. As only one of the thirty or more candidates can win, the local campaign is a popularity bout among aspiring big men at home. Some proudly say, "I came in third." One's name matters within the tribe and clan. It is a modern version of the traditional exchange and feast system, relevant to the tribe and its neighbors.

> For most of the candidates, candidacy itself is the goal. It demonstrates local popularity, makes a big man, shows how the candidate measures up against local rivals for clan and tribe leadership. In this competition, candidacy itself, having one's name on the ballot, posters, cars, supporters is an indication of being a local big man. Secondly, success is measured by obtaining votes of the subclan, clan and tribe. Electoral success, that is, achieving office, against thirty or forty rivals cannot be expected. In the local contest the one who achieves the largest number of votes demonstrates that he has at least a local following.[10]

Elections are times of great interest in Simbu. In 1987 in Kundiawa, many of the candidates were nominated with a parade of clan and tribe supporters, and assumed a flamboyant style of campaigning. Candidates own or hire cars and campaign on the roads, loudly playing musical tapes and speaking through loud-hailers, or bullhorns. Roadside meeting places and small markets become platforms for speeches, and the close followers of a candidate hitch rides and drink and dispense beer in the area. Some large food and beer distributions are made, and there is much talk of buying, selling, and delivering votes. Expectations are high in most candidates and contesting ballot counts on suspicion of false returns is common. There were many candidates who hardly appeared in public but said they met in local communities and spoke in men's houses of the need for governmental responsibility and change. Candidates who traveled into parts of the area dominated by enemies of their tribe were sometimes attacked.

For nearly twenty years highlanders have disregarded the pacification that was thought to be completely successful by the kiaps of the 1930s, 1940s, and 1950s. As independence was planned and highlanders saw that their country would be ruled and administered by Papua New Guineans, often the educated elite of coastal and island Melanesia, they repudiated their avowals of peace and began to fight their neighbors and nearby tribesmen over local insults, injuries, land, and other disputes. The pressures of self-government were intensified by mistrust of the police and administrators, and the police in turn have been unable to control fights and warfare. In the past few years intertribal disputes and attacks have escalated with modern weapons. Another form of violence—which is present in urban areas, on highways, and in communities—takes the form of holdups, robbery, rape, beatings, and sometimes killings by raskol gangs. These groups of young men are often members of the same community; in towns they may be recruited from among migrants.

Despite frequent enforcement of curfews, declared emergency areas, and strong measures by riot police armed with mace and guns, tribal warfare and gang attacks continue throughout the parts of Papua New Guinea where potentially hostile groups are close neighbors and strangers travel the highway. Papua New Guinea towns are often the scenes of violence and robberies of residents and stores. Looting of shops and houses has become a common practice during mass gatherings for celebrations, funerals of important persons, and, as now reported, following the volcanic eruptions of September 1994 in Rabaul.

Europeans with long experience in the area, both administrators and missionaries, looked back to hail some achievements and deplore some new developments. A seasoned government administrator observed changes after independence when most of the Australian public service officers had gone home. He noted lax discipline in the Papua New Guinea public-service officers, and inefficient government and courts. He also found dishonesty and easy spending of government money among elected officials.

Independence, the end of kiap rule, has been followed by distrust of government and police and the use of guns by rural and urban gangs. New sources of knowledge and authority, and young people's mobility and exposure to opportunities beyond the valley have greatly weakened traditional family and community controls.

9

Simbu Voices

*Kiap Taylor chose me to carry the mail from Goroka to
Kundiawa because I was a brave man and a strong runner.*
—NONOVI SABARAI 1987
   (Interviewer Paula Brown) This Eastern Highlander
   was a mail carrier during World War II.

As the many interview excerpts and quotations above show, storytelling,
personal narratives, and self-accounts are a popular genre for the Simbu.
Men especially take delight in recounting their exploits and adventures.
Each person has a memory store of experiences, self-images, views of the
past, the events in his/her life. I found that Simbu tell their life stories with
pride and humor, and elaborate on their memories of fights and travels. I
will present some stories of the Naregu people of Bamugl and Mintima,
and others I know well from many field trips made from 1958 to 1987. I
also quote directly from life stories, personal experiences, and attitudes collected from people known in the communities of interviewers. In this way
I hope to avoid a biased report of what Simbu thought they should tell
me. Some stories are taken partly from an interview that I joined, some
entirely from interviewers; the situation is indicated. Most of the interviewers chose elders and people of some distinction; the lives of young villagers
and *rabisman* (P. worthless people; S. *yagl tom, ambu tom*) are poorly represented.

   Here I retell some abbreviated and condensed life stories. This is not a
collective biography, but rather an array of career accounts and reminiscences of individuals. The general course of Simbu history provides the context for memorable experiences in the life of the speaker. Every life is unique:
there is no typical life, although some age-group cohorts may have had similar experiences, such as labor migration, warfare, or holding elected office. I
have placed quotations from interviews in the appropriate chapters to demonstrate the breadth and variety of these recollections as reported to me and
to interviewers.

Life Stories

Wamugl, Waim, Waine, and Kum are longtime Mintima friends; they have told me about their memorable experiences, and I have observed them over many years. I put together the story of Wamugl, a Sunggwakani Naregu, from the many conversations we had over twenty-nine years. Born around 1922, he was an orphaned boy living at Kogai with his mother's relatives, as was Kondom when they were both young. They went about together to visit girls and singsing with them. One time they had to run away when Wauga men grabbed them. They broke Wamugl's arm and cut him on the leg, neck, chest, and head, then threw him in a stream and went away. He washed the blood off in the water, waited, then escaped. He was treated by the missionaries and recovered. In personal fights he was considered a troublemaker and told he should be a policeman. Wamugl began to work on the road and joined the police in about 1940, when Downs was at Kundiawa. Then, as a policeman in World War II, he was sent to Kokopo and New Britain.[1]

After his adventures in the war, when some of his fellows rejoined the police, Wamugl returned to Simbu. He worked at Kundiawa, Hagen, Nondugl, and Kerowagi as a bosboi building airstrips. Back at home he acquired land at Yuagl, then unused land belonging to the Maimangaumo group. Here he built up an estate with cash crops and extensive coffee planting. When I met him (in 1958) he was the leading man at Mintima, a coffee grower and promoter of business development with three wives and many pigs but no sons or staunch followers to continue his enterprises. A follower of Kondom and a pidgin speaker, he had friends among non-Simbu government clerks and workers in Kundiawa. In 1958 he was an entrepreneur at Mintima and was named as school komdi (P. committeeman, leader) in charge of organizing volunteer labor and plank cutting for Wandi school. In the following years he became a leading local government councillor, being reelected from 1959 through 1969 as the council expanded and councillors represented increasingly larger groups. Wamugl was one of the first men to have a successful trade store and kept it for many years. He organized the Chimbu Players, a theatrical group that performed traditional pantomimes and plays for tourists arriving by bus at Yuagl. This continued for over twenty years after he aged and retired from the council; Wamugl died in 1990.

Waim, a subclan brother of Wamugl, born about 1920, says that he learned pidgin from Kiap Taylor and became a work boy, then a turnim tok. Waim remembers when the two missionaries were killed. Kiap Downs took him to be a policeman, and he is mentioned in patrol reports of the 1940s. During the war he was stationed in Rabaul and in Wau, escorted Australians and evacuees from Kainantu and Mount Hagen, and fought the Japanese at

Lae, Wewak, and Madang. After the war he was trained at Port Moresby and promoted to corporal. During many years of police service he was stationed in the highlands at Goroka, Tari, Kainantu, Kundiawa, Hagen, Wabag, and Mendi. In 1970 Waim retired and in 1973 became a Mintima storekeeper, buying land from Maimangaumo at the roadside. In the 1980s the government made him a member of a peacemaking committee that attempts to stop fights and arrange settlements in intertribal disputes.

His many children by two wives have all been to school. Of wife Dan's ten children in 1976, some were married, some worked outside the area, and others were in school. In 1984 the sons were working in towns and the daughters were married, several living in towns. His wife Moro's two daughters married. Aina (Kathy) worked at a Mount Hagen bakery and Goroka coffee shop; in 1990 she accompanied her schoolmate Ambassador Margaret Taylor to Washington, D.C., as housekeeper and visited me in New York. Waim's son Apa George had several cars and a bus service attached to Waim's store; he became a candidate for the National Parliament in 1987, but died during the campaign.

Waine of Bamugl, Naregu, born about 1930, was one of the first men to be recruited in the Highlands Labour Scheme. He went to work copra with many men of Mintima. They were taken by plane from Kerowagi to Madang, then to Karkar Island plantation. Some cut grass, others made copra (see Chap. 8). Waine returned to Bamugl in the 1950s, before my first visit to Mintima. He says that, after his return, he went around with Harry (H. Brookfield) and me as turnim tok in our fieldwork.

When Waine was ready for marriage, his father had died, and two older men of his subclan, Tagubo and Binde, helped him with the bride-price; he was very grateful and named his first son Tagubo and the second son Binde. We knew Waine as an energetic householder and skilled flute player. He had established considerable coffee land, and when a young married man in the 1960s and later, he supported his mother, his wife's mother, his father's second wife, his father's brother's son's family, and his own wife and family of three sons and one daughter in a self-contained estate of houses, food gardens, and coffee. His sons were educated in high school and beyond—one in agricultural college and another as a teacher. Two of them suffered accidental deaths while in their twenties. In recent years Waine has been a magistrate, until his participation in a tribal fight in 1981 disqualified him for this office, and in the 1980s he was an electoral scrutineer.

Kum of Mintima, whom I first met in 1958 when he was cook to the A.D.O. in Kundiawa, was a man in his sixties when I recorded his story in 1987. He said:

I was a little boy when the first plane and white man came. The patrol came to Damar, stopped one night, then took cargo up to Yuagl, Nokun, Gamba. I saw them eat tin meat, red tomato sauce; I looked through a hole and saw them eating. They got some food—banana, *kaukau* from us; we didn't have tomato, onion, potato at that time.

(Then he told the story of the theft at Kunabau; see Chap. 3.)

I went to school at the mission at Dimbi. They gave me a piece of laplap cloth. Then a Madang teacher hit me and I ran away. They took my laplap away—the Father sent boys to get it. I didn't return to school. I worked when Japanese were at Wewak—worked for kiap, went to Madang. We carried goods, walked on tracks—there were no roads—during the war. I learned pidgin about 1950. Later I became a cook and worked for the kiaps, taught others to be cooks. After years as a cook in different places, I returned home and I have lived at home since the 1960s.

Kum's interest in white men's food may date from his peek through the tent hole and led him to a career as a cook.

Danga Mondo was born around 1920 at Pari in the Simbu valley. He had no formal schooling but worked as government interpreter at Kundiawa in the 1940s. Then he worked on roads and as a carpenter, and later came to Kerowagi and to Minj in 1946–1947. As cash cropping developed in the 1950s, he established a homesite and was the first Simbu to acquire a large area of land on government contract, which was near Kerowagi fellow tribesman. This had been avoided land, unclaimed by any person or group, and Danga built up a family enterprise with food and cash crops, coffee and cattle. He later obtained an Agricultural Bank loan and successfully met its requirements. His activities include cattle raising and plantings of cardamom and peanuts, as well as coffee.

In 1976 Danga had a car he used for buying coffee. He had three wives and a large family of educated children; several were employed outside the province as doctors, teachers, government employees, soldiers, or policemen. He and a son have been unsuccessful political candidates several times. After the death of Kondom in 1966, Danga was president of the Kundiawa Coffee Society.

Danga is well known as a long-established successful agricultural developer and businessman. For some years he has served as a peace negotiator, and was appointed to be a salaried member of the peacemaking committee (along with Waim). When a fight is threatened or begun, the committee is called by the administration to talk with fight leaders to arrange for the end of tribal fighting. As explained to me by Danga, the peace committee negotiates with the involved parties, pointing out to tribal leaders that fighting will destroy houses, crops, and businesses, and trying to arrange payments of compensation for death in pigs and money. In the 1980s these compensation payments were K4,000–5,000 (about $5,000–6,000), which was to be collected from tribesmen involved in the fighting. According to Danga, the peace committee advises the parties to pay when coffee money comes in. Danga was a leader in collecting compensation money for fights when Kamanegu were involved. Danga is an active member of the Seventh-Day Adventist church in Kerowagi. He has a modern house made of metal with a raised floor and modern furniture, cars, and a thriving cash-crop business.

I here summarize the life story of Geregl Gande, a Silku (Siku) from Kerowagi, from the profile written by Paul Dage in 1986:

> Geregl was born at Kup in 1930, when his mother fled from tribal fighting. He remembers the first missionary at Mingende and white man at Kundiawa and later Kerowagi. He was taken to the kiap by his father, and first became firewood boy for the kiap, learned pidgin, began to interpret at the age of ten. Became interpreter and wanted to teach people that he believed the kiap government was better for the people to learn and obey. He was aggressive and used physical force by punishing the men and women so they would do anything the kiap wanted them to do. At age sixteen Geregl was the top interpreter at Kerowagi. At nineteen he was a policeman on patrols and conducting census, and learned to shoot a rifle. Geregl was considered rough on the people. In the Second World War he was taken to join Australian troops, and stationed in the highlands, in Morobe, Markham valley, and fought Japanese. After the war he became a medical orderly so that he could remain in one area and get married. He trained at Mount Hagen and traveled with a whiteman doctor who said that whiteman medicine is better than traditional. He would share things with people who came to the aid post. From 1946 for five years he was aid post orderly at Boko. Geregl wanted to become a leader to his people as he knew the people respected him. He wanted to organize the people and lead them in speech making, a *kaungo yomba* (S. orator). Then he acquired land, wives, and became rich. Geregl heard about coffee and money from the agricultural officer, and became a coffee bosboi supervising planting, told people how to pick and wash coffee, dry beans, and make money. He saw that people bought salt, cloth in stores. Then returned to own village to grow coffee. People respected him for his knowledge of white man's laws, as a leader. Dage says: "He was qualified to be a leader in the sense of solving any problems, issues and decision for the good of the people." In the early 1960s Geregl was elected a councillor, to decide the real work of the people when cash economy and money were vital. Geregl had a close relationship with kiaps and patrol officers. When village

courts were established he was elected magistrate, chairman of village court. Now he has three wives and fifteen children.

Joseph Teine Iuanga was interviewed by Lawrence Gigmai and me in 1987 and was known to me for some years. The following combines our notes.

I was told that I was about two years old when the white man came. From the age of seven, schooled at Catholic mission at Kumbo, I was taught basic alphabet and arithmetic in pidgin—which I did not fully understand but picked up quick enough that I was selected to be a mission teacher. I was catechist for fifteen years from 1947 until 1962. Then I was elected councillor 1962 in Waiye-Digabe Council; to the House of Assembly (later National Parliament) for Kundiawa district 1972–1976.

(Joe was in the opposition, and at the time of independence he was against it, but everyone forced independence.)

In 1982 I was elected to Simbu Provincial Assembly and I had the intention of becoming premier. Mathew Siune was the premier then but later he led the government to corruption.

Finally I'm a Catholic myself and still playing politics and currently a member of the board of directors of the Simbu Holding Enterprises, a business arm of the Simbu Provincial Government. I believe that the true wealth of the nation is in land, but that youngsters now don't touch the land. The mission schools should be supported by the government, as they are able to produce brainy people, create jobs and provide vital services.

Joe Teine has ten children by one wife, all educated and most working outside the area. Two of his sons are lawyers. Alphonse Yer, born in 1953, was schooled at Kondiu, National High School, and University of Papua New Guinea, and became a law graduate in 1977. Alphonse was a public solicitor, then a lawyer in private practice in Mount Hagen. Unlike his younger brother, Joe Mek, Alphonse told me in 1987 that he has no political ambitions. Joe Mek Teine is also a law graduate; he was public solicitor in Mount Hagen but resigned to stand as candidate for Parliament 1987. Teine said his son, at age twenty-six, is too young for office. Joe Mek told me that if he lost (which he did), he would not stand again; but in fact he did stand as Simbu regional candidate for Parliament in the 1992 election, and again failed. Two other children of Joe Teine are a teacher and a corrective institution officer, and the youngest were studying at school or teachers' college. In later years Joe has become a farmer and businessman, owning coffee gardens, livestock, and a bus. Although he represents the first mission-educated men who have won leading political offices, he holds strong traditional and Catholic values and believes in the work ethic. He deplores declining respect for elders and lawlessness, and sees a need for strong leaders.

Karigl Bonggere of Simbu valley (interviewer Apa Tobias):

> Karigl is from Denglagu; born near Gembogl about 1932; saw airplane, missionaries. Heard that kiaps and police were shooting people and pigs because of death of two early missionaries. After mission school he was catechist at Goglme. Became a good shot and had license to shoot animals in Gembogl. Then District Advisory Council Gembogl. Trade store and first car in area. Coffee gardens, club. Was president of Mt Wilhelm Local Government Council; elected to House of Assembly (then Parliament) for two terms 1968–1976; continues to stand but not elected.
>
> Karigl Bonggere's wife was in school, and they married after her baptism. They had seven children. John, born 1952, went to Goroka Teachers' College; died. Vero Kaglme studied at Port Moresby Teachers' College and is now a teacher. Toby attended University of Papua New Guinea and is now a lawyer in private practice in Kundiawa. Joan went to Holy Trinity Teachers' College and is a teacher in Simbu. Joe attended Laloki Business College, and is now Business Development officer Simbu. Kumi, born 1963, stopped at grade 8. Dominic, born 1978, was in grade 3 in 1987.

Several men of the small subclan Komunkngaumo in Naregu achieved distinction. Kaglwaim has been mentioned and quoted several times; his career from renowned warrior to tultul to respected Christian elder spans sixty years. Another elder, Ombo, received an old-age gift on 12 June 1976, which I observed. His kinsmen from Kombugo provided a large money payment, stated to be over 2,000 kina, stacks of beer, and a big food presentation that was shared by all.

In 1987 Bruce Mondo Kair recorded the life story of Ombo's son, Kair Ombo. Kair's son (Ombo's grandson), Bruce, has benefited from his schooling; he prepared excellent interview reports and was an active football player while living in his home community. I summarize here:

> Kair was born in the early thirties and joined the police in 1952 . . . became a policeman while still illiterate . . . patrolling in Goroka. . . . He got leave and came home, where he got married and then went to Okapa where he stayed for about 15 years. . . . Children were born in Okapa and Madang, and all went to school.
>
> When stationed at Chuave the people of Elimbari were still savages so he was once beaten up near the station while on duty. He left the force in 1975

and retired. He said: "Back at village I preserve my culture and tradition. . . . I really am glad and appreciate my pension because I'm old and am back in the village. . . . My mates and I are the pioneers of today's developments."

Kimbe Monguwai, an Endugwa, was interviewed by me and Paul Ambani of the Lae University of Technology in 1987. He was a boy when Kiap Taylor came; was taken to work as a carrier, but was scared and ran away. Then, when he learned the white man was not a spirit, he worked cutting bush for salt and other things. Kimbe was made a tultul by the kiap; after the local government council began, he was a komdi. Kimbe worked with Kondom, built roads, planted coffee, and introduced livestock.

Lawrence Gigmai recorded the life story of Baundo Kir, an Endugwa:

> I was just a child so I couldn't recall seeing the first missionaries. I attended mission school at Mauraugl. I married a wife from Mindima who had children 2 twin brothers and a sister and a small brother. The inlaw is Dokopa. Before I was a councillor during Kondom's times. I have never entered politics. I had plenty of coffee trees but all chopped down by Kamanekus during the tribal fights.

The story of Bandiyagl of Naregu was recorded by Michael Mugua. It can be summarized as an account of the events of a village life. His father was killed in a war when he was a child, before he saw white men. When his mother died, he and his sisters lived with relatives at Bamugl; he and other boys stole food and pigs and took them to the men's house. He was arrested by a patrol officer and made to walk to Goroka and work there. He married; his children were born at Bamugl and went to school at Mingende mission. One became a teacher and later joined the Papua New Guinea defense force. Bandiyagl has visited Mount Hagen, Lae, and Madang to buy feathers, shells, and possum fur for women to make string bags, which he sells in the village. He has planted coffee gardens and has about four to five hundred trees. He is a simple man, but the people of his village call on him to discuss marriages and stop quarrels. He has seen many new things and styles.

Women's Lives

For the life stories of women, who are rarely recognized leaders, I asked both men and women to interview and in many cases joined in the interviews or conducted them myself. I collected a number of life stories from rural women that followed a local pattern of youth, courting parties, marriage, family and home life. The aim was to learn how women have lived and how they see their lives as individuals. The three women portrayed here represent three different age groups. For all, the church offered the opportunity for training and leadership; there was no precontact counterpart.

Ninmongo, born about 1918, leads Catholic prayer meetings of men, women, and children. I knew her father in his last year,[2] and in 1958 heard his stories of wars, defeats, and the migration of his tribe, Naregu, from the Simbu valley to Mintima and Damar. Ninmongo remembers moving from place to place as a child because of fighting. She is the eldest child; her younger sister and brothers were born after they settled at Damar. She married Miane, moved a short distance to his adjacent clan territory, and has been in the area her whole life. Ninmongo and her two brothers Goiye and Bomai are all intelligent, outgoing, active members of their local group; Ninmongo does not speak pidgin. I extract from the story that I obtained (10 June 1984) and also a life history taken by Michael Mugua (1987).

> I lived at Yuage with my family. I looked after my small brothers and sister when my mother went to the garden. In those days there was no school and mission or kiap station. We just lived in our village and we had no games for us to enjoy so what we used to do was we looked for frogs, insects, wild fruit, honey, lizards, and nests. What I saw during my life was that my village people have a lot of ceremonies and tribal fighting; ceremonies of pig killing, wedding, funeral, food ceremonies, singsing with boys. They had this when I was a child and have it now. My father went to tribal fighting; all the tribes were fighting with ours. We never visited our friends from other clans, just lived in our village.
>
> When I was about to carry leg [P. go to courtship parties] one day I heard people say there were two ghosts coming out of grave to Kundiawa they were both white men. Some people said they were their ancestors or relatives who died long ago. This time I was not married yet. Word came that they were coming out. My people were waiting at the road when they came to my place our people gave them food. They went to Mt Hagen, came back. Message came that they had killed a lot of people from Wauga. So keep away from them. Then word came that there was another spirit or ghost coming with three men from Siambugla clan. They settled at Dimbi, then down to Mingende. It was father Separ [Schäfer]. I was married to Miane at Bamugl. Two of us live for some time and then I give birth to a daughter but she died. After a while I have a son we named him Dokoba William. When he grew up he went to school Mingende Catholic mission, then Kondiu, then worked as superintendent of the malaria service but he died in 1971 in Madang. In my childhood I haven't travelled but by transport I have been to Madang, Lae, Goroka, Mt Hagen. What we women do is very very hard in our life time. We cook for pigs and our family, gardening, clearing, planting, with care for babies. We women had a hard time; it is the culture that men should not spend time with his wife. So it was hard.

Ninmongo's brothers Goiye and Bomai are fluent speakers of pidgin; both have had some years of schooling and have worked outside the area. Goiye worked as a laborer in Kavieng for three years as a copra bosboi, at Kagamugl and Banz as a cook, and at Bulolo. He has been a local magistrate for some fifteen years as well. Bomai worked for years as cook-houseboy, including for me on many visits from 1959 to 1987. During one season, Dokoba, his sister's son, was a manki in our household. Ninmongo's husband, Miane, whose clan adjoins that of Ninmongo's family, is prominent and responsible but not a "big man."

For many years Ninmongo has been a regular parishioner at the Catholic mission in Mingende. She said they called her for the Legion of Mary, and she goes to church meetings on Tuesdays. She brings men and women together for talk and prayer. She tells the people to behave well, not to fight or steal, to talk of the Lord Jesus, pray. She brings news of the work of the mission, attending all special meetings and serving as a women's and community leader. Nowadays she leads prayers in the evening when men and women gather in the men's house, and she is also called upon whenever there are women's activities in the area. Many girls of Bamugl and Mintima have been named Ninmongo; such naming (S. *dina*) indicates that the parents felt that she had been a particular friend and helped the mother in childbirth and home care. She is respected, the first woman people think of when problems arise in which the mission may be involved. In the community there is no more important woman; Bamugl people have not been involved in many provincial activities; their chief distinction is performing as "Mudmen" in tourist entertainments, in which Ninmongo is an occasional performer.

Kal Mondo was born perhaps twenty-five years after Ninmongo. In 1984 and later, I often saw her at the office of the first business development officer for women, who promoted cash-raising activities at home, shops selling handicrafts, and canteens (P. haus kaikai). At Ku, located on the highway a few miles east of Kundiawa, Kal was the energetic, pidgin-speaking leader of a women's club project that received the support of the business officer and welfare department. In 1984 I visited Ku in the company of a (male) social development officer and was shown two buildings: the women's clubhouse, for its twenty-seven members; and a canteen where food was served and sold. At that gathering the group was planning to begin sewing, a poultry project, and the expansion of artifact and doll making for a tourist shop in Kundiawa. I was told that the main purpose of the club was to help the blind, the lame, and women, especially widows and wives who had been divorced when their husbands were required by the church to embrace monogamy. They saw the facts that widows had no one to help them and to build their houses, and that unmarried mothers were now living in the village, as new problems. The several clubs I visited in Simbu Province had a few men speaking, and often directing, the meetings.

Kal's life story was taken down for me by Moro in 1985, and I have added to it some notes and observations from my talks with her during 1984–1987. After the 1984 provincial election, Kal was appointed as women's representative in the Provincial Assembly. In 1987 I saw her frequently in the provincial office, the only woman in the premier's inner chamber. She frequently sat with the men in informal conversation. Because of her I felt able to enter and talk with the men. (I was at that time doing interviews of parliamentary candidates and politicians.)

The life history recorded by Moro, an educated young women, states that Kal's father was a luluai and that there were no schools in her community of Sinasina. Her first marriage (about 1962) was to a domestic servant at Lufa; then, divorced, she married Mondo, also a domestic servant, and worked for the Chimbu District Officer. She then returned to her husband's home village of Ku, where she had two children. They are baptized Lutherans, and Kal was a church leader in the 1970s. She now lives with her husband, has one married daughter, and says she has adopted a young girl. She was chosen chairwoman of the Simbu women's business group, which maintains a craft shop and cultural center at Kundiawa. Her fluent pidgin and experience gave her a prominent leading position. I saw her frequently in Kundiawa, sometimes with a child in hand, always nicely dressed and moving between the women's business development office and the provincial government office, attending meetings and talking with women from all over the province. She frequently represented Simbu Province in regional and national women's association meetings. Although Kal was confident enough to be the only woman to go into the premier's inner sanctum, I have never seen her speak out or make any comment in the general discussion with the men.

The final line of Moro's interview is "She says even though I'm not educated I can take up any opportunities which will be given through my experience." I read that in 1990 Ku, her village, was the center of an adult literacy campaign, and I am sure that she was involved in its promotion.

Lynn Womba, principal of the provincial nurse training school, is one of a small group of Simbu professional women now working in official positions in the province. I found her at the nurses' training school on my last day in Kundiawa in 1987. She began to give me her life history as a curriculum vitae, speaking in fluent English about her father, a Lutheran pastor, who encouraged Lynn and her brother to seek scholarships. By that time I had interviewed a number of female schoolteachers and health workers. Many of them had reached a conflict with their husbands and raised their children themselves while pursuing their careers. Lynn was another; her career had been a series of schools, jobs, training programs, and postings to new workplaces. She had supported her child and, for some of the time, a husband with technical skills who has worked as a contractor in various places. She speaks with professional concern of the curriculum and training programs in nursing and community health that the school is developing.

After working as a nurse and teacher in many places, Lynn prefers to live in Kundiawa near her family; she is active in the Lutheran women's group and close friends with other professional women. Her job, with its professional responsibilities, the church, and her friends are her life. She is firmly outspoken about her wishes and standards, which do not include making a home for her husband. Her son is now in high school, and she has adopted a relative's child. She will not allow drinking or smoking in her house and holds to her principles. She refused to help a relative pay compensation for killing a woman on the highway and will not be swayed by the claims of her kinsmen. She says that she does help women who come to her, gives money to the church and to causes she approves of. Her decisiveness was, to me, almost unique in a woman. She thinks men manipulate women. On the subject of women in politics, she says she respects them and their goals, and thinks there's a place for women today. "Men don't understand how women feel." Her interests and support depend upon her own Christian principles and standards, and she makes up her own mind on every issue. None of the women I interviewed was as independent and autonomous as Lynn.

These women are of three different age groups and differ greatly in education, career, and activities. If they are leaders who have departed from their contemporaries, in each case circumstances and opportunities were offered through the missions or government schools and programs; none owes her position to indigenous development. The three women are outstanding members of the small set of women in positions of significance, local and provincial. Their places in their communities, their qualifications, and their knowledge demonstrate the rapid change of Simbu life. Simbu women's demeanor and style, even those of leaders, contrasts with the oratorical manner of leading Simbu men.

The diversity of these lives, within a Simbu context, demonstrates a range of personal situation, chance, the impact of introduced mission and government education, job opportunities, and political circumstances, combined with the abilities, training, and interests of the individual persons. The education and careers of children reflect both the parents' and the child's choices and ambitions.

How the Simbu View Change in Their Lives

These selfless Missionaries, who were known as the Fathers of soft bows because of their meekness and kindness, were supported by the gallant Kiaps, the Fathers of the strong bows, for their sternness and toughness, combined forces of meekness and sternness in conquering the Highlands and made the people tame.
—KILAGE n.d.:37–38

When I prepared questions to guide the life-story interviews these were included: What do you think of the changes you have seen? Is your life better than before? What is good? What is not good? Some also responded to the question: Do you think the government can make things better? How? As written up by interviewers, the responses take different forms, yet it will be seen that they have much in common.

Western technology, knowledge, and what they see as a western way of life have been admired and desired by Simbu for more than two generations. These are mentioned in nearly every interview over many years. In the Upper Simbu valley in 1959 I was told:

We had stone axes and tools, and did not walk alone at night because we were afraid of attacks by enemies. We went courting by stealth, and some girls came to their friends. There were enemy groups, and when the fighting stopped they were friendly and would court and marry. In wartime we went out to kill. Now we have schools and work.

And in Kerowagi:

Before the kiap came we had wars. Then the kiap came to Kundiawa. He said to make a government station, and gave us rings and brass medals. The policemen burned our wood and stone weapons and gave us steel. This is good. Three missions have come: we follow their teaching. The government has shown us coffee, peanuts and food, and now we work. There will be a council. Now we are all peaceful here.[3]

The oldest Simbu can remember precontact times of tribal warfare, fleeing the enemy, hunger, and the killing of family members. Along with the benefits of peace and western goods, many elders see a loss of moral and social control, a deterioration in community support and cooperation, increasing crime, the raskols, and political chicanery. I begin with elders' statements emphasizing the benefits of the white man and colonial experience, such as new and more reliable foods, improved tools and household goods, roads and cars, clothing, health, education, and stabilized community life.

Simbu of the next generation, of course, know the stories of the old days and have lived with kiaps and missionaries all their lives. A number of men and women who did not experience precontact tribal warfare contrasted colonial times and the recent period of independence.

When we asked women their opinions of the changes they have experienced, they often said the good things are roads, manufactured goods, clothing, bedding, education, religion, and medical care. They think other things introduced by the white man—alcohol, disco, prostitution—are bad, and they deplore the abandonment of traditional custom, loss of ceremony, and what they see as selfishness among young people.

Some of the statements are "wish lists" and relate also to the parliamentary elections, which were to be held shortly after our field inquiries in 1987. It is clear that many commentators, agreeing with senior Australian public servants, feel that violence and dishonesty have come about with the end of Australian colonial administration and mistrust their fellow countrymen and their elected representatives. Simbu say that among the failures of recently elected members of Parliament is their failure to bring news and inform their constituencies of legislation and issues that may concern them. The announcing role of politicians is a Simbu requirement, and some leaders fail at this.

What Simbu Elders Say about the Present

Agl Gandi, a Pagau of Kerowagi (interviewer Jenny Aglai):

> Today's life is very enjoyable and people have a lot of freedom to move around, live in good houses, travel in fast moving transports. But before—in my days we had a terrible life. The only transport we had was land transport. We walked from one place to another.

Kombani Kundie of Bogo, Kerowagi (interviewer Naur Awi Philip):

> To conclude, he said that life before was hard. A brother killed his own brother, and people lived in great fear, but now life is free. He said today we have good means of food, health services, transportation, education, housing and clothing.

Martin Nombri, a teacher of Naregu, wrote this in 1987, and it was collected by Paul San:

> The government has done tremendous things. The government has guided us through hard and easy times. The government makes decision and solves prob-

lems on our own disregard of good or bad. Being independent to me is good. We can govern our self as we wish and not by the white countries.

The change I have seen is magnificent. Some of the changes which I have seen is the rapid westernization of Papua New Guinea and Simbu and is adopted fast by the people in a peaceful way without shedding of blood like some other countries. I like the fast changes. But the foreign cultures should be systemise with our culture. The resources we have should be exported in bigger portion. The cheap selling of our culture and the misusing of the western culture is disliked by me.

Epema Drua of Kamanegu, a church elder of Ega Lutheran mission who was baptized in 1947, was interviewed in my house (with translation by Ruth Kega) on 13 April 1987. After baptism she went around with a native pastor, led a Christian life, and is now a Lutheran women's group leader.

My young life was good, I still enjoy life. Living before, we had rules. Knew each other, lived well, no stealing or damage or there would be tribal fights. We obeyed the clan and family rules. There was no running around like today. We shared everything. No one was left out when there was something to share. Today is different. People run here and there. The girls leave at marriage, it is selfish living. Food is not shared. We have laws of the government but it doesn't work right.

Talaba Sinne of Masul, eastern Simbu (interviewer Fred Eremuge):

I am very happy to see all these changes because these have changed a lot of our old lives. It gives us a lot of freedom to go to some other parts of the country. It brings in a lot of things such as machinery—in the olden days we normally use our hands to do all the work, but nowadays we use machinery.

The change which is not good or which we don't want to see is that our physical environment is destroyed, which means we won't be able to get trees to build houses and so on and at the same time we won't be able to hunt birds and animals because there won't be any more bushes for us to hunt and no more land.

This man was one of the few who spoke of land and environmental pressures, which have been observed throughout northern Simbu Province for many years. Our studies at Mintima show the loss of shared group territory and cooperative work in fencing and garden preparation (Brown, Brookfield, and Grau 1990).

Mondo Ola of Ombondo, Simbu valley (interviewer Paul San):

When we talk about independence we don't like it because during Australian rule we were better off but today when we are independent it seems that independence is only for the young ones and we old are being forgotten. . . . The changes I like are clothes, food of a different type, health centres . . . the bad is the behaviour of our young ones. They turn to rascalism and prostitution are what I don't like.

Porongo Kunma of Bogo, Kerowagi (interviewer Naur Awi Philip):

Porongo said, he has seen many changes with his own eyes. These changes were due to the influence of western culture. Young people today are not interested in participating or keeping the traditional rituals and that's why the traditional rituals are slowly fading away. Young people today are interested in following western culture. Because of these many changes, the living standard is also changing. He said living standard today is much better than before. We have good means of health services, which we did not have before. We have good food which nourishes our body daily, with less sickness. Before we ate same quality of food every meal. Today we have short means of transportation, but before walking was the only means of transportation in the highlands. Also today people are free to move around as they wish without much fear of attacking. Today we have good system of education where many Papua New Guineans are highly educated which means they are just in line with the Europeans. Also our young people know more of the outside world. Also we today have good housing and clothing. There are few things he doesn't like. He said, today young people are not respecting their leaders. He also said the life today is free but he doesn't like this rascalism fashion. And lastly he doesn't want this elite system to be practiced in Papua New Guinea. He said, this is a young country and people should be all equal. . . . He believes the Government will still make the things better, because we are already independent of the colonial powers. . . .

Porongo has received several medals for his hard and dedicated work to the people of Kerowagi. He is now a respected man, and his dedication and services will be remembered for ever.

Mondia of Siambugla (interviewer Francis Kombugum):

"Is it better since independence or not?": When Europeans of Australia looked after us we got money enough and they did well for us. We were happy with Australian government. Now our own people look after us. They don't do anything for us. No money; it goes into their own pockets. I don't like our own government.

What Simbu Say They Want

Gull of Endugwa (interviewer Harry Godfrid):

> To name the changes I like would be those of schools, hospitals, roads (basically all forms of development). I would also be prepared for the use of army in controlling the numerous tribal fights in the Province to maintain peace. But at same time I do not like prostitution, discos, and criminal activities. They are replacing some of our traditionally valued activities such as *kuanande* (S. carry-leg courtship) and various initiation activities that are gradually vanishing. In discussing the 1987 general election, he said after the election the new Parliament should do the following:
> —use army to control crime and tribal fighting;
> —put more emphasis on the people to improve their living standards;
> —free secondary education;
> —provide funds for rural projects, roads, and during famine;
> —free electricity;
> —good housing;
> —decrease the cost of goods in stores.

Mondo Gunama of Toromambuno, upper Simbu valley (interviewer John Karl):

> I want big factories, many airstrip, many jobs that can be created so that our child in school can work and also we want Development.

Michael Prul of Hagen, Western Highlands District (interviewer Talaba Kulga):

> I can see changes which are good and others which are not. My life is better than before. The good things I could say is that we've got good medical care, less tribal fighting, meeting different people, and have the opportunity in visiting other places, and bad sides are rascal activities in urban centres, creating classes of people—that is rich people and poor people. And unemployment, urban drifters and squatter settlers in urban centres. What the government could do to improve problems:
> —set up projects in villages where young people can run it;
> —let foreign companies to invest in this country which could create jobs for young people;
> —introduce an education system which equip students more suited in their village resources;
> —jobs which could be handled by us should be localized.

Kua Bogia of Kangrie, Simbu valley (interviewer Joseph Mondo):

The changes I have seen have made me think deep and I come to the conclusion that the rich get richer while the poor get poorer. I would like revolution.
The whole system and government is not good. Changes to be made are many
and diverse but a good start would be to change the style of leadership from one
of money-hunting egotistic politicians to self-sacrificing honest statesmen.

Karigl Bongere, former member of the House of Assembly, of Gembogl,
Simbu valley (interviewer Apa Tobias):

He wants to see his people keeping some of the good traditional customs as well
as some of the good western culture. He said roads, bridges etc are good changes
but rascalism, drunkenness and prostitution are bad. Controlling beer, stop taxation, controlling inflation to minimize prices of goods and services, and chan-
nelling more funds to small businesses, severe treatments to law breakers,
improvement in health services and a good dose of detailed knowledge to students at Tertiary level with better and more advanced learning facilities will
stop most of the social, economic and political problems of today and tomorrow. "I wish I was still in Parliament so I can solve these problems today which
I didn't see yesterday."

Election Campaigns and the View of the Future

When candidates make speeches, they seem to transform the "wish list" of a
Simbu into that of a spokesman enunciating policy. In 1984 we interviewed
candidates for office in the Simbu Provincial Assembly, and in 1987 the candidates for the Papua New Guinea Parliament. Candidates for office in
Simbu Province were very numerous, and for the most part young, educated
more than the average, and with some experience in government and business Standish 1983, 1992; (Brown 1987a). As many of them stand for provincial and national office when elections are held, and have the support of
their local group and often some leaders in the tribe and district, the candidates represent the sophisticated elite of Simbu Province.

When interviewed by Paula Brown in 1987, John Nilkare stressed the
importance of and need for experienced managers and trained manpower in
both private and public sectors. He has worked with expatriate associates in
his businesses. Nilkare said the country has huge undeveloped resources and
that, as the Australian subsidy is reduced, he would ask developed countries
of the world to give aid for specific projects. The Simbu people, he said, are
short of land for agriculture, resettlement is required, and forestry needs to be

developed. Simbu is far from markets and unsuitable for industrial development, but the abilities of the Simbu people can be cultivated with practical
training.

In my report on the 1987 Parliamentary campaign I said:

> Every candidate questioned stated that his political program, even if little
> enunciated in his public addresses, was to improve the life conditions of Simbu
> Province: roads, business, investment, educational and health facilities for the
> people. The 1987 catchword was "grassroots." Few mentioned national or inter-
> national issues, and these rarely arose in public discussion. Problems of corrup-
> tion, bribery, law and order in Simbu, curing the ills of former governments,
> were also raised. Some manifest little knowledge of the powers and capacities of
> Parliament to deal with local or national problems. Very few candidates stated
> any party allegiance in terms of political issues. However, party support in the
> form of funds and materials was received by some and expected by others. Many
> take the position that:
>
> I'm independent and stand on my personal popularity and character. The
> voters will choose me because I am well known, well liked, honest, trustworthy,
> and have a strong group of supporters in my clan and tribe. If I win I may join
> the winning party, hold a ministry and bring great benefits to my community,
> tribe, district and province. (Brown 1989:249)

These 1987 candidates, sophisticates, young men who attended school
and university, played football, traveled around Papua New Guinea and in
many cases overseas for training and experience, all looked to the future of
Simbu Province. They know that opportunity for agriculture is restricted by
the large population and limited land. A few successful independent businessmen and professionals serve as models for the ambitious, and are often
candidates for provincial and national office. Simbu assess the present and
future in terms that might be used almost anywhere, evaluating the experience of their people and reflecting on the leaders and forces of change.

Simbu put some hopes in the government to solve problems, as a legacy
of the days when the Australian administration was the bearer of progress
and the main source of money and skills. In the midst of the good things
brought by the white man, Simbu increasingly are discouraged by lack of
economic progress and by the political corruption and violence of their fellows—all of which is seen as having come since independence. Though
Simbu today speak in many voices, all see their life as changed—for good
and for ill—by the forces of the Australian administration, the missions, and
the experiencing of the world beyond their mountain valley.

In their statements about change, good and bad, Simbu show strong
agreement. Western goods, health facilities, foods, roads, vehicular transpor-

tation, and education are marked improvements over the precontact conditions of life still vividly recalled by the elders. Money and cargo are the means to this style of life, and no one would return to the past. Today some long-term mission adherents, teachers, elders, and officials deem their better life a Christian one.

In 1987, twelve years after independence, most of the elders and the middle-aged colonial cohort found fault with postcolonial life. They praised the kiap order, the leaders of the past, and distrusted their new leaders. However, the elders had faded from formal leadership. Recently, most men elected to political office have been under forty years of age, educated, and successful in the postcolonial period. This new elite is highly competitive, and the fast turnover of officeholders shows the voters' dissatisfaction with their elected representatives.

10

Isolation, Intrusion, Inclusion

Kondom taught us how to plant and how to take care of coffee.
He had good thoughts.
—GENDUA OF BAMUGL, NAREGU, 1987
  (interviewer Paula Brown)

After his [Iambakey's] death, the meaning and significance of his
name persists and grows because of the events of his life and
how they are remembered by the people of Papua New Guinea.
—RYDER 1992:7

Transformation

In their sixty years of contact and interaction with newcomers, Simbu social horizons have extended from isolation to inclusion in a new nation, to the world economy and participation in the United Nations. The transformation has affected Simbu values and relationships between them and outsiders in their social world.

The precontact life of the Simbu was no peaceful communal subsistence and pastoral existence. Each local population pressed upon its neighbors because of dense settlement and contention for land. Simbu intergroup relations are competitive; among each group and its neighbors conditions oscillate between war and exchange. To take Clausewitz' epigram, "war is the continuation of politics by other means" (1832):[1] for Simbu, politics may be equated with intergroup exchange. The whole productive effort and drive toward prestige of Simbu is embedded in exchanges among tribes, clans, and groups, led and managed by big men. Preparations for a large feast require the combined efforts of the entire group, and the rewards are shared. In war, allies are sought among kinsmen and exchange partners in other groups.

The limits of expansion, population growth, and fluctuations in alliance and warfare effected an unstable, non-equilibrium system, even during periods of little fundamental innovation in technology or political relations (Brown 1979a). Intercommunity, interclan, and intertribe relations alter-

nated between competition and cooperation, marital and intergroup exchange, fights and wars. Precontact times are seen by kiaps, missionaries, and
Simbu alike as times of ecological and social stress, and most older commentators say that they welcome the coming of the white man as the bearer of
peace, improved living conditions, and community stability. But the first
view of the white man did not promise these better times.

The lives of individuals are contextualized by the general conditions
and culture of Simbu Province. This includes the Simbu view of the important and heroic people of recent history; these heroes' lives are grounded in
the same soil. Some, as will be seen, have attained a local legendary character, a place in history as Simbu see it. The named people and places mark
turning points and events. Simbu lore and storytelling include many tales
about the acts and performances of persons who lived in the past and did
wonderful things.

Some heroes of the past are described in thorough and circumstantial
detail by their relatives, friends, and associates, and are seen as having played
a significant role in their time, as prophets and innovators. In Simbu it is significant to say, "I saw it with my own eyes"; this is regarded as a test of
authenticity. Other stories may only suggest eyewitness accounts and have
extraordinary, magical incidents. These include the stories of the nonhistori-
cal personages Magruai (Rambo 1990) and Kurara Yagl (Hughes 1988:67–
68). These two are inimical characters, magical and unpredictable.

Magruai appeared from the east, it is said, shortly before the first white
man was seen. He had many features of a rabisman: he was short and ugly, a
homeless wanderer whose behavior, notably singing and eating rat heads,
was eccentric. When visiting among strangers he could speak their language.
Magruai makes food multiply and performs a miracle: he brings plenty; but
this is in the form of vegetable greens, not favored foods. Now, the legend of
Magruai, an unkempt wanderer, has made him into the herald of Christianity and events to come (Rambo 1990).

Discovery and First Contact

The first sight of airplanes, the Taylor-Leahy patrol, missionaries, and other
stories of patrols are everywhere described as wondrous events.[2] By their
accounts, Simbu were agog when they first saw the white men, their clothes,
dogs, and goods, New Guinean police and carriers, and the goods they
received from them when they gave them food. These things were amazing:
were they men or spirits? They had and gave shells and other greatly valued
objects. Simbu sought ways to obtain the goods of the newcomers and, if possible, to exclude other Simbu from the advantages. Simbu, and many other
highlanders, were quick to accept the trade goods that patrols and mission-

aries offered for food and pigs. They invited mission, government, and private settlers to build houses and live among them.[3] My data suggest that this
was a typically opportunistic Simbu act—they welcomed newcomers in the
hope that these rich strangers would be friends, allies, and providers of shells,
knives, axes, cloth, and other new goods. The presence of armed allies on
the borders of tribal land would be a barrier to the raids and invasions of
enemy groups.

The beginning of the Catholic mission at Mingende, which for sixty
years has been a major force for education and religious change, assumes
dramatic form in the stories Simbu tell of Kawagl and Fr. Schäfer. They per-
sonify the transformation for Simbu, especially those of the central area
around Mingende.

Kawagl and the Catholic Mission

Kawagl is renowned as the man who brought Fr. Schäfer and Christianity to
the Simbu and is a hero for the Catholics of the area. I collected a number of
accounts of the role Kawagl played in the entry of Fr. Schäfer into Simbu. He
was already aged in 1958, when I first saw him, and his son Asiwe had taken
over leadership of the Siambugla-Wauga as luluai and later councillor.

My field notes of interviews at Dimbi with two elders, Witni and Mondia, in 1976 and 1985, are eyewitness accounts of the first meetings of
Kawagl and the Siambugla with Fr. Schäfer. I visited the site of Dimbi ceremonial ground and settlement with Bomaiambu Clara and Witni Michael, a
daughter and son-in-law of these elders of Siambugla.[4] I summarize my notes:

> Siambugla ancestors were at Womkama and then migrated to Kogai, through
> Gena to Dimbi. When Witni was young, he went to Bundi, visiting his sisters
> and a brother married there. When these old Siambuga men, with Kawagl,
> were at Bundi, Fr. Schäfer came. They took the Mondia road and brought Fr.
> Schäfer to Dimbi. They showed the father the nose holes for feathers, which
> are made on Simbu children. When Fr. Schäfer asked they said they have
> gardens and nut pandanus trees; the Bundi had taro, manioc, marita [P. oil pan-
> danus]. Fr. Schäfer wanted to come with them to Dimbi. When they brought Fr.
> Schäfer kunai [P. grass] for his house they were given small shells, and then also
> kina shells. Kawagl's son Asiwe was going to fool the Bundi, took bilas (P. deco-
> rations) and ran away. Fr. Schäfer took small shells to his house, and Kawagl
> thought they had been taken, fought the Bundi. The next day all of them car-
> ried Fr. Schäfer's cargo and brought it down to Dimbi. Fr. Schäfer and Witni
> could communicate in the Bundi language. They traveled through Toromam-
> buno, where a brother shot a pig, which was cooked and eaten; paid for with
> girigiri shell. In trade, they got shells, steel axes, yombagl (S. lesser bird of para-

dise) feathers. The marriage of their sisters with Bundi were to further trade; Bundi got pig and Simbu got shells and feathers. In earlier days, shells were not wanted, but only feathers. Later, shells and steel axes were traded.

I returned to Dimbi in 1985 with Bomaiambu Clara to talk again with Bomaiambu's father, Mondia, and the other old men, who had remained there since the *bugai ingu* (S. pig feast) in 1976. They told the same story:

Their ancestors came from Womkama and found Dimbi. Womkama was a stone place, and the Simbu—Nauru, Bandi, Kumai, Pagau, Gena, all came from there and went to many places. After a fight with Gena, Siambugla joined the Wauga, Siku, Kamanegu. When Kiap Taylor came through, Witni showed them the road; asked about the bird (S. *kua:* plane). They built a house, and then went to Hagen. When they returned a man took a bush knife and ran away; Taylor shot a lot of men to retaliate.[5] It was after that they (Kawagl, Witni, and Mondia) went to Bundi. Some people thought the priests and white men were *gigl* (S. spirits); that the Siambugla brought a *gigl* to Mingende, and those at Gembogl were afraid. At Bundi they met Fr. Schäfer, brought him to Dimbi. After this they went to Mingende, which is Wauga land. Later they went again and brought cattle. People wondered what these animals were, and if they would kill them. It was later that they called him Father, and all good things came; before that the land was full of enemies. Witni and Mondia were strong and went to Bundi. Witni could speak Bundi language, learned as a child with his father there. Kawagl did not know the language. Kawagl tried to take the wife of Dilu, Mondia's older brother; then he was afraid of Dilu and escaped to Bundi and met Fr. Schäfer. Asiwe's mother bore him at Bundi, then died and was buried there. Kawagl, Witni, and Mondia came into Simbu with Fr. Schäfer, and Mondia gave Fr. Schäfer his land at Dimbi. At that time they were afraid to be with or eat the food of Gena and Nauru, but Fr. Schäfer had them go to school together.

Francis Kombugun's interview of Mondia in 1987 elaborates on his role:

Went to Bundi with his brother Kawagl. Went to Hagen with missionary Fr. Ross—thru the bush where airstrip is now. They came back and relatives bought him a wife Maria. Then to Bundi to get Fr. Separ [Schäfer]. Witni of Siambugla was at Bundi; the three came back with Fr. Separ to Dimbi. Then Kiap Taylor came to Kunabau and a person stole an axe. Taylor got angry and told his policeman to shoot Siambugla Wauga people; killed two to three hundred at Kunabau. Later Witni translated talk of the Father with Mondia and Kawagl; told Fr. Schäfer that they had all kinds of food at Dimbi; then the Father came to Dimbi. Kawagl's wife died at Bundi and was buried there. But Kawagl dug out bones and carried them back to Simbu. The Siambugla men carried Father Schäfer's goods in bags to Simbu, and were given goods and red laplap for it. They built a house at Irpui, and then school, brought kids to school. Appointed mission bosbois in Naregu—Ti, Gandi, Komun, Palma, others. Built houses for mission, then schools. Naregu Arime, Gande, Waine, Kondom went down to Madang to get the cows for the mission.

Guwand Kombugon of Gena (interviewer Harry Godfrid) tells another story of Kawagl and his actions. Outside of the Siambugla-Wauga, I find no mention of Mondia and Witni; only Kawagl is remembered.

Kawagl is a Siambugla Wauga man. He lived at Dimbi near Mingende. An old time warrior, Kawagl was a great leader of the Siambugla Wauga people. Many people in those days feared and respected him because he was the one who associate himself with the missionaries. The others wouldn't because they were frightened. Kawagl was attending what is claimed to be a funeral somewhere in the Gerel (Bundi) area when the first missionaries came. Everyone there was scared including the most feared Gerel people (because of their magical powers). Kawagl however decided not to be scared and started getting himself associate with the new comers. It is believed it was Kawagl who told the missionaries about Mingende and eventually brought them over to Mingende via Mondia, Golme, Guiye, and Nendi. He then gave all of his land to the missionaries to camp there. Today the center of the Roman Catholic Church in Simbu Province is Mingende.

If Kawagl were alive, he could be a great religious leader today.

Gull, an Endugwa interviewed by Harry Godfrid, tells a similar story, giving Kawagl a special role as peacemaker and church leader:

He was from Dimbi near Mingende. The most significant thing that he did was he introduced the missionaries all the way from Bundi area to his place at Mingende and that is where the missionaries are now. He was also an influential man. A peacemaker as well as an old time warrior. Kawagl said "those white people with white skin are friends from the dead" and he was the only one who had close ties with the missionaries. Many believe that if he was still around today he would have been a very significant church leader in the Province and probably the highlands region as a whole.

In an original essay, Schäfer describes Kawagl as the man who met him at Bundi and invited the mission to his home area at Dimbi. He was known in Simbu as a strong man, a man of physical strength, independent. Schäfer (1938:108) says he is "kein Tyrann" (German: not a tyrant) but discusses everything with his colleagues; he says, rather, "we will do." Self-confident, quick-tempered, and dangerous in a rage, he killed many enemies and also two wives. But, Schäfer continues, he is not only a wild man of force; he is a great orator and raconteur. His status among the Siambugla was as a formidable warrior, a persuasive speaker, and a friend of Fr. Schäfer. Although some anthropologists (Salisbury 1964; Feil 1987) have interpreted this description as indicating despotic big men in Simbu, I cannot agree (Brown 1990b).

In interviews, my informants have called Kawagl a peacemaker, an influential man, and, most importantly, the one who brought the Catholic church to Simbu. Unlike his traveling companions, he was not afraid of the white men and made friends with them. Fr. Nilles (1987a:13ff.) makes a point: Kawagl was visiting the relatives of his Bundi wife when he saw the material benefits of whites and wanted them for his people. He saw that a pig was bought with shells, salt, and a large steel axe. Kawagl asked the missionaries to come to Dimbi so he and his people could obtain this wealth. In this interpretation, Kawagl was an opportunist, reaching out to welcome the missionaries as human friends whose trade goods might benefit their Siambugla hosts. The heroic role of Kawagl in bringing the Catholic church to Simbu is a later addition to the story.

These reports of Kawagl depict a many-sided big man. His fellow clansmen at Dimbi and Fr. Schäfer had rather different views of him. His quick grasp of the potential of friendship and host relations with the mission brought Fr. Schäfer into the Simbu area, established the mission on his ground, and ensured its benefits to the community. Although Kawagl first acted merely as guide and host to Fr. Schäfer, he later led the people of his tribe in acceptance and adherence to the mission. In the 1950s he was often to be seen at the mission house at Mingende. His reputation as a great church leader came after many years of attachment to the mission and persists in legend beyond Mingende.

Father Schäfer

Fr. Schäfer's pioneering is well documented in his own writings and those of Fr. Nilles, as well as mission records. My first visit to Simbu was in 1958, when Fr. Schäfer was back in Germany, ill; his death was announced and a memorial service held for him on 25 August 1958. My field notes record statements which describe him as a heroic figure, beloved by all Simbu of the area, a man who learned their language and lived for a long time among them (whereas other priests and kiaps were there for shorter periods). The funeral mass, led by the bishop, was a truly extraordinary gathering of Simbu from a large area; it was attended by planters, missionaries, and government officers from all over the highlands. The sermon was delivered in pidgin and translated into Kuman Simbu.

Simbu wailed and smeared mud on themselves, as they do when mourning a dead friend or relative. Each clan carried a long pole from which chickens, pineapples, gourds, and other foods were suspended, and huge piles of food were displayed, to be distributed. My 1958 notes show that many people told me of their feelings toward Fr. Schäfer. They said:

> He gave us school, and was truly our father. He spoke our language, went out at night and in the rain to baptize people when they were dying. Before Father Schäfer we did not know the people in other tribes and were afraid to visit; since the mission was at Mingende all came together. Before we were wild savages, did not stay straight in one place, fought constantly. The white man taught us to live right; now we are a little straight, we can walk on the big road safely, we have more food, better food, and we do not fight. He took the boys and taught them prayers, held their hands to show them how to cross themselves. One man said: "He said he would come back, but he died at his home place. We cannot see his face. I cannot eat now."

Fr. Nilles (1987a) describes Fr. Schäfer and his work at Mingende without heroic attributions, pointing to the quality of teaching at Mingende, the establishment of advanced schools and training of teachers, the use of the vernacular in church, and the instituting of Christian leaders as liaison between the people and the church, and of the women of the Legion of Mary who lead prayer meetings. Many of his recommendations to the church—the use of aircraft and building airstrips, pack horses, and the extension of schools into the rural area—were important to Mingende's preeminence. His role was as initiator, director, and long-term priest of Mingende. The mission school at Kondiu became a high school and now will be a senior high school. Many Simbu officials and men who attended university were educated there.

For the Simbu, cargo connotes western life.[6] From their first view of the white man, his goods were highly desirable, and monopoly of access gave the newcomers an unattainable advantage. In the 1930s airplanes began to bring mission and government visitors and goods to Simbu. Rather than the cargo ships of coastal Melanesia, planes landing on airstrips became the source of cargo. In both cases the origin of cargo was unknown.

In the period 1933–1940 Simbu first learned of the existence of the western world, the Australian administration, and missionaries. The patrols and mission establishments had close contact with only a few; most Simbu knew of them from brief glimpses and through stories of the white man, police, and large dogs, and the strange things they wore, carried, and ate.

Government officials and missionaries conveyed their culture into Simbu, along with the policies and principles of their parent organizations.

To the Simbu, the beginning of their transformation was personalized in Kiap Taylor and Fr. Schäfer, icons of the white man who brought peace, government, and church to their valley. Their images now represent two powerful forces, the church and the government.

Kiap Jim Taylor: A Legend in the Highlands

Taylor's legend is of particular interest, as it supports the entire foundation of discovery and administrative control in many areas of the highlands. My interview in 1991 with his daughter Meg, then ambassador to the United States, provided new insights. In colonial and postcolonial Papua New Guinea highlands lore, "Jim Taylor" symbolizes an event, initiating the episode of awakening, pacification, and the beginnings of Australian colonial government. To a million people of the Papua New Guinea highlands, Kiap Jim Taylor brought western civilization. The process of creating a hero and fabricating a legend discloses both Simbu and Australian viewpoints. In pidgin it is said, *Em i brukim bus na painim ol Simbu*—"He broke through the bush and discovered Simbu."

Taylor was born in 1901 and attended schools in Sydney. As a teenager he joined the Australian army in World War I, then spent a year at the University of Sydney and served in the New South Wales police force for three years. When Taylor joined the New Guinea administration in 1926 he was a patrol officer in Morobe District. Earlier chapters describe his role in the Bena-Hagen patrol, the theft and shooting at Kunabau, and the investigation of killings of the two missionaries in 1935.

Jim Taylor's predominant place as explorer of the highlands, and as an official at various highland posts, is well documented. He was highly regarded and put in charge of a major government exploratory expedition, the Hagen-Sepik patrol of 1938–1939. After these he earned renown as a great explorer and peacemaker.[7] He served as major in ANGAU during World War II, as director of native labor 1945–1946; then was "District Officer of the Highlands region until 1949, when he resigned to become a pioneer coffee farmer near Goroka" (Griffin 1986:11).

He married Yerima, the daughter of a Wahgi valley highlander friend. She was born at the time of his early patrols and was fifteen or sixteen at the time of their marriage in 1949. She has been called "a woman of great personal ability and strength of character, who became the Highlands first national woman business person, plantation manager and driver."[8] Taylor resigned from the Papua New Guinea administration in the early 1950s, settled in the highlands, and began growing coffee on a plantation near

Goroka. A "loving, kind and generous person,"[9] Taylor was a founding member and first president of the Highlands Farmers and Settlers Association in Goroka in 1955, and continued as a leader in coffee development (the main source of income for hundreds of thousands of highlanders) into old age.

To the highlands people of Papua New Guinea, the two exploratory patrols of the 1930s and Taylor's continuing role in administration, and his subsequent life as a coffee farmer, are heroic events that are responsible for their first knowledge of the white man and progress. From the government's point of view, the purpose of the Taylor-Leahy exploratory patrol in 1933 was to make contact with the native inhabitants and prepare them for colonial government control.

My fieldwork was mostly in Simbu Province, where the story of the patrols was told to me many times from 1958 to 1987. Kiap Taylor represented the Australian administration as an explorer responsible for the first use of guns, arrests, killing Simbu natives, and also as a trader of shells for food, potential ally against enemy tribes, punisher of warriors, and dispenser of justice. People recounted their experience thusly: "Kiap Taylor put salt on his hands so we could taste it." Many Simbu remember accompanying him on patrols.

In Simbu stories, Kiap Taylor appears as the first stranger who befriended them or as the kiap who arrested and punished thieves and warriors. Even though (as the reports show) there was a succession of kiaps at Kundiawa, and the pacification program was implemented by Kyle, Bates, Vial, Downs, and others, when the Simbu tell of this period and its changes no other kiap is named. Kiap Taylor signifies the Australian administrative presence in the highlands.

The kiap represents the Australian administration, with its power and command of police and rifles. He is the owner and giver of shells, metal, cloth, great wealth, and powerful goods. Taylor, as the embodiment of the white man and first colonial administrator, has become the agent of the white man's way. The concept is reminiscent of cargo-cult beliefs (see Lindstrom 1990a, 1990b) and also applies to native heroes such as Magruai, Kondom, and Okuk.

Interviews in 1987 in the Eastern Highlands brought out specific personal ties: the first native coffee planter in the Goroka area said: "Kiap Taylor showed me how to plant coffee, then I showed all the people of the eastern highlands. He made friends with us." These recollections and tales are personalized and take a form common to other stories of relations with white patrons. Simbu say: "Masta told me that I would be paid; masta said there would be a school, a factory."[10] These stories also carry the idea that the colonial white man was all-knowing and all-powerful; Kiap Taylor personally brought great benefits.

Taylor describes his organization and management of the Hagen-Sepik patrol.[11] At each step he told people to put down their arms and accept the visitors. At each opportunity he demonstrated the power of the rifle by shooting at shields and trees. Taylor observed that natives were only occasionally hostile at first, but always dangerous after a visit by a European who did not show his strength and was thought to be afraid or weak. Many different people and language groups were met on this long patrol. Taylor proposed establishing police posts, so that the resident policeman would bring peace to a community.[12] He stated that the natives needed friendly white men and missionaries, and swift justice, to correct their faults. If this was done, he believed, the highland people would maintain a happy village life, and would develop, progress, and become loyal and faithful assistants to the administration.

Stories told in New Guinea and published in Australia further developed the Taylor saga—that he came as a great white stranger into a land of miserable, warlike, fierce, hungry highlanders, bringing white man's goods, healthy food, and peaceful and fearless living to the people of a vast inland highland and valley region. His report of the Hagen-Sepik patrol of 1938–1939 makes it clear that Taylor was concerned to make the white man's power and gun symbols of authority, to prevent thefts and attacks on his patrol group, and enter each new area in peace, buying food for the patrol group with shells, and continue on. The purpose of the patrol was to discover, observe natural features, map, and prepare the people for administration. Settlement by Australian planters and businessmen was his vision for the future of the highlands, in analogy to the Kenya highlands.[13] He found the missionaries both too critical of and determined to change the natives, making them ashamed of their evils, as well as insufficiently firm in their dealings with them to prevent theft and attacks.

The report of the Hagen-Sepik patrol makes recommendations about the way to develop and control the area, and generalizes about native thinking and social life. These ideas strongly influenced Australian attitudes about the inland peoples of the highlands and Sepik areas. When the colonial administration was returned after World War II, the Taylor policy was renewed with a program of reestablishing administration of the highlanders contacted before the war and extending control into new areas. Australia developed a stance of benevolent colonialism based on the Taylor saga: "Kiap Taylor" represented the beginning of peace and progress as the kiap who brought civilization to the highlands.

At his death in 1987, Taylor was hailed and eulogized as the man who discovered the highlands and was responsible for its development. The Prime Minister, opposition leader Somare and his wife—along with leaders from Wahgi, Simbu, Goroka, and Enga—walked with the coffin. A pidgin eulogy was read by Leo Hammett. It was said that Papua New Guinea had lost a real father, leader, and businessman who had raised the region to its present position. Goroka shops were closed (out of respect and against looting).

I have been privileged to see articles and letters written by many who had known Jim Taylor during his long service and residence in Papua New Guinea, including many received by Taylor's family after his death (M. Taylor 1991). His personality and achievements are described by former colleagues and friends. The writings attest to lasting esteem for him on the part of fellow officers, Papua New Guinean officials, and friends.

Ian Downs, writing in the Retired Officers' Association Newsletter:

> I recall him as an impressive personality. A big handsome man who never failed to create excitement amongst the people when he toured the highlands before the war. He was generous in his help to junior officers. His flair and style in first contact situations made many memorable occasions, but he never allowed the people to underestimate the power and authority of the goverment he represented. Jim Taylor had a better educational background than most of his superiors. He was a romantic intellectual, emotionally involved in the country and with the people. His thoughts for their future were years ahead of those in central administration. I much admired the manner in which he blandly ignored the demands of paper-work and any instructions from headquarters which he found tedious.
>
> Apart from his achievements in exploration, Jim Taylor was a model of courtesy, dignity and understanding in his dealings with the people. A model which became the basis for the control and pacification of the New Guinea Highlands before the Japanese war.

Freddie Kaad in the Retired Officers' Association Newsletter:

> When I think of Jim Taylor I think of humanity, humility, kindliness, a gentle firmness, vision, intellect.

John Black's letter to the family:

> In the old hierarchical pre-war New Guinea set-up Jim was very much Mr. A.D.O. J. L. Taylor—and a senior one at that and I and my contemporaries of the same batch—lowly cadets. He was the first intellectual I encountered in the service and he made me aware that a patrol officer's life was something

more than a glorious boy scout adventure. I respected his dedication to the Highland people and to establish a non-racist relationship based on mutual respect in the process. He became my most loyal and understanding friend in Papua New Guinea.

Jean McCarthy (widow of J. K. McCarthy, a former Director of Native Affairs and member of the Legislative Council):

Jim was a very fine man whom both my husband and I admired and respected— he lived his own life as he wished and sought no accolades. . . . Another great man of Papua New Guinea has gone—can only hope their wonderful achievements perhaps will be remembered. . . . Both Jim and Keith had a wonderful understanding and compassion for the people of Papua New Guinea.

Ivan Champion (letter to the family):

It is with sincere regret that we heard of the death of your father. I never heard him say an ill word of anyone. In all the years he has remained a silent figure, never boasting about his great achievements. The highland people will miss his wise advice.

Richard Leahy (letter from the son of Michael Leahy):

Jim was dad's greatest friend and had only the fondest memories of their association over all those years. What a really great life they both had though. Watching the country evolve from the stone age to a democracy in a little over a generation.

Julius Chan, a leading member of the government who was prime minister in 1994 (letter to M. Taylor):

Your father was a great man. He did for the highlands people a great service as a *kiap* in the 1930's and will be remembered by many Papua New Guineans.

David Inaho, medical faculty, University of Papua New Guinea (letter):

Your Daddy is great man and a man full of hope, ambition and strength, so I . . . express my respect . . . I know you will follow his foot steps to be a great lady.

Walter Nombe, premier of the Eastern Highlands Provincial Government (letter):

My government sympathized the loss in [*sic*] one of the prominent public figures in the sense of Highlands development in politics social and economic
fields. The late Jim Taylor's memory will always be remembered for many years
to come as he was (to me) the father of Highlands development and dignity.

There can be no final word on the significance of the Taylor legend for
the people of Papua New Guinea. Its interest to me resides not only in the
man and his reputation, but in the demonstration of how the highland
people have personalized the experience of discovery by the white man and
the establishment of administrative control in the name of Kiap Taylor. His
name stands for the kiap of the 1930s and the beginning of administrative
control. The letters and articles of people who knew him support his symbolic and actual role in early contact. It was Taylor's peaceful approach—
backed by the demonstrated power of guns—to the control of tribal fighting,
thefts, and attacks which prevailed and advanced pacification. The officers
who manned government posts throughout the highlands in the 1930s
followed his policy. To the highlanders, he was the great discoverer and
bringer of white man's treasures; in the eyes of his white successors in highlands administration, he originated peacemaking and put an end to tribal
fighting.

Pacification and Change

Avid for the goods that the newcomers possessed, Simbu brought food and
pigs to trade, offered women to patrols, and worked on roads that would
bring in visitors and trade. At this time the mission wanted settlement sites
to begin evangelizing and teaching. When missionaries built houses on
offered land, Simbu expected alliance and a permanent favorable exchange
relationship. Thefts and attacks, and most particularly the killings of Fr.
Morschheuser and Br. Eugene, provoked their first experience of colonial
domination: the shooting of Simbu in defense of officers and police, arrests
and imprisonment of Simbu. The incidents in which response to theft or
attack was shooting began a period of fear of guns and police, but not resistance. The crowds that came out to work building roads, requests of men and
women to accompany government patrols, huge welcoming parties at patrol
stops, and offerings of food and pigs, surely had different meanings for Simbu
and white men: the Simbu were seeking cargo; the whites, local supplies and
acceptance of administrative control. What the missionaries and kiaps saw
as acts that were welcoming civilization to Simbu were moves toward the
opportunity to acquire the wonderful goods of the white man.

For the administration, the major goal from 1935 onward was pacification. Government officers stopped intertribal conflicts and prevented wars; often they brought together the opposing leaders to arrange peace ceremonies, burn weapons, and exchange food. This introduced a new concept of compensation to the injured party in any fight or encounter. Before this, enemies retaliated when they could; only allies injured in the course of aiding friends had formerly been compensated with pigs, valuables, and sometimes a bride.

At some distance from Kundiawa, missions were established at Mingende, Kerowagi, and Toromambuno. Employment opportunities, church meetings, and religious schools began to attract Simbu. For mission adherents, Fr. Schäfer, the Catholic priest, or Rev. Bergmann, the Lutheran pastor, signified the new message of Christianity and things of the white man. Fr. Schäfer and Fr. Nilles became accomplished speakers of Kuman, preaching sermons and making announcements in the native language. Church teachings were often called the "good news."

By the end of the 1930s, people of "inner Chimbu" had seen and provided food and firewood for patrols of kiaps and police; made roads to connect their settlements with the government office at Kundiawa; worked on airstrips and seen visitors and goods arrive by airplane; received seeds and interbred pigs to improve agriculture; seen horses, cows, and new forms of building at missions; had their tribal territories and boundaries mapped; built rest houses and assembled for meeting officers and for census; laid down their weapons, promising to keep peace; and obtained shells, metal tools, and implements from the white man. Some had been examined by medical officers; served prison sentences; eaten new foods; worn cloth; used steel tomahawks, shovels, and knives; carried goods for the patrols; worked as interpreters or policemen; had sexual relations with the newcomers; gone to mission schools and churches; been appointed bosboi or luluai; reported fights and attacks or taken disputes and homicides for arbitration to the kiap, and paid compensation to victims on a kiap's ruling. A few had worked for the missions or the government. Among these, the close association with the newcomers—white and black—was an intense experience, in part directed toward specific work and techniques, religious teacher training, and policing. These began a transformation in technology, the structure of power and authority, the exchange system, ways of reestablishing friendly relations with other tribes, the value of labor and local production, knowledge, and the system of ritual and belief—everything was changing. The forces of change, both mission and government, were personalized in individual relations and the heroizing of Father Schäfer and Kiap Taylor.

Colonial Dependency

By 1950 the fear of kiap and police power and the craving for western goods and benefits had become a form of colonial dependency. Many adult Simbu still believe that the white man is better informed and equipped than themselves to guide progress. This reflects the prevailing view of the conqueror, the missionary, and the administrator; Simbu took it up as transmitted through the police, laborers, and native leaders. Mission workers and converts spread a Christian form of the message of white man's superiority.

Chimbu was a subdistrict of the Eastern Highlands, with Goroka—which had become an important air station, commercial and coffee center, and administrative post—as the district headquarters. The tradition of patrol officers as general administrators and announcers of the Department of District Services and Native Affairs' intentions to the people continued. Patrols were routinized by stops at designated rest houses, assemblies of people, census, evaluation of tultuls and luluais, displays of the flag, and lectures on specific subjects, conveying administration plans and priorities to the people. Simbu saw the kiap as a supreme authority, the image of power in their colonial life. Individual kiaps were rarely identified in Simbu statements, and they were rarely known by name.

After 1950, the Australian government directed its attention to the political and economic development of Papua New Guinea. They accepted highlanders as plantation laborers on contract and made coffee the main cash crop. Whereas economic development in the Eastern and Western Highlands districts included the alienation of land for European-owned coffee plantations, because of the density of population in Simbu, the only land leases allowed were for government use, for mission churches and schools, and for small commercial establishments.

In Chimbu Subdistrict, the 1960s brought elected local government councils and representation in the House of Assembly. There were new government schools, more medical-aid posts, enlarged hospitals, and clinics. Political and economic development programs were stabilized and expanded, and roads improved. On my first visit to Mintima in 1958, visible evidence of western influence was everywhere.[14] The rural people were, on the whole, unfamiliar with shops. Then Simbu began to use money earned in work or cash cropping for household goods, clothes, food, beer, and all forms of exchange. But their hopes for cargo were never achieved.

The elders, including most of the officials, and women of all ages rarely had any outside experience. Some middle-aged and many younger men attended mission and catechist schools, traveled to the coast as labor migrants, and spoke pidgin. Young married men and women often had a brief

period of mission school, were regular churchgoers, knew that they should go
to the kiap's court to settle fights; and many made some use of health facilities. Mintima area luluais and tultuls saw that they were responsible for keeping the peace and assembled people for government work on roads and to
meet with visiting officers.

Kondom

Kondom dominated the Simbu and had great influence throughout the area.
Under the guidance of Kondom they placed strong emphasis on and
approved of what they considered progress—colonial obedience, doing what
the kiap and Father (priest) advised, *wok bisnis* (P. work/business; here, growing coffee), and the end of traditional ceremony.

I knew Kondom well in my early years of fieldwork. Because of my
interest in politics and social change, the Chimbu Subdistrict Officer at
Kundiawa in 1958 suggested that we make our field site among the Naregu at
Mintima Rest House. Luluai Kondom, an administration favorite, lived at
Wandi, three kilometers away. Kondom was clearly the most important man
in the four Waiye tribes, with a population of about ten thousand people,
that formed the first highlands local government council a few months later.
His unwavering loyalty and attachment to the govman (P. government) was
rewarded with appointments, assistance, and visits to view economic and
political development projects, which he brought to the Simbu. Older
adults, especially in Naregu, see Kondom today as the great innovator, the
hero of a golden age of Australian patronage. He appeals to the Simbu as an
ideal personification, a really huge, heroic man.

When I first knew Kondom he was a driving, progressive leader whose
reputation and influence extended well beyond his tribe. He adjudicated disputes, urging people to follow the white man's ways of peace and business. In
the 1950s, as a young luluai, he became a favorite of the Australian District
Officers, being presented to visiting dignitaries and taken on junkets and to
congresses in Papua New Guinea and the Pacific Islands. From appointed
luluai he became the highlands' first elected local government council president in 1959. When the appointed Legislative Council was transformed in
1961, he was the first, and at the time the only, elected highlands member
(see Whitaker 1975:116–117).

As I saw Kondom's role at the time, when the Australian administrators
wanted to promote cash crops, build roads, institute elections for local government councils, and introduce coffee growing and later a coffee cooperative, Kondom was shown or told about it, and then demonstrated and
explained it to the people. At Wandi his was the first planting of coffee and

introduction of a machine for coffee pulping in Simbu. He encouraged the Naregu to select land and prepare plots for individual coffee blocks, which were beginning to produce fruit in 1959.

After Kondom lost the 1964 House of Assembly election (he was opposed by several Simbu), his last years were dedicated to being the first chairman of the board of the Kundiawa Coffee Society. For a time, under his direction, each Naregu subclan organized and supervised the cooperative pulping, washing, and drying of coffee in the area, greatly improving its quality. During his travels to projects and towns Kondom grasped opportunities: when he saw buildings, schools, medical facilities, and economic ventures, he asked that they be brought to his home area and to the highlands. As the kiap's favorite Simbu leader, he became the agent for all forms of political and economic development. He was a tireless orator and demonstrator of new ways. This is the basis of the present legend that has made him a hero in his tribe, throughout Simbu Province, and in the highlands region. He combined a big-man role of great influence at home with that of intermediary, mediator, and spokesman for the administration in relation to his tribe, local government council area, and region. He made the most of opportunities in bringing new facilities and programs to the people. Kondom was a great public speaker who directed the Simbu into a new world of coffee bisnis and elected government.

Kondom's career ended, when he was about forty-five to fifty, as a result of a Daulo Pass motor accident when he was returning home from a political meeting in August 1966. Nearly every Simbu knows this: some time afterward the driver's tribe paid a very large compensation to Naregu in a huge ceremony. His timber-frame house, which was built in 1959, the first in Simbu, and his grave and memorial billboards stand by the roadside at Wandi. The Simbu Provincial Office Building in Kundiawa is prominently signposted "Kondom Agaundo House."

My interviews with older Naregu fill in details of his life and activities, colored of course by memory. As one might expect, the accounts often disagree in particulars: they seem to reflect the experience and values of the person interviewed. What stands out is the aura of greatness: Kondom is the heroic big man of Simbu. These personal reminiscences both elaborate on his role and explain his importance.

Kagl Bruno of Kangrie, Simbu valley, told Arnold Nai:

> Kondom was a true born leader in Simbu, and due to his untiring efforts to bring big developments to Simbu and the highlands as a whole, his name was well known from east to west. As a result, he was appointed as a highlands representative to attend meetings and discuss other important things and make

decisions and so [*sic*] in the House of Assembly down in Port Moresby. That's where he stayed till his tragedy in a car at Daulo pass.

Kugame Tange, an Endugwa (interviewer Lawrence Gigmai):

I worked with Kondom Agaundo and I knew him very well. During tribal fights when he was small he lived at Koglai for a while and then he came back to Wandi. He was jealous about Wenambe Arime's luluai badge and falsely reported to kiaps of Arime and kiaps were tired of Arime and gave the badge to Kondom. When Kondom had the badge he was really on top of everyone. He did very good work around so people called Kondom *kua kande* (S. big bird). He called meetings every now and then and during those meetings he said he will ask the kiaps if they could build a school for us. His request was answered and schools were built and he appointed me as chairman of board of management. After schools he then asked the kiaps again for Local Government Council system and again request fulfilled and with the introduction of Council system bosboi and luluai systems were dissolved. He then built roads both highway and feeder roads. After completing roads and bridges he told the people that we will be rich and we'll see big trucks full of cargo travel on the road. Whatever you name like coffee, pyrethrum and passionfruit are all brought in by Kondom Agaundo. Even stacking firewood along the road sides for sale was all Kondom's idea. He introduced the village system and told us to fight hard during council meetings so that the kiaps can bring beer for us to drink. I drank first beer for 3 shillings in that time when first introduced but after 3 bottles I really got pissed. He also worked closely with health inspectors and established aid posts in remote areas.

He even expanded his work to east and west and people at those places they reckon he must be a white man but when he visited them in person they bow down to him and respected him. I used to be his carrier when he travelled around. He liked everybody alike. Wherever he goes they shouted from mountain tops that *yagl kande* (S. big man) Kondom is coming. Kondom's grandfather was called Kondom *kigla kumugl* (S. strong; hawk young man) who was pretty wealthy and a recognized leader who initiated pig killings and other important events and so people all around followed his ideas. The grandfather Kondom also married many wives and had many pigs. Kondom's father was just another man who followed his father's footsteps and liked everybody alike and so Kondom Agaundo followed in the line. But now Kondom's sons have failed miserably to carry on the good name of Kondom and will never as far as I am concerned.

According to my field notes of 1958–1959, Kondom's father was a young warrior when he died. He was thought to have been a victim of enemy poison sorcery during tribal warfare. After his death Kondom lived with his mother's people at Kogai. Quite often in my family records, a war widow takes her small children to live with her relatives after the death of a father. Both Kondom and Wamugl, Naregu orphans, lived at Siambugla Kogai as youths and were close friends throughout life (see Brown 1963, 1967, 1972, 1990).

Gull of Endugwa (interviewer Harry Godfrid):

> He had influence over the people. The kiaps, the missionaries and other white men around respected him as well. I will quote some of his words: Today I introduce coffee. This plant will bring you new advantages. The one with many coffee trees will later have more money. If you are an old man and have a lot of coffee trees, you will be able to marry a very young girl because she will want money and you will have it. The road you build now will not last. Later, the roads will be sealed with a black thing (tar) and not everyone will clear the roads but only a few and they will be paid with money. Money will be so important that young boys who cannot get it will become rascals and girls will be prostitutes all aiming to obtain easy money. The one with a lot of cattle will have a high prestige in the village. During feasts he may be able to contribute more meat. He can also sell his cattle to obtain money which he could use for other things.

Mondo Ola of Ombondo, Simbu valley (interviewer Paul San):

> When Kondom was a leader there was peace among us but today with present leaders there is plenty of fighting and "rascal passion" and many other happenings. Kondom was a chosen leader by God. All highlanders obey him. The old ones still tell stories about him and his work. We today still wish there was another leader like him.

Kondom's importance was indicated by the fact that all addressed him as "Masta President," a designation ordinarily confined to white men. Later he was addressed as "Memba" (P. member of the Legislative Council) as well as "Masta."

Stories about Kondom were collected from schoolchildren and adults all over North Simbu. Some said "everyone obeyed him. The kiap said to obey him. People were afraid to disobey him." "He said that the kiaps brought good things, and that all the people should build these roads and buildings." Others said that he was a good leader, not greedy or selfish as many leaders are today: "He had a heart to do things for his people." People say: "Kondom began everything we have. If he had lived he would have brought wonderful new things, but since he died we have had nothing. If he hadn't died, Simbu would be important and wealthy today. If he were still alive he would be prime minister or governor-general."

In the legend, Kondom helped everyone, not just himself and his local group. He was generous and unselfish, bringing developments to all the people from Kainantu to Hagen. "He was a great man who brought people out of the dark ages." By his own efforts in planting coffee, introducing coffee machines, improving processing, starting cattle and pig projects, and other kinds of wok bisnis, he set a model for the people. He asked for schools so his children would have jobs; for machines and health centers to improve highlands life. He promoted a new way of life, wok bisnis, and prohibited fighting, stealing, and tribal ritual exchanges as being bad old ways. He was a harbinger of a new way of life, but since his death the economy has stagnated, tribal fighting has grown destructive, beer distributions and compensation payments consume resources that could be used to improve living standards. The great age of Kondom has been followed by a bitter new age of distress and a feeling of abandonment by the Australians. The Kondom legend serves Simbu demands for a hero.

A Second Transformation and Its Leaders

The long-established Lutheran and Catholic missions extended their school, church, and community activities into many localities. Children in these communities have been baptized, given European names, attend church services and activities, and many have gone to mission or government schools. Simbu were determined to accept the new ways of mission and government, especially as they hoped to attain the goods and benefits of western life.

In retrospect, the period of my early field visits, 1958–1965, had two phases: in the first years people believed that this was a good colonial time of peace and progress brought by the Australians; in the next phase, because coffee sales and the local government council did not make them rich, there was some disappointment, especially among young and middle-aged Simbu.

Hope mixed with worry in the 1970s. Iambakey Okuk's strong drive for national independence reached Simbu in the form of increased power in the central government. Many highlanders feared that the loss of Australian kiaps would leave them poorer and dominated by Papua New Guineans of the more developed coastal and island regions. Papua New Guinean officers, teachers, medical workers, agricultural development officers, technicians, and businessmen began to replace Australians and other foreigners. Tribal conflicts and local competitions began to become more violent, and the police were not feared. The friendly kiap no longer patrolled and stopped in rest houses to talk with local leaders. Colonial dependency is still preferred by some older Simbu.

My interviews asked for other very big men of Simbu, and quite a few were named. A man may be seen as a person of great importance within his home group; he initiates, organizes, directs memorable activities, and this performance marks events.

Iambakey Okuk

Iambakey Okuk was a famous politician whom I interviewed in 1984 (see Chap. 8). Born in 1944 at Pare, after his father died he was adopted by his father's brother, Palma Okuk, and grew up as a policeman's son at Mount Hagen. His schooling continued at Goroka, Sogeri High School, and Idubada Technical School; he held a Queensland diploma in mechanics. He then apprenticed at Rabaul, and also worked in Port Moresby and Mount Hagen. He felt unrewarded by his white employers. Iambakey objected to the large differential in pay for Papua New Guineans and Europeans. He was a grass-roots organizer, a leader among students and coworkers, captain of a soccer team, and organized apprentices for a protest march (Ryder 1992).

After incidents of disagreement with the European managers of the workshops, Iambakey left employment and took up business interests—coffee buying and selling at Mount Hagen and Simbu, stores, a coffee factory, real estate. He stood for national office in 1964, at the regional election in 1968 in Mount Hagen, and at every subsequent election. In 1972 he was elected to the House of Assembly for Simbu, and became Minister of Agriculture under Somare. In 1973–1975, when he was Minister of Transport, he secured the completion and upgrading of the highlands highway to the longest sealed road in Papua New Guinea, which has been renamed the Okuk Highway. He was Deputy Leader of the National Party in 1974, Minister of Education in 1976, and Parliamentary Leader of the National Party in 1977. As Leader of the Opposition in 1978–1980, he challenged Somare's leadership with motions of nonconfidence and succeeded in becoming Deputy Prime Minister. He was knighted in the 1980s and came to be known as Sir Okuk, now "late Sir Okuk." He lost the 1982 election in Simbu to John Nilkare and claimed that it was fixed. In his last years, attempting to regain a position in Parliament, he contested the seat at his wife's electorate in Unggai-Bena; a success at the polls, he was declared ineligible for this office. The issue was under appeal when he died.

Iambakey Okuk was a dynamic political figure, always appearing in national newspaper headlines, assembling candidates and voters for his party organization, building a power base, opposing and blocking the actions of others. When the 1984 Provincial Assembly results were announced, he took the newly elected members into the Chimbu Lodge to sign up as members of his party, and also attempted to recruit other provincial leaders to the party.

Iambakey's political vision was monumental; it encompassed plans for youth, national development, industry, education, and free enterprise. He is remembered for developing and completing the Okuk Highway, and for bringing large "dash seven" planes to Papua New Guinea. When he was an active businessman with coffee enterprises and shops he employed European managers. He fell ill with liver cancer in 1986 and was taken to Australia for diagnosis and treatment. When he died in Port Moresby in November 1986 there were widespread riots and looting. His Kamanegu tribesmen went on a rampage, destroying property.[15] Okuk's body was taken to Goroka and Mount Hagen before burial in Kundiawa, where a tomb was placed.

In 1987 his father, Palma, guarded the tomb in Kundiawa; I interviewed him with Lawrence Gigmai. Palma was a boy when the first white men came and joined the police as a young man. After numerous postings, and when Iambakey won the 1972 election, he resigned from the police in order to take care of the family, living on his pension. He feels that Iambakey had great goals, which were fulfilled, changing the government and bringing good things to the people of Papua New Guinea. Palma said: "Late Sir Okuk wasn't in Parliament just to increase our wealth or start businesses for us but he was the man who thought about everyone in Papua New Guinea." Wagluo Goiye said: "Sir Okuk fought for his people and [was] a true nationalist. A colourful politician and a firebrand."

The Simbu provincial government voted a grant to preserve Okuk's tomb, but I understand that the tomb has not been maintained since Palma died in 1991.

Independence

In the first years of independence (after 1975), the activities of local government councils declined and magistrates' courts dealt with local disputes. Commerce, roads, markets, and government services expanded in Kundiawa town. In the 1980s, the provincial government, with funds from the national government, took charge of financing services and development. One remaining Australian kiap in Simbu noted laxity of government officers, inefficiency of government courts, and dishonesty of officeholders. Since 1975, in the absence of Australian officers, Simbu are a provincial people in the new nation, where they see themselves as disadvantaged in two ways: they have limited land for economic development and lagging educational achievement that would enable them to take a leading role in national affairs. Rural Simbu mistrust government and police and feel detached from national politics. The officers of government seem increasingly remote from the rural communities, and community activities have declined as individuality in work and enterprise has expanded. The modern nation and bureaucracy of Papua New Guinea are rent by rivalry, regionalism, and factionalism.

Individuation and personal control of resources in land and goods now predominate, and the traditional group land holding, with the office of *magan nim* (S. ground father), has lost out. Within the tribe, and even in small local groups, there is great rivalry and many contend for each elected position. Simbu remains a place of tribes and rural people, whose big-men leaders are educated entrepreneurs and successful politicians. The greatest entrepreneurs are largely detached from their rural community ties, except insofar as these are the constituency in elections. This is, however, of the greatest importance; for the display of largesse in feasts that distribute purchased food and beer in great quantities is essential to electoral success. Candidates pay voters for their support in elections. Tribal solidarity under big men is found only when the elected officeholder is an effective local leader as well.

The elders often speak of the loss of cooperation and social control of youth. Young people are characterized as "school leavers" who have little knowledge or prospects for employment. Today stratification through education, jobs, and business enterprise prevails over local community organization. Successful business and professional Simbu have friends and business ties with expatriates, travel extensively by private plane and car, and frequent hotels, bars, and sports events. Overseas posts in the United Nations and other international organizations are achieved by a few who keep home ties through occasional visits.

As a result of increased travel and road traffic there is much mobility, and attacks on strangers are frequent. Throughout the province, houses, stores, property, and people are destroyed by arson and gunshot in tribal fights. Accidents, automotive injuries, and injuries by drunken drivers bring demands for compensation in large payments from the tribe of the driver or assailant. These escalated to the point that in 1991 Parliament outlawed threats accompanying compensation demands and set limits on payments for accidental deaths. As local opinion favors large payments for the honor and esteem of both donors and recipients (Dage 1985), I do not believe that this move toward restriction is likely to be effective, any more than had attempts to limit bride-price in the 1960s.

In a time of cultural self-consciousness following independence and closer association with other third world nations, some Simbu, concerned for the preservation of their cultural heritage, would like to establish a museum, display and sell crafts, and write articles and books about Simbu traditions.[16] At the same time, some educated highlanders speak disparagingly of their primitive ancestors and turn toward westernization.

Religion is an accepted part of life for many Simbu, who flock to church on Sunday, confirm marriages, take their children to be baptized and send them to mission schools. New church groups in some parts of the province attract adherents. Government and church-sponsored programs for women and families have an uneven record. The women's groups of *wok meri* (P. women's work) (Sexton 1986) seem limited to the Daulo area, while Lutheran church women's groups were active in Chuave District in the 1980s.

A legacy of the colonial period, strongly adhered to in the 1980s, is that education is the way to higher income and government service. Many young people find mission schools the first step toward economic achievement. Government positions, payments, and jobs dominate the Simbu economy and are seen as the source of wealth and power. In provincial and in national government, ministers control large funds that can be used to award followers and pay for projects in their areas. Simbu, who want the white man's goods and the money to get them, are especially dependent upon government resources, and the people of the province know it.

Traditional themes—tribal solidarity, competition, and rivalry—thrive on new goals and achievements. Money and power dominate interpersonal and intergroup relations. Politics and economic success are still joined together when a leader finances a flamboyant political campaign, feasts the voters and delivers services, development contracts, and cash disbursements from the central government. The source of cargo is now trade and government funds.

In 1987 my acquaintance with young people from many parts of the highlands allowed me to see Simbu in a regional perspective. Most striking were the opportunities and interests of educated Eastern Highlanders. Some young men draw upon large land holdings acquired from former expatriate coffee plantations, and one of them wondered whether it was worthwhile to complete teacher training and take a job that would pay less than he could make during the season when coffee is ripe. Another debated the value of continued help from the Europeans, looking for ways to select and incorporate benefits into new activities for the highlanders. Some professionally educated highlanders had sophisticated goals and hoped to lead their less-educated fellows into a new era of democratic cooperation. A few business and political leaders are urban elite and employers of expatriates.

Transformation through Heroes and Events

In Simbu eyes, heroic performances and pronouncements create events, which are historic markers. In Simbu community affairs, when a leader makes a public statement or directs an exchange ceremony, the whole group participates in and experiences his performance. He stands for the group and asserts the conditions, situation, position, relationship with another person and group, the beginning or ending of hostilities; the performance is an event, fixed by place and person. The context is structure, culture, antecedents (as may be recognized, recalled, or seen as significant), relationships of the actors and groups, and any other situational considerations. An event is never isolated and singular; however, it can mark a turning point, a development that is seen as significant. The event, the speech—or, as Marilyn Strathern would say, the artefact—becomes a historical marker. The image of Strathern (1988, 1991) and Wagner (1991) of a fractal, dividual person, is then a characterization of the big man as group spokesman and actor. Each actor performs; each reporter in retrospect states his/her recollection and interpretation. They report their personal experiences of an event. As Sahlins says, interpretations vary (1985:153; see Chap. 1).

Throughout these chapters, the statements of Simbu, of writers about Simbu, and my own observations and notes relate memories of the past sixty years. The statements and acts of individuals—especially leaders—events, and experiences remembered are the substance of Simbu history. I follow the standpoints of Parmentier, Gewertz and Schieffelin, and Andrew Strathern, as discussed in Chapter 1, in explicating Simbu historical thinking.

I perceive some key events and turning points in early Simbu contact as indicators of historical change: the theft and deaths at Kunabau, the first sightings of the airplane and interpretations of it, the deaths of Fr. Morschheuser and Br. Eugene and their aftermath. These stand out in memory and are recalled by many, in varying ways.

In Simbu, three heroes—Kawagl, Kondom, and Iambakey Okuk—embody major historical events. Kawagl represents the coming of the mission and new things to central Simbu; Kondom, the introduction of local and national government and economic projects of cash cropping, which brought money to Simbu; and Iambakey Okuk, independence and the linking of Simbu to the central government of Papua New Guinea. These momentous developments are personified and viewed by Simbu as having been created by their heroes.

In the stories and memories of Simbu, places and persons locate groups and actions in time and space. Events are identified in legend and tale through personalization; this is their way of memorializing events. Statements of memory and life-story views of Simbu place the events. Fr. Schäfer brought the benefits of a Christian life to the Simbu of the Mingende area. Kiap Taylor personifies the first view of the outside world, pacification, and coercive control. Kondom represents the introduction of coffee, money, and local government. Iambakey Okuk led Simbu into national government and independence and gave them the road to the coast. The politicians of the 1980s, Iambakey Okuk and John Nilkare, through education and entrepreneurship, achieved a Simbu ideal of wealth and a white man's living standard. Each hero takes the Simbu beyond their valley to a new view of Simbu life.

These tales and reminiscences tell a many-sided story. The heroes are agents of history, known to the speakers, remembered in their performance and through the elaborations of and tales about their words and deeds. The heroic image is a cumulative effect of many Simbu observations and recollections.

My conjecture about new goals for Simbu is optimistic. With education and investment, and the use of the great riches in Papua New Guinea—minerals, fisheries, timber, hydroelectric power, and agriculture—the Simbu capacity for competition may make the highlands a center for advanced technology. The heroes of such a transformation, identifiable now only to their peers, may emerge from those now training in schools and colleges, fostered by the political leaders of the present generation. The dark side of the future involves existing warfare, robbery, gangs, and political venality. I am confident that the new heroes will deal with these issues just as the old ones confronted the problems of their times.

NOTES

Preface

1. From the first discovery, the people, river, and area were known as Chimbu. However, since the 1970s the province has been known as Simbu, and now the people also refer to themselves and prefer the spelling Simbu. I conform to this usage. In the text as required, Simbu words and phrases will be indicated by (S.) and pidgin by (P.).

2. Early work by Fortune, Salisbury, Reay, Read, R. and C. Berndt, Meggitt, Bulmer, Glasse, Ryan, and Watson is described in Hays, ed. 1992 and in Pawley, ed. 1991. Participants in the 1956 conference believed they knew the main outlines of highlands social structure. I could characterize the theme thusly: "We have met the highlander, and he is patrilineal." Such a confident assumption demonstrates the authoritative voice of 1950s ethnography. However, Barnes (1962); Langness (1964); A. Strathern (1982); Lederman (1990); Modjeska (1991); Ryan (1992); Glasse (1992); and many later field-workers disagree. (See also Brown 1962, 1964).

3. W. Bergmann's writings, to which I refer later, were done after his retirement to Australia in the early 1970s.

4. A method taught me at the University of Chicago in the 1940s.

5. In the 1980s, Marilyn Strathern (1988, 1990b) was to identify the key Melanesian characteristic as gift exchange.

6. Pidgin English or pidgin is the common lingua franca of New Guinea. It was sometimes called Neo-Melanesian before independence. Today, *Tok Pisin* or *pisin* is more common. There is a highlands dialect, but spelling will attempt to reproduce the form used generally in Papua New Guinea. It differs from Bislama and other Melanesian Pidgins in some vocabulary and pronunciation and, like every vernacular language, is constantly changing.

7. Recent commentary on ethnographic method (Marcus and Cushing 1982; Clifford and Marcus 1986; Carrier, ed. 1992), proposes and evaluates forms of ethnographic experimentation, collaboration of ethnographer and "informant" or native member of the community (Bulmer and Majnep 1977), biographical/autobiographical volumes taken down and translated by the ethnographer (Keesing 1978; A. Strathern 1979; Shostak 1981), and polyphony.

8. This procedure proved tedious, and once I was satisfied with the accuracy of the recording and translations we dispensed with it in later interviews. I have written records of interviews in Kuman, pidgin, and/or English.

9. In 1992 he wrote to me:

Paula, mi amamas long harim olsem yu pinis (retired) *long wok blong yu. Yu bin wokim bikpela wok pinis na nau yu ken malalo gut tru.*

Thank you for spending most of your time for the Simbus. Being a Simbu I'm ever so proud that you have cared about us. Please don't forget us. I will not forget to remember special people like you.

Cheers

Lawrence Gigmai.

10. The material is hardly controversial, although often limited to local matters, and the content was not likely to discomfort the interviewee or interviewer. This method and its goal differ greatly from that followed by Herdt and Stoller (1990).

11. For example, the beliefs about and reactions to the first sight of an airplane became a special interest, and it now would appear that this has become a significant event to the Simbu, entailing a number of different local interpretations and mythological elaborations (see Chap. 3). It may take a self-deprecatory tack, telling how foolish and ignorant the Simbu were in their first encounters with outsiders and showing how sophisticated the present generation has become (see Strathern 1992).

Paul Dage wrote some twenty-five essays for me between 1984 and 1989, some of them over fifty pages long. They include topics I requested, material from interviews with elders, and his own views of these many subjects.

Chapter 1: Introduction

1. Strathern considers the event, for example, the first appearance of Europeans, as an image: "I suggest that Melanesians may have seen the advent of Europeans in the form of an artefact or performance" (1990a:26). Artefacts become events of history: when they exchanged shells and pigs in the first encounters, Hagen people came to regard the first Australian visitors as human because they were exchangers. Strathern (1992) sees the reactions of Hagen people embedded in traditional definitions of human or nonhuman beings based upon their behavior in an encounter.

2. The more extended discussion explains the roles of the creators of a performance, the witness as an agent.

3. Reviews and comments on Obeyesekere point to still further differences in interpretation. See Book Review Forum, *Pacific Studies* 17 (1994):103–155; Sahlins 1995.

4. Watson was puzzled by the apparently different interpretations and reactions of villagers, a magician, and himself to the violent rainstorm that followed his introduction to rain magic in 1955 (Watson 1990). Blong found a significant legend in some places of the tephra fall from the Long Island, Papua New Guinea, volcanic eruption long ago, whereas no legend was recorded in other areas where geological evidence shows a distinct tephra layer (1982).

5. For example, Poyer's (1988) demonstration of how the Sapwuafik massacre has become crucial for ethnic identity. Netting (1987) considers the Kofyar's reaction to war and massacre an event of magnitude. Keesing (1986) examines documentary sources and oral tradition of the Kwaio attack upon the *Young Dick* recruiting ship in the Solomons one hundred years earlier to show the different interpretations of the event.

6. For example, Taussig 1980 and 1987. Keesing (1992) describes the long history of Kwaio resistance.

7. See Lurie 1961; Fenton 1952. The anthropologists' and ethnohistorians' tasks are said to be to discover and write the facts and histories of native peoples (Trigger 1982) or

folk histories (Carmack 1972). The sources to be used include documents and oral and ethnographic materials; Sturtevant would also include linguistic, comparative, and archaeological evidence (1966).

8. This oral history approach to clan or tribal history, reconstruction, and authorization of a native history has been prominent also in Papua New Guinea studies by Lacey (1981), Waiko (1981, 1986), Oram (1981), and others (Denoon and Lacey, ed. 1981). The problems are discussed by Neumann (1989 and 1992).

9. Carrier defines authenticity thus: "This is the concern to discover and describe an authentic Them, a radically alien and different society that is free from the corrupting influence of contact with Us" (1992:12).

10. See, for example, Howe 1984; Parmentier 1987; Borofsky 1987; Dening 1980, 1988a; Gewertz 1983; Gewertz and Errington 1991; Carrier and Carrier 1989; Keesing 1993; Keesing and Corris 1980; A. Strathern 1984, 1991; Linnekin and Poyer, eds. 1990; Jolly and MacIntosh, eds. 1989; Neumann 1992.

11. A document which is Fox's reconstructed diary of the brothers' gold prospecting expedition in 1934 makes it possible to locate campsites; interviews with Huli of the area provide descriptions of the people and interactions.

12. Fentress and Wickham define social memory as "recalled past experience and shared images of the historical past that have particular importance for the constitution of social groups in the present" (1992:xi).

13. In the present-day legend of Magruai (Rambo 1990), he is interpreted by the Simbu as a precursor to the white man who entered from the east and departed from the west, and as a first appearance of Jesus. Hughes (1985, 1988) recorded folktales of Simbu tricksters and other personified characters.

14. Events such as killing of the missionaries and stealing at Kunabau are, as I shall show, indelible memories of early contact for Simbu of the central area and Simbu valley. From these arise further legends and convictions—for example, the punishing police and the first jail. Kiap Taylor is personalized as the one first *kiap* (P. government officer) who discovered Simbu and brought in Australian control.

15. As has been noted (Carrier, ed. 1992: see in particular Carrier, Jolly, Thomas, Keesing, Barker).

16. See Errington 1974; MacDowell 1985, 1988.

Chapter 2: The Simbu and Their Traditions

1. Most of the interviews quoted are translations made by young people who served as my research assistants in 1987, as I discuss in the Preface. Notes and dates are given if the interview was done at a different date or circumstance. Godfrid Harry commented, "I would like to thank you sincerely because while doing your job I also have learnt a lot about my own people and their origin."

2. Studies and published reports from 1933 until recently use "Chimbu" for the people and the language. This chapter delineates some enduring Simbu characteristics; I use the present tense, although there have been some changes and individual Simbu vary in their beliefs and practices.

3. Chimbu is the largest Papuan language family, made up of Kuman, Dom, Gumine (Golin), Salt-Yui, Chuave, and Sinasina (Foley 1986:237). Other languages included by Wurm (1971) are Nagane, Nondiri, Elimbari, Nomane, and Kaire. Besides Chimbu, there

are speakers of Siane, an Eastern Highlands language, and small populations of Mikaru or Daribi and Pawaia speakers in the Karimui district of South Simbu Province.

4. Peter Golla recorded Sinasina and Numai traditions of origin for me in 1984.

5. An important exception are Wagner's studies of Daribi (1967, 1972).

6. Parmentier (1987:11–15) might term these "signs of history." Another, more recent discussion of the importance of location and names is Kahn (1990), who describes stones that serve as monuments. The long-lived trees of Simbu ceremonial grounds and cemeteries bear witness to those who planted them.

7. Aufenanger's many works are rich in these stories; also see Bergmann 1971: vol. 3. Nilles (1977:165–166) has published a version of this origin story, and some also appear in the patrol reports when officers were directed to obtain anthropological information. My young research assistants collected many different personal and family stories from elders in 1987.

8. A version of the story is in Bergmann 1971, 3:31–34. Others were obtained by research assistants in 1987. This version was given by a Sinasina, Yal Essy Miamu, collected by Walkaima Essy:

> Once upon a time a man had many sons and daughters. Each morning he would dress up each of his sons for the day. They would go and do the day's work and return in the afternoon. Upon returning other sons except the elder son would demand for food to fill their hungry stomachs. The elder son would stay as though he was not hungry and in fact he never demanded food. Another peculiar thing about the elder son was that they would discover rubbish amongst his feathers and at his back. When the brother asked where he collected all this rubbish, he would reply that the rubbish must have fallen on him while going to the bush to excrete. This continued for some time.
>
> One day the other brothers became suspicious and were very curious about the activities of the elder brother. When they were dressed up and sent away, the rest of the brothers followed the elder brother into the bush. They always stay at a distance so that their presence was not felt and seen.
>
> When the elder brother reached the thick bush, he removed his costume and turned into a pig and started digging up the soil looking for worms. When the pig was some distance away from the costumes the youngest brother walked quietly to the place where he left the costume, stole a feather and returned to the rest of the brothers.
>
> In the afternoon when the elder brother came home, the rest of the brothers tease him saying words like worm eater. They ended up with a big quarrel and the father intervened and stopped everyone. The rest of the brothers told the story to the father and showed the feather as evidence. The elder brother was so ashamed that he bent his head down and was silent. That night the village leaders were called together, killed some pigs for the elder brother, took the liver and hearts of the pigs and offered them to the spirits and destroyed all the feathers and belongings and received him as one of them.
>
> After this ceremony he never turned into a pig. Due to this legend pigs are known as elder brother.

9. O'Hanlon, whose study in the Wahgi valley included people who trace their origin to Simbu, reports similar beliefs (1989, 1990, 1991, 1993).

10. A summary story of Siambugla local origin is that Bandi and Paglau lived at

Womkama. They quarreled because Paglau did not share cuscus marsupial meat with Bandi. They killed a dog, and then a Paglau man beat up a Bandi man. Gena people came in with flowers to fight, and the Bandi were chased away. But one Bandi came later and founded Gena Goglmba. Siambugla settled at Koglai, then Bobni, Bagkal, and Kair. Then one shot a bird at Dane, where Naregu are. A boy went to Niur with Damagu, then went on next day.

Denglagu, at the head of the Simbu valley, say that the Siaku group migrated from the east to Goglme. Tribal fighting in this densely settled area forced movements and migrations in the valley area, and the Siaku Denglagu moved to the upper valley (Raphael Kindua Kumugl of the upper Simbu, interviewed by Tobias Apa).

11. The first missionaries and government officers noted that some Simbu valley people, a part of the Inau group, spoke an Eastern Highlands dialect known as Nakane ka; this is called Nagane by Wurm, who noted that it was being superseded by Kuman Simbu. There were close ties of exchange and marriage to highlanders to the east.

12. These tales become authoritative statements of tribal leaders, the social memory of the group (Connerton 1989).

13. Bandua Monguai interviewed by Paul Ambani. The story told by Guri, an Endugwa, to Godfrid Harry in 1987 is more detailed. It recounts that a small group of four hunters and gatherers were found and captured by the Naregu. They were shown how to build houses and make gardens by their Naregu hosts, given wives, and founded the Endugwa clans.

Kugame Tange of Endugwa (interviewer Lawrence Gigmai):

> The man returned to Kogo with good food gifts. The Endugwa were wild so they didn't want to come any closer to the Kombalkus and one of their friends so they (the Kombalku) left the food at a clearing and went home to Pari. After a while the Kombalku came back to their Endugwa friends and took them up to Kogo and built houses for them and made gardens for them and make them settle there. Some said we originate from Womkama but I don't believe them. We Endugwa originate from Kogo. The Kombalku instructed Endugwa on aspects of gardening and house building and even to the extent of explaining to them to sleep with women and reproduce even their children. The list of clans and subclans follows.

14. The story continues: they found that food grew well and brought other Endugwa there to Gondoma Morugl. (This is *gondoma*, a vine and root, probably *pueraria*, and a tree that is grown to support it.) Nauru often tell the same story of their origin. In the several versions of this story as recorded by educated Simbu, the wife is sometimes said to have "dated" Bengande; sometimes she was raped; and sometimes she mistook Bengande for her husband because they looked and had voices so alike. Although the Endugwa tribes were once allies, fights between the several subtribes of Endugwa have also occurred, and since 1984 the Naregu have been allied with the Nauru in their fights against the Endugwa and the Siambugla.

15. Story told by Garen Gelua to Joe Gelua.

16. See discussion of *kumo* witchcraft, note 23 below.

17. *Yombagl*, in its dialectic variant, *iambakey*, is the name chosen by the Simbu politician Iambakey Okuk as a child (Ryder 1993). He used this powerful lesser bird of paradise symbol on his airplanes and as personal identification.

18. They were known, of course, from the early writings of Malinowski (1922) and Mauss (1925). For further discussion of exchange in Melanesia, see: A. Strathern 1971;

Gregory 1982; Lederman 1986; Appadurai, ed. 1986; M. Strathern 1988; Thomas 1991; and Weiner 1992. M. Strathern says, "Melanesia appears to endorse a form of gift exchange as a fundamental principle of social life" (1990:206).

19. In the Eastern Highlands, by contrast, small pigs were killed at more frequent ceremonies, and in the Western Highlands and Enga, transactions of live pigs were a phase of the feasts.

20. The ritual is also described by Bergmann (1971, 4:92–118).

21. Pigs are often named for the circumstances of their acquisition, such as the price or goods given for them, or the place of origin (Brown 1986b). In this way pig names are markers of events.

22. It is most fortunate for my understanding that Nilles reported these trade relations in early contact (Nilles 1944:10–13). Sale of manufactured goods, salt, paints, etc., by mission and trade stores soon made these local markets decline. However, I saw trade between unrelated visitors in the Kerowagi area following a pig feast in 1959.

23. Simbu have no tradition of cannibalism and regard it as a horrible practice of witches and some outside peoples.

24. See Warry (1987) for a description of first reactions in the Chuave area of Simbu.

25. In his discussion of compensation, Paul Dage (1985) remarks that today few girls are willing to become brides in such circumstances but the gift is still appropriate.

Chapter 3: White Spirits and Cargo

1. At this time in the New Guinea administration, a District Officer (D.O.) was in charge of a district; an Assistant District Officer (A.D.O.) was in charge of a subdistrict or on special assignment. A Patrol Officer (P.O.) was an experienced officer, whereas a Cadet Patrol Officer (C.P.O.) was usually on his first assignment. These abbreviations will be used throughout. The pidgin term *kiap* is used for all government officers.

2. Australian Archives, A/518/1; K840/1/3.

3. Leahy's diaries are in the manuscript collection, National Library of Australia.

4. Report in Australian Archives A7034/1, item 31, by Samson, Roberts, Penglase.

5. This view was expressed in many situations. It is mentioned by J. Flierl, one of the pioneer Lutheran missionaries, when referring to people of the Finschafen area (1927:19ff.).

6. C. Marshall 1983:109.

7. Peter Munster 1975:4.

8. Fox diary, Papua New Guinea collection at the University of Papua New Guinea.

9. This study and the retracing of the Hides and O'Malley expedition in highland Papua (Schieffelin and Crittenden 1992) detail native memories of great dangers and many deaths, an entirely different view of early contact than that presented by Australian writers.

10. These notes and quotes are from my notebook and tape recording of the interview.

11. Connolly and Anderson 1987, photographs on pp. 248, 251.

12. The employers often favored men from certain areas, and many refer fondly to their Waria or Markham "boys," close companions in strange territory.

13. In 1958–1960, when we drove a jeep on small dirt roads into Simbu settlements,

children came up to touch the metal; vehicles were still unfamiliar in places away from the highlands highway.

14. Okuk Palma tells of early days with Rev. Bergmann and the first landings at Kundiawa airstrip (see Chap. 6).

15. I had several talks with Witne and Mondia, Siambugla men of Dimbi on May 8, 1976 and May 24, 1985 (information from my notebooks, Witne Michael translator). In 1987, Francis Kombugun of the Mingende area interviewed elders at Dimbi, and a translation of the taped interview was made. I discuss Kawagl's legendary character in Chapter 10.

16. Also spelled Kote, Kotte, Kôte; it is a language of the Finschhafen area used by the Lutheran mission teachers and in schools.

17. Leahy's diary became the basis of several articles and books, differing in some ways to emphasize his discoveries and adventures for different audiences. See Brown 1994.

18. This was repeated many times by people of the area.

19. This remark is taken from my notebook of 1959 when visiting the Kerowagi area.

20. My field notes of different times name Dege or Gege as the thief. I cannot say if this is due to my mishearing or to different informants' statements. My notebooks name the object stolen as a knife or an axe; at that time, either may have been called *di maima* (S. cutting implement of iron or metal).

21. J. R. Black, patrol Report B. 16 of 1934. The observation stands out in contrast to McCarthy's patrol into Menyamya: "I insisted that all food be purchased at one spot. . . . We would not allow more than half-a-dozen of the club-bearing Kukukuku . . . at one time" (McCarthy 1963:97).

Chapter 4: Discovering the Gun

1. Rev. Bergmann kept a journal for many years. After his retirement to Queensland he wrote up this journal as *Vierzig Jahre in Neuguinea*. I am indebted to Bob Heuter for the microfiche of this eleven-volume work, and to Norbert Weisinger for help in translation.

2. See also Bornemann 1939.

3. There are alternate names and spellings throughout these reports. Denglagu, Dengaragu, and sometimes a more inclusive group, Denglamagu or Dengla-Maguagu, are a tribe (sometimes called clan) at the head of the Simbu valley, where Keglsugl (also called Toromambuno) airstrip was later built; Keglsugl became a Catholic mission center. The Inau are sometimes called Inaugu or Inauhu; Kukane may be Kukani, Kuglkane, or Kokane; Womkama may be Womatne; Goglme may be Gorime, Gogol, Gorgme, etc. Fr. Morschheuser's name is spelled in many ways. Kundiawa, Ega, and Tema are places where the Lutheran mission, the government post, and the airstrip were established. Now Ega and Tema refer to the mission and airstrip, Kundiawa to the government headquarters.

4. This statement that there was a post at Goroka is incorrect; Goroka became an airfield and then a government station in the 1940s. The speaker evidently knew nothing about the Morobe headquarters at Salamaua. Goroka became the Eastern Highlands District headquarters after 1950.

5. It is not possible to be certain of identification; this seems rather far from Tropper, but it may be.

6. In Salisbury's discussion of Siane, he says that the new goods resembled valuables and were accepted as such. Big men were recipients. When white men wanted a pig, they offered valuables; Siane saw this as exchange, not purchase (1962:115). Girigiri (P. cowrie shells) brought by the strangers from the coast cost them only 6d. per pound, which was two to three hundred small cowries. Fr. Ross comments that at Wilya natives worked for a few cowries a day, and that he bought a pig for a bushknife or small axe and a large pig for a shell worth twenty-five cents (Ross 1968, 1969).

7. Fr. Nilles' information is based upon diaries, and talks with Fr. Schäfer, Fr. Tropper, mission helpers, and Simbu who had been present at these events.

8. Taylor's legend is further examined in Chapter 9.

Chapter 5: Establishing Control

1. Some patrol reports of 1936–1937 to District Office Madang are preserved in the J. K. McCarthy Papers, Australian National Library; the microfilm is also in the Pacific Manuscript Bureau and other archives. Vial published articles about Simbu in the Australian journal *Walkabout* (1938–1941). Diaries and other notes have been consulted when possible.

2. See discussion of police in Chapter 6.

3. I do not have these reports and could not find them in archives.

4. John J. Murphy, personal diary, first four volumes, in Simbu from 8 August 1936 to 3 March 1937, photocopied from Fryer library, University of Queensland. I met Murphy at the university in April 1993, and his conversation filled in a little more information.

5. The incidents and inquiry are discussed by Connolly and Anderson (1987:208–214); in Leahy's writings the incidents are described as attacks upon him and shooting in self-defense.

6. I was able to make some notes on their reports years ago, but little survives. This information is from my old notes.

7. At this time an official hat was given to native officials as an insignia of office.

8. The practice is discussed by Radford (1977) in the Eastern Highlands.

9. Dilu Deck writes: "*awage goglkwa* is a place near my village which means Jim Taylor and early colonial kiaps ordered the people to burn their traditional fighting weapons. The name means 'shield burn' " (1992).

Chapter 6: Securing Control

1. The Australia New Guinea Administrative Unit (see Chap. 7).

2. This institution of compensation payment reinforced, if it did not initiate, the idea that pigs and valuables might be equivalent to human lives. This practice of the 1930s may place Strathern's concept of substitution (1988) historically.

3. "We mustered two thousand unarmed men from the Siambuga Waugwa and Kamanagu and advanced with considerable noise on the Yongamugl who retired in their traditional fashion to the safety of their limestone caves above the Chimbu gorge. Our operation had been carefully organized and for two days we ignored people and concen-

trated entirely on rounding up and fencing in what must have been very close to their entire resources of livestock. Then we sat down with our screaming hostage of five thousand pigs and demanded that the Yongamugl give up all their fighting leaders, which they did" (1986:120). According to another statement (Downs in Griffin, ed." 1978:238), 1,500 pigs were taken. I cannot verify either of these statements. Downs writes with dramatic force, and the pigs could hardly have been accurately counted in this action.

    4. Tribal fights over such frozen boundaries have become common in the province.

    5. Annual Report, 1940:6.

    6. Patrol Report, 1–11 January 1939, p. 2.

    7. Downs in Griffin, ed. 1978:237.

    8. Patrol Report, 16–19 May 1940:2.

    9. Monthly Report, August 1940.

    10. Patrol Report, 3 September 1940:2.

    11. Monthly Report, July, 4 August.

Chapter 7: Simbu Dependence

    1. Burridge (1960) defines a triangle of relationships: *kanaka,* missionary, and administrative officer. It applies somewhat differently to the highlands, where native loyalty has been a matter of some contention.

    2. My fieldwork began in 1958. Some of the patrol reports of 1941–1973, available through the Papua New Guinea Archives Accession no. 496, series Kundiawa and Chimbu, are sources for this chapter. Some additional reports are in the Australian Archives (A7034/1). The reports, some of which contain census records and maps, are far from complete, and the context or other matters of the time may be missing. I can fill in some particulars and context for the period in which I was a frequent visitor. Hide, in his discussion of land titles and litigation (1973) cites many reports now unavailable. He also shows great differences between native concepts of land rights, government principles, and the observations of Fr. Schäfer and anthropologists.

    3. Ubom Street, as told to P. Munster in 1975.

    4. See life story in Chapter 9.

    5. My first house at Mintima was built on the border of two clans. Of the two rooms, each was built by the clan on whose land it stood.

    6. Birth dates and infant mortality were not recorded, and migration could include marriage and divorce. The compilation of village books by administration officers did not indicate demographic trends with any accuracy (see Brookfield 1960).

    7. Reports of Sina Sina confirm that village settlement is a postcontact pattern (Hatanaka 1972:8–9).

    8. Papua New Guinea Archives, Kundiawa patrol reports, Accession no. 496, vol. 1; on microfiche.

    9. Winterford reported that three plants are eaten: *munaguna* causes barrenness; *kombukakau,* of which the fur on leaves coats ovaries; *kuku* applied with massage causes abortion. This ethnobotanical note did not provide information that would enable one to identify the plants or in any way test their properties.

10. See also Hatanaka 1972, M. Strathern 1985, and Podolefsky 1992.

11. New Guinea flag used by the government.

12. See Hassell (1991:29). The Tommy Kabu movement was doomed to fail because of European control of money. Government interfered with native and mission attempts at enterprise.

13. Hayano (1990) provides a vivid picture of his dependence on a local employee.

Chapter 8: Old Ways to New

1. Some of the information in this chapter has been presented in greater detail elsewhere: see Brown 1962, 1964, 1965, 1966a, 1966b, 1969, 1972, 1978, 1979a, 1979b, 1982a, 1982b, 1986, 1987a, 1987b, 1988, 1989, 1990, n.d.; Brown, Brookfield, and Grau 1990. Nilles (1939, 1940, 1943, 1944) describes traditional beliefs and ceremony; his later works (1950, 1953) discuss changes.

2. By five years of age, children were two kilograms heavier in 1981 than in 1956, when Simbu infant malnutrition was considered a serious problem. Cereals, protein foods, and trade-store foods now comprise a significant part of the Simbu diet (Harvey and Heywood 1983a, 1983b). Simbu child health is close to the Papua New Guinea national average (Townsend 1985).

3. We supplied them with food, clothing, and personal necessities. One year the two men were dressed in white T-shirts and blue laplaps for the visit of David Hodgkin, the ANU registrar. He observed the colors and said, "I see you have provided them with the livery of the ANU."

4. I describe his later career and life story in Chapter 9.

5. The very different situation of the Eastern Highlands, with their abundant land, large plantations of coffee, and an active commercial center, is evident in Howlett (1962), Finney (1973, 1987), Good and Donaldson (1980), Grossman (1984), Donaldson and Good (n.d.).

6. This information comes from field inquiries and patrol reports. There are also reports from other researchers: see Hatanaka 1972:56; Warry 1987; and Podolefsky 1987, 1990 for field descriptions of councillors' activities.

7. Careers of Simbu statesmen are described by Standish (1992).

8. I had no opportunity to meet him and present this as it was written by the interviewer. This man was interviewed separately by two young men, quoted in several places here.

9. The subject is far beyond the scope of this book (see Hegarty, ed. 1983, Oliver, ed. 1989, and Standish 1992).

10. Brown 1989:251.

Chapter 9: Simbu Voices

1. See above, in discussion of World War II, Chapter 7.

2. Wamugl 1; see story of Naregu in Chapter 2.

3. From 1959 notebooks.

Chapter 10: Isolation, Intrusion, Inclusion

1. In 1938, Mao elaborated upon this: "Since ancient times there has never been a war that did not have a political character . . . politics is war without bloodshed while war is politics with bloodshed."

2. Here my Simbu informants would differ from Marilyn Strathern's interpretation of the nonchalance of Hagen highlanders and their first views of airplane and strangers. Whereas planes often landed in Hagen in 1933 and thereafter, they were rare in Simbu and there was no regularly used landing field until later.

3. These hopes persisted. In the 1960s Harold Brookfield and I were offered land for a house at Bamugl by the landowners. The house was built by the Australian National University and was used for the next twenty years by several research field workers. To the people of Bamugl it was a source for the sale of produce and employment of servants and guides.

4. It may be noted that the name Witni is common to these two men, and that Mondia is a place-name, a pass from Bundi into Simbu, and the name of the other old man. Children are named for friends of the parents and sometimes for places with which they are associated.

5. This is a reference to the incident at Kunabau described in Chapter 3.

6. Wagner (1975:31–32) explains how differently westerners and natives have conceptualized cargo. However, "cargo" is not the word used by Simbu; rather, they speak of white man's goods, specifying metal, clothes, foods, and cars. Today, "developmen" (P.) is in general use, meaning western goods, industry, roads, and other forms of "modernization."

7. There are articles, films, and books about the patrols: see the *Pacific Island Monthly* for 1940, Leahy's photographs, and his daughter's film *My Father, My Country*, on the Hagen-Sepik patrol. Other historical works are reported to be in progress (Gammage 1990).

8. From dedication of Jim Taylor Memorial Drive, Mount Hagen.

9. From dedication of Jim Taylor Memorial Drive, Mount Hagen.

10. The film *Angels of War* depicts this belief and faith in the white man's promises made during World War II and the sad disappointment of Papua New Guinean war veterans in the lack of fulfillment years later.

11. Microfilm and MS in archival collections.

12. Bill Gammage (1991, 1992) states that the police had a more decisive influence in the highlands than has been recognized.

13. This is, of course, as the Kenya highlands were viewed in 1940.

14. Simbu used steel axes, knives, shovels, nails in houses, wore some clothing, used matches to make fire, and smoked tobacco rolled in newspaper. When I spoke with Rev. Bergmann in 1976 about change in Simbu, he confirmed my impression that the greatest changes had occurred in the first years, before 1950.

15. I cannot fully explain looting that occurs at the death of an admired leader. It may be that people express their grief by taking payment for it. Looting in Rabaul after the volcanic eruptions of 1994 and the evacuation of residents seems, rather, to be another example of the phenomenon reported from communities where a natural disaster or power failure has weakened normal security precautions.

16. By 1985, two shows, Chimbu Players and Chimbu Mudmen, were available to

tourist groups stopping at Mintima and Bamugl on bus tours of the highlands. They were presented on specially constructed stages where the visitors could sit on log benches to view the performances. When I asked why those particular themes and playlets, which resemble the traditional *gitn darkwa* (S. spirit plays), were presented to tourists, I was told that these were the ones the tour organizers chose. Simbu seemed able to design their repertoire in response to these preferences. The groups also sold locally made artifacts, necklaces, and carvings of traditional and nontraditional design. Some of these were fashioned after the tourist crafts better known in the Sepik area (see Gewertz and Errington 1991).

GLOSSARY OF PIDGIN TERMS

baiim meri	marriage payment, bride-price
balus	airplane
belo	lunchtime bell
belo bak	time to return to work
big lain	big work line
bikhet	arrogant, stubborn, disobedient
bilas	decorations
bilum	net bag
bisnis	business, commercial enterprise
boi	native male, usually adult
bosboi	headman, foreman
developmen	development, westernization
girigiri	small cowrie shell
govman	government
gutpela pasin	good customs/ways
harim tok	listen to the leaders' talk
haus kaikai	restaurant, canteen
kanaka	native, often from a backward area
kaskas	scabies
karim leg	carry-leg, a Simbu courtship practice
kaukau	sweet potato
kiap	government officer
kina	goldlip mother-of-pearl shell; now currency of Papua New Guinea, worth one U.S. dollar to $1.25 in the 1980s
komdi	ward committeeman, leading local person
konsel	elected councillor
kot	court, hearing
kunai	grass
laplap	cloth, usually a wrapped skirt
luluai	government-appointed native official; in Simbu, head of a tribe or large clan
manki	native boy
manki masta	domestic servant, cook
marita	oil pandanus and its fruit
masalai	spirit
masta	white man
memba	elected member of official body, such as Legislative Council
meri/mary/mari	native woman
nupela pasin	new ways

pasin bilong Satan	heathen (satanic) way
pitpit	reed, cane
ples balus	airstrip, airfield
rabisman	worthless person
raskol	"rascal" gang
sangguma	magic, sorcery
singsing	festival, ceremony
sumatin	Catholic pupil
tambu	small cowrie shell
tultul	appointed native official, assistant to luluai, head of clan or subclan
tumbuna	ancestor
turnim tok	interpreter
wara	water, river
wok bisnis	work/business
wok meri	women's organization of eastern Simbu
yar	casuarina tree

BIBLIOGRAPHY

Appadurai, Arjun, ed.
1986   *The social life of things*. Cambridge: Cambridge Univ. Press.
Ardener, Edwin
1989   The construction of history. In *History and ethnicity*, edited by Elizabeth Tonkin, Maryon McDonald, and Malcolm Chapman. ASA Monographs 27. London: Routledge.
Aufenanger, Heinrich
1960   The kanggi spirit in the central highlands of New Guinea. *Anthropos* 55:671–688.
1962a   Sayings with a hidden meaning (Central Highlands, New Guinea). *Anthropos* 57:325–335.
1962b   The sun in the life of the natives of the New Guinea highlands. *Anthropos* 57: 1–44.
1965   The Gerua cult in the highlands of New Guinea. *Anthropos* 60:248–261.
1971   The dinggan spirit of disease in the central highlands of New Guinea. *Ethnomedizin* 1:373–396.
Axtell, James
1979   Ethnohistory: An historian's view. *Ethnohistory* 26:1–13.
1992   *Beyond 1492*. New York: Oxford Univ. Press.
Bailey, L. W.
1954a   Chimbu patrol report 11, June–July, Koronigl. Australian Archives ACT. A7034/1, item 118.
1954b   Chimbu patrol report 3, Yonggamugl, Australian Archives ACT. A7034/1, item 122.
Ballard, Chris
1992   First contact as non-event in the Papua New Guinea highlands. Unpublished paper for American Anthropological Association conference.
Ballard, Chris, and Bryant Allen
1991   Inclined to be cheeky. Unpublished seminar paper, Australian National University.
Barnes, John A.
1962   African models in the New Guinea highlands. *Man* 62:5–9.
Bates, C. B.
1936   Patrol reports. National Library of Australia MS 5581. Box 14, folders 40–45.
Bergmann, Wilhelm
1971   *The Kamanuku*. 4 vols. Mimeograph. Mutdapilly, Queensland.
N.d.   *Vierzig Jahre in Neuguinea*. 11 vols. Mimeograph.
Biersack, Aletta
1991   Introduction to *Clio in Oceania*, 1–36. Washington, D.C.: Smithsonian Institution Press.

Black, John R.
1934   Patrol report B. 16: Finintegu, Bena Bena and Purari. MS. Pacific Manuscript
        Bureau, Canberra, Australia.
1935   Diary. MS.
Bloch, Marc, and Jonathan Parry
1989   Introduction to *Money and the morality of exchange*, edited by Jonathan Parry and
        Marc Bloch. Cambridge: Cambridge Univ. Press.
Blong, R. J.
1982   *The time of darkness*. Seattle: Univ. of Washington Press.
Book Review Forum
1994   *Pacific Studies* 17:103–155.
Bornemann, Fritz
1939   *Missionar in New-Guinea. P. Karl Morschheuser SVD 1904–1934*. Missionsdruck-
        erei St. Gabriel, Wien-Mödling.
Borofsky, Robert
1987   *Making history*. Cambridge: Cambridge Univ. Press.
Boyd, David
1981   Village agriculture and labor migration: Inter-related production strategies
        among the Ilakia Awa. *American Ethnologist* 8:74–93.
Brison, Karen
1992   *Just Talk*. Berkeley and Los Angeles: Univ. of California Press.
Brookfield, Harold
1960   Population distribution and labour migration in New Guinea. *Australian Geogra-
        pher* 7:233–242.
Brookfield, Harold, and Paula Brown
1963   *Struggle for land*. Melbourne: Oxford Univ. Press.
Brown, Paula
1960   Chimbu tribes. *Southwestern Journal of Anthropology* 16:22–35.
1961   Chimbu death payments. *Journal of the Royal Anthropological Institute* 91:
        77–96.
1962   Non-agnates among the patrilineal Chimbu. *Journal of the Polynesian Society*
        71:57–69.
1963   From anarchy to satrapy. *American Anthropologist* 65:1–15.
1964   Enemies and affines. *Ethnology* 3:335–356.
1966a   Kondom. *Journal of the Papua and New Guinea Society* 1, no. 2:26–34.
1966b   The Chimbu political system. *Anthropological Forum* 2:36–56.
1969   Marriage in Chimbu. In *Pigs, Pearlshells and Women*, edited by Robert Glasse and
        Mervyn Meggitt, 79–95. New York: Prentice-Hall.
1972   *The Chimbu: A study of change in the New Guinea highlands*. Cambridge, Mass.:
        Schenkman.
1974   Mediators in social change: New roles for big men. *Mankind* 9:224–230.
1977   *Kumo* witchcraft at Mintima, Chimbu Province, Papua New Guinea. *Oceania*
        48:26–29.
1978   New Guinea: Ecology, society and culture. In *Annual Review of Anthropology*
        7:263–292. Palo Alto: Annual Reviews Press.
1979a   Change and the boundaries of systems in highland New Guinea: The Chimbu.
        In *Social and ecological systems*, edited by Philip Burnham and Roy Ellen, 135–
        151. ASA Monograph 18. London: Academic Press.

1979b   Chimbu leadership—to the beginning of Provincial Government. *Journal of Pacific History* 14:100–117.

1982a   Chimbu disorder: Tribal fighting in newly independent Papua New Guinea. *Pacific Viewpoint* 23:1–21.

1982b   Conflict in the New Guinea highlands. *Journal of Conflict Resolution* 26:525–546.

1984   Long-term research. In *Ethnographic research: A guide to general conduct*, edited by Roy Ellen, 241–247. London: Academic Press.

1986a   Simbu aggression and the drive to win. *Anthropological Quarterly* 59:165–170.

1986b   What do you call your pig? Who is your namesake? *Names* 34:432–436.

1987a   New men and big men: Emerging social stratification in the third world, a case study from the New Guinea highlands. *Ethnology* 27:87–106.

1987b   From birth hut to disco. *Bikmaus* 7, no. 1:15–24.

1988   Gender and social change: New forms of independence for Simbu women. *Oceania* 59:123–142.

1989   The Simbu election. In *Eleksin: The 1987 national election in Papua New Guinea*, edited by Michael Oliver, 245–252. Port Moresby: Univ. of Papua New Guinea.

1990a   No dialogue: Premises and confrontations in intercultural encounter, Papua New Guinea. *American Anthropologist* 92:468–474.

1990b   Big man, past and present: Model, person, hero, legend. *Ethnology* 29:97–115.

1992   Chimbu and stranger. *Ethnology* 31:27–44.

1993   On telling and retelling a story. *Reviews in Anthropology* 22:285–295.

N.d.a   Adolescence in Chimbu. MS.

N.d.b   Property in Chimbu. MS.

Brown, Paula, and Harold Brookfield

1959   Chimbu Land and Society. *Oceania* 30:1–75.

Brown, Paula, Harold Brookfield, and Robin Grau

1990   Land tenure and land transfer in Chimbu, Papua New Guinea, 1958–1984: A study in continuity and change, accommodation and opportunism. *Human Ecology* 18:21–49.

Brown, Paula, and Aaron Podolefsky

1976   Population density, agricultural intensity, land tenure, and group size in the New Guinea highlands. *Ethnology* 15:211–238.

Bulmer, Ralph

1962   Chimbu plume traders. *Australian Natural History* (March), 15–19.

Bulmer, Ralph, and Ian Majnep

1977   *Birds of my Kalam country.* Auckland: Oxford Univ. Press.

Burridge, Kenelm

1960   Mambu: A Melanesian millennium. London: Methuen.

Burton, John

1983   A dysentery epidemic in New Guinea and its mortality. *Journal of Pacific History* 18:236–261.

1984   Axe makers of the Wahgi. Ph.D. diss., Australian National University.

Carmack, Robert M.

1972   Ethnohistory: A review of its development, methods, and aims. In *Annual Review of Anthropology*, 2:227–246. Palo Alto: Annual Reviews Press.

Carrier, James G.

1992a   The gift in theory and practice in Melanesia: A note on the continuity of gift exchange. *Ethnology* 31:185–193.

1992b   Introduction to *History and tradition in Melanesian anthropology*, edited by James Carrier. Berkeley and Los Angeles: Univ. of California Press.

Carrier, James, and Achsah Carrier
1989   *Wage, trade, and exchange in Melanesia*. Berkeley and Los Angeles: Univ. of California Press.

Christie, Marion
1980   Changing consumer behavior in Papua New Guinea: Its social and ecological implications. Report No. 3, Center for Resource and Environmental Studies. Canberra: Australian National Univ.

Clausewitz, Karl von
1832   On War. In *Oxford dictionary of quotations*, edited by A. Partington, 205. Oxford: Oxford Univ. Press.

Clifford, James
1988   *The predicament of culture*. Cambridge, Mass.: Harvard Univ. Press.

Clifford, James, and George Marcus, eds.
1986   Introduction to *Writing culture*. Berkeley and Los Angeles: Univ. of California Press.

Cochrane, R.
1966   Success at Kundiawa—a triumph of cooperation. *Australian Territories* 6, no. 2 (April): 16–22.

Cohn, Bernard
1980   History and anthropology. *Comparative Studies in Society and History* 22:198–221.
1981   Anthropology and history in the 1980s. *Journal of Interdisciplinary History* 12: 227–252.

Colman, J.
1954   Patrol report 3, Sinasina. Australian Archives ACT. A7034/1, item 123.

Connerton, Paul
1987   *How societies remember*. Cambridge: Cambridge Univ. Press.

Connolly, Bob, and Robin Anderson
1987   *First contact*. New York: Viking.

Dage, Paul
1985–1989   Private communications, interview, and report manuscripts.

Deck, Dilu
1991, 1992   Private communications, letters.

Dening, Greg
1980   *Islands and beaches*. Honolulu: Univ. of Hawai'i Press.
1988a   *History's anthropology*. Association for Social Anthropology in Oceania Special Publication no. 2. Lanham, Md.: Univ. Press of America.
1988b   *The Bounty: An ethnographic history*. History Department, Melbourne Univ.
1991   A poetic for histories: Transformations that present the past. In *Clio in Oceania*, edited by Aletta Biersack, 347–380. Washington, D.C.: Smithsonian Institution Press.

Dennis, J. C.
1945   Patrol report from Chuave. Papua New Guinea Archives Kundiawa patrol reports Accession no. 496, vol. 1.

Denoon, Donald, and Rod Lacey
1981   *Oral sources and the history of Papua New Guinea*. Port Moresby: Univ. of Papua New Guinea.

Donaldson, Michael, and Ken Good.
N.d.   The Eastern Highlands: Coffee and class. In *A time to plant and a time to uproot*, edited by Donald Denoon and C. Snowden. Port Moresby: Institute of Papua New Guinea Studies.

Downs, Ian
1939–1940   Annual report, monthly reports, patrol reports. In Downs Papers, Pacific Manuscripts Bureau no. 607.
1980   *The Australian Trusteeship 1945–75.* Canberra: Dept. of Home Affairs Australian Government Publishing Service.
1986   *The last mountain.* Brisbane: Univ. of Queensland Press.

Economic Consultants
1979   *Simbu Province rural development study.*

Epstein, T. Scarlett
1968   *Capitalism, primitive and modern.* Canberra: Australian National Univ.

Feil, Daryll
1987   *The evolution of highland Papua New Guinea societies.* Cambridge: Cambridge Univ. Press.

Fenton, William M.
1952   Training of historical ethnologists in America. *American Anthropologist* 54: 328–339.

Fentress, James, and Chris Wickham
1992   *Social Memory.* Oxford: Blackwells.

Finney, Ben
1973   *Big men and business.* Honolulu: Univ. of Hawai‘i Press.
1987   Business development in the highlands of Papua New Guinea. Research report. Pacific Islands Development Program Series No. 6. Honolulu.

Flierl, John
1927   *Forty years in New Guinea,* trans. M. Wiederaenders. Chicago: Wartburg Publishing House.

Fogelson, Ray
1989   The ethnohistory of events and non-events. *Ethnohistory* 36:133–147.

Foley, William A.
1986   *The Papuan languages of New Guinea.* Cambridge: Cambridge Univ. Press.

Fortes, Meyer
1953   The structure of unilineal descent groups. *American Anthropologist* 55:17–41.

Fowler, N. F.
1952   Patrol report, Kup and Dom. Australian Archives ACT. A7034/1, item 112.

Fox, Jack
1934   Diary MS. Papua New Guinea Collection, Univ. of Papua New Guinea.

Gammage, Bill
1991, 1992   Private communications, letters.

Gande, J. A.
1974   Chimbu pig-killing ceremony. *Oral History* 2, no. 9:6–14.

Gauci, J. A.
1954   Kerowagi patrol report 1, Koronigl, Kup. Australian Archives ACT. A7034/1, item 120.
1955a   Patrol report 12, Koronigl. Australian Archives ACT. A7034/1, item 130.
1955b   Patrol report 13, Kerowagi. Australian Archives ACT. A7034/1, item 131.

1955c   Patrol report 1, Upper Chimbu. Australian Archives ACT. A7034/1, item 119.
Gewertz, Deborah
1983   *Sepik River societies*. Cambridge: Cambridge Univ. Press.
Gewertz, Deborah, and Frederick Errington
1991   *Twisted histories, altered contexts*. Cambridge: Cambridge Univ. Press.
Gewertz, Deborah, and Edward B. Schieffelin
1985   Introduction to *History and ethnohistory in Papua New Guinea*. Oceania Mono-
         graphs 26. Sydney: Univ. of Sydney.
Giddings, Rick
1990   Personal communication (letter).
Gigmai, Lawrence
1987   Personal communications, interviews.
1992–1995   Personal communications, letters.
Glasse, Robert
1968   *Huli of Papua*. Paris: Mouton.
1992   Encounters with the Huli: Fieldwork at Tari in the 1950s. In *Ethnographic pre-
         sents*, edited by Terence Hays, 232–249. Berkeley and Los Angeles: Univ. of Cal-
         ifornia Press.
Gluckman, Max
1940   *Analysis of a social situation in modern Zululand*. Rhodes-Livingstone Papers no. 28.
Godelier, Maurice
1982   *La production des grands hommes*. Paris: Fayard.
Godelier, Maurice, and Marilyn Strathern
1990   *Big men and great men*. Cambridge: Cambridge Univ. Press.
Golla, Peter
1984   Personal communications, notes.
Golson, Jack, and D. S. Gardner
1990   Agriculture and sociopolitical organization in New Guinea Highlands prehis-
         tory. In *Annual Review of Anthropology* 19:395–417. Palo Alto: Annual Reviews
         Press.
Good, Ken, and Michael Donaldson
1980   *Development of rural capitalism in Papua New Guinea*. Institute of Papua New
         Guinea Studies no. 1.
Gregory, Christopher A.
1982   *Gifts and commodities*. London: Academic Press.
Griffin, James
1986   *The Times of Papua New Guinea*, 26 December 1986.
———, ed.
1978   *Papua New Guinea portraits*. Canberra: Australian National Univ. Press.
Grossman, Lawrence
1984   *Peasants, subsistence ecology, and development in the highlands of Papua New
         Guinea*. Princeton: Princeton Univ. Press.
1992   Personal communication.
Harding, Thomas G.
1967   *Voyagers of the Vitiaz Strait*. Seattle: Univ. of Washington Press.
Harvey, Philip W. J., and Peter F. Heywood
1983a   *Nutrition and growth in Simbu*. Research report of the Simbu land use project,
         vol. 4. Boroko: Institute of Applied Social Research.

1983b   Twenty-five years of dietary change in Simbu Province, Papua New Guinea. *Ecology of Food and Nutrition* 13:27–35.

Hassall, Graham
1991   The failure of the Tommy Kabu movement: A reassessment of the evidence. *Pacific Studies* 14:29–52.

Hatanaka, Sachiko
1972   *Leadership and socio-economic change in Sinasina, New Guinea highlands.* New Guinea Research Bulletin No. 45. Canberra: Australian National Univ.

Hayano, David M.
1973   Individual correlates of coffee adaptation in the New Guinea Highlands. *Human Organization* 32:305–314.

1979   Male migrant labour and changing sex roles in a Papua New Guinea highlands society. *Oceania* 50:37–52.

1990   *Road through the rain forest.* Prospect Heights, Ill.: Waveland.

Hays, Terence E., ed.
1992   *Ethnographic presents.* Berkeley and Los Angeles: Univ. of California Press.

Haywood, M. R.
1955a   Patrol report 7, Salt. Australian Archives ACT. A7034/1, item 127.

1955b   Patrol report 11, Dom and Sinasina. Australian Archives ACT. A7034/1, item 129.

1955c   Patrol report, Gumine. Australian Archives ACT. A7034/1, item 134.

1955d   Patrol report, Maril. Australian Archives ACT. A7034/1, item 133.

Hegarty, David, ed.
1983   *Electoral politics in Papua New Guinea.* Port Moresby: Univ. of Papua New Guinea.

Herdt, Gilbert, and Robert J. Stoller
1990   *Intimate communications.* New York: Columbia Univ. Press.

Heuter, Bob
1990   Personal communication.

Hibbard, W. J.
1954   Patrol report 12, Dom. Australian Archives ACT. A7034/1, item 121.

Hide, Robin
1973   *The Land Titles Commission in Chimbu.* New Guinea Research Unit Bulletin No. 50. Canberra: Australian National Univ.

Hide, Robin, et al.
1984   *South Simbu: Studies in demography, nutrition and subsistence.* Research report of the Simbu land use project, vol. 4. Boroko: Institute of Applied Social and Economic Research.

Hides, Jack
1936   *Papuan wonderland.* Glasgow: Blackie & Sons.

Howe, Kerry E.
1984   *Where the waves fall.* Honolulu: Univ. of Hawai'i Press.

Howlett, Diana
1962   A decade of change in the Goroka valley, New Guinea. Ph.D. diss., Australian National Univ.

Howlett, Diana, et al.
1976   *Chimbu: Issues in development.* Development Studies Centre no 4. Canberra: Australian National Univ.

Hughes, Ian
1977   *New Guinea stone age trade*. Terra Australis 3. Department of Prehistory. Canberra: Australian National Univ.
Hughes, Jenny
1985   Chimbu worlds: Experiences and change by a Papua New Guinea highlands people. Ph.D. diss., La Trobe University, Australia.
1988   Ancestors, tricksters and demons: An examination of Chimbu interaction in the invisible world. *Oceania* 59:59–74.
Jayawardene, Chandra
1987   Analysis of a social situation in Acheh Besar: An exploration in micro-history. *Social Analysis* 22:30–46.
Jolly, Margaret, and Martha MacIntosh, eds.
1989   *Family and gender in the Pacific*. Cambridge: Cambridge Univ. Press.
Kagl, Toby Waim
1984   Kallan. In *Two highland novels from Papua New Guinea*, edited by T. Kagl and M. Mel. Boroko: Institute of Papua New Guinea Studies.
Kahn, Miriam
1990   Stone-faced ancestors: The spatial anchoring of myth in Wamira, Papua New Guinea. *Ethnology* 29:51–66.
Keesing, Roger
1978   *Elota's story*. New York: St. Martin's.
1986   The *Young Dick* attack: Oral and documentary history on the colonial frontier. *Ethnohistory* 33:268–292.
1990   Colonial history as contested ground: The Bell massacre in the Solomons. *History and Anthropology* 4:279–301.
1992   *Custom and confrontation*. Chicago: Univ. of Chicago Press.
Keesing, Roger, and Peter Corris
1980   *Lightning meets the west wind: The Malaita massacre*. Melbourne: Oxford Univ. Press.
Keesing, Roger, and Margaret Jolly
1992   Epilogue to *History and tradition in Melanesian anthropology*, edited by James Carrier. Berkeley and Los Angeles: Univ. of California Press.
Kelly, W. J.
1955a   Patrol report 5, Central. Australian Archives ACT. A7034/1, item 124.
1955b   Patrol report 6. Australian Archives ACT. A7034/1, item 134.
Keogh A. M.
1953   Patrol report 11, Upper Bomai. Australian Archives ACT. A7034/1, item 111.
Kilage, Ignatius
N.d.   *My mother calls me Yaltep*. Port Moresby: Institute of Papua New Guinea Studies.
Kiste, Robert
1992   Introduction to Klaus Neumann, *Not the way it really was*. Pacific Island Monograph Series no. 10. Honolulu: Univ. of Hawai'i Press.
Kituai, August
1974   Bundi history. *Oral History* 2:8–15.
1985   Taped interviews of Ameri and Tawi. MS.
1988   Innovation and intrusion. *Journal of Pacific History* 23:156–166.
Kondwal, A., and Garry Trompf
1982   The epic of the Komblo. *Oral History* 10, no. 1.

Kroeber, Alfred L.
1939   *Cultural and natural areas of native North America.* Univ. of California Papers in American Anthropology and Ethnology 38.

Kyle, A. F.
1937   Patrol reports. National Library of Australia MS 5581, Box 14, folders 40–45.

Lacey, Rod
1981   Traditions of origin and migration: Some Enga evidence. In *Oral traditions in Melanesia,* edited by Donald Denoon and Rod Lacey. Port Moresby: Univ. of Papua New Guinea.

Langmore, Diane
1989   *Missionary lives in Papua 1874–1914.* Pacific Islands Monograph Series no. 6. Honolulu: Univ. of Hawai'i Press.

Langness, Lewis
1964   Some problems in the conceptualization of highlands social structures. In *New Guinea: The Central Highlands,* edited by James B. Watson (Special Issue). *American Anthropologist* 66:162–182.

Leahy, Dan
1987   Personal communication.

Leahy, Michael
1930–1934   Diaries. National Library of Australia MS 384.
1935a   Letter to Leo Tracey MS.
1935b   The central highlands of New Guinea. Paper read to the Royal Geographical Society in November 1935. Australian Archives ACT. A7034/1, item 55.
1991   *Explorations in highland New Guinea 1930–35.* Tuscaloosa: Univ. of Alabama Press.

Leahy, Michael, and Maurice Crain
1937   *The land that time forgot.* New York: Funk & Wagnalls.

Lederman, Rena
1986   *What gifts engender.* Cambridge: Cambridge Univ. Press.
1990   Big men, large or small? Towards a comparative perspective. *Ethnology* 29:3–16.

Lindstrom, Lamont
1990a   Big men as ancestors: Inspiration and copyrights on Tanna (Vanuatu). *Ethnology* 29:313–326.
1990b   *Knowledge and power in a South Pacific society.* Seattle: Univ. of Washington Press.

Linnekin, Jocelyn, and Lin Poyer, eds.
1990   *Cultural identity and ethnicity in the Pacific.* Honolulu: Univ. of Hawai'i Press.

Lurie, Nancy
1961   Ethnohistory: An ethnological point of view. *Ethnohistory* 8:78–92.

MacDowell, Nancy
1985   Past and future: The nature of episodic time in Bun. In *History and ethnohistory in Papua New Guinea,* edited by Deborah Gewertz and Edward Schieffelin. Oceania Monographs 26. Sydney.
1988   A note on cargo cults and cultural constructions of change. *Pacific Studies* 11:121–134.

Malinowski, Bronislaw
1922   *Argonauts of the Western Pacific.* London: Routledge & Kegan Paul.

Manning, H. J.
1959   Golden voiced Vial. *South Pacific* 10, no. 4:86–92.

Mao Tse-tung
1967   *Quotations from Chairman Mao Tse-tung.* New York: Bantam.
Marcus, George, and Dick Cushman
1982   Ethnographies as texts. In *Annual Review of Anthropology* 11:25–70. Palo Alto: Annual Reviews Press.
Marshall, Charles
1983   The Chimbu expedition New Guinea—February 1933. *Australian Natural History* 21:103–115.
Mauss, Marcel
1954 (1925)   *The gift.* London: Cohen and West.
McCarthy, J. Keith
1934   Report from Madang. Australian Archives P518 841/1.
1963   *Patrol into yesterday.* Melbourne: Cheshire.
Meggitt, Mervyn
1958   The Enga of the New Guinea highlands: Some preliminary observations. *Oceania* 28:253–330.
Mellor, R. H. C.
1953   Patrol report 15, April–May, Upper Chimbu and Koronigl. Australian Archives ACT. A7034/1, item 113.
1955   Patrol report 7, Chuave. Australian Archives ACT. A7034/1, item 126.
Mennis, Mary
1982   *Hagen saga.* Port Moresby: Institute of Papua New Guinea Studies.
Modjeska, Nicholas
1991   Post-Ipomean modernism: The Duna example. In *Big men and great men,* edited by Maurice Godelier and Marilyn Strathern. Cambridge: Cambridge Univ. Press.
Moore, Philip Kai
1985–1987   Personal communications.
Morpeth, Tim
1970   Interview with M. Leahy. MS.
Mosko, Mark
1991   Yali revisited: The interplay of messages and missions in Melanesian structural history. *Journal of the Polynesian Society* 100:269–298.
Munster, Peter
1975   Three men from Morobe. MS.
1979   Makarai. M.A. thesis, Univ. of Papua New Guinea.
1983   Notes from an interview with J. Taylor. MS.
Murphy, John
1936–1937   Diaries MS, Fryer Library, Univ. of Queensland.
1949   *The book of Pidgin English.* Brisbane: Smith and Peterson.
1992   Personal communication.
Netting, Robert M.
1987   Clashing cultures, clashing symbols: Histories and meanings of the Latok war. *Ethnohistory* 34:352–380.
Neumann, Klaus
1989   Not the way it really was. *Journal of Pacific History* 24:209–220
1992   *Not the way it really was: Constructing the Tolai past.* Pacific Island Monograph Series no. 10. Honolulu: Univ. of Hawai‘i Press.

Nilles, Fr. John
1939   Madchen reifefeier bei den östliche Waugla im Bismarckgebirge Neuguineas. *Anthropos* 34:402–406.
1940   Eine knaben-jugendweihe bei den Ostlichen Waugla im Bismarckgebirge Neuguineas. *Internationales Archive für Ethnographie* 38:93–98.
1943   Natives of the Bismarck Mountains, New Guinea. *Oceania* 14:104–124.
1944   Natives of the Bismarck Mountains. *Oceania* 15:1–19.
1950   The Kuman of the Chimbu region, Central Highlands, New Guinea. *Oceania* 21:25–65.
1953   The Kuman people: A study of cultural change in a primitive society in the central highlands of New Guinea. *Oceania* 24:1–27;119–131.
1977   Simbu ancestors and Christian worship. *Catalyst* 7:163–190.
1987a   *They went out to sow*. Rome: Analectica SVD 62. Apud Collegium Verbi Divini.
1987b   Personal communication.
1990   Personal communication.
Obeyesekere, Gananath
1992   *The apotheosis of Captain Cook*. Princeton: Princeton Univ. Press.
O'Hanlon, Michael
1989   *Reading the skin*. London: Crawford House Press, British Museum.
1990–1991 Personal communications.
1993   *Paradise: Portraying the New Guinea highlands*. London: British Museum Press.
O'Neill, Jack
1979   *Up from South: A prospector in New Guinea*. Edited by James Sinclair. Melbourne: Oxford Univ. Press.
Oram, Nigel
1981   The history of the Motu-speaking people according to their own traditions. In *Oral sources and the history of Papua New Guinea*, edited by Donald Denoon and Rod Lacey, 207–230. Port Moresby: Univ. of Papua New Guinea.
Ortner, Shelly
1984   Theory in anthropology since the sixties. *Comparative Studies in Society and History* 26:126–165.
Parmentier, Richard J.
1987   *The sacred remains*. Chicago: Univ. of Chicago Press.
Pawley, Andrew, ed.
1991   *Man and a half*. Auckland: The Polynesian Society.
Pegg, H. S.
1953   Patrol report 6A, Central. Australian Archives ACT. A7034/1, item 116.
Podolefsky, Aaron
1987   To make the belly cold: Conception of justice in the New Guinea highlands. *Anthropology* 2:35–54.
1990   Mediator roles in Simbu conflict management. *Ethnology* 29:67–82.
1992   *Simbu law*. New York: Harcourt Brace Jovanovich.
Poyer, Lin
1988   History, identity, and Christian evangelism: The Sapwakfik massacre. *Ethnohistory* 35:209–233.
Radford, A., and A. Speer
1986   Medical tultuls and aid post orderlies. *Papua New Guinea Medical Journal* 29:165–182.

Radford, Robin
1977   Burning the spears: A peace movement in the Eastern Highlands of New Guinea
        1936–7. *Journal of Pacific History* 12:40–54.
1987   *Highlanders and foreigners in the Upper Ramu*. Melbourne: Melbourne Univ. Press.
Rambo, Karl
1990   Jesus came here too: The making of a culture hero and control over history in
        Simbu, Papua New Guinea. *Ethnology* 29:177–188.
1993   Economic change and differentiation in Kerowagi (Papua New Guinea). Ph.D.
        diss., State Univ. of New York, Stony Brook.
Read, Kenneth E.
1951   The Gahuku-Gama of the Central Highlands. *South Pacific* 5:202–207.
1965   *The high valley*. New York: Scribner's.
1986   *Return to the high valley*. Berkeley and Los Angeles: Univ. of California Press.
Reay, Marie
1959   *The Kuma*. Melbourne: Melbourne Univ. Press.
Reitano, V. F.
1946   Patrol report, Upper Chimbu. Papua New Guinea Archives Kundiawa patrol
        reports Accession No. 496, vol. 1. On microfiche.
Ross, Fr. William
1968   The Catholic mission in the Western Highlands. In *The history of Melanesia*,
        edited by Marion Ward, 319–327. Canberra: Australian National Univ.
1969   The growth of Catholicism in the Western Highlands. *Journal of the Papua and
        New Guinea Society* 2:59–64.
Ryan, D'Arcy
1992   Meeting the Mendi. In *Ethnographic presents*, edited by Terence Hays, 199–231.
        Berkeley and Los Angeles: Univ. of California Press.
Ryder, Elizabeth
1992   Iambakey Okuk. Ph.D. diss., UCLA.
Sahlins, Marshall
1981   *Historical metaphors and mythical realities*. Ann Arbor: Univ. of Michigan Press.
1983   Other times, other histories. *American Anthropologist* 85:517–544.
1985   *Islands of history*. Chicago: Univ. of Chicago Press.
1991   The return of the event, again; with reflections on the beginnings of the Great
        Fijian War of 1843–1855 between the kingdoms of Bau and Rewa. In *Clio in
        Oceania*, edited by Aletta Biersack, 37–100. Washington, D.C.: Smithsonian
        Institution Press.
1992   Comment: First contacts in Melanesia. MS for American Anthropological Asso-
        ciation meetings.
1995   *How "natives" think about Captain Cook, for example*. Chicago: Univ. of Chicago
        Press.
Salisbury, Richard F.
1956   Asymmetrical marriage systems. *American Anthropologist* 58:639–655.
1962   *From stone to steel*. Melbourne: Melbourne Univ. Press, for Australian National
        Univ.
Salmond, Anne
1991   *Two Worlds*. Honolulu: Univ. of Hawai'i Press.
Schäfer, Fr. Alphons
1935   Report to McCarthy 2 January 1935. Australian Archives CRS A 518 p841/1.

1938   Kavagl, "der Mann mit der Zaunphalkeule." *Anthropos* 33:107–113.
1981   Christianized ritual pig killing. *Catalyst* 1, no. 11:213–223. Original in German
        Steyler Missionschronik, 1959.
Schieffelin, Edward B., and Robert Crittenden, with contributions by Bryant Allen and
        Stephen Frankel, Paul Sillitoe, and Lisette Josephides and Marc Schiltz
1991   *Like people you see in a dream.* Stanford: Stanford Univ. Press.
Schieffelin, Edward B., and H. Kurita
1988   The phantom patrol. *Journal of Pacific History* 23:52–69.
Schütte, Heinz
1991   Stori belong wanpela man nem bilong em Toboalilu. *Pacific Studies* 14: 69–96.
Seefeld, P. A. F.
1956   Patrol report no. 7 of 1956/7, Central census sub-division Chimbu Sub-District,
        Eastern Highlands District MS.
Shand, F. N. Warner
1941   Patrol report, Papua New Guinea Archives Kundiawa patrol reports Accession
        no. 496, vol. 1. On microfiche.
Shostak, Margery
1983   *Nisa.* New York: Vintage.
Simpson, Colin
1964   *Plumes and arrows.* New York: Barnes.
Sinclair, James
1981   *Kiap.* Sydney: Pacific Publications.
Singh, S.
1974   Cooperatives in Papua New Guinea. *New Guinea Research Unit Bulletin* 58:128-
        145.
Standish, Bill
1983   They want to be highest always. In *Electoral politics in Papua New Guinea*, edited
        by David Hegarty. Port Moresby: Univ. of Papua New Guinea Press.
1992   Simbu paths to power. Political change and centralization in the Papua New
        Guinea highlands. Ph.D. diss., Australian National Univ.
Sterly, Joachim
1987   Kumo: *Hexer und hexen in Neu-Guinea.* Munich: Kindler Verlag.
Strathern, Andrew
1971   *The rope of Moka.* Cambridge: Cambridge Univ. Press.
1979   Gender, ideology and money in Mount Hagen. *Man* n.s. 4:530–548.
1984   *A line of power.* London: Tavistock.
1991   Struggles for meaning. In *Clio in Oceania*, edited by Aletta Biersack, 205–230.
        Washington, D.C.: Smithsonian Institution Press.
———, ed.
1982   *Inequality in New Guinea highland societies.* Cambridge: Cambridge Univ.
        Press.
Strathern, Marilyn
1972   *Women in-between.* London: Seminar Press.
1985   Discovering "social control." *Journal of Law and Society* 12:111–134.
1988   *The gender of the gift.* Berkeley and Los Angeles: Univ. of California Press.
1990a   Artefacts of history: Events and the interpretations of images. In *Culture and his-
        tory in the Pacific*, edited by J. Siikala, 25–44. Transaction 27, Finnish Anthropo-
        logical Society, Helsinki.

1990b   Negative strategies. In *Localizing strategies*, edited by R. Fardon, 204–215. Edinburgh: Scottish Academy Press.
1992   The decomposition of an event. *Cultural Anthropology* 7:244–254.
Sturtevant, William
1966   Anthropology, history and ethnohistory. *Ethnohistory* 13:1–51.
Taussig, Michael
1980   *The devil and commodity fetishism in South America*. Chapel Hill: Univ. of North Carolina Press.
1987   *Shamanism, colonialism, and the wild man*. Chicago: Univ. of Chicago Press.
Taylor, James L.
1933   Mt. Hagen Patrol. Australian Archives CRS A7034, item 218.
1935a   Patrol report. Australian Archives CRS A518 item p841/1.
1935b   Reports on patrol and added notes to District Office. Australian Archives CRS A 518 item p841/1.
1939   Report of the Hagen-Sepik Patrol. MS.
Taylor, Meg
1991   Personal communication.
Thomas, Nicholas
1991   *Entangled objects*. Cambridge, Mass.: Harvard Univ. Press.
Toren, Christine
1989   Islands of history. *Critique of Anthropology* 8:113–117.
Townsend, Pat
1985   The situation of children in Papua New Guinea. Boroko: Institute of Applied Social and Economic Research.
Trigger, Bruce
1982   Ethnohistory: Problems and prospects. *Ethnohistory* 29:1–19.
Tueting, Dorothy
1935   *Native trade in Southeast New Guinea*. Bishop Museum Occasional Paper 11, no. 15.
Ulbrich, P. Josef, ed.
1960   *Pioneer auf Neuguinea. Briefe von P. Alfons Schäfer SVD*. Rome: Steyler Verlagsbuchhandlung.
Umba, Benjamin
1976   The fires of dawn. In *Three short novels from Papua New Guinea*, edited by M. Greicus. Auckland, N.Z.: Longman Paul.
Vansina, Jan
1985   *Oral tradition as history*. London: James Currey.
Vial, Leigh G.
1939   The Kaman. *Walkabout*, 1 May, 17–22.
1941   Down the Wahgi. *Walkabout*, 1 July, 16–20.
Wagner, H., and H. Reiner, eds.
N.d.   *Lutheran Church in Papua New Guinea*. Adelaide: Lutheran Publishing House.
Wagner, Roy
1967   *The curse of Souw*. Chicago: Univ. of Chicago Press.
1972   *Habu*. Chicago: Univ. of Chicago Press.
1975   *The invention of culture*. Chicago: Univ. of Chicago Press.
1989   Private communication.

1991   New Ireland is shaped like a rifle and we are at the trigger: The power of diges-
        tion in cultural reproduction. In *Clio in Oceania*, edited by Aletta Biersack, 329–
        346. Washington, D.C.: Smithsonian Institution Press.
Waiko, John
1981   Binandere oral tradition: Sources and problems. In *Oral sources and the history of
        Papua New Guinea*, edited by Donald Denoon and Rod Lacey. Port Moresby:
        Univ. of Papua New Guinea.
1986   Oral traditions among the Binandere. *Journal of Pacific History* 21:21–38.
Walstab, J.
1924   Report on tribal fighting in Sepik area. Australian Archives ACT. A/518/1, item
        K840/1/3.
Warry, Wayne
1987   *Chuave politics: Changing patterns of leadership in the Papua New Guinea highlands.*
        Political and Social Change Monographs 4. Canberra: Australian National
        Univ.
Watson, James B.
1990   The sorcerer's rainstone. In *The humbled anthropologist*, edited by Phil DeVita.
        Belmont, Calif.: Wadsworth.
1992   Personal communication.
Weiner, Annette
1992   *Inalienable possessions.* Berkeley and Los Angeles: Univ. of California Press.
Whitaker, J. L., et al.
1975   Kondom Agaundo, a Chimbu orator, speaks for the highlands people in the Leg-
        islative Council, Sept. 1963. In *Documents and readings in New Guinea history:
        Prehistory to 1899*, 116–117. Milton, Queensland: Jacaranda.
Whiteman, Daryll
1983   *Melanesians and missionaries.* Pasadena, Calif.: William Carey Library.
Williams H. C.
1946   Patrol report Minj-Kerowagi-Kundiawa. Papua New Guinea Archives Kundiawa
        patrol reports Accession no. 496, vol. 1. On microfiche.
Willis, Ian
1969   An epic journey. M.A. thesis, Univ. of Papua New Guinea.
Winterford, H. L.
1945   Patrol upper Chimbu and Gembogl. Papua New Guinea Archives Kundiawa
        patrol reports Accession no. 496, vol. 1. On microfiche.
Wohlt, Paul B., and Anton Goie
1986   *North Simbu. Simbu land use project*, vol. 5. Boroko: Institute of Applied Social
        and Economic Research.
Wurm, Stephen
1971   The Papuan linguistic situation. In *Current trends in linguistics. Linguistics in
        Oceania*, edited by T. A. Sebeok, 547–559. Paris: Mouton.
1975   *New Guinea area languages and language study. Vol. I: Papuan languages and the
        New Guinea linguistic scene.* Pacific Linguistics Series C. Canberra: Australian
        National Univ.

INDEX

ABOUT THE AUTHOR

PAULA BROWN received her Ph.D. from the University of London. Over the course of a distinguished career she has held positions at University College London, UCLA, University of Wisconsin, Australian National University, Cambridge University, and for twenty-four years at State University of New York, Stony Brook, where she is presently emeritus professor of anthropology. Her major works include *The Chimbu: A Study of Change in the New Guinea Highlands* and *Highland Peoples of New Guinea*.